W9-AQY-128

PN
4784
.C75
B3
Copy1

Bastian, George C.
   Editing the Day's News.

890 21984

**Galveston Community College
Library**
Galveston, Texas

Editing the Day's News

Associated Press Photo by Joe Rosenthal

OLD GLORY ON MT. SURIBACHI. A classic news picture, this Pulitzer prize-winning photograph was made by Joe Rosenthal on Mt. Suribachi, Iwo Jima, Feb. 22, 1945 (Feb. 23, Iwo Jima time). Then an Associated Press photographer, Mr. Rosenthal made the pool picture on the fifth day of the battle. He recorded for posterity the episode of the Marines raising the banner to replace a smaller flag. This photo has been copied for stamps and statues.

An Introduction to Newspaper Copyediting,
Headline Writing, Illustration, Makeup
and Small Magazine Production

EDITING THE DAY'S NEWS

GEORGE C. BASTIAN

Late Copyeditor on the Chicago Daily Tribune *and Lecturer in Editing, Medill School of Journalism of Northwestern University*

LELAND D. CASE

Publication Consultant; Former Assistant City Editor, Paris Edition of the New York Herald Tribune; *Assistant Professor of Journalism, Northwestern University; Editor of* The Rotarian

FLOYD K. BASKETTE

Professor of Journalism, University of Colorado; Copyeditor on the Denver Post; *Former Copyeditor on the Atlanta* Constitution

FOURTH EDITION

NEW YORK   *The Macmillan Company*

Fourth Edition © Copyright, The Macmillan Company 1956

All rights reserved. No part of this book may be reproduced or transmitted in any form or by any means, electronic or mechanical, including photocopying, recording or by any information storage and retrieval system, without permission in writing from the Publisher.

Eighth Printing, 1967

First, second and third editions copyright 1923, 1932 and 1943 by The Macmillan Company.
Copyright renewed 1951 by Laura M. Bastian.

Library of Congress catalog card number: 56–7287

The Macmillan Company, New York
Collier-Macmillan Canada, Ltd., Toronto, Ontario

Printed in the United States of America

GALVESTON COMMUNITY COLLEGE LIBRARY

To the Copyeditor,

Unsung Hero of the Newsroom

Preface

Scores of books had explained and extolled the reporter's techniques, but few if any had detailed the copyeditor's role in American newspapering when, in 1922, Harry Franklin Harrington, then director of the Medill School of Journalism, persuaded the late George C. Bastian to write *Editing the Day's News*. It was a task to which Mr. Bastian brought a sincere desire to perform "some slight service to the craft that has claimed his wholehearted devotion for twenty years." His success is attested by three decades of classroom use of the volume, which he started on its way.

In the present edition, we have endeavored to retain the aims of the original and of previous revisions:

First: to record newspaper methods accurately and to visualize them for the student.

Second: to make them teachable by setting them down simply, beginning with elementary things; then progressively working into the more technical problems.

Third: to give the student a conception of the materials, both tangible and intangible, that enter into newspaper production, and to supply the requisite background understanding of the newspaper as a product and an institution.

This edition has been revised from front to back to keep abreast of new mechanical developments—from the teletypesetter to photocomposition—which have occurred since the previous edition appeared. Where these developments have affected editing, they have been treated fully. The present revision, for example, not only explains the TTS operation in detail but describes the various methods used by newspapers in editing copy by TTS.

The new edition reflects current editorial trends. Worth special mention are: emphasis on clarity and precision in news copy, attention to semantics, use of the one-idea one-sentence principle rather than the old five w-and-h pattern. Many of the "shoptalk" tidbits, culled from memoranda issued by newspaper offices and associations, are used to illustrate some of the down-to-earth problems of copy-handling. These will be especially evident in the section, "Tips to Copyeditors," in the chapter on Various Kinds of Copy.

A distinctive approach will be found in the emphasis on small city paper practices. This usually is the starting point, after which discussion moves to the more highly developed techniques of the big city paper.

Recognizing the growing importance of the newspaper's local magazine supplement, the present volume offers a detailed description of small magazine editing and production, an innovation for textbooks on newspaper editing.

Newspapering is more than a bag of technical tricks a smart boy or girl can master during a few months in a newspaper office. In its broader meaning, editing calls for a mastery of a craft and an understanding of the principles which, as they are intelligently applied, progressively justify the special prerogatives given the press by society. The authors, therefore, have chosen the term *copyediting* rather than the traditional *copyreading* to describe the work of the deskman. The term is used deliberately to help the beginner realize that editing is something more than mere "copy-fixing."

One of the striking features of the present edition is the organization of material to fit the needs of the classroom and laboratory. It plunges immediately into the two basic skills of the copyeditor—preparing copy for the printer and writing headlines. This is intended to give the student enough instruction so that he can start to develop his skills in the laboratory immediately. Then the student is led into the more comprehensive procedures of perfecting copy and mastering headlines. After he is acquainted with these techniques, he moves along to typography and makeup, then, finally, to the higher policy level—reader research techniques and their findings; ethical considerations in newspaper editing and copydesk administration.

The revision follows the original plan of providing abundant material for a full academic year of instruction in editing. Perhaps sufficient attention is given to news values and perfected copy to make it usable also as a textbook for reporting in colleges offering limited instructions in journalism. Both the elements of news and the arts of news writing are treated fully.

"Many persons and many newspapers have aided in the compilation of this book," wrote Mr. Bastian in the preface of the original edition. This has been true also of the revised editions, including this one.

Collaborating on this edition are two authors, one of whom twice before had the task of revising this book. They acknowledge a profound debt to many persons who have aided with previous editions, especially to DR. GEORGE H. GALLUP, director of the American Institute of Public Opinion.

Among those contributing generously of counsel to the present edition are:

GIDEON SEYMOUR, late executive editor of the Minneapolis *Star* and *Tribune*.

WARREN MORRELL, editor of the Rapid City, S.D., *Journal*.

DOUGLAS D. MARTIN, former managing editor of the Detroit *Free Press,* now head of the department of journalism of the University of Arizona.

Acknowledgment also is made of the help and inspiration received from staff members and executives of the Denver *Post* with a special word of appreciation to the following:

E. RAY CAMPBELL, attorney for the Denver *Post* and president of the Post Printing and Publishing Company, who gave valuable counsel on the chapter on the newspaper and the law.

BILL HOSOKAWA, editor of the Denver *Post Empire* Magazine, who reviewed the chapter on magazine editing.

The authors are indebted to JOHN JAMESON, chief of the Denver bureau of the Associated Press, who gave many helpful suggestions on wire editing.

Grateful acknowledgment also is made of the generous permission given by individuals, publications and associations which have permitted reproduction of text and pictures as well as office memoranda, as noted throughout the book by references and by credit lines. Especially helpful in the preparation of this text were materials selected, with permission, from the *AP Log,* the *AP Style Book, Editor & Publisher,* the *Bulletin of the American Society of Newspaper Editors, Nieman Reports* and many other sources.

The responsibility for all statements of fact or opinion in this book rests, of course, entirely with the authors and not with any of the persons or organizations named above.

Tucson, Arizona   LELAND D. CASE
Boulder, Colorado   FLOYD K. BASKETTE

Contents

VI. 'SITTING IN' AT THE EDITOR'S DESK

APPENDICES

PART I

News Makes the Newspaper

1 News Makes Newspapers

A newspaper exists only because it is the purveyor of news. If it ceases to publish the news in a reasonably complete form, it presently ceases to exist, for the public doom it to a swift or a lingering death, and rightly so.—Charles H. Dennis (1860–1943), *ex-editor emeritus of the* Chicago *Daily News.*

We rarely meet a man who can tell us any news which he has not read in a newspaper, or has been told by his neighbor. For the most part, the only difference between us and our fellow is that he has seen the newspaper or been out to tea—and we have not.—Henry David Thoreau (1817–1862), *American author.*

Why Read Newspapers?

The English newspaper magnate, Lord Northcliffe, observed that there are only two reasons for buying newspapers—curiosity and habit. Some readers gratify their news curiosity in five minutes. Others take much longer to pore over their newspaper.

Most readers can absorb a lot of information and entertainment from a newspaper in 18 minutes—the average newspaper reading time in the United States—because, from habit, they know where to find what they want to read. Nothing irritates a reader more than to miss an item from the place he is accustomed to reading it. That explains why an editor keeps the weather report in the same position in the newspaper every day.

The reader usually reads at the same time and in the same place every day. If he prefers not to read his paper, that is his prerogative. But if the paper is not available at the time he usually reads it, his routine is broken and he often becomes irritated enough to call the paper or the carrier.

That helps explain why a *deadline* is the most sacred rule in a newspaper office. An act of God (such as a blizzard) or a mechanical breakdown are justifiable excuses for a newspaper's delay. But no editor will tolerate a staff that can't meet the paper's deadline.

No One Reads Everything

The reader reads selectively—using the headlines to direct him to the topics of his interest. He absorbs news, often without having to read details. Even a headline sometimes suffices. "I see they've caught the robber," he muses, but he doesn't care about the details, so he passes on to another item. On a big running story he might pass it by for a few days, then decide it must be worthwhile. So he starts reading the story. That explains why the paper always includes enough background to bring readers up to date on a continuing story.

It's likely that some readers read their newspapers because they're afraid not to. Perhaps they're not ashamed if they are not in touch with the juicy divorce trial that is the talk of the neighborhood. And surely they're not afraid to admit they didn't know the Dodgers got knocked off the top perch in the National League. But they're afraid they'll wake up some morning to find their community or their nation in a crisis and they would hate themselves for not having known it was coming.

The executive editor of the Winston-Salem *Journal and Sentinel,* Wallace Carroll, put it this way, "We must produce a newspaper which will help the reader work out his answer to the question, 'What must I do to be saved?' For years, editors have been producing a newspaper for spectators; today the newspaper must be produced for the citizen who is no longer sitting in the grandstand but is down playing on the muddy field."

The reader has a conscience about news. He cares about newspapers because they bring him the news—in detail, in depth and in perspective. He feels that reading a newspaper is a good citizen's duty.

The Rewards of Reading

The reader selects news in expectation of a reward, either immediate or delayed, in the opinion of Dr. Wilbur Schramm, journalism research expert. Discussing the nature of news in a *Journalism Quarterly* article, Dr. Schramm maintained that the immediate or pleasure reward is derived from news of crime and corruption, accidents and disaster, sports and recreation, social events and human interest stories. In these, the reader shares a vicarious experience without having to undergo any of the actual dangers. He shudders at the brutality of a murder but often forms his opinion about who committed the atrocity long before the detectives have issued an arrest warrant.

Delayed reward, says Dr. Schramm, comes from news of public affairs, economic matters, social problems, science and education. Here the reader reads for information and preparation, then retreats from the world of threatening reality toward the dream world.

If there were a person who had the solitude of a Robinson Crusoe and the personal adequacy of a dictator, he would neither need nor desire a newspaper. But no such person exists. From the moment a baby opens his eyes, the outside world is borne in upon him. As he matures, his life is increasingly conditioned by physical and social environment. His successful adjustment depends upon his awareness and understanding of what happens about him. To help him in this, newspapers were invented. "Journalism," Kipling summed it up, "meets the first tribal need after warmth, food and women."

News Is the Essential Ingredient

Whatever the newspaper reader's reason for reading—habit, curiosity, fear, duty, reward or escape—the editor accepts it as his responsibility to give his readers the latest and most accurate account of selective social events. In short, to give the news.

Canny Benjamin Harris sensed that many stay-at-home Bostonians of 1690 would like to know what was being talked about in the coffee houses and along the waterfront. On September 25, he pulled from his press PUBLICK OCCURRENCES *Both Forreign and Domestick.* He was to be a historian in the present tense and stated his purpose succinctly:

It is designed, that the Countrey shall be furnished once a moneth (or if any Glut of Occurrences happen, oftener,) with an account of such consider-able things as have arrived unto our Notice.

In order hereunto, the Publisher will take what pains he can to obtain a Faithful Relation of all such things; and will particularly make himself beholden to such Persons in Boston whom he knows to have been for their own use the diligent Observers of such matters.

Harris was born with a nose for news. First in his pattern of purpose was "a Faithful Relation" of what happened. But he also was concerned:

That people every where may better understand the Circumstances of Publique Affairs, both abroad and at home; which may not only direct their Thoughts at all times, but at some times also to assist their Businesses and Negotiations . . .

News first, then as its byproduct comes editorial guidance: That was Harris' dictum. And it still stands.

Harris' formula for America's first newspaper was echoed nearly two centuries later by Charles A. Dana when he took over the New York *Sun* in 1868:

The *Sun* will always have all the news, foreign, domestic, political, social, literary, scientific and commercial. It will use enterprise and money freely to make the best possible newspaper, as well as the cheapest.

It will study condensation, clearness, point, and will endeavor to present its daily photograph of the whole world's doings in the most luminous and lively manner.

It will not take as long to read the *Sun* as to read the London *Times* or *Webster's Dictionary,* but when you have read it you will know about all that has happened in both hemispheres. . . . We shall endeavor to make the *Sun* worthy of the confidence of the people in every part of the country.

Making the news product worthy of the people's confidence is the supreme challenge of journalism. News is not a comprehensive array of all the world's activities in a day or a week but a balanced, audited account of the "glut of occurrences."

Newspapers Are Edited

A heavy volume of material flows into the newspaper office. On the average day the larger daily receives eight million words of copy from wire services, feature syndicates, correspondents and special and staff writers. Yet it can use only about 100,000 words of reading matter. It buys not one wire service but several. The Houston *Chronicle,* for example, subscribes to the services of the *Associated Press, International News Service,* Chicago *Daily News,* New York *Times,* Chicago *Tribune, Reuters* and the New York *News.* It buys or has available more than 100 photographs daily, exclusive of cartoons, but it can use only 25 to 30 photos.

All the material available to a newspaper has to be filtered before it is funneled to the readers. This filtering is done by editors, subeditors and *copyeditors.*

Newspapers have one or more editors, someone to redact, revise, draft or design the product. On the small publications the editing is done by the editor and his reporters. On larger papers the culling and refining are done by departmental editors and a staff of specialists called copyeditors.

Writers, whether or not they have the added responsibility of editing others' copy, should practice copyediting. That is, they should correct their story once they have committed it to paper. Teach a reporter to edit others' copy and he will become a better writer. Let him struggle to convert another's prosaic account into polished prose and he will begin to pay more attention to his own style of writing. Challenge him to summarize a story in a half-dozen headline words and he will start writing leads that get the story underway immediately. When he has had to undergo the tedious task of verifying facts, he will be more scrupulous with truth and accuracy in his reporting.

There Must Be Teamwork

One person gathers news and writes the story but many have to work on it before it reaches the reader. Rewriting and editing have become as important in newspaper production as fact-gathering and writing. Here is a story under a Washington dateline appearing in the local daily. The story was covered by a wire service staff member who called in the story to a rewrite man in the Washington office. The story was then edited and filed on a wire to a regional bureau. There it was edited again before it was placed on a state wire and sent to a newspaper. And once more it was edited before it appeared in the paper.

At the local newspaper plant many hands were needed to get the story to the reader. The story first went to an executive who evaluated it and designated it for a particular position. It then moved to the copydesk where it was refined, pared to specifications and headlined. From there it went to the mechanical department where it was transformed into type, fitted into a page form and made ready for the press.

This processing, with variations, is done by all media of mass communications. Writing a story is only the first step; the second step is shaping it for presentation to the news consumer. It is put into one mold for the newspaper reader, another for the radio listener, another for the TV viewer, another for the magazine reader and still another for the newsreel viewer.

Not only is news selective, it is refined. Not everything presented in a newspaper is significant or important, but everything that appears in print is there to give the paper balance, variety and acceptability. The editor is under no compulsion to present everything he has available, nor are readers compelled to read what is presented to them. Both exercise their right to decide what is fit to print and what is fit to read.

Selectivity and emphasis change with the times. But news, as news-

FROM REPORTER TO READER: A SIMPLIFIED STORY

THE REPORTER'S COPY GOES TO THE EDITOR →

WHO "DEALS" IT OUT TO ONE OF HIS COPY EDITORS WHO PERFECTS IT AND WRITES THE HEADLINES

IT IS SET IN TYPE (LINO)

A PROOF IS PROOFREAD WITH THE COPY

THE MAKEUP EDITOR DRAWS UP A SCHEDULE FOR ALLOCATION OF IT, AND THE OTHER STORIES

THE TYPE PAGE IS MADE UP IN A FORM CALLED A CHASE

A MOLD IN HEAVY CARDBOARD (MAT) IS MADE UNDER PRESSURE AT THE STEAM TABLE

A CURVED METAL CASTING OR STEREOTYPE IS THEN MADE

ALL PAGE STEREOTYPES ARE PUT ON THE PRESSES

THE PRINTED PAPERS ARE HURRIED TO DISTRIBUTION POINTS

AND TO YOUR DOOR

Cartoon by John Norment

8

papermen understand the term, has basic qualities and elements. Unless a newspaper worker understands news, he has no place on a newspaper whether it be a metropolitan daily or a community weekly.

News is the *sine qua non,* the *raison d'être,* or, in the revived Elizabethan idiom, the *guts* of the modern American newspaper. Take news from it and you may have a magazine, a review or a picture paper; it is not a newspaper. The beginning and end for a newspaper is news.

2   What Makes News

The story of an individual is generally more interesting than that of a group, for the reason that the reader identifies himself with an individual.—F. P. Adams (1881–   ), *columnist.*

Begin with a clear conception that the subject of deepest interest to the average human being is himself; next to that he is most interested about his neighbors. . . . Do not let a new church be organized or new members be added to an existing one, a farm sold, a new house raised, a mill be set in motion, a store be opened, nor anything of interest to a dozen families occur without having the fact duly though briefly recorded in your columns.—Horace Greeley (1811–1872), *famed editor of the* New York *Tribune, advising a young newspaperman.*

News Versus Opinion

To avoid confusion, the beginning newsman should learn to distinguish between straight news and opinionated writing.

A straight newsstory is an account of what happened, told as factually and as accurately as a trained reporter, aided by the copyeditor, can make it. It is cast simply, briefly, accurately. It draws no conclusions, makes no gratuitous accusations, indulges in no speculations, offers no opinions. It may arrange facts with an eye to their importance or dramatic values. It may report in depth, supplying a factual background to help the reader understand. But it should never distort, misrepresent or falsify facts and quoted statements, even by implication.

Interpretive reporting can be misunderstood. Perhaps *explanatory writing* is better. This means putting the news in its proper context or putting meaning into the news. It means full (or depth) reporting, not shallow, one-sided reporting. Placing a particular event in the larger flow of the news, providing background so the reader can have a better understanding—this is the new dimension in reporting.

At the opposite pole from straight news is the editorial. It is opinion. In effect it says, "You have read the facts; now here is what the 'editorial we' think about it." News gives the facts. The editorial gives the value judgment about the news. Although in practice there is a gradation from straight news to opinionated writing, yet this differentiation is fundamental to an understanding of American journalism.

News Is Relative

Newsmen often appear dogmatic to the layman. "There's no news in that," they will announce, or "That's news!" They mean, but don't say, "for *this* newspaper *today*."

Consider a newspaper published for that little community called a campus. Much space is devoted to items that do not appear in the downtown paper. The collegiate reporter's nose for news leads him to offices and classrooms entirely sterile in news interest for off-campus publications.

Now pass to another community, a village. Its weekly newspaper will chronicle the fact that William Smith, the garageman, smashed a finger, or that the banker's automobile had two blowouts as he was riding home from the First National. The finger and the tires are of no significance to a metropolitan newspaper because in a large city such incidents are multiplied to infinity. Of the 250 or more homicides in New York each year, not half are mentioned in the daily press though details of almost all are known in editorial offices.

Furthermore, news values vary from day to day and even hour to hour in the constant battle for space. Typically, small community papers are 40 to 50 per cent advertisements; metropolitan dailies, 60 to 65 per cent, sometimes higher. Into the remaining *news hole* is packed an amazing quantity and variety of information and entertainment. A single issue of a large daily often will carry 50 major stories, 100 brief items, 50 photographs and comics, as well as a dozen features including syndicated columns. A study of Indiana newspapers showed that the small daily runs 13 columns of news daily, the larger daily 106 columns. About half the news hole is devoted to departmentalized news: sports, society, editorial page, etc.

Broadening News Coverage

Newspapermen sometimes assume that almost all major happenings of interest to newspaper readers center on certain public officials such as the mayor, chief of police, county clerk. On some days these offices are barren of news. General reporters are expected to fill in the gaps not listed with

the official fulcrums, but usually these are events the city editor can antici-
pate. Readers do not get a well-rounded picture when too much emphasis
is placed on city hall, Washington or foreign capitals to the neglect of other
areas of news. One political writer thought that American newspapers
missed the boat on the 1948 presidential election because reporters were
too preoccupied with the candidates themselves and not enough concerned
with the voters.

Reporters today have broken away from the mold of routine affairs and
are investigating wider interests and discoveries. Science, religion and the
arts, for instance, are being offered as news, not because these are more
newsworthy now than they were in the past but because we have more
editors and reporters with vision and understanding who can see the news
potentials in these subjects.

An Arithmetic of News

News is full of quirks and oddities. It has an arithmetic all its own.

There is news only for the village paper in a $10 fire, but add a $3
canary and cause it to be rescued by its little girl owner, and you have a
good story even for a New York daily.

Metropolitans are little concerned about a $10,000 burglary, but add
the fact that a $2 mongrel bit the burglar and did his best to save his
owner's property, and you have a story rich in interest for the newspaper
reader, anywhere.

Here are examples in news arithmetic that illustrate graphically, if
rather satirically, what does and what does not constitute news for a city
newspaper.

```
1 ordinary man + 1 ordinary life = 0
1 ordinary man + 1 extraordinary adventure = News
1 ordinary husband + 1 ordinary wife = 0
1 husband + 3 wives = News
1 bank cashier + 1 wife + 7 children = 0
1 bank cashier − $10,000 = News
1 chorus girl + 1 bank president + $10,000 = News
1 man + 1 auto + 1 gun + 1 quart = News
1 man + 1 wife + 1 row + 1 lawsuit = News
1 man + 1 achievement = News
1 woman + 1 adventure or achievement = News
1 ordinary man + 1 ordinary life of 79 years = 0
1 ordinary man + 1 ordinary life of 100 years = News
```

When News Becomes NEWS

Take a recipe for making bread. If it is a new recipe, it contains a news element of low grade. If it also cuts the cost in half, the news values increase greatly. If it is a recipe that calls for *ersatz* flour made of sawdust, it is freak news. There is no transcendent news value in any of these items. Yet bread is indispensable, the staff of life and its ingredients have a supreme news value, just because they go into the making of bread.

Wheat, for instance. Almost any story about it gets a place in a small newspaper in a wheat-producing community. Every large newspaper in the world has a daily story on wheat, its supply and its prices.

But the daily story of the breadstuffs and grains and meats and produce is not normally metropolitan front-page news. It is merely routine news that assumes great importance only under threat of catastrophe, such as imminent or actual famine, or unusual prices, or unexpected drains on the supply. Then breadstuffs become vital news to all papers, large or small.

This sample progression of events and of news values reveals that news consists not so much in the action recorded as in its reaction on human kind.

What Makes News

Elements of news can be stated in various ways but generally they are:

Action	Beauty and romance
Combat or struggle	Adventure and pathos
Suspense and mystery	Numbers and size
Immediacy	Property
Nearness or propinquity	Timing
Significance	Novelty and humor
Names or identity	Children
Achievement	Animals
Sex and scandals	Places

Action. In jungle days, when self-preservation often depended upon quick bodily response to the lateral threat of, say, a tiger, close inspection of an object served a less vital purpose than awareness of movement. So ingrained is this neurophysical response to movement that a skillful hand instantly lures the eye, as every orator and magician knows. If the reason for the observed action is not apparent, curiosity is aroused.

Pictures-in-the-mind—yes, but preferably moving pictures. Intuitively wise are attention-seeking public figures who, like "Teddy" Roosevelt, the apostle of "the strenuous life," permit no news pictures to be taken of them in repose. Even suggested action has an elemental appeal to the mind—an appeal shared by words to the degree they suggest movement.

News today seems to have more action than it did a century ago because both the headlines and the stories suggest movement. A static picture on television is flat. As one executive put it, "If it doesn't wiggle, it isn't television."

Combat or Struggle.   Action opposed makes combat—a common denominator of news interest to be found in every issue of every newspaper throughout the world. It may be the clashing of minds, of wills, of ideas, of classes, of nations or of man against fate. It is a basic element of fiction as it is of news.

Combat abounds even in routine news. The rivalry of sports has an atavistic interest, even to a grandmother knitting in her rocker as she watches grunting wrestlers over television. There is combat in lawsuits, in political campaigns, in the drives against public indifference for better schools or cleaner back yards. Sometimes it is so hidden that it takes skillful reporting and editing to make the reader conscious of it, but if overlooked by the newsman, he has thrown away one of his best tools to pry open the mind's eye of his reader.

Suspense and Mystery.   Suspense is the vital news element in combat, for man is an inquisitive animal. Skilled copyeditors often inject suspense into an otherwise prosaic story by use of a word like "suspicious" or "unexplained." The more the suspense, the greater the newsstory becomes. Lindbergh's flight across the Atlantic and the kidnaping of the Lindbergh baby both had that vital element of suspense. In the first instance, readers eagerly grabbed the papers to find out if the lone flier had landed safely; in the second instance, the readers waited breathlessly to find out if the baby would be returned to the parents. No detective fiction can offer the degree of suspense found in great stories of real life.

Occasionally the life cycle of a news event unfolds like a fictional "whodunit." Here is one which might be called "The Great Pearl Mystery" with chapter titles drawn from headlines:

Chapter I. Pearl necklace mystery in suit over $380,000; perfect string of 389 will figure in vivid story.

Chapter II. Who has it? Who bought it? At what price? Matchless rope of pearls still a mystery.

Chapter III. Detroit holds secret of pearl necklace owner; bought by a millionaire there, but who?

Chapter IV. $1,500,000 gem left to wife by $5-a-day man; pearl necklace now Mrs. H. E. Dodge's.

Chapter V. U. S. probes sale of the $1,500,000 pearl necklace; import duty paid only on $825,000, report.

Chapter VI. Pearl necklace enigma solved; price $825,000; Dodge executor admits purchase of gems.

Chapter VII. Mrs. Dodge gave pearl necklace to her daughter; once wore gems on the street unguarded.

Suspense holds readers' interest in news. Suspense invites readers to share vicariously—they enjoy playing the role of detective. Who committed the Brinks' holdup? Did Shakespeare write the plays attributed to him? Readers form their own hypotheses, then await the solution.

Immediacy: Is It New? What has just happened is new—and probably news. The nearness of an event *in time,* its immediacy, is the most important factor in the relativity of news values. As news ages, it loses potency. That is the rule. But it must be interpreted by the principle, once stated by Addison in the *Spectator,* that *All matters of fact, which a man did not know before, are news to him.* A newspaper should be edited for its readers and not its competitor. News is news to a man who has not read the account in another newspaper or heard it on radio or seen it on television.

Immediacy is of sharpest importance to dailies in large cities. There, the latest news is usually given preference, especially if it is a scoop over rival newspapers. The pressure is less intense on smaller papers, however. A weekly will give a detailed account about an event that happened the hour after it last went to press, though it may have been reported by neighboring city papers or by radio. To most of its subscribers, it still is news.

Nearness or Propinquity. Closeness in time of an event must be considered in relation to other factors, especially its closeness in space—its propinquity. The connotation of this word is close neighborhood, and refers especially to personal vicinity. Often the newsworthiness of an event is in direct ratio to its physical nearness to the public served by the newspaper appraising it.

Readers at Sleepy Eye, Minn., would hardly care to read a story of comings and goings of inhabitants of Columbia, S.C., absorbingly interesting though it might be to Columbians. Yet something could happen at Columbia which would make headlines from Portland to Portland.

Significance.   To nearness in time and space must be added nearness in *personal concern*. You and everybody else almost every day say, "That's news to me!" The emphasis always falls on *me*. Though social conditioning may modify one's egoism, it is generally true that the perpendicular pronoun is equivalent to No. 1 in the individual's scale of interests. A newsstory will have reader appeal, no matter what its point of origin, as it has (a) personal, (b) family, (c) community, (d) national or (e) international significance.

To Speculator Jones, quotations on Brazilian manganese may be the news of the day; not so for Widow Smith whose son is wounded on a foreign battlefield. Thousands upon thousands of chemists are at work upon experiments, but let a wise editor get wind of a discovery to cure the common cold and every city and hamlet will have a story of transcendent interest.

Significance includes background material for a current event. As news becomes more complex, the need for background or interpretation becomes greater if the reader is to have a complete, comprehensive understanding of the news. Details provide the depth that the overt news lacks. Background and explanation may help the reader have the whole truth about the news.

Names or Identity.   "Names make news" is an axiom of journalism, yet the news value of names, like all other news ingredients, is relative. An old newsroom yarn illustrates the point.

"Cover the fire at Farmer Brown's," the editor told his cub reporter, "and don't forget to get names." The reporter duly turned in this story: "Three cows lost their lives in a fire that destroyed John Brown's barn last night. Their names are Susie, Mary Jane and Arabella."

Even a great metropolitan daily is influenced by the neighborhood news idea. The difference is that in the city, various yardsticks of selection are applied: wealth, social position, achievement, business success, etc. That is why the metropolitan daily will devote much space to society and club events, to schools, to amateur theatricals, to community enterprises, to campaigns for funds and to businesses and clubs with long lists of "among those present." And the "folksy" type of column popularized by O. O. McIntyre and Walter Winchell is confessedly but a citified version of the village weekly's "locals."

Some personalities are so widely known that in themselves they make news in papers large or small. Henry Ford was a prime news source for many years. Today, Queen Elizabeth II has the power to charm news columns. Even trivial happenings to prominent men and women have news values. So do their opinions on some quirk of fashion or social usage, some new public problem or international situation or any subject that has timely interest.

News turns unknowns into familiar personalities, whether they be heroes or gangsters. News centers on individuals simply because they can be identified easily by the reader. You cannot visualize "the German people," but you can see Hans, and through episodic treatment centering on one character, you can appreciate the personal problems of a whole community. Identity is an aspect of news. As an individual continues to appear in news, he becomes more familiar to the reader until finally the reader is casually referring to him by nickname as if he were a long-time acquaintance. In World War II, readers became acquainted with General Dwight D. Eisenhower; at the opening of the 1952 presidential campaign they read about Ike. And when President and Mrs. Eisenhower arrived in Colorado for a vacation, the Denver *Post* cheered in 120-point type, *Welcome Ike, Mamie.*

Achievement: Position and Wealth. Usually names make news because position or wealth is associated with them. A comparatively unknown professor becomes a "name" when he is elected president of an important university. The Nizam of Hyderabad became a news name, not because he was ruler of an Indian state, but because he was the wealthiest man in the world. No city newspaper would print a line about the ordinary ill-running affairs of an ordinary department-store clerk. But with his or her $50,000-a-year employer it is different. A big salary is regarded as a symbol of substantial achievement and the reader likes to participate vicariously in successes or, perhaps, to gloat in superiority over failures.

Why devote hundreds of words to the wedding of the Biltmore heiress? Because the shopgirl who reads the story can experience, vicariously through the newspaper, the type of wedding she herself can never have.

When the Associated Press was asked what the Sheppard murder trial had that raised it above hundreds of others, the agency spokesman replied: "It seems a fairly familiar formula—Murder x Sex x Society."

Sex and Scandals. Old orders change and so do taboos, mores, customs and conventions. Whipped up by modern psychology, public interest in sex has led the press to a frankness unknown in Victorian days. Whether the handling is prurient or it emphasizes social reform is dependent upon those who direct the newspaper's policies.

But known long before Freud was the interest of people in the relations of men and women. The news-reading public of a century ago was stirred with curiosity about polygamists. Back-chamber affairs of royalty have always had an audience and misalliances of Greek deities undoubtedly still contribute to an interest in mythology.

The scandal story may be ascribed to modern man's curiosity about his neighbor. It is characteristic of the city, where sheer numbers afford a certain anonymity to the principals, detachment to the reader and impersonality for the reporter. But scandal stories, let it be recalled, are not unknown to village journalism also. Laws of libel set legal boundaries for stories in this field, but editorial policies that trespass too far on readers' concept of decency soon or late hang themselves in the circulation department.

News deals with human foibles and weaknesses as well as with human strengths and achievements. When a big department store calls for an audit after a trusted officer has committed suicide, the reporter knows that a story could be brewing. He writes the facts, leaving it to the reader to put two and two together. If the investigation shows that funds are missing, the story is played for all it is worth. Newspapers don't make news (most of the time); they report the news.

But newspapers have, or should have, a character and when they compromise for the sake of sales they pander to the public's lowest taste. Can newspapers survive without sex? Yes, said August Heckscher, editorial writer for the New York *Herald Tribune,* in a debate recorded in the *Saturday Review,* June 24, 1950:

This emphasis on sex many friends of *The Post* (New York) find disconcerting. It must be presumed that these friends are not actually averse to sex itself, that they do not lack a sympathy for outcasts or unfortunates, and that they are not unwilling to pursue any social problem to its roots. If they object it is on the practical grounds that they do not like being compelled to leave their favorite evening newspaper on the train, or otherwise dispose of it, before entering homes where growing children are entitled to be protected against at least the most brutal and the most sordid facts of life. They object, on moral grounds, to having their sex dished up as bait.

Beauty and Romance.   Psychologists have their own explanations, but it is a patent fact to anyone that the reading public is interested in beauty— especially beautiful women. If proof were required, one need but cite the pretty-girl pictures used to advertise products ranging from peaches to beer.

Cheesecake is now a part of the daily fare served by many papers to their readers.

However, a newspaper's use of this appeal is bounded on one side by taste and the other side by common sense. It is a boomerang for a newspaper to call a woman pretty and then publish an extremely homely picture, or to dub every woman beautiful.

We are a sentimental, romantic public and cherish a love for romance, no matter how commonplace our own lives. Entertainment is one of the major functions of the newspaper. But it is not fiction that the newspaper uses in news columns: it is real life romance of Mrs. Simpson and the then King Edward VIII, who renounced his throne and became the Duke of Windsor.

Adventure and Pathos.   Under this heading come narratives of adventure and achievement published in the newspapers with a nice sense of historical duty as well as of what constitutes good reading. Such stories include chronicles of arctic explorations, scientific discovery, invention, excavation of ancient and forgotten cities, art and archaeological treasures and scores of others.

Under this heading can also be classified those numerous stories, humorous and pathetic, which the newspaperman groups under the rather vague title of *feature* or *human-interest stories*. Many of these are little masterpieces of writing, comparable to the best of the short stories of fiction and often reaching the dramatic heights of a great novel.

Numbers and Size.   Numbers make news. A train wreck in which all passengers escape without injury is not worth much space in a city paper unless improved by some other *angle*. A wreck in which a number are only slightly injured is not worth much more. A wreck in which several persons were killed or badly hurt grows in space value. A parade witnessed by hundreds of thousands of persons is always worth a story. The attack launched by a speaker before an audience of 12 is not nearly so good news as is the philippic before 10,000. A man who carves a mountain into a statue will always be worth a headline.

How many? How high? How far? These are questions readers ask. When building permits reach a new high, it is front-page news. When the thermometer dips to a winter's low or soars to the summer's high, readers want the figures. When the price of coffee drops two cents a pound even the non-coffee drinkers are interested in reading the story.

Property.   Property is always news, of course, in the real-estate department of a newspaper. But in a city without skyscrapers, the building of the first one is an event worthy of front-page space; in a city there are many, one more or less does not matter much, unless it is to be a church built in the form of a skyscraper, or a skyscraper built on the spreading-tree principle, or one like Radio City that compels attention because of its sheer size.

Building reflects progress, an element of news. Erection of a new hotel is news in any community because it signifies growth and progress in the community.

Real-estate landmarks are news at times. Historic tracts also may figure in the news, but the sale of some common or garden acreage and the building of an apartment make but routine business-page items.

Timing.   The hour of an event may decide its news importance. A midnight elopement and marriage is better than a prosaic marriage at noon. The elopement kept secret for a year is a good story, with an added element of attraction if the bridegroom has been a football star in a university that forbids campus nuptials or if the bride is in society. The transcontinental train, or ocean liner, or automobile, or airplane, or horse, or man, figuring in a speed record, is news, decidedly.

Much news is seasonal in character. Sports news is such. Weather furnishes news—storms, bathing beaches, summer resorts, icy sidewalks, fatalities from extremes, vacation sports, gardening and poultry news and news of the fashions. Fads, foibles, tendencies or any new movement of changing times make news.

Stories about fire hazards in a community can be considered newsworthy. Released immediately after a serious fire in another community, they become more timely, thus more newsworthy.

Novelty, Humor.   The average reader, perhaps just a bit bored with routine, pounces with delight upon news that titillates his bump of credulity, or makes him smile. Hundreds of such stories are published because of their freakishness, but an attempt is made to avoid the distasteful or horrible.

A champion archer slays a bear with his bow and arrow; an adventure-minded maiden reads of his exploits; they marry, and we have a pleasant little tale that has news value because of its oddity. The story of the farm woman who reached under the front porch to extricate what she thought was the family cat only to discover it was a skunk gets a chuckle from readers.

The novelty or human element of these yarns is not always in the event itself; often it lies in the way the story is told. Skillful writers often turn out bright little pieces by giving a new twist to something commonplace in the hands of another. A good copyeditor can either preserve the humor or suspense with a clever headline, or he can ruin the story by giving away the point in the headline.

Children.   The naivete of children, their wistfulness, their pathos and joys, are sure fire. No romance or tragedy appeals to emotions of adults more than the one that involves youngsters, as motion picture directors so well know. The core of the Christmas appeal is The Child—and all children. No "classic of the press" is more often reprinted than Frank P. Church's reply, in the old New York *Sun* of Sept. 21, 1897, to 8-year-old Virginia O'Hanlon's appeal, "Please tell me the truth, is there a Santa Claus?"

Stories about children have a multiple psychological appeal. They may bring nostalgic recollections of the reader's own childhood; they may create sympathy through the medium of the experience transferred to a parent's own child; they may release forgotten emotional reservoirs through a twinkle of the eye, a tear or a check to a crippled children society.

Animals.   Hardly a less refreshing break in routine is afforded by bright little stories about animals, birds and fish. A boy-and-dog story is perennially good, especially where these two principals emerge victorious from a clash with municipal ordinances.

When a university campus correspondent was annoyed by repeated early morning rat-a-tap-taps of a puzzled woodpecker on the tin roof, he turned his musings to account with a short feature story about the "bird alarm clock" that awakened inmates of his fraternity house each day in time for 8 o'clock classes. It made the front pages of metropolitan newspapers from coast to coast.

So, too, did the story of an 11-year-old dog protector of Monroe, La., who liberated his pet at gunpoint after his school principal locked the dog in a closet.

Places.   Where a thing happens is important. Among spots that do not seem to lose their lure are: Broadway, the Gold Coast, Timbuktu, the Loop, Hollywood, Montmartre, London, Bali, Tibet, South Africa. The district in which wealthy and fashionable persons reside, the great hotel, the suburb filled with the homes of millionaires, the mansion, these are also attractive. Little Italy, the Ghetto, Death Corner, the Latin Quarter, Times Square, Chinatown, Wall Street, Pine Ridge Reservation, Moscow: scores of places with such names and associations add picturesqueness to a story.

Suicides are not big news in New York, where an average of three persons take their own lives daily. But when a discouraged clerk poised on the ledge of the 14th story of a hotel, finally plummeting to the pavement, his "slow suicide" made front-page headlines over the nation.

So, the News

News is the record of the most interesting, important and accurate information obtainable about the things man thinks and says, sees and describes, plans and does.

The media for news communication are newspapers and magazines, radio, television and newsreels.

Reader interests may be narrow or they may be broad. The purpose of media like newspapers is to satisfy his immediate curiosity and to invite him to expand his interests and his understanding.

PART II

The Copyeditor
and His Two Basic Skills

GALVESTON COMMUNITY COLLEGE LIBRARY

3   Meet the Copyeditor

Confidence is the *raison d'etre* of a newspaper's well-being. The same people don't spend money day after day to be fooled day after day. Even Barnum knew that. But, enter the copyeditor. He is the private detective and the F.B.I., the motorcycle cop escort, nay even the army, navy, marine corps, and air force to the newspaper's most treasured possession: The Confidence of Its Readers.

Wherever the newspaper goes, the copyeditor's long pencil is as a rod and a staff. When reporters slip, the copyeditor puts on the chains. When wires stutter, the copyeditor—well, he does more than cuss. He puts his nose into the gazetteer or encyclopedia and gets the right dope. When storks mix memoranda, he directs them aright. When befuddled grooms stammer, he delivers to them the right blushing brides. When folk good or bad die, he buries them decently. He is the copyeditor.

He wears neither star nor chevron, and his bosom never bulges with gold medals nor his pocket with coins, but he is the lifeguard of the newspaper office. Let bricks shatter windows, let irate subscribers beat up editors. It avails naught, for any hardware merchant can replace the window, and editors are spawned overnight.

But the good copyeditor! He is the salt of the earth, and a joy forever. *Selah!—An Editor.*

The Copydesk Funnel

Every means known to civilization, from pen, ink and paper to the airplane and the radio, is used for the transportation of news from the place of origin to the newspaper. All comes to the man at the copydesk. None is considered a complete newspaper product, worthy of publication, until it passes under the copyeditor's pencil.

Striking evidence that the pages of the modern newspaper are as accurate as human effort can make them within the brief time available is offered by a study of the methods the copyeditor employs in editing the various kinds of copy that come to his hand. Every step of the way, no matter what kind of copy he handles, or whether he is on a morning, afternoon, Sunday or weekly newspaper, the copyeditor must make accuracy, speed, alertness, vigor, good judgment and common sense his watchwords.

So, the Copyeditor

The art and the profession of conditioning copy for publication is known in the United States as *copyediting* (formerly *copyreading*) or the British equivalent, *subediting*. For the copyeditor does edit the day's news. His desk is an extension of the desk where the editor charts policy, evaluates events and plans the day-to-day coverage of news. And many a renowned editor and publisher is most proud that he is a competent copyeditor.

How copyediting is done varies from paper to paper. A large metropolitan daily may have a dozen or more copyeditors assigned to editors responsible for such breakdowns of news as local, society, sports, state, telegraph. On smaller dailies, news executives themselves may read the copy that comes from reporters, correspondents or by wire. Every reporter should be a copyeditor in the sense that he should edit his own copy carefully before he submits it to the city editor. On some dailies reporters edit their own copy and write their own headlines. But so essential is a critical review by a second mind that even on a weekly it is common practice to have someone other than the writer "look over" the reporter's copy.

A Specialist in Variety

Not all newsmen make good copyeditors. The copyeditor must have what may be called a bifocal mind—one that can be shifted instantly from meticulous examination of details to the overall view. A good copyeditor should be able to write good English and to edit it into stories that lack it; he should be acquainted with all important events and tendencies; he should know his own paper and its policies; he should be alert to the times; he should know books, plays, the magazines and reviews, the legalistic and governmental machinery; names, localities, political and other social relationships; geography, history, human nature, life. He should have a sense of literary fitness and of news fitness; he should be a master of detail; and he should be gifted with a high degree of ordinary common sense.

As a trusted and versatile lieutenant, a copyeditor may be called upon do so almost any job on the news side of a newspaper—from writing a story to supervising page makeup. But the usual functions of a copyeditor are these three:

1. To correct errors and improve copy assigned to him.
2. To write headlines.
3. To carry out his newspaper's policy.

Each of these functions—as well as *makeup* on which copyeditors sometimes help—will be detailed in chapters to follow, but first a quick preview of the above three duties.

1. Correcting Copy. Men and women who write are fallible. Even the best of them occasionally make errors ranging from spelling, grammar, capitalization, punctuation, abbreviation, to fact. To correct them is the first and most obvious task of the "second mind" known as the copyeditor.

Every newspaper has—or should adopt—a *stylebook,* which prescribes for its columns such mechanics of writing as capitalization, spelling, punctuation and abbreviation. It's the copyeditor's job to see that the paper is consistent in usage.

Errors of fact are more serious. Writers are of all degrees of professional maturity. Some are merely young. Others persist in carelessness, emotionalism, faulty perspective, stupid exaggeration or plain faking until discovery eliminates them from the profession. That more mistakes do not go through, in the tension and rush of producing even a small daily, is because the American newspaper has a more elaborate system of insuring accuracy than any other business in the world. And at its core sits the copyeditor.

Four courses are open to him when he encounters a dubious statement of fact. (1) He may consult any of the standard reference works—the dictionary, *Who's Who in America,* the encyclopedias, the histories, the city directory, the telephone directory, the almanacs, and others—for verification. (*See Appendix.*) (2) He may refer the story to the writer, that the statement may be checked and its authority stated. (3) He may challenge the story to the head-of-the-desk and ask that executive to pass finally upon it. (4) He may eliminate the statement, provided this process does not destroy the value of the story as news. "When in doubt leave it out."

1A. Improving the Story. Copyediting calls for creative imagination. There can be as great a thrill in sculpturing a good story out of a poor one as there is in writing one. Each manuscript offers its peculiar problems which the copyeditor must solve to the story's betterment. The good copyeditor has both seasoned judgment and creative imagination. Every story challenges him to improve it, retaining as far as possible the words of the writer. Often the story needs no textual change, but if it omits important facts the copyeditor sees to it that they are inserted.

He polishes sentences until each is so clear, compact and interesting that even a child may read and understand.

To the cub he may be the soulless butcher of literary masterpieces but to the experienced reporter he is a friendly backstop and a constructive partner. And to the editor he is an essential lieutenant who is trusted to put final touches on copy before it meets the eye of the critical customer. He is a key man in the production of the modern newspaper. That is why he usually ranks a notch higher than reporters on newspaper salary scales.

2. Headlines.   By the time the copyeditor's pencil has gone through a story, the chances are the headline has written itself in his mind and he needs but to transfer it to paper. He grasps the whole story, then uses half a dozen words to catch the reader's attention and invite his perusal of the story.

Every newspaper has standardized its chief headlines. They are usually listed on a schedule and keyed with numbers, letters or names. The head of the desk simply designates on the upper lefthand corner of a sheet of copy the kind of headline he wants the copyeditor to write. The copyeditor knows, without being instructed, to write a *jump* or *runover* head if he's handling a long page-one story and to insert subheads at appropriate places in longer copy. Should his paper carry an index or news summary of leading stories, he also writes its component items in longhand but on separate sheets. They are sent with their stories to the composing room, there to be assembled in the order in which they are to appear in print.

3. Carrying Out 'Policy.'   The good newspaper seeks to tell the day's or week's story honestly, fairly, intelligently. It's the copyeditor's special but delegated responsibility to help it do that. He must be on guard against publication of stale news, cheap news and advertising matter disguised as news. He eliminates statements that are absurd, trivial, improper, irresponsible, anonymous, dangerous, libelous or that may bring needless trouble. He eliminates all editorial expression from news columns, except that allowed by his paper's policy, such as signed articles and columns. He should know how to distinguish between propaganda masquerading as news, and the real thing.

His news sense should be so acute that he will recognize possibilities for localized tie-ins on stories coming over the wires and other ways of expanding new interest in the copy that passes before him. If he is "doubling in brass" as an editor, he should alert the executive responsible for circulation to probable unusual demands for papers because of interest in big news of the day.

To summarize, the good copyeditor takes every measure possible to uphold the standards of truth and common sense—the price of freedom of the press as well as of the safety of the individual newspaper. He is the direct representative of the editor—if, indeed, he is not the editor himself.

Know the Paper's Operation

The unwritten rule on any newspaper is to keep copy moving to the composing room. Fodder must always be plentiful for the typesetting machines. When the copy hook is empty, the operator is idle. Because a newspaper's production is geared to the full and steady output of the composing room, the paper is delayed if the operators are idle. This explains why a mediocre story, if handled early, gets into the paper while a good story, arriving late, is discarded or held over to the next day.

Newspapers operate on a tight copy schedule, something every copyeditor must appreciate if he is to hold his job. Copy itself must move on schedule. On an afternoon paper, for example, editorials must be in early so the editorial page can be *made up, plated* and out of the way for other pages. Sports, society and other inside news pages all have to clear the stone and stand by for the final, furiously paced effort, the front page.

Copyeditors also should learn the edition times of the newspaper and the areas served by each edition. A story destined for an edition serving a particular area is worthless unless it makes that edition.

Advertising Versus News

Advertising, not the available news, usually determines the size of the paper. A weekly editor assesses the amount of advertising sold during the week, then announces, "Sixteen pages and it will be tight."

That means all nonadvertising material will have to be kept to within about 60 columns. The editor could go 20 pages but his equipment can't handle it. His alternative is to leave out some advertising or to eliminate some of the news, features or editorials. He'll do the latter, always.

So, too, on a city daily. The number of pages is determined by the amount of advertising sold. Each department is allotted its quota of space and it must hold copy to the space allowed. Of course, if one department has a light day some of its space can be given to another department. Editors have a relatively free hand in selecting copy, but whatever is used must conform to the space allotted. This includes not only text, but headlines, pictures and drawings as well. If the editor can't keep within the space allotted to him, the result is overset material, a luxury most newspapers won't tolerate.

The trick to stay within space limitations is to keep a copy schedule. Some editors keep an accounting of copy lines, with an allowance for headlines. Others measure copy and headlines in terms of column inches. Still others use a "book" system, each half page of copy constituting a "book." In most cases, the responsibility for measuring the depth of copy rests with the copydesk.

The most accurate method of fitting copy to space is by character count—totaling characters in each line of type. The system is used mostly in magazine and book editing. The system can be used on newspapers if reporters write line-for-line—a typewritten line for each type line. The average typewritten line consists of 11 or 12 words, and makes two lines of 8-point type. In the old days, type was set by hand in small metal receptacles called *sticks*. That term is still used to indicate roughly two column inches of type, some eight to ten lines of usual newspaper type.

The ordinary newspaper column is approximately 21 inches long. The following scale is approximate, but usable:

Ordinary Typewritten Lines	*One Inch of Type in Size:*
6	6 point
5	7 point
4	8 point
3	10 point
2	12 point

Trimming on Manuscript

The head-of-the-desk, mindful of the space available for his department, often orders a copyeditor to *trim to space*. For example, a story three-fourths (75 per cent) of a column long has been scheduled with the *makeup editor* who has allotted space for it. When the slotman receives the manuscript, however, he notes that it runs a full column. As a direction to the copyeditor, he scribbles at the top of the first sheet of copy: "Trim to .75" or simply ".75". If the paper uses a line count of five typewritten lines to the inch, the notation refers to 75 lines of copy (including allowance for the headline). The copyeditor understands he is to trim the manuscript so that it and its headline will take up but three-fourths of a column.

The order *trim* or *trim for words* is used on stories fat with verbiage. *Boil* or *boil it down* is a more severe order. It instructs the copyeditor to prune each sentence and each unimportant detail. The order to *cut* usually means to delete specific parts until the story is just as short as the facts will allow.

The Copyeditor in Action

Once the story is in the hands of the copyeditor, the detailed process of editing begins. Spreading the manuscript before him, he reads the story carefully, alertly and with all the intelligence and experience at his command.

Some excellent copyeditors read each story three times, once to grasp its general import, once to check on facts and language, and once to formulate headline ideas. Others go over their copy twice, once for corrections and once for headlines. The usual method, however, is to edit a story completely in one reading.

The copyeditor weighs each sentence, each statement of fact and the common sense and credibility of the story as a whole. Here he crosses out a badly chosen word and writes in a better one. There he recasts a sentence or merges some paragraphs. He transposes, combines, corrects errors in English, spelling, punctuation, capitalization, and wherever possible makes the story smoother and more lucid.

The good copyeditor is the friend and helper of the writer and makes no alterations simply to please himself. His job is to help the writer tell a better, clearer story that may be grasped quickly by the reader. Any tampering with facts is, of course, highly dangerous.

The Copydesk

The copyeditor's place in the news machine is midway between that of the reporter and that of the editor.

Especially designed for copyeditors' efficiency and convenience is a horseshoe-shaped table known as the *copydesk*. Highly organized newspaper offices may have four, presided over, respectively, by the city, telegraph, cable and sports editors. Each such executive is a *head-of-the-desk*, popularly called *chief,* and sits in the center or *slot,* his copyeditors around the *rim.*

Medium-sized dailies call their copydesk a *combination* or *universal* desk, because over it passes all kinds of news copy—local, telegraph, state, markets, sports. Still smaller newspapers may have but one or two copyeditors who, in the absence of a copydesk, use conventional tables or desks,

Photo by Albert Moldvay, Denver Post

THIS FAMILIAR HORSESHOE-SHAPED DESK is the copydesk of the Denver *Post,* a universal desk that handles all news copy except sports and society. The slotman sits at the center of the desk. At his left are tubes to convey copy to the composing room. At the extension of the desk are news and wire editors.

probably with typewriters at their elbows. Some newspapers have experimented with a J-shaped desk where departmental editors sit at the extended arm of the desk and work their own copy but yet are part of the universal desk.

Each newspaper perfects its copyediting equipment as its needs and means permit. The tendency of the smaller papers is to adopt and to adapt to their requirements not only the tools but the methods which have been developed in more prosperous metropolitan offices and plants.

METROPOLITAN NEWSPAPER ASSEMBLY LINE

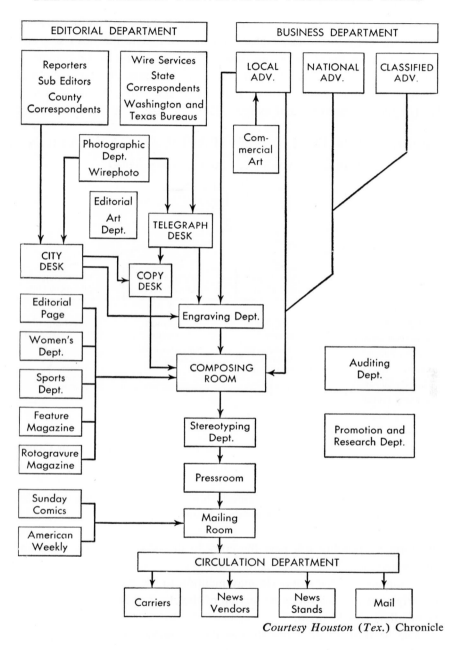

Courtesy Houston (*Tex.*) Chronicle

33

Starting at the Slot

When a reporter on a metropolitan paper finishes writing a story, he delivers the copy to the city editor who may designate the head size and page number for the story before passing the copy along to the copydesk. The head-of-the-desk, or slotman, scans it to judge its accuracy and credibility, to fix its value as news. If it is a routine story, the slotman may *slug* (or name) the story and assign a headline size. If it is a major story

HOMETOWN DAILY NEWSPAPER ORGANIZATION
[SIX DAYS A WEEK, CIRCULATION 8000]

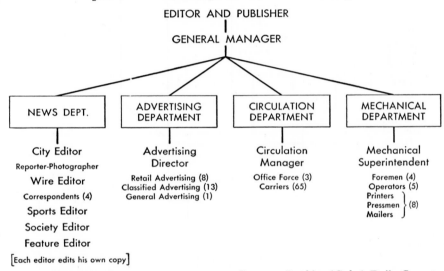

EDITOR AND PUBLISHER

GENERAL MANAGER

NEWS DEPT.	ADVERTISING DEPARTMENT	CIRCULATION DEPARTMENT	MECHANICAL DEPARTMENT
City Editor	Advertising Director	Circulation Manager	Mechanical Superintendent
Reporter-Photographer	Retail Advertising (8)	Office Force (3)	Foremen (4)
Wire Editor	Classified Advertising (13)	Carriers (65)	Operators (5)
Correspondents (4)	General Advertising (1)		Printers, Pressmen, Mailers (8)
Sports Editor			
Society Editor			
Feature Editor			

[Each editor edits his own copy]

Courtesy Boulder (*Colo.*) Daily Camera

Total Number of Fulltime Employes (including Commercial Printing Staff of 15)—67
Services: News Wire (TTS), Syndicated News Features, Syndicated Comics, Plastic Engraver, National Advertising Agency

the slotman probably will pass the copy to the news editor for head and page designation. Before dealing the copy to the copyeditor, the slotman has a fair appraisal of the story. He may mention to the copyeditor to be particularly alert to a questionable section of the story or he suggests an angle the headline should stress.

The head-of-the-desk usually has discretionary power over copy. He may kill the copy as unfit for publication or he may take the copy back to one of the departmental editors and ask for a better story. Since editing is his responsibility, the head-of-the-desk usually has some authority over copy selection.

Most stories are complete when they come to the desk, but when time presses they often come in short installments (or takes) to be discussed in detail later.

Certain copyeditors are adept at handling feature stories; others are experts in politics, municipal affairs, national affairs, war, economics, finance, markets. A top-notch copyeditor is an all-round man, skilled in handling all kinds of copy. The head-of-the-desk knows the powers and limitations of his copyeditors and distributes stories to those who will handle them best.

If Copyeditor Jones has edited the first of a series of stories dealing with a flood, the chances are he will handle succeeding stories concerning the flood, on the theory that he is the man most familiar with names, dates, places, developments and is best equipped to insure accuracy.

Nearing the Presses

Edited copy, together with the headline, goes back to the slotman who studies both the headline and the copy. If he is satisfied with the editing job, he schedules the story and headline on his schedule sheet, then places the copy into a conveyor which takes it to the composing room. If the editing is faulty, the slotman either fixes it himself or returns the copy to the copyeditor for more work.

When copy reaches the composing room, a copy handler distributes the story copy to one operator, the head copy to another. If the story copy is long, he cuts it into segments, labeling each with a code letter, then distributes segments to various operators so that one typesetter does not hold up a long story.

Type is set up in long, strip-like metal boxes called *galleys,* and hence proofs *pulled* from it are known as *galley proofs.* Complete sets are rushed to each editor, from the managing editor down. These men go over them to detect blunders, to eliminate unfit stories and to fix relative values of the various items. Galley proofs occasionally are used by the copyeditor when he is called upon to go to the composing room to *trim at the forms.* This is necessary when the printer, packing the type into the allotted space, finds it too long. He calls for a news editor who trims it by marking on the proof the type to be killed.

Copyediting: A Summary

This chapter has sketched the copyediting process. Now, a motion-picture-in-words summary. It is from a writer on *Time*:

Nineteen minutes before a big city newspaper's first edition goes to press. Page by page, a story starts coming across the city editor's desk.

The city editor reaches for the phone, calls the makeup editor in the composing room. "How are we doing?" he asks. "The City Hall story looks pretty hot."

"We're going to be tight. Keep it down," warns the makeup editor. "We can't squeeze the Washington story another inch."

"Okay," responds the city editor. He looks at the penciled layout for Page One, scribbles some figures in the upper corner of the sheet of copy, and with an expert twist sends it sailing onto the big horseshoe desk next to his own.

"We're tight, Mac," he calls to the man in the slot. "Cut it a third."

Seventeen minutes now to the deadline . . . only ten for cutting, editing, headline writing. For those vital ten minutes, the responsibility rests on the shoulders of the man in the slot . . . newspaper parlance for the head of the copy desk.

A dozen considerations flash their chain lightning patterns across the slotman's mind. Tyler's story . . . Tyler, the brilliant and touchy. He got it out of that certain municipal department which is giving off a faintly gamy odor. The boss will want it in all editions. This isn't the big break though, just another build-up to it. Damn good story . . . real stuff in every paragraph. Hard to cut. Needs a headline with sock. Who's to handle it? Ward's fooling around with that zoo story . . . Won't do, his cuts make Tyler sore. Colihan's a better bet.

"Colihan," says the man in the slot. One of the furious pencil-wielders around the rim of the horseshoe looks up. "Cut this a third and put a 36 head on it in time for the bulldog."

All this has used up 15 seconds.

Colihan has nine and a half minutes to cut and edit and write a top headline and subheadline. Every line of both headlines must count exactly so many characters and spaces, figuring *i* as a half and *m* and *w* one and a half characters. Then the slotman will take just 15 seconds more to review Colihan's work, change "banned" to "curbed," sniff the whole concoction for traces of libel, and shoot it to the news editor in the composing room. It is a shorter story than Tyler's original, and a better one—keener of edge, swifter of impact, yet complete in every essential detail.

Watch what a copyreader [copyeditor] is really doing—you'll see agility and speed to make an Olympic skier look musclebound. Clearing hurdles of phrases in one long broad jump of the pencil. Untying sloppy granny knots, retying the thought strands square—and always on the dead run. Swooping over a field of facts and leaning out to pick the tallest one. Doing the cross-word puzzles called headlines against a time limit and for high stakes.

The slot is not a glamorous job. It hasn't been discovered by Shubert Alley or the fiction magazines. To the cub reporter, eager for bylines and self-expression, the whole copydesk looks backwater. It takes maturity—grasp of the whole art of news presentation—to appreciate the little miracles that a good copydesk passes.

4   Preparing Copy for the Printer

POWER OF THE PRESS

When a doctor makes a mistake he buries it.
When a garage man makes a mistake he adds it on your bill.
When a carpenter makes a mistake it's just what he expected.
When a lawyer makes a mistake it was just what he wanted, because
he has a chance to try the case all over again.
When a judge makes a mistake it becomes the law of the land.
When a preacher makes a mistake nobody knows it.
But when an editor makes a mistake—the trouble starts.
—Tid Bits (London).

I.   COPYEDITING MARKS

The Copyeditor's Tools

Physically, the copyeditor's equipment is not impressive. The copydesk has been mentioned. Add to it a pair of long shears, a handful of soft-lead pencils, an eraser, a drooling pastepot, a "chunk" of copypaper, spindles called *spikes,* a voracious waste basket, a typewriter (if duties include rewriting) and his kit of visible tools is complete.

But in his head he has equipment far more important: the shorthand of the copydesk called *copyediting marks.* Their skilled use is the mark of a professional copyeditor. A student should learn and practice them until his fingers respond with them to an error in copy as automatically as a violinist's fingers take their cue from a musical score. Knowing copyediting marks does not make a copyeditor, but no one can be a professional copyeditor—qualified to sit on the rim—without them.

Guidelines

For very short items, headlines usually are readily set by the same machine that sets body type. Such headlines are written by the copyeditor with generous spacing, above the text.

Larger heads are set separately. These are written by the copyeditor on a separate sheet. To guide the printer, who assembles the type of the headline with that of its story, both sheets are keyed by the head-of-the-desk (or by the copyeditor) with a labeling word. This word or phrase (name of the reporter and story subject) is called the *guideline* or *slugline* or the *guide* or *slug*. Usually the guideline is written at the upper left-hand corner of the copy. The guideline is set into type but is discarded by the makeup man when the headline and the story are brought together.

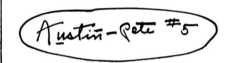

> It was a stolen car, but University of Arizona students had a lot of fun with it last night without harming it, and the owner wasn't angry, so no complaints were filed.
>
> The car was a yellow Austin, a seven-year-old bantam model belonging to Gerald B. Chapeau, 200 East Drachman st. Chapeau parked it on the university

Some newspapers use the first two words of the headline as a guide. (One advantage is that it need not appear on the headline proof.) Thus, a slug might be: MAYOR QUIZZED—1-24-3. (The numerals indicate the head is to be set one column wide, in three lines of 24-point type.)

This system probably finds more favor with smaller dailies than with metropolitan newspapers because on the latter the city editor, news editor or telegraph editor—not the copyeditor—supplies the guideline.

When time presses, a copyeditor often speeds the copy to the typesetter and writes his headline later. In such cases he jots HTK (Hed to Kum) below the guideline.

Letter Changes

The simplest errors of copy are typographical. In ordinary typewritten copy the copyeditor rectifies them in these ways:

Connect letters.	campu s at 8:15 p. m. and
Transpose letters.	went no about his business.
Insert letters.	Son afterwards a group of
Capitalize letters.	students took it to cohise
"Knock down" capital letters to lower case.	Hall, men's dormitory. The
Kill dead letters.	entirfe population soon

Verbal Changes

Similar marks are used for alterations involving whole words, as follows:

Separate words.	pouredout of the hall and
Transpose words.	gathered and around played
Insert matter.	with the machine until after
Kill copy.	near to midnight.
"Run in" copy.	Then the head resi-
Kill corrections.	dent suddenly appeared

Copy is folded in half as it is placed on the typesetting machine. It is held in place on the machine by a copy-holder. Editing marks should be made within the typewritten line or above the line, if possible. Do not edit with arrows. If a paragraph near the bottom of the page of copy is to go near the top, clip and paste rather than draw arrows.

If an entire paragraph is to be deleted, draw a box around the paragraph, mark an X or vertical arrow through the box so the typesetter can find the *pickup* quickly:

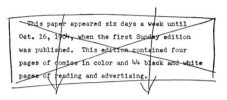

This system is better than crossing out each line because the material remains legible in case the copyeditor later decides to use the paragraph. If he does, he simply writes *stet* beside the paragraph he deleted. Or if his marks have been light, he may simply erase them.

If several successive paragraphs are to be deleted, the copyeditor should use a tear rule and pastepot, ripping out the unwanted copy and closing up the manuscript again. Making copy easy to follow saves money for the paper.

Typographic Instructions

Written English, few people stop to realize, is really two (or four) languages. Children must learn two complete printed (and corresponding written) alphabets, one of small letters and one of capital letters.

This duality is a heritage from old Rome. There the tradesmen and other common folk who could write used cursive letters; but on their stone monuments, patricians had text incised in capital letters such as is still used —with the V for the U—on public buildings. By the time printing was invented in 1440, both kinds of letters were employed; but soon thereafter capitals were limited to present usage.

Type then being set by hand, the capital letters were segregated in an upper pigeon-holed *case* and the small letters were arranged in a case nearer to hand. Thus it is that to this day, capital letters are by printers called *upper case* and small letters *lower case*.

Typesetting machines offer the choice of *caps* and lower case and other variations such as: *small caps,* simply a small capital letter; and *bold face,* a blacker version of regular type in both capital and lower case letters; and *italics*. The latter simulate handwriting—a reminder of the manuscripts (*manu,* hand, *scriba,* to write) of the common people of old Italy.

How copyeditors instruct printers to make use of these special forms of type is indicated below:

Capital letters.	the word Caesar in large letters so that
Small capital letters.	all Rome would know a new conqueror had
"Caps and small caps."	Sleepy eye, Minn.--The one legged
Bold face.	Special to the Evening Call
Italics.	a message vital to all Americans who are

Starts and Stops

Paragraphs and periods are relatively modern inventions. The text of early manuscripts of the Bible, for example, is run together—offering the scholar nice problems of editing, alongside which solving crossword puzzles is a kindergarten exercise. Writings of ancient times were for the highly educated few, but the modern newspaper is for the man-in-the-street and every device is utilized to make it quickly intelligible even to him who reads as he runs.

The cue is taken from spoken language which has full stops (periods), pauses (commas and dashes) and half stops (semicolons). Paragraphs serve a double purpose. They aid the eye with "hooks" of white space—that is, the indentions—and guide the mind by dividing stories into logical units.

Latitude is offered the copyeditor in indicating such punctuation marks omitted by the reporter. Some copyeditors simply insert with pencil the missing mark; others meticulously use a *caret,* ∧, with a line from its apex encircling the added symbol, as:

the right to print the news an inalienable right according to the speaker of the

Another technique is to use the caret over inserted commas, but inverted for apostrophes—ringing the marks. (Some desks prefer not to ring inserted material.)

the news of Mary Jones suicide. Why it was asked, was the detective so eager

Inserted periods should be ringed also. The copyeditor uses a small x instead of the conventional dot:

to solve the mystery?" The prisoner hesitated⊗ The judge repeated the question in a

Three marks are used for paragraphs—the last one shown being preferred.

¶ The old man hesitated   ⨅ To go now was the best   ⌊Slowly the clock intoned

When a paragraph has been indicated in the copy by the usual indention, but no paragraph is wanted, either of two methods can be employed to direct the printer to *run in* the text:

to stop the racket. The verdict was   he could ride any thing with four feet
given at once.⌐   he said.
⌐ The prisoner lifted his head   *NO* ⅋ But he looked with doubt in his
as the words came. No surprise   eyes ⸱as the steed was led before him

Many a slip in countless newspapers has been avoided by the little word "more," always ringed. It is a red lantern to the compositor, warning him that other pages are coming from the copydesk—or have been mislaid. It is used at the bottom of every page of incomplete copy, and, if not typewritten by the reporter, the copyeditor adds it in longhand—circling it in either case. Reporters should not *break over* a sentence from one page to another, but frequently do. Careful copyeditors handling such copy not only use "more" at the bottom of the page, but run a diagonal line from the last word to the margin; on the next page another diagonal tells the compositor to *pick up* the next word of the sentence.

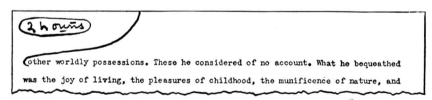

The reporter ordinarily indicates the end of a story by striking the diagonal key on his typewriter thrice, the marks then being ringed by the copyeditor. If this end symbol is lacking, the copyeditor informs the printer "That's all of this one" by writing in the numeral "30" (with which old-time telegraphers are said to have closed dispatches) or this symbol, #:

'Quotes,' Numbers, Abbreviations

Careful copyeditors call the compositor's attention to quotation marks this way:

Horses have fallen on her and with her -- "/I'm always trying to hold 'em in my lap,"
she used to say. She could ride anything that had four legs and hair. Her death re-

Ringing, as is now obvious, is a favored device of the copyeditor. In addition to its eye-attracting use, it is employed to indicate contraction and expansion. When arabic numerals are encircled, they are to be spelled out; when spelled-out numbers are encircled, figures are to be used. The same principle applies to abbreviations. Thus:

Spell out number.	Teetor caught ②trout that day
Use arabic numerals.	while his guide got (twenty). The
Spell out word.	(prof.) had a roaring fire ready
Abbreviate word.	and (Doctor) Fred Carpenter eagerly

Very seldom does the ringing of inserted matter cause any confusion. In the case of abbreviations, it may be desirable not to enclose them completely within the ring. That method, preferred by some copyeditors, gives this result:

two bantam hen in ʌJacob Edges barn ᶜaring for four tiny kittens. The happy family

Special Instructions to Printer

Occasionally stories are to be set in unusual type. It may be that the headline for a Christmas feature story or an editorial is to be set in *Old English*; it may be that the first few paragraphs of an important piece of news are to be set in large type; it may be that text in typewriting type is needed to simulate a letter. In all such cases, instructions to the printer are carefully written by the copyeditor or head-of-the-desk, either in the margin or on a separate sheet and ringed.

"Letter space" is a command to the compositor to *throw in* a slight amount of space between letters, sometimes needed to balance two lines in a headline. Some copyeditors use this mark: "ltr #."

Four seldom used, but generally understood, marks are *folo* and *folo lit.,* *hold,* and *lead out.* They are used on copy in all or part already printed—clippings, excerpts from books, etc. "Folo" on copy tells the compositor to follow all signs, symbols, figures, italics, abbreviations, idiomatic words, but to observe office rules on capitalization, punctuation and compound words. "Folo lit." (follow literally) means to reproduce the text exactly, even with its errors. "As Is" or "OK" or a check mark ($\sqrt{}$) over or following unusual words are sometimes used for the same purpose.

"Hold" or "hold for release" tells the printer not to allow the copy to be printed until special orders are given. "Lead out" means to insert metal *leads* (pronounced *lĕds*; *see Appendix*) between the lines of type, an easy way of giving prominence to text.

Writing Subheads

Not all newspapers use subheads. Some papers require the reporter to write them, but usually they are inserted longhand by the copyeditor. Tabloids may use subheads only a few lines apart, but the general rule for stories more than 200 words in length, is to interpolate a subhead wherever one phase of the story is finished and another begins—on the "natural breaks." This is not always possible, however, and a more exact practice is to place a subhead at intervals of every 125 or 150 words, a system that makes for uniformity and some degree of typographical beauty. Occasionally this method will necessitate the "forcing" of a paragraph, but not often, as the rule is not to be taken too literally.

As a rule, stories of 200 words or fewer do not require subheads. Some newspapers have a rule against using only one subhead in a story.

Subheads must say something. They should never be flat, dead, lifeless labels. They are subject to the same rigid but necessary standards as the major headlines. With a little thought and effort, copyeditors can make subheads a decided attraction to the reader, adding one more inducement to attract the eye farther into the body of the story. A bad subhead interrupts the story; a good one enhances its value, causing no perceptible break.

Methods of inserting them vary, but the following form is in general use. The symbols ⌐ ⌐ indicate the line is to be centered "Bflc" means "bold face [caps and] lower case." Some copyeditors write it "fflc," the "ff" signifying "full face." Or the wavy underline can be used, as already noted.

include Clyde Kelly, Corrine Kearney, Karl Krueger, Ray Schmitz, and other members

of the club. ⊕flc ⌐ Krueger to head ⌐

⌐They will join the celebrants in a fiesta evening commemorating the

shift two years ago from a two column to a three column format. Krueger, master of

Or *subhed* may be written out or abbreviated (S.H.) to make positive the printer understands:

puppetry, will stage the show. "Dessert Worth Price"

(Subhed) ⌐"I want it distinctly understood," he declared, "that while no admission

is charged, the dessert alone will be worth the entire price of the meal." When

Telegraph Copy

Before the advent of the teletypesetter, most telegraph copy came to the desk in capital letters. The copyeditor treated it as though it were entirely in lower case; underscoring letters to be printed in caps. Here is a bit of edited wire copy for a typical metropolitan newspaper:

CHICAGO, NOV. 19--COUPLES WHO MARRY TO "SETTLE DOWN" ARE LIKELY TO BE

HEADED FOR DIFFICULTIES, SAID DR. PAUL POPENOE, DIRECTOR OF THE INSTITUTE OF

FAMILY RELATIONS, LOS ANGELES, IN AN ADDRESS HERE.

⌐MOST MARRIAGE DIFFICULTIES ARE CAUSED BY IMPROPER BALANCE OF NORMAL

HUMAN NEEDS," POPENOE SAID. "THESE ARE THE NEEDS FOR SOCIAL ACCEPTANCE,

A FULL EMOTIONAL LIFE, AND SOME OUTLET FOR INDIVIDUAL CREATIVE IMPULSES."

On many copydesks, the triple underscoring symbol is simplified to one line. Some small papers have trained compositors to capitalize proper words without the copyeditor marking them.

Longhand: A Caution

Few copyeditors have a Spencerian hand. To avoid mistaking a "u" for an "n," they always underscore the former and overscore the latter when they appear in longhand. Some go so far as to underscore "w" and "a" and overscore "m" and "o" for the same reasons, though most copyeditors think such refinements unnecessary.

Reasons

Back of the copyeditor's arbitrary marks are reasons rooted deep in experience. The typesetter has a monotonous job, yet often works under pressure. He must be given every aid possible for quick and accurate work. Furthermore, corrections in type cost money. *Copyeditors should make every correction conspicuously obvious.*

Omit No Marks

Many beginners omit paragraph marks and neglect corrections in spelling, capitalization and punctuation. Such practices constitute a wholly mistaken idea of copyediting.

The good copyeditor leaves nothing to chance or to the other fellow. There must be no opportunity for error, however slight. The copyeditor who neglects paragraphing will neglect other things. Correct spelling is just as important to the dignity of the paper as correct statement of facts. If a paper is slovenly in language and general style, the plain implication is that it also is slovenly in reporting the news.

Capable copyeditors have so mastered their marks that inserting them is second nature. Indeed, they ofttimes find themselves vaguely ill at ease while reading poorly printed or edited magazines or books until they pencil in the needed corrections.

The Edited Copy

Here follows a little feature story as it appeared after leaving the copyeditor's hand. The instructions were to "trim." Note carefully the explanations of the marks at the side.

Guideline, reporter's name, and headline number.

Byline to go in bold upper and lower case.

The copyeditor has checked on the reporter. The name is "Leigh" not "Lee."

A sentence is killed and broken lines are linked.

Word killed; letter changed.

Paragraph. Always mark quotes as indicated.

Another trim.

Dead letter deleted.

Use figures; period and quotes inserted. A trim.

Paragraph; missing letter supplied.

Paragraph and quotes.

Capital and lower case letters. Story not ended. The diagonal line indicates a continuation of the sentence on the next page.

GODIVA--Jack   #6

By A. Jack

Thomas Leigh, 20 years old, 1535 N. Mansfield ave., was out of breath last night when he rang the rear doorbell of his home. He was out of clothes too and perhaps of courage. He was out of everything else, it seems, too, except goose flesh.

"Quick," he gasped, "give me a blanket and stir up the fire and put some coffee on. Believe me or not but the plain facts of the matter are that I am playing the Mr. Godiva role with short hair and no horse and the thermometer stands at thirty three degrees exactly, if you will but take the trouble to look at it. #"

After he had been wrapped up and thawed a little he told his story.

"I was going by the alley near Custer and Sitting Bull streets, eight

more

Page number, guideline, reporter identification. The carry-over line indicates no paragraph.	2 GODIVA --Jack
Letter corrected.	blocks soᵁth of here when three big men
Quotes.	with guns stopped me," he said.
Paragraph and quotes.	"They forced me to the alley and took the 89 cents I had. Then one of them said:
Paragraph and double quotes.	"You must think we are in this business for fun. We'll show you we are out to make a profit on every deal."
Letter elided, period, and half-quotes.	
Paragraph and quotes.	"Then they took off my topcoat and my suit and my shoes and whatever else I had on and told me to beat it. It is dix difficult
Dead letters out.	
Words separated.	to explain my state of mind as I dashed
Words transposed.	from ash barrel to barrel ash, from shadow
Text killed by mistake restored.	to shadow, wondering what the neighbors
Quotes.	would think if they saw me."
Paragraph and inserted apostrophe.	One witness to Mr. Leigh's escapade has been found, but he refused to comment.
Quotes indicated —and elided.	"I am a friend of Tom's" was all that he would say.
One way of trimming or killing at the end of a paragraph. Note the text is so clear that if the copy-editor changes his mind it can be restored by writing "stet" in the margin.	Police are searching for the bandits who made Mr. Thomas an unwilling polar bear.
Closing mark. Always use one.	///

II.   THE STYLEBOOK

Every Newspaper Has 'Style'

Style has a special meaning for those who process words to be used, whether in book, magazine, newspaper or radio and TV scripts. It is a catch-all of rules for spelling and capitalization, abbreviation and punctuation and other details. These rules are set forth in a *stylebook* or *stylesheet*. If a newspaper doesn't have one, the reporter and copyeditor are expected to study the paper so as to recognize its style.

Learn the Stylebook

It is a point of pride on any well-conducted newspaper to be consistent in style. And the first task of a copyeditor on a new job is to learn his paper's rules and special instructions.

Most stylebooks start by telling the reporter of basic requirements of preparing copy. These also pertain to copyediting. The instructions that follow are typical:

Use a typewriter and regulation copypaper for newsstories. Never write them in longhand.

Type on one side of the sheet only and double space.

Begin your story about the middle of the first page.

Indent deeply (at least five spaces) the beginning of each paragraph.

Stories should be identified on the first page with a slugline—the name of the reporter, and a word identifying the story.

Each page thereafter also carries the page number.

If the story requires more than one page, type the word "more" at the bottom of each page except the last. There you indicate its conclusion with the sign: # or ///.

If a story is written in "takes"; *i.e.,* sending along one page at a time, slug the second page: add 1–Fire, the second: add 2–Fire, and the last take— last add–Fire.

All copy added to, inserted in, or preceding the original story should carry the slug of the original story.

Many newspapers require one or more carbon copies of stories.

Instructions to Copyeditors

Use a soft black pencil.

Write your corrections, changes, subheads and headlines so they can be read quickly and correctly.

Overscore with your pencil longhand "n's" and "m's" and underscore "u's," and "w's."

Ring the reporter's name and "more"—and all instructions to the printer.

Erasing penciled marks that you wish to cancel usually is better than crossing them out.

If changes make the copy illegible, retype it—or see that someone does. Then go over it again for errors.

Turn out legible copy always. And make it as neat as possible.

If you're not sure what the instructions mean, ask the head-of-the-desk or the person who wrote the instructions.

Never forget your responsibility: *When copy leaves your hands it should be in its final form.*

Typical Stylebook Practice

Language is made less by grammarians than by usage. Newspapers vary in practice, but those that capitalize sparingly are downstyle. Many editors insist that consistency is more important than style peculiarities. And on a few papers, style is the way the compositor sets the type. Obviously the only way to bring uniformity in a newspaper is to devise a printed stylesheet and insist that all departments, including the composing room, follow it.

Photo courtesy the Associated Press

NERVE CENTER of the *Associated Press* is the bureau in New York. At right front is the general desk and at right rear is most of the bureau's TTS operation.

Adherence to a specific style saves space and time. Every finger stroke on a typesetting machine costs money. To make a capital letter requires one more motion than a lower case letter. To spell out words, which would be just as well understood if used in figures or in abbreviations, not only consumes more time at the typesetting machine but requires additional newspaper space. Thus, newspapers have gradually eliminated all time and space-consuming niceties not absolutely essential to quick and exact transmission of information from the printed page to the reader's mind.

Newspapers using *teletypesetter* copy (received on tape from a wire service) are compelled to use the style of the wire service for wire copy. That style thereby becomes standard for local copy also. This trend was given impetus in 1953 by a stylebook issued by the *Associated Press*. The following is adapted (with permission) from it.[1]

CAPITALIZATION

Capitalize:

All proper names, days of the week but not seasons: *Monday* but *spring.*

Titles preceding names: *Secretary of State John Foster Dulles* but *Dulles, secretary of state.* In titles, ex- and former are lower case: *ex-champion, former President Harry S. Truman.*

Heads of government when the person, not the office, is meant: *President, King, Pope,* etc. Hence: *He told the Prime Minister* but *as a candidate for president of the United States.*

Positions of authority as titles: *Umpire Bill McDermott* but *McDermott, umpire.* But not occupational or "false" titles: *day laborer Hodge Percival* or *Yankee southpaw Phil Saunders.*

Legislatures both as nouns and adjectives: *Senate, House, Legislature, General Assembly, House of Lords,* etc. Hence: *The Senate voted on the House bill.* (This rule also applies to City Council and such groups.)

Legislative committees, Cabinet, and specific courts: *Senate Foreign Relations Committee* but *the committee and its subcommittee; the Court of Appeals* but *the court.*

Federal and state departments: *U.S. Department of Agriculture, USDA,* but *the department, New York State Thruway Authority* but *the authority.*

Political parties: *Democrat, Republican, Communist* as *He is a Republican* but *a republican form of government.*

Synonyms for countries: *Union, Republic, the Colonies* (referring to the original 13) but *federal, nation, government* except in official titles.

[1] Single copies are available, price $1, from the Traffic Department, The Associated Press, 50 Rockefeller Plaza, New York 20, N.Y. Special rates for quantities are available to schools and libraries.

Specific military groups: *U.S. Navy, Army, Air Force, Marines.* It is *soldier* and *sailor* when they stand alone, but *Marine* always. Other special groups also are capitalized: *Evzone, Swiss Guard, Bengal Lancer, etc.,* when alone.

Wars: *World War I,* but *the first World War, War of Independence, Korean War, the Revolution* (U.S. and U.S.S.R.).

Special events and holidays, fanciful appellations: *Mothers Day, Reformation Day, National Safety Week, Old Glory, Leatherneck, Galloping Ghost.*

Descriptive terms for regions or geographical features: *the Buckeye State, the Deep South,* the *Arctic Circle, the Orient, East* or *West Germany* (as political entities), *the West.* Mere direction is not capitalized: *He started west, in south Germany, the southernmost counties.*

Words denoting the Deity, the Bible or other sacred writings, all confessions of faith and adherents, and Satan specifically: *the Scriptures, Divine Father* but *divine guidance; Hades* but *hell.*

Astronomical bodies as such: *Mercury, the Sun, Venus, the Earth* but *the moon is smaller than the earth.*

Races and racial groups: *Caucasian, Negro, Oriental, Occidental* but *white, black, yellow, red* (never *colored*).

Proper names of fauna: *Hereford cattle, Plymouth Rock hen, Dalmatian dog* but not the kinds as *bantam chicken, a terrier,* etc.

No names or derivatives of proper names that have acquired an independent meaning or are not associated with their source: *dutch oven, brussels sprouts, paris green, plaster of paris.*

Degrees when abbreviated: *B.A.* and *Ph.D.* but *bachelor of arts* and *doctor of philosophy.*

Fraternal organizations: *Knights of Columbus, K. of C., Ancient Free and Accepted Masons, AF&AM* (note different abbreviations), *B'nai B'rith* (no abbreviation).

Organizations and recognized events: *American Legion, Boy Scouts* but *the legion* and *the scouts; the seventh annual South Dakota Fair* but *the seventh annual fair; the Kentucky Derby* and *the Davis Cup* but *the derby* and *the cup.*

Military decorations: *Congressional Medal of Honor, Silver Star, Croix de Guerre.*

Books, plays, songs: *"The House by the Side of the Road"* (usually *a, the, of, in,* and *by* are capitalized only at the beginning or end).

First words of direct or indirect quotations when they make a complete sentence, usually after a comma or colon: *Franklin said, "A penny saved is a penny earned."* and *He replied: "Fly a kite."* and *The question is: Do we change our rules?*

Most abbreviations (see section on abbreviations).

Common nouns that are an essential part of a proper name—but they are lower case when standing alone: *Hoover Dam* but *the dam, the Missouri River* but *the river, the Blue Room, Macalester College* but *the college, Custer County Courthouse* but *the courthouse* and *the county.*

Van in Dutch names usually but make it *von, d', da, della,* and *de* in foreign names except where the person prefers it otherwise. Examples: *Justice*

Van Devanter and *Irenee du Pont* but *Samuel F. Du Pont.* The spelling a man wants, he should get.

Trade names and trademarked names with the noun usually in lower case: *Peace rose* and *Foamite extinguisher, Sabrejet* and *Coca-Cola* and *Coke.*

Capitalize fanciful appellations: *Keystone State, South Side.*

ABBREVIATIONS

These save time. But be sure the reader understands them. If in doubt, spell out the name when first used.

Abbreviate:

Without space or periods, the shortened names of certain government agencies, military terms, radio and television stations, time zones, organizations and corporations. Here usage rules. Examples:

ECA, TVA, ICC, AWOL, MP, KP, GI, GI's, MIG MIG's, NBC, WABC-TV, EST, EDT, AFL, CIO, YMCA, YMHA, DAR, B&O, AT&T, AP, UP, SPAR, WAVE (organizations), *Spar, Wave* (members).

These business names: *Corp., Co., Bro., Bros., Inc., Assn., Ltd.* (but *Twentieth Century Limited,* a trade name).

Addresses: *St., Blvd., Ave., Sq., Ter., Pl., Rd., N., E., S., W.,* but *NW* and *SE,* etc., as *163 W. 43d St.* and *164 B, NE* and *807 Reba Pl.* and *9900 E. Broadway at 22nd,* but *the paving on West boulevard.*

Lower case these—with periods: *m.p.h., f.o.b., c.o.d., a.m.,* and *p.m.* but in measurements use *mm* or *mm.* for millimeters.

These states when following cities, airbases, airports, etc.:

Ala., Ariz., Ark., Calif., Colo., Conn., Del., Fla., Ga., Ill., Ind., Kan., Ky., La., Md., Mass., Mich., Minn., Miss., Mo., Mont., N.C., N.D., Neb., Nev., N.H., N.J., N.M., N.Y., Okla., Ore., Pa., R.I., S.C., S.D., Tenn., Tex., Va., Vt., Wash., Wis., W. Va., Wyo. (but not *Idaho, Iowa, Maine, Ohio, Utah*).

Also these territories and possessions: *C.Z.* (Canal Zone), *P.R.* (Puerto Rico), *V.I.* (Virgin Islands); but not *Alaska* and *Hawaii.*

These Canadian provinces, likewise when preceded by a place name: *Alta., B.C., Man., N.S., Que., Ont., Sask., Nfld., N.B.;* also *B.W.I.* (British West Indies).

No countries (it is *Canada, England, India,* etc.) except *U.S.* when it is part of a name as *U.S. Junior Chamber of Commerce* and *US* for ships as *USS Missouri* and (in a series) *USIS* for *U.S. Information Service.* The *United States* is always spelled out as a noun but the *Union of Socialist Soviet Republics* may be shortened to *U.S.S.R.*

United Nations as in *U.N. Educational, Social, and Cultural Organization,* or *UNESCO.*

Degrees after the name of an individual—in this order: religious or theological, earned academic, and honorary academic (consult appendix of dictionary for proper terms) as *Jedediah Smith, D.D., Ph. D., D. Lit.*

These titles: *Mr., Mrs., Dr., M., Mlle., Mme., Rev., Prof., Dist. Atty., Sen., Rep., Dep., Asst., Msgr., Atty. Gen., Lt. Gov., Gov. Gen.,* and *Supt.* (Never use *Rev. Smith.* Make it *the Rev. Mr. Smith.*)

These Air Force and Army officer titles: *Gen., Lt. Gen., Maj. Gen., Brig. Gen., Col., Lt. Col., Maj., Capt., 1st Lt., 2nd Lt.*

These Army designations for enlisted men: *M. Sgt., Sgt. 1.C., 1st Sgt., Sgt., Cpl., Pfc., Pvt.*; also *C.W.O.* (chief warrant officer) and *W.O. (j.g.).*

These Navy officer titles: *Adm., Fleet Adm., Vice Adm., Rear Adm.,* (no abbreviation for *Commodore*) *Capt., Cmdr., Lt. Cmdr., Lt., Lt. (j.g.), Ens.*

These Marine designations: *T. Sgt., S. Sgt., C.W.O.* (commissioned warrant officer).

Months, when followed by specific dates (except March, April, May, June, July)—*Sept. 3, 1954, September 1954.*

Abbreviate St. and Ste. (except *Saint John, N.B.*): *St. Louis, Sault Ste. Marie.*

Do Not Abbreviate:

Christmas to *Xmas.* (*Yule* permitted.)

Christian names. Make it *Robert, Charles, Alexander,* etc., except in cases where the person prefers it abbreviated: *Alex. O. Potter, Jeff Williams, Tom J. Davis.*

University, court, or district.

Brothers, railroad, railway, company, or corporation except when they follow a name (or are abbreviated in official name): *Pennsylvania railroad, Lever Bros., Crane Co.*

Cents: Make it *35 cents,* not *35¢,* except on market pages.

The United States of America, except to *U.S.A.* or *U.S.N.* written after names of army or navy men and women.

Fort or Mount, when part of city names: *Fort Myers, Mount Vernon*; but *Mt. Everest, Ft. Douglas.*

Port, point, detective, commandant, field marshal, general manager, postmaster general.

Days of the week.

PUNCTUATION

The Period (full stop):

The period is the most useful mark of punctuation for newspapermen.

Omit it after headlines, captions, subheads, figure and paragraph numbers, single-line heads, Roman numerals, letters used in formulas, the word *per cent,* compass points, and radio stations: *KDKA, NNE* (but N. latitude).

Use a period with abbreviations: *Dr. Ainsley Rosen, Col. Robert L. Barnes.*

Use a series of periods (in this case called leaders) to indicate omission of quoted matter: "in the beginning . . . the darkness was upon the face of the deep. . . ."

The Comma (pause):

Wherever the lack of a comma renders the meaning doubtful, use one:

Use no comma in: *5 feet 11 inches; 7 hours 36 minutes 13 seconds*; and *Northwestern 2, Notre Dame 2.*

Punctuate lists of names with cities or states thus: *Thelma Crosbie, Peoria; David Morris, Park Ridge.*

Omit the comma before *of: Georgette Marseille of Paris.*

Omit the comma before "and" and "or" except where such omission makes the meaning confusing. *Fish abounded in the lake, and the shore was lined with deer.*

Omit the comma between name and abbreviation of persons, before the ampersand, dash, in street numbers, years and serial numbers: *John Jones Jr., Smith, Jones & Co., 1628 Oak St., A16503421.*

Use commas to set off parenthetic words, phrases or clauses and appositions: *The work, he said, was exacting. Smith, the favorite, won handily.*

Punctuate: *At the Zion Memorial church, Paul Teetor, pastor, services were held.*

If the introductory clause is short it need not be followed by a comma. If the clause is so long that a comma would make it more readily understood by the reader, the comma should be used. (This paragraph illustrates the point.)

Restrictive clauses—that is, clauses that restrict or "tie down" the word they modify—should not be separated from this word by a comma: *The boy who is willing is in demand.* Nonrestrictive clauses, that add some explanation or comment, should be set off by commas: *The boy, who saw what was going on, hesitated and then ran.*

The Colon (the anticipative stop):

Use a colon after a statement introducing a direct quotation of one or more sentences. In such cases the material following the colon is usually paragraphed.

Or to introduce a series of results: *Those elected were: Hector Hinojosa, president*; etc.

A colon should be used to introduce a formal resolution of a deliberative body: *"Resolved: Whereas revenues . . ."*

Use a colon between chapter and verse in Scripture references: *John 3:16.*

If the colon introduces a complete sentence, capitalize the first word: *He made this point: The county needs the money.*

Use a colon in extended clock time and in time sequences: *6:30, 1:24:30:1* (hours, minutes, seconds, tenths).

The Semicolon (half-stop):

Use a semicolon to separate coordinate clauses of the same sentence when they are not separated by a coordinate conjunction: *There are the Indians; we should have taken the other trail.*

A semicolon should be used to separate a series of names and addresses, or to replace commas in any series for the sake of clarity: *Homer P. Shepherd,*

Lyndhurst, N.J.; Altman Read, Leavenworth, Kan.; and *apples which had been purchased in New York; California pears;* etc.

Commas are too weak to punctuate the end of a paragraph of an uncompleted list. Dashes call undue attention to the break. Use a semicolon preceded by *and* as in the following:

John Norment, Frances Fuller, Donald Mills, Dean Nauman, John Taylor Arms, Arthur William Brown, and Peter Paul Ott; Lynn Bogue Hunt, W. T. Benda, Devitt Welsh, Harvey Dunn, etc.

The Dash:

It is easy to overdo the dash. Try to use commas or parentheses instead.

Use the dash after a name at the beginning of a quotation as: *Barnes—I have no statement to make.* (Use no quotation marks for this form.)

Use the dash after question and answer in verbatim testimony: *Q.—How old are you? A.—Twenty-three.*

Use a dash in these cases: *First—, Second—, and Table 2—Continued; and Note—.*

A dash (without a period) may denote the unfinished state of a sentence: *"Well, I hardly—"*

Or for an emphatic pause: *He fired the cannon and hit—nothing.*

In announcing sport events: *shot put—Casey, first; Wojinski, second;* etc.

To replace parentheses: *He claimed—and no one denied it—priority.*

The Apostrophe:

Use an apostrophe to mark an omission: *I've, can't, don't, it's, (it is), '95.*

Use the apostrophe for possessive except in pronouns: *the boy's clothes, Burns's poems;* but *its, ours, yours, theirs.*

Use no apostrophe in such common abbreviations as *varsity, phone, bus.*

Use the apostrophe in making plurals of letters, but not plurals of figures: *early '90s; four A's.*

Use the apostrophe in making plurals of Greek letter societies: *Pi Kappa Delta's; the Beta's.*

If the singular ends in s, add apostrophe and s, unless the second s makes pronunciation difficult: *Lois's book,* but *Moses' leadership, Jones' hat.*

If the plural ends in s, only the apostrophe is added: *The girls' books, the Joneses' houses.*

Use the official form in geographic, institution, firm or organization name: *Johns Hopkins University, Reader's Digest, Court of St. James's, Harpers Ferry, Harper's Weekly.*

Use but one apostrophe to indicate common possession: *Norvell and Robert's glider.*

Quote:

All quotations when they are to be set in the same type and measure as the rest of the text, but not when they are in narrower measure or smaller type.

A quotation within a quotation requires single quotation marks; a third quotation reverts to double quotation marks.

Put "weak" punctuation marks—periods and commas—inside quotation marks, but the "strong" ones—question marks, exclamation points, colons and semicolons—outside, unless the punctuation is a part of the quotation.

All direct testimony, conversation and interviews given in direct form, except when the name of speaker or Q. and A., with a dash, precedes, as: *Mannel Hahn—I have nothing to say; Q.—What is your name? A.—Marjorie Hough.*

To set off a word of unusual meaning or an unfamiliar, ironic or coined word: "lame duck" amendment.

Names of books, dramas, paintings, operas, songs, subjects of lectures, sermons, magazine articles, including the initial "A" or "The."

Use quotation marks at the beginning of each paragraph of a continuous quotation of several paragraphs, but at the end of the last paragraph only.

Do Not Quote:

Names of characters in plays: Peter Grimm, *in "The Return of Peter Grimm."*

Names of newspapers or periodicals: Manchester *Guardian.*

Names of vessels, animals and sleeping cars.

Common nicknames, as: Deadwood Dick; when they are used with the full name use parentheses: *Richard (Deadwood Dick) Clark.*

Parentheses:

Avoid parentheses as much as possible in news copy.

If an entire sentence is enclosed in parentheses, the period should come before the last curve.

If any mark is required after the portion of the sentence preceding the parentheses, put it after the second curve.

When the name of the state, though not a part of the title of a newspaper, is given with the title, use this form: Mankato (Minn.) *Free Press.* Omit the name of the state after large cities: New York *Times.*

When parenthetical matter makes more than one paragraph, start each paragraph with a parenthesis and end the final paragraph with a parenthesis.

The Question Mark:

Use this at the end of all expressions containing a question, rhetorical or otherwise.

The Hyphen:

Use the hyphen in measures only if used as adjectives: *3-inch valve, 7-foot plank;* but *3 inches long.*

Write as one word: *baseball, basketball, football, today, tonight, homecoming, textbook, thunderstorm, cannot, bookcase, downstate, upstate, snowstorm, lineup, newsstory, copypaper, newsman, writeup, makeup, nationwide, weekend.*

Use the hyphen with all prefixes joined to proper names: *un-American, anti-Legion, pre-Raphaelite.*

Words compounded of the following prefixes and suffixes usually are written without the hyphen: *a, after, ante, auto, bi, demi, ever, grand, holder, in, inter, intra, less, mid, mis, non, off, on, over, post, re, some, sub, super, trans, tri, un, under, up, ward, wise, with.*

Words compounded with the following prefixes and suffixes are hyphenated (except in cases where familiar usage indicates otherwise): *anti-, able-, brother-, by-, cross-, -elect, ex-, father-, great-, half-, -hand, mother-, open-, public-, quarter-, -rate, self-, semi-.* Do not hypenate *vice president, commander in chief, sergeant at arms,* etc.

Do not use the hyphen when one word is usually made of subjoined words and used as an adjective: *brotherhood, faraway, cottonseed, hardwood, hardworking, nearby, redhot, tumbledown,* and *wornout.*

The tendency is toward combining words and eliminating hyphens. When a proper name is an element in a compound word, however, or when an odd combination would result from omission of the hyphen, the hyphen is used. Examples: *Judas-like, bell-like, re-echo, pre-empt* but coordinate.

Use the hyphen in double occupation or office: *poet-artist, secretary-treasurer.*

Use hyphens to differentiate between words of similar or identical spelling but different meaning: *correspondent, co-respondent; overall, over-all; resent, re-sent; recover, re-cover.*

An adverb ending in "ly" never takes a hyphen when used with an adjective to form a compound adjective: *newly chosen.*

FIGURES

Spell out numbers from one through nine; 10 and above may be used as figures. Note exceptions below.

Use *3:45 p.m.; sailing at 9 a.m. Friday.* (Never *9 a.m. this morning.*)

Use *July 28, 1951.* Omit the st., th., rd., etc., after dates.

Use figures for all sums of money: *$5.* Not *$5.00.*

The dollar sign is not used in round sums of millions or billions. Spell instead: *one million dollars, 20 billion dollars.* But: *$1,657,318.*

Casual figures may be spelled: *I wouldn't touch it with a ten-foot pole.* But: *The flag hung from a 10-foot staff.*

Fractions are confined (in figures) to eighths: ⅛ ¼ ½ ¾ Other fractions are spelled: *three-sixteenths.*

Decimalized fractions are avoided except in tabular matter. In textual matter: *2½ million.* But *2,333,000,* not *2⅓ million.*

Use figures for street numbers: *807 Reba pl.*

Use figures for scores, degrees of temperature, telephone numbers, automobile numbers, latitudes and longitudes, distances, times in races, betting odds, votes, percentages, prices, dimensions and in a series of related expressions: *90 degrees, 65 per cent, 90 x 120 feet; 60-foot beam. Means had 3 suits, 12 pairs of shoes, 65 shirts, 102 ties, 2 overcoats and 1 trunk.* But: *There were ninety 4-room houses, six 8-room houses.*

Use figures for sporting records: *Yale 14, Harvard 6.*

Use figures for ages: *He was 21 years old; 2-year-old Bobby.*

Avoid beginning a sentence with a figure. If you must use a number to start a sentence, spell it: *Seventy members of the club,* etc.

Ordinals above 10 carry the th, nd, rd, and st: *33rd, 57th, 22nd.*

Ordinals below 10 are spelled out except in classifying orchestra instruments or voices, in addresses or in political or military divisions: *1st Army, 1st Ward, 1st violin, 2nd tenor, first contingent.*

Use Roman numerals for personal sequences, wars, Popes, royalty, yachts and horses: *Pope Pius XI, John Jones III, Shamrock IX, Hanover II, World War II.*

CHURCH USAGE

Follow official usage in church titles and terms.

ROMAN CATHOLIC—*the Rev. John Smith. Father Smith* (never *Mr.*).

Rt. Rev. Msgr. Jones, Msgr. Jones.

The Most Rev. John Jones, bishop of the Denver diocese; Bishop Jones.

Francis Cardinal Spellman, archbishop of the New York archdiocese; Cardinal Spellman.

Sister Mary Joseph (never *Sister Jones*).

EPISCOPAL—deacon or priest: *the Rev. John Jones, the Rev. Mr. Jones.*

A dean: *the Very Rev. John Jones, the Rev. Mr. Jones, Dean Jones.*

A bishop: *the Rt. Rev. John Jones, the Rev. Mr. Jones, Bishop Jones.*

An archbishop: *the Most Rev. John Jones, the Rev. Mr. Jones, Archbishop Jones.*

(In "high church" dioceses the terminology is the same as for Roman Catholic prelates.)

JEWISH—*Rabbi James Wise, Rabbi Wise, Dr. Wise.*

Cantor Harry Epstein, Cantor Epstein.

CHRISTIAN SCIENCE—Practitioner, Lecturer, Reader (never reverend in any form).

SEVENTH DAY ADVENTIST—*Elder John Jones, Elder Jones.*

METHODIST—Pastor, Minister, Preacher, Bishop. Use of "the Rev. Mr." in surname form is correct.

LUTHERAN—*Pastor John Jones, Pastor Jones; the Rev. Mr. Jones.*

Scandinavian usage follows same form as Episcopal.

LATTER-DAY SAINTS (do not use *Mormon church* but its members may be called *Mormons*). *Pres. David O. McKay, Pres. McKay; Elder Harold B. Lee, Elder Lee; Presiding Bishop LeGrand Richards, Bishop Richards; Bishop Joseph L. Wirthlin of the Presiding Bishopric, Bishop Wirthlin.*

Church Terms:

Mass is celebrated, said or read. High Mass is sung (never held). The Rosary is recited or said (never read). Services close with the Benediction of the Blessed Sacrament.

Various segments of the several religions are diocese, area, presbytery, synod.

TITLES

Always give initials or first names of persons the first time they appear: use both initials or first names; never *Mr. Howard Potter,* or *Mr. H. Potter,* make it *Mr. Potter* or *Howard Potter.*

Give first name of unmarried women, not initials only: *Miss Lily Pons,* not *Miss L. Pons.*

Make it: *the Rev. Robert Chapler,* or *the Rev. Mr. Chapler.* Do not omit *the.*

Never say: *Mrs. Doctor Struthers,* or *Mrs. Professor Hines.* The husband's title belongs to him alone. If the wife has the title, she is *Prof. Katrinka Struthers* or *Professor Hines.*

Avoid long and awkward titles before a name: *Superintendent of Street Cleaning Smith. Paul Smith, superintendent of street cleaning,* is much better.

Avoid the use of such titles as *Attorney Arthur Neu* or *Colonel* (for auctioneer) *Karl Franke.*

Properly speaking, titles belong to the office and not the officeholder. When Judge John Walsh leaves the bench, he becomes John Walsh or former Judge John Walsh. Military titles of the grade of captain and above are an exception to this rule [especially in the South].

Write it: *Mr. and Mrs. Roscoe Page,* not *Roscoe Page and wife*; and *Prof. and Mrs. E. H. Hahne,* not *Mr. and Mrs. Prof. E. H. Hahne.*

FOREIGN TITLES

The following are approved forms for English titles:

King	Queen
the Duke of	the Duchess of
the Marquis of	the Marchioness of
Earl (or *the Earl of*)	Countess
Viscount	Viscountess
Baron	Baroness
(More commonly, *Lord* and *Lady*)	
Sir John Bennett	Lady Bennett (Never use her given name
(Thereafter, *Sir John*)	unless she has the title by birth)

Baronet is a hereditary title. Its holders are distinguished from *knights* by the abbreviation, *Bart.* or *Bt., as Sir Samuel Higbee, Bart.*

Use *the Right Honorable* rarely. Say *Captain Sir Edward Jones*; thereafter in a story make it *Sir Edward* or *Captain Jones.* The wife of a *Lord Mayor* may be called the *Lady Mayoress.* It is *Sir Winston* and *Lady Churchill.*

LATIN NAMES

The first of the double Latin name refers to the father's family name and the second to the mother's. It is *Guillermo Martinez Marquez*; thereafter, *Mr. Martinez* (not *Mr. Marquez*).

5 Writing the Simple Headline

When you stop to think how few people read beyond the headlines and how much of public opinion is made by headlines, you begin to realize the enormous influence exerted by the journalist who sits at a desk and writes the headlines.—Glenn Frank (1887–1940), *educator, editor* and *commentator.*

He [the copyeditor] must be master of the art of headline writing, one of the most difficult of the arts, and the least acclaimed and appreciated, even in newspaper offices.—Neil MacNeil (1891–   ), *assistant managing editor,* the New York *Times.*

Creating the Headline

Headlines compact the gist of newsstories into a few eye-snaring words. A skillfully turned headline tells a story, or enough of it, to arouse or satisfy the reader's curiosity. It is like a highway marker that catches the motorist's eye and gives him a message as he speeds along the road.

The most momentous event of the year or of the decade is first shouted in two or three headline words:

U.S. at War   **F.D.R. Dies**   **Germany Surrenders**

Who hasn't chuckled over or been sobered by heads like these?

8 Pairs of Glasses Required by Lasses In Quest of Passes

CINCINNATI, Nov. 29.—(*P*)—
The well dressed young lady who wears eye glasses simply must have eight pairs to be correct, an expert said today.

M. J. Julian of New York, president of the Better Vision institute made that assertion.

Outmoded, he declared, is that little old rhyme which says:
"Men never make passes
"At girls wearing glasses."

DRIVER SAVING MINUTES PAYS PRICE IN BLOOD

Tries to Pass on Curve and 3 Cars Crash

The headline becomes a vital part of the story once copy leaves the reporter's hands. All stories in the paper, except the short fillers, must be headed. All headlines have the same essential function: to tell the reader what the story is all about.

The Copyeditor's Domain

The width of a single newspaper column does not afford much room in which to gambol with the alphabet; it will accommodate only a few letters and symbols, only three or four short words cast in unyielding metal. Yet this scant area is the copyeditor's domain. The reporter creates the story; the copyeditor creates the headline.

First, he must mentally summarize the vital facts or the feature of the story; then he must weave these into the most telling combination of words that his vocabulary and ingenuity will yield; he must employ his imagination, his knowledge of synonyms and antonyms, his learning and his familiarity with current events.

Lastly, is the problem of spacing. The headliner must make word and phrase slip easily into the narrow space between column rule and column rule, and the lines should be symmetrical, or fairly so. If they are too long, they cannot be set in type; if one is too short and the other fills the column, an ugly effect is produced; if all lines are too short, the headline again is defective.

'Counting-In'

Space available for a headline depends upon the width of the headline and the typeface used. Some letters are regular, some are thin and some are fat. Usually the head-writer can allow one unit for each letter, punctuation, figure and space between words. Take this example:

Texas Mother Reunited
With Kidnaped Infant

The top line counts 21 units, the bottom line 20. In the top line, *M* is a *fat* letter, *i, r* and *t* are *thin* letters. In the bottom line, *W* is fat, *I* and *f* are thin letters. To get a precise count, the head-writer will use a scale like this:

$1\frac{1}{2}$	1	$\frac{1}{2}$	1	1	$\frac{1}{2}$	2	1	$\frac{1}{2}$	1	1	$\frac{1}{2}$	$\frac{1}{2}$	$1\frac{1}{2}$	1	1	1	$\frac{1}{2}$	$\frac{1}{2}$	1	1	= 20
T	e	x	a	s		M	o	t	h	e	r		R	e	u	n	i	t	e	d	

2	$\frac{1}{2}$	$\frac{1}{2}$	1	$\frac{1}{2}$	$1\frac{1}{2}$	$\frac{1}{2}$	1	1	1	1	1	1	$\frac{1}{2}$	$\frac{1}{2}$	1	$\frac{1}{2}$	1	1	$\frac{1}{2}$	= $17\frac{1}{2}$
W	i	t	h		K	i	d	n	a	p	e	d		I	n	f	a	n	t	

In some type faces, the only fat letters are *m* and *w,* with *i* being the only thin letter. This usually is true also when faces are set in all caps:

$$1 \quad 1 \quad 1 \quad 1 \quad 1 \quad \tfrac{1}{2} \quad 1\tfrac{1}{2} \quad 1 \quad 1 \quad 1 \quad 1 \quad 1 \quad \tfrac{1}{2} \quad 1 \quad 1 \quad 1 \quad 1 \quad \tfrac{1}{2} \quad 1 \quad 1 \quad 1 = 20$$
T E X A S   M O T H E R   R E U N I T E D

$$1\tfrac{1}{2} \quad \tfrac{1}{2} \quad 1 \quad 1 \quad \tfrac{1}{2} \quad 1 \quad \tfrac{1}{2} \quad 1 \quad 1 \quad 1 \quad 1 \quad 1 \quad 1 \quad \tfrac{1}{2} \quad \tfrac{1}{2} \quad 1 \quad 1 \quad 1 \quad 1 \quad 1 = 18$$
W I T H   K I D N A P E D   I N F A N T

Unless the headline pushes the allowable maximum, the system of counting one unit for each letter, figure or punctuation mark will suffice. On newspapers where copyeditors compose headlines on the typewriter, the one-unit principle is used. If the line contains several fat letters or figures (0 usually takes more space than other numerals and 1 usually takes less) the head-writer makes the necessary allowance.

If it takes 18 units to fill a line of 24-point, it is better to keep the count to a maximum of 16 units than to crowd the line. Even in a *stepped-head* in which each line should be approximately the same length, it is better to be under the maximum rather than crowd the head. Adjustments can be made on a short line (letter-spacing) but nothing can be done about a crowded line.

The head-writer should make sure the head will fit. If it doesn't, the head comes back to the desk for a rewrite, a waste of time and effort. Some compositors will cooperate by letterspacing to fit the line into type; others won't. The responsibility for making heads fit rests with the headline writer, not with the compositor. And it usually is unsafe to encourage compositors to change wording to make the headline fit.

Even with *flush-left* heads, copyeditors prefer to keep the lines fairly uniform. Note the difference in appearance:

PHOTOGRAPHER WINS   **PHOTOGRAPHER WINS**
MEDAL   **MEDAL FOR WAR DUTY**

The Anatomy of Headlines

Each section of a headline is known as a *bank* or a *deck,* except those which stretch across several or all columns of a page and are known as the *ribbon,* the *banner,* the *streamer,* or simply *the line.* A line above the nameplate is called *skyline.* A deck accompanying a multicolumn line is called a *bank* or *read-out.* A short line over the main headline is termed *overline* or *kicker.*

25 Killed in Chicago Skid Row Fire

**Human Torch
Believed Cause
Of Hotel Blaze**

Chicago, Feb. 12 (AP)
Fire, believed started by a
panic-stricken human torch, sped
through a crowded Skid Row hotel
subroom cold early today
least 25 men. Fifteen
two firemen,

EIGHT-COLUMN LINE (ALSO BANNER OR STREAMER OR RIBBON) WITH ONE-COLUMN READ-OUT.

Airliner Missing, 29 Aboard

Story in Column 5

Voice of the
Rocky
Mountain
Empire **THE DENVER POST** CITY EDITION

SKYLINE

Tish-sue! (Gesundheit)

Lowly Cold Bug Flits Hither and Yon, Bites Ike, His Mrs. and Shah of Iran

—Washington *Post and Times-Herald*

OVERLINE OR KICKER

A headline over a story continued from another page is called a *jump* or *runover* head.

When the lines of a top deck are spaced to fill, it is a *full-line* head:

Chandler Bond
Action Taken

When lines of a headline are *ragged* on the right but line up evenly on the left, they are known as *flush* headlines. Obviously, they do not require as careful a count as do those that are *staggered* symmetrically and, for obvious reasons, called *stepped-line, step* or *dropline* heads.

Hizzoner
On Toot?
Plot Seen

Seminole County
Drunken Driving
Arrest Is Blasted

—Oklahoma City *Times*

FLUSH HEADLINE

Village Venuses
Glut the Market
In Cinema Cities

Trek of Pulchitrude to Hollywood
Usually Ends in Lost Hopes
and Hard Work.

—Paris edition of New York *Herald Tribune*

DROPLINE

The lower deck in the flush example above also is flush; that below the dropline is an *inverted pyramid*. Used as a lower deck for both step and flush heads is the *hanging indent*:

MOTHER TELLS OF POISONING
MATE AND CHILD; PLANNED
TO KILL HER SON ALSO

Headlines come in many varieties. They may have the appearance of a square, a parallelogram, a pyramid, an inverted pyramid or a combination of these.

Now see what happens when the newspaper employs a single and a double line on the same line:

Yup, It's a Horse!

Elijah Decides
To Stay Aloof

A line centered in a column is known as a *crossline* or a *keyline*:

| STATE JOINS FIGHT |

Numerous combinations are possible. The following examples are a few of many varieties:

Atomic Explosion BidRejected By Top Nuclear Brass
—Oregon *Journal*

Five-line Flush Left

It Won't Be Long Until Men Can Take It Easy
—Denver *Rocky Mountain News*

Centered Middle Line

Motorists Terrorized by Armed Indian

Centered Top Line

Almost any kind of headline can be *boxed*. Boxes range from two heavy lines, one above and one below, to partial and complete enclosures with a plain or fancy rule:

TIGERS AND REDS BATTLE TODAY FOR WORLD TITLE

The Headline Copy

Most newspapers have *head skeds* (*headline schedules*) or *hed charts* which assign a number to the various headlines used. Thus the copyeditor simply calls for "line" or "No. 1" or "No. 5" or whatever he desires. (*See Appendix.*)

This designation is written on the upper left corner of a fresh sheet of copypaper with the story's guideline. Below this, the copyeditor writes the headline, *word for word and line for line,* as it is to appear in print. More than that, he draws guiding lines to make clear instantly to the typesetter that the head is a dropline, a hanging indent or whatever it may be.

Here is the way typical headline copy looks just before it is sent to the composing room:

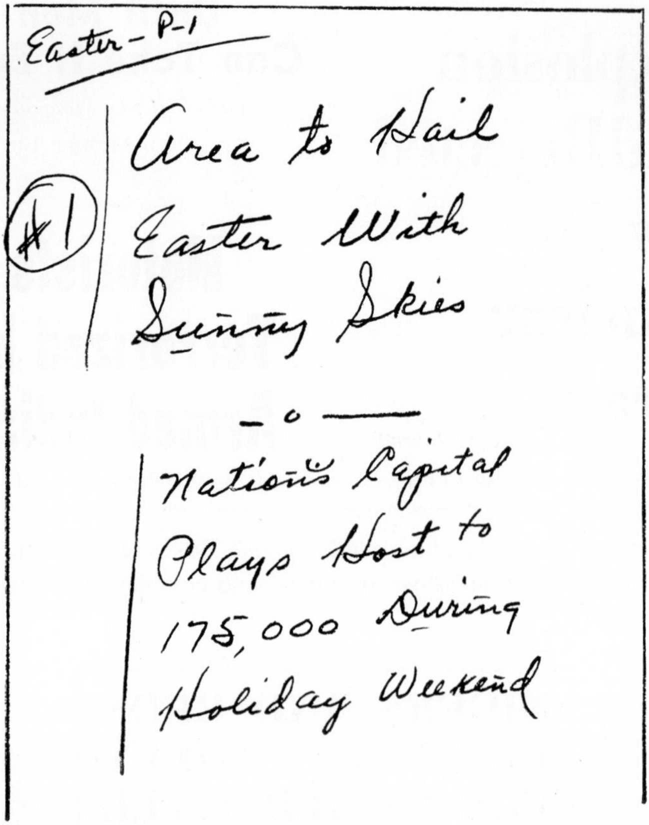

[Handwritten headline copy:]

Easter – P-1

#1

Area to Hail
Easter With
Sunny Skies

— o —

Nation's Capital
Plays Host to
175,000 During
Holiday Weekend

Phrasing the Headline

The newswriter thinks in terms of sentences; the headline writer phrases his ideas. Here is the opening paragraph of a story:

WASHINGTON, Feb. 14 (UP)—A Jewish couple Monday lost their supreme court fight to invalidate a Massachusetts adoption law which prevented them from adopting 3-year-old twins of a Roman Catholic mother.

That is enough for a headline. The lead has key elements the head-writer can use: *Couple, lost, court, fight, adoption, twins.* Two phrases are suggested: *Couple Loses* and *Court Suit*. But the third phrase is too long. *Twins* can be dropped, leaving:

Couple Loses
Court Suit
On Adoption

If the phrase of each line carries a complete idea in itself, the reader grasps the story idea the headline is trying to convey. Compare these:

STOCK MARKET PRICES CLOSE
HIGHER DESPITE LATE SELLING

STOCK PRICES CLOSE HIGHER
DESPITE LATE SELLING FLURRY

The story said that lightning decapitated and felled the statue of Miles Standish, hero of the Pilgrim fathers, that stood in the public square at Green Mountain, Vt. The headline phrasing becomes:

LIGHTNING FELLS STATUE
OF MILES STANDISH

By turning the headline around to put Miles Standish in the top line, the head-writer gets:

MILES STANDISH STATUE
WRECKED BY LIGHTNING

Many newspaper editors insist that deskmen make each headline word count and not pad the lines with superfluous words like *is, are, and, the.*

WORST BLIZZARD OF THE YEAR
LEAVES 4-FOOT DRIFTS IN WNY

Sometimes a single phrase in a story makes the headline. The alert copy-editor will search for these few telling words, which frequently paint a picture for the reader that no amount of labored description could achieve. Here is an example:

Jacob Buske, arraigned before Judge Joseph LaBuy today on a larceny charge, was sentenced to the House of Correction for 60 days and fined $10 and costs. Buske, arrested 21 times before on charges of larceny and burglary, is known as the "crying bandit" because of his laments following each arrest.

It is apparent that the words *crying bandit* should go into the headline, together with *22 arrests* and the fact that the man has been jailed at last, despite his weeping.

'CRYING BANDIT,' ARRESTED
FOR 22D TIME, GETS 60 DAYS

Digging Out the Feature

The key word or phrase of the story is preserved in the headline. If the story has a feature or human interest angle, the head-writer seeks out the feature elements for the headline.

Newark, N. J.—A dog owned by Felix Carbone bit a boy and the health officer ordered the animal tied up for observation. As Felix was carrying out the order the dog bit him in the left leg. Felix only smiled. It's a wooden leg. The dog was shot.

Here is one that relies for its news value on a single word, "wooden." Eliminate it, and this item becomes a commonplace not worth newspaper space, for the action recorded is trivial. Obviously the headline must set forth the fact that the dog decreed its own death by biting its owner's wooden leg. Therefore:

DOG DOOMS SELF BY NIP
AT OWNER'S WOODEN LEG

Dover, N. J.—Sèvres vases, rare paintings, tapestries, and the like were thrown aside today by bargain hunters when a ton of pea coal made its appearance at an administrator's sale. The ton finally was knocked down for $22. The buyer paid $3 to have it carted to his bin and established a new high level for pea coal.

Oddity makes both news and headlines. Reverse the facts in the item reproduced herewith and the story loses its oddity—in other words, its feature. It is the fact that the auction bidders ignored the art works to bid for a ton of coal that gives this story the right to occupy a bit of newspaper space. If the bidders had ignored the coal to bid upon the art works, there would have been no item. So the headline is formulated as follows:

AUCTION PATRONS SPURN
ART WORKS TO BID ON COAL

Following is a filler item that offers a new problem for the beginner in headline writing. It has two phases of action—plowing and milking—and one big, all-important feature—the ages of the persons in the story. Somehow, the copyeditor must pack this essential but complex information in the narrow space of a one-column headline. This is how the three news elements were neatly stowed away in two lines:

> Abrams, Wis.—Mrs. James Bell, 106 years old, milks seven cows daily for exercise, and her husband, 108 years old, plows for the same reason. The couple have just celebrated their eighty-ninth wedding anniversary.

MAN, 108, PLOWS FIELDS;
HIS WIFE, 106, MILKS COWS

> Addison Jones, 3216 Wentworth ave., angered when his proposal of marriage was rejected yesterday by Miss Lucille Sheppard, 3154 Indiana ave., shot her in the left arm. Policeman Philip Duncan was slightly wounded during a struggle to get possession of Jones' revolver.

The next story increases the headline problem slightly by offering three phases of dramatic action: The man has been scorned by a woman; angered, he shoots her; when a policeman arrives, he offers battle and wounds the latter. Carefully examine this headline in which the copyeditor told the three phases of action in six words.

SPURNED, SHOOTS WOMAN,
THEN WOUNDS POLICEMAN

When Details Grow

Simple little stories call for heads that usually are easy to write. It is when details pile up that the beginner finds heavy going. His trouble usually lies in insufficient elimination of minor details, or it may be that he views the story from a wrong slant. There is, however, encouragement in the fact that any reasonably well-written story can be stripped down to essential headline elements by a bit of systematic thinking.

Take this one from Chicago's (downtown) Loop as an example. With a pad and pencil at your elbow, read it through. Then jot down the facts that you consider worthy of being placed in a headline. Suppose the notes read about as follows:

Unidentified man.

Jumps into river.

Loop bridges—crowds.

Policeman to rescue in boat.

Efforts vain—man dies.

Tried to swim to safety.

Current too strong.

Brought to shore—too late.

Here are far too many items to be fitted into a short headline. Which ones, then, may we eliminate without material loss of news?

The man is unidentified, so there is no significant name to carry any news; the policeman's rescue failed, so this is a negative element; the man's own struggle also had a negative result. Dropping these, there remains only this positive action for the headlines: man jumps into river; Loop bridges; crowds; victim dies later.

With the text of the story reduced to these few essential words a headline almost writes itself: "Man jumps into—River as Loop—Crowd watches." But this headline omits the essential news of his death.

In view of scores of pedestrians and autoists who lined the railings of the Randolph and Washington street bridges, Policeman Charles Gainor yesterday pulled out of the water an unidentified man who had leaped into the river. His efforts were of no avail, however, for two hours later the man died in the Iroquois Memorial hospital of exposure.

The man, about 45 years old, from whose clothing all marks of identification had been removed, climbed up on the rail of the Randolph street bridge and plunged into the icy water.

Persons attracted by the shouts of the bridgetender saw the man come to the surface and begin swimming, apparently attempting to reach the bank.

He made little headway, however, and he was carried by the current toward the Washington street bridge. Policeman Gainor ran under the bridge and jumped into a rowboat, reaching the struggling man just as his head sank beneath the water. He pulled him into the boat and took him to shore, where he was carried to the hospital.

The man was unconscious when taken from the river, and he died without regaining consciousness.

At the Central undertaking rooms, 422 South Clark st., all efforts to identify the body were unavailing. All tailor marks had been cut from the clothing, which was of poor material, and there was nothing in the pockets which would lead to identification.

We try again: "Jumps in river—As Loop crowd—watches; dies." This time the headline tells the news of the story, but in a flat, commonplace, and awkward way. How can it be improved? "Leap" is a more vigorous action word than "jump"; "leap to death" is even more striking. It dramatically tells what took place, so we start:

LEAP TO DEATH —

Where? From a skyscraper? The answer is, No—into the river; so we answer that question in the next line:

IN RIVER — — —

A third phase is still unaccounted for. The man leaped from a bridge in Chicago's crowded Loop, with scores pausing to look and scores hurrying on unawares—a dramatic feature we should not deny the reader. This fills out both the second and third lines:

— — — — VIEWED
BY LOOP CROWDS

But the headline has not yet told the identity of the victim, if known, and the lower part, or *bank,* is yet to be written. Going back over the original notes, we find a choice of material, but possibly a statement of the fact that the victim is unidentified will bring some friends to the morgue to claim him. So the next *deck* becomes:

Unidentified Man Dies
In Hospital

The completed headline now reads:

LEAP TO DEATH
IN RIVER VIEWED
BY LOOP CROWDS

———

Unidentified Man Dies
In Hospital

You can extract the vital facts necessary to the headline from any ordinary newsstory by this method. It is simply a matter of eliminating the details and limiting attention to the important action that took place. Nor need you limit yourself to the lead of the story for headline facts if better material is to be found lower down.

Headlines in themselves are interesting, entertaining and good to look at; they comprise as vital a feature of the newspaper as any of its news or editorial text. Much hard work goes into their composition and much talent. They must justify their existence for the limelight beats upon their narrow, cramped quarters more fiercely than it does upon any other portion of the paper.

Not all headlines merely summarize. Some by adroit phraseology seek to arouse and suspend curiosity, thereby luring the reader into the story. Humor and play on words are favorite devices for this type of headline which usually appears over feature or news-feature stories. Examples:

■

In Scotland,
Guy Like Him
Can Get Kilt

MARSHALLTOWN, IOWA— (AP)— When Jon Ramsey, 23, started to remove his trousers while getting ready for bed, things happened.

His feet got tangled. He stumbled backwards against a cedar chest beside the bedroom window.

When his knees hit the chest they folded, p i t c h i n g him through the window.

His pants came off as he fell and followed him down to the concrete driveway 16 feet below.

Ramsey was hospitalized with two broken ribs, a black eye and a gash on the forehead.

He had some advice Saturday for men:

"Sit down before you take your pants off."

■

—Minneapolis Sunday *Tribune*

LET DER HAIR GROW ON DER WEST LONG, BERLINERS TOLD

BERLIN, Feb. 24. —(Reuters)— The Communist regime in East Berlin Tuesday banned West Berliners from getting haircuts in the east sector of the city. The decree also prohibits eastern watch repairers from working on western watches.

The ban follows a recent edict forbidding westerners from patronizing Eastern food stores. Westerners long had taken advantage of the lopsided exchanges rates (six East marks for one West mark) to hunt bargains in the East.

—Denver *Post*

What Headlines Do

Headlines flag the reader's eye. They're set up to say: "Mr. Reader, here are the minimal essentials of what you should know about this event. The size of the type and the position on the page give you a clue to its importance. If you want more information, *read on!*"

Analyze their functions, and you'll see that headlines: (1) inform the reader briefly; (2) grade and organize the news of the day; (3) lure the reader into stories; (4) make the newspaper attractive.

To turn out brisk heads that do those four jobs requires study and practice. Copyeditors habituate themselves to "think in headlines" as they read; they sift out interesting and significant facts, then cast them into phrases. With the introduction to the headline-creating art given in foregoing pages, the student may start at once to write simple heads as preparation for the more complex problems to be discussed in Chapter 14.

The beginner can teach himself to retell a story in headline words. He clips from his newspaper a handful of stories, removes the headlines, shuffles the clippings and tries his hand at writing the headlines. He then compares his efforts with the headlines used on the stories originally. Soon he will discover for himself the "knack" of arranging a few words to produce an impelling, readable headline.

PART III

Perfecting the Copy

6   Sharpening the Lead

Words are like sunbeams; the more they are condensed the deeper they burn.—Robert Southey (1774–1843), *English poet.*

Begin at the beginning, go through to the end and then stop.—The Red Queen in *Alice in Wonderland* by "Lewis Carroll" (1832–1898), *English novelist.*

Compression is the first sign of the master.—Johann Wolfgang von Goethe (1749–1832), *German author.*

I.   GETTING STARTED RIGHT

The All-Important Start

"A story well begun is half done" is a commonplace in newsrooms. Young reporters often spend more time on the opening paragraph than all that follow; even oldtimers have been known to use their wastebaskets a half dozen times before getting on. They know that the first few words will lure the reader into the story or his roving eye will swing to something else.

A quick getaway is as important in the news column as on the track. The introductory paragraph—known to newsmen as the *lead* (leed)— plays the main role. It must tell what happened, or make the reader so curious he will want to read on to find out what happened. The lead should lead. It should lead to or into something. It aims, guides, conducts, directs, begins. It sets the emotional tone, telling the reader right off whether the story is matter-of-fact, humorous, pathetic. It is the all-important start of a newspaper story.

The experienced deskman can tell from the first 50 words of a story whether the reporter understands what he is writing about and whether the writer is communicating the essentials of a story to the reader. Learn to write a lead and you're on the way to becoming a good newswriter. Back into the story or wind up like a pitcher before throwing the ball and the story will stall. Cram all the main facts and details into the beginning and you confuse the reader and kill his interest.

The world's best seller has the world's best lead: "In the beginning, God created the heaven and the earth."

When young Tom Paine wanted to set the world afire with a frenzy of democratic fervor, he started his tract with these words: "These are the times that try men's souls."

If the lead is sluggish, the copyeditor should quicken its pace. Inserting a bright word here, removing a worn one there, rearranging a phrase— these minor changes sometimes suffice. But if the lead requires complete rewriting, that should be done. And if the first page or any part of it merely marks time, kill all to the point where the story starts.

Speaking Versus Writing

Think what an advantage a public speaker has over a writer. Give him an audience, and though his first words do not take, he is exposing those who sit before him to a continuous barrage, some of which, usually, takes effect. The radio story often starts by catching the listener's ear before giving him the essential facts. It says, "A former cabinet member in the Truman administration died at his home in Texas this morning. He was. . . ." But the eye sees what the ear may miss so the newspaper writer starts abruptly—"John Doe, former cabinet member in the Truman administration, died at his home in Texas Tuesday at the age of 70."

Radio uses sound to call the listener to attention; television uses sound and motion. But the newspaper has to do the trick with cold type and silent words.

The haste-maddened reader's roving eye focuses momentarily on the writer's product. Will he read it? The fate of the writer rests upon the answer. Editors have little sympathy to squander on roses blushing but unseen, nor violets—no matter how coy—if hidden by mossy stones. The lead is the prey for the hawk-like reader swooping over the page. It must grab his attention, force him to direct his interest on this tiny morsel. Will he pass it by, or will the writer's words lure him into the article?

News used to be more leisurely and literary than it is today. Then the world was moving slowly; the reader had the time (and the patience) to read a 2,000-word story in 6-point type. Notice how Julian Ralph in the New York *Sun* opened the story of the famous blizzard of March 1888:

It was as if New York had been a burning candle upon which nature had clapped a snuffer, leaving nothing of the city's activity but a struggling ember.

At little after 12 o'clock on Sunday night, or Monday morning, the severe rain that had been pelting down since the moment of the opening of the church doors suddenly changed to a sleet storm that plated the sidewalks with ice. Then began the great storm that is to become for years a household word, a symbol of the worst of weathers and the limit of nature's possibilities under normal conditions.

That would be enough for today's readers. They would switch to radio or television to find out what happened. Fifty trainloads of passengers were stuck on the main lines, electric power was cut off—these are the facts the modern reader wants—and quickly.

News and Feature Leads

Leads take their tempo and form from the story to be told. If it is timely, such as a battle, an accident, an election, births, deaths and so on, it ordinarily will be introduced by a straight-news lead. If the quality known as *human interest* predominates, and the writer's purpose is less to inform than it is to entertain, it will be a *feature story,* or *article* if it runs to some length. But feature handling can be given to straight news, and thus, a hybrid type emerges: the *news-feature story.*

Note this example—straight news in content and treatment:

A predawn fire took three lives at 1820 Monument Ave., yesterday, and within 90 minutes firemen were fighting to control a spectacular blaze that gutted three buildings at 1217-19 East Main St.

—Richmond *Times-Dispatch*

Now take another routine newsstory and notice how the writer creates a dramatic effect with the lead:

Train No. 884 came tearing down the track after the railroad said it wouldn't, the plaintiff alleged yesterday in a $41,500 personal injury lawsuit that went on trial in superior court before Judge Lee Garrett and a jury.

—Arizona Daily (Tucson) *Star*

Sometimes copyeditors can liven a newsstory by giving it a feature slant, if the story justifies that treatment. The story itself may be trivial or whimsical, but handled right, it makes good reading:

CHICAGO, Ill. (AP)—Santa Claus was rescued from a menacing crowd and hauled away to jail Friday.

Traffic Policeman James Mullen said the merry old fellow was standing at State and Monroe streets, ringing his bell to solicit coins for a charity, when a 15-year-old lad grasped a handful of false whiskers and pulled. The elastic band about Santa's head stretched. Then the boy let go.

Hopping in rage and pain, Santa let the bell whiz through the air and strike Frank Bush, 12, cutting the innocent youngster in the forehead.

Shoppers booed Santa until the patrol wagon arrived. Santa identified himself as James Hogan. He was charged with disorderly conduct.

A "twist" has the effect of whetting the reader's appetite even on a story that has no news value. It is strictly a human-interest feature:

NISQUALLY, Wash. (NEA)—Earl McDermitt claims the title as the world's champion baby-sitter.

From now until next winter, war or no war, farmer McDermitt will nurse-maid 8,000,000 "babies"—tiny Douglas fir trees in the unique nursery of the forestry conservation committee of the Pacific northwest forest industries. He has completed his sowing operations, using certified seed for the first time. . . .

Structural Types

Most straight newsstories start with what short-story writers would call the climax and would place last. They present in the first few words the most interesting element—*the feature of the story*. This is not only to catch the reader's eye, but to retain the gist of the story in case makeup exigencies make it necessary to lop off succeeding paragraphs.

Suspended-interest stories follow the short-story scheme of development. They lead off with words intended to arouse curiosity which is not immediately satisfied.

Both basic types may be fixed in the mind by thinking of them as built on a pyramid plan, illustrated by the following:

BOSTON, April 9.—(AP)—Umbrellas were in style in most of New England today, as rain and snow flurries dampened the Easter parade.

Even early church-goers failed to escape a dampening, for the first drizzle fell from the cloud darkened skies before 8 a.m. By 10 o'clock, the rain turned into quick melting snow. A slight rise of the mercury changed it back to rain at noon.

McCOOK, NEB., Dec. 14.—(AP)—Mrs. Peter Karthauser is one of the best window washers and polishers in her neighborhood.

When she finished washing a window in the front room of her home it apparently was invisible to a strange dog. The dog jumped through the window and landed in the parlor amid shattered glass.

The Identification Principle

The lead can be likened to a spearhead with each attention-getting element a barb to be hooked into the reader's consciousness. The shaft should be tipped with something new, but the experienced reporter and copyeditor are always on the alert to reinforce the reader's interest in the new with facts already known in some degree.

This is the *principle of identification,* instinctively grasped by every successful teller of stories.

A reader may know all major developments to date in, say, a criminal hunt. Then the desperado is caught. In writing of the event, a reporter will slip in unobtrusive but informative references to previous events in order to correlate the new to the old and make for a coherent story. These are called *second-day elements* and make the item a *second-day story.* It follows that the deskman must know what was reported yesterday or last week. On the second-day story, he must let the tone indicate that today's newsstory is a followup to a previous story; but he also must remember that many of the newspaper's readers missed the original story.

Most large newspapers have a rule that any individual mentioned must be identified at least by his address, thereby enabling the reader to orient him. Age, criminal records, relationship to better known persons, achievements, titles, professional standing—these are a few of the ways of tying up a news personality to facts the reader already knows or readily comprehends. When an expression of individual opinion is given, it should be identified with its authority. Here are a few illustrative leads, weak and strong in identification:

WEAK: If a man will not buy his share of charity certificates, knock him down, say some of the leaders in the Associated Charities campaign in Milltown.

STRONG: "Knock down the man who will not buy his share of charity certificates." This recommendation was made early today by John T. Richards, chairman of the Milltown Associated Charities.

WEAK: Milltown should have a building and loan association, according to views expressed today by some of its most prominent citizens.

STRONG: William H. Thompson, president of the Commonwealth Manufacturing company, this morning got behind a movement to launch a building and loan association in Milltown. Or (and better): A building and loan association is to be launched in Milltown, according to William H. Thompson, president of the Commonwealth Manufacturing company, who will head the campaign as chairman.

Discovering the Lead Material

The man who edits copy must know news values and factors of taste and policy that govern what appears in his newspaper. He should be able to disinter leads buried by hasty or unskilled reporting. He should be a master of the art of making dull leads sparkle.

What is the best of many possible leads for a specific story? Often it is the one that jumps to the mind of the reporter as the most natural way of relating what he has seen. But it may be necessary to dig.

Here is a hypothetical situation but it will illustrate the problem of finding the right lead. The following facts are supplied by Midtown's chamber of commerce:

National Research Laboratories
Drug and vaccine research
One of the largest of its kind in the world
To hire 500 workers
Cost: One million dollars
Main office to be in Midtown
Square mile of land for plant and employe homes
Dr. Meyer Rothstein, president
Dr. Jonas Salk, laboratory director

How should the writer begin a newsstory concerning this laboratory? Suppose he starts with the *source:*

Secretary George Hope said today the chamber of commerce has just landed another—

No—that will never do because Secretary Hope and the chamber of commerce are not the news. This writing is provincial.

Another start, this time to add some "color"—

Midtown, queen city of the plains, is to have another giant—

No. This is "goon" writing, the style used on resort and travel folders. Try again with this:

It is rumored that the National Research Laboratories—

Worse and more of it. The reader wants a quick focus of facts, something positive and definite, not irresponsible gossip. So:

Dr. Meyer Rothstein, president of the National Research Laboratories, said today his firm may—

Somewhat better, except that "may" news is poor news. All news worth its ink is positive and specific. This introduction is wooden. Now let's try to answer the essential question—*what happened?*

National Research Laboratories will build a million dollar laboratory in Midtown and will move its main office here.

That's better, except that National Research Laboratories is not identified. What does it do? Visualize the opening paragraph in terms of the headline. What would it say? Probably something like: Midtown To Get Million Dollar Laboratory. The deck would contain the idea: Dr. Jonas Salk Will Direct Plant. So we try this for the lead:

Midtown has been selected as the site for a million dollar drug and vaccine research center, Dr. Meyer Rothstein, president of National Research Laboratories, announced today. Dr. Jonas Salk, discoverer of anti-polio vaccine, will direct the Midtown laboratory when it is completed early next year.

Many Ways to Do It

There are several right ways of phrasing the lead of this story. All will seek to answer the readers' main question, what happened?

Now let's take an actual newsstory and examine some of the alternate leads. Twenty Trappist monks from the monastery of Our Lady of the Gethsemani in Kentucky arrived in Georgia to start a monastery on a farm near Conyers. Here are the ways the Atlanta newspapers, a wire service and a national news magazine opened the story:

Morning daily:

Twenty members of the Trappist Order of the Catholic church passed through Atlanta yesterday on their way to a farm near Conyers, Ga., where they will establish Georgia's first monastery of the ancient organization and the fourth in the United States.

The wire service rewrote the story under a Conyers dateline and put the story on the national wire:

CONYERS, GA., March 22 (AP)—Twenty monks and brothers of the Trappist order arrived here from the monastery at Gethsemani, Ky., today to establish the fourth foundation of the order in the United States.

For the radio wire:

CONYERS, GEORGIA—Twenty members of the centuries-old order of Trappist monks have taken possession of an old barn near Conyers to establish the fourth foundation of the order in the United States. The monks and brothers are from the monastery of Our Lady of Gethsemani at Trappist, Kentucky, which was established in 1848.

Afternoon daily:

CONYERS, Ga., March 23—A new life of poverty, chastity and obedience began Thursday at "Our Lady of the Holy Ghost"—the first established Georgia monastery, situated in a barn on a 1,465-acre tract near Conyers.

Time magazine:

A cinemactress's southern plantation last week became a Trappist monastery. To Conyers, Ga., 30 miles northeast of Atlanta, came 20 monks (10 priests, 3 clerics or students, 7 lay brothers), all members of the Roman Catholic Church's strictest monastic order (Trappists do not converse with one another).

II. TYPES OF LEADS

Classifying Leads

Most experienced newsmen don't think in terms of leads by types or names. They just write 'em—and they know when they've done a good one. But it's smart practice for the beginner to pull some leads apart to see what they're made of—then to group them by kinds. Here are examples to start the process:

Summary Lead. Commonest of all news leads is the one in which the whole story of what happened is summarized for the reader. If this can be done in crisp, clear sentences, the reader can get a swift comprehension of the essentials. If it tries to cram too many of the answers to *who, what, when, why, where* and *how* into one compact capsule, the reader loses his way. When the writer lumps action, source, consequence into one tightly-compressed sentence or paragraph, he runs the risk of making the story top-heavy. The copyeditor can save the day by breaking up the story into separate elements.

The old-school rule of five-w-and-h pattern left its mark on newspaper style in the form of "hugger-mugger" leads, top-heavy structure and involved sentences. Today's style is more like a rifle shot intended to get the reader into the story quickly. The newsstory seldom if ever needs an introduction; it tells the reader immediately *what happened* or *what is going to happen.*

The summary lead must tell what happened, but not necessarily all that happened:

MILAN, N.H. (AP)—Searchers found a wrecked Northeast Airlines (NEA) plane atop snow-covered Mount Success Thursday. Two of its seven occupants—marooned since noon Tuesday in near zero temperatures—were dead.

That's enough for one breath. Now follow with details:

Five survivors . . . were removed by helicopter and taken to a hospital.
The victims were . . .
The survivors are . . .

Comprehensive Lead. This provides an overall picture of a number of events, each having a common relationship to a central fact. Sometimes they are called *roundup* leads. The following example is to be classed as a comprehensive lead, but in it can also be seen a summary lead, a second-day lead and a feature lead. The *when* element is stressed in the opening sentence presenting the essence of the news, followed by a recital of the salient facts:

WASHINGTON—A distinctly Democratic trend was discernible in yesterday's elections.
The Democrats captured three of the five congressional seats. . . .

The second paragraph of such a lead sometimes numbers the important facts, 1–2–3 style, becoming a sort of secondary lead, with the rest of the story detailing each of the enumerated points.

Accident Lead. A combination of the comprehensive and summary leads is utilized in stories carrying lists of names so important they must precede other details. This *who* element is inserted after the briefest possible account of what has happened.

Two young sisters were injured critically shortly after noon today when they were struck by an auto on Kenmore Ave. near Starin Ave. Buffalo police issued a summons to the driver. The injured girls are:

Mary Ellen Brennan, 7, in Emergency Hospital with probable skull fracture, left arm fracture, rib and pelvic injuries and other internal injuries.

Bonnie Brennan, 11, in Kenmore Mercy Hospital, head injuries, leg fracture, chest and pelvic injuries. The girls are daughters of Mr. and Mrs. Robert J. Brennan of 537 Park Ave. . . .

—Buffalo *Evening News*

Punch Lead. This lead meets the frequent requirement that the lead paragraph must start with the biggest feature in the story—with a *punch*—and that each sentence and paragraph must be introduced by important facts. Examine the following and review the other leads cited with this principle in mind:

Tiny little legs, seared and blackened by third-degree burns, have been "rebuilt" by medical science for four-month-old Sandra Brown.

For more than a month the child, daughter of Mr. and Mrs. Clarence Brown, 1426 E. Grand ave., has been on her back at Iowa Methodist hospital, her heavily bandaged legs held in the air.

Severe burns that at first threatened to take her life—burns so deep blood vessels were destroyed—presented doctors with a huge task. But . . .

—Des Moines *Register*

Guidance, Amusement

But stories may be written obviously to give the reader guidance and entertainment, as well as information. Their leads may be serious or light, provocative or startling.

New Year's Eve is expected to be meteorologically dry and socially wet. . . .

—Murray Shumach in the New York *Times*

Crusade Leads. Following is a crusade or campaign lead, so named because it is typical of leads used by newspapers in crusading against some abuse or evil.

Only four of the 48 states are without some state agency with authority to regulate the rates of electric and gas companies. Mississippi is one. The others are Iowa, Minnesota and South Dakota. Such agencies are found in all the other states.

—Jackson (Miss.) *State Times*

Astonisher Lead. This lead is exclamatory—but if it takes an *astonisher* (exclamation mark) to arouse reader astonishment, the chances are it is weak.

Casting a bombshell into the county commissioner race, Mrs. J. O. Miller, a former state president of the League of Women Voters, today revealed a six-year secret, that Sen. William D. Mansfield and David L. Lawrence played undercover roles in bringing about the arrest of County Commissioner Joseph G. Armstrong.

—Pittsburgh *Press*

Notice in the foregoing lead that every possible inducement is present to make the reader read more of the story.

Cartridge Lead. The cartridge lead is explosive. It is the shortest way of telling a bit of news.

"Whaler Bill" Muldoon is in jail.

This eccentric character, whose long beard and tall tales have enlivened the water front for many years, has been sought by police for three weeks as an accomplice in the murder of two sailors . . .

You-and-I Lead. Some stories are told effectively by dropping into an informal you-and-I tone. Often they amuse or entertain. Or they may with varying degrees of subtlety seek to direct the reader's thinking, in which case they may become editorialized news and, preferably, carry a byline. Observe the deftly restrained use of this technique in an excerpt from a Damon Runyon story:

WASHINGTON, Dec. 1—You are in Washington, District of Columbia, the capital of the nation, and you see in the middle distance the contour of the building that is called the White House.

You should be reflecting on the historical background and the significance of this building which to our 130,000,000 stands as the symbol of a free government. Instead, you find yourself thinking of it as Heartbreak House.

You think of it as the place where, at regular intervals, we install one of our well-meaning citizens as the leader of. . . .

—© by *King Syndicate*

Suspended-Interest Lead. The suspended-interest type of newsstory, as has been noted, is similar to the short-story form of fiction. It begins with minor events and reserves its climax to the last. Often a time-order sequence is followed, in which the events are related in the precise order that they happened. This is one of the most natural ways of telling a story and many times is an economizer of space as well. It is useful for the historical-type feature as well as the crusade type:

Abraham Lincoln never saw the state he helped create, although he got as far west as Kansas Territory at one of the low points of the rigorous career of privation and defeat which prepared him for and led him to the White House.

—Robert Perkin in the Denver *Rocky Mountain News*

Almost from the day that Peter Minuit bought Manhattan from the Dutch for the equivalent of $24, there have been attempts to avert fires by safety legislation. The problem has grown with the city.

It lies dormant for long stretches at a time. . . .

—Sydney Gruson in The New York *Times*

Interpretive Lead.   The reader knows the broad outline of a newsstory, but he doesn't know its significance or how it will work. The simplest lead for an explanatory or background story might be:

Here's how the new income tax structure will affect individual taxpayers—

Or on a *sidebar* (story with another story):

Police Chief John W. Polcyn said Thursday he was investigating a reported four-hour delay in broadcasting to the state radio network a message that Richard Netzel was wanted here for shooting and wounding his wife.

Bylined interpretive reporters use various devices to give meaning or significance to news. Here is one method:

Moscow is carrying out a significant revision of its policy towards China and towards the East European members of the Soviet block. A new course, contrasting sharply with the practice of the Stalin era, has been initiated. Its purpose is . . .

—Isaac Deutscher in The Manchester *Guardian Weekly*

Grammatical Forms

A story may be started with any part of speech, any grammatical form known. The following examples are illustrative, but it should be noted that each can be fitted into categories already cited.

Infinitive Lead.   Here is an infinitive lead—a device for introducing a minor note of suspense. It is useful to avoid having all leads begin alike:

To get food and clothing for his children, Robert E. Lanich, aged 32, of 1263 Indianola avenue, planned to turn burglar, he admitted to police Tuesday. Lanich is the suspect who broke away from . . .

—Columbus (Ohio) *Evening Dispatch*

Participial Lead.   The participial lead also avoids beginning a story with the articles "the," "a," and "an," and suggests action from the first word on:

Rejecting an 11th hour Indian bid to widen talks on President Eisenhower's plan for a peaceful international atomic program, western sponsors pushed Saturday for final acceptance of the program . . .

Question Lead. As useful to the workman as a crowbar is the question lead to the newsman. It gets a quick bite under a corner of a fact, and, with the reader's curiosity as a fulcrum, pries selected information out of a mass of details. It must challenge, titillate, or pique reader interest at once or it fails. And because it is so easy to use, some reporters employ it too frequently, giving their stories a monotonous sameness. A question lead usually tries to answer the question raised:

BOSTON (AP)—Should 4-year-old Hildy McCoy, born a Catholic, be taken from her foster parents because they are Jewish?
That question was raised in the Massachusetts Supreme Court today as Mr. and Mrs. Melvin B. . . .

Quote Lead. Another overworked beginning for interviews or for stories of events featured by speeches is a quotation. An official of a news agency said of quotation leads, "Show me a newsstory that begins with a quotation, no matter how striking it is, and I will show you how it could be improved by taking the quoted statement out of the lead and placing it in the body of the story." Nevertheless, a quote lead is effective, especially if it lends drama to the story.

JOHANNESBURG, South Africa, March 9 (AP)—"They'll be coming soon to take us away. Then they'll destroy this house like the others. What are we to do?"
The Negro doctor stared through the window toward heaps of rubble where once men, women and children laughed and cried and died.
At his side a gray-haired Negro woman in her 50s finished her husband's thoughts: "I guess we're all sure heading for no-good in these parts."
They are the Xumas, Alfred and Madie, an African and an American who, over the years, have carved a life and a home for themselves in the doomed Negro township of Sophiatown four miles from the heart of Johannesburg.

Here is one of many ways to avoid the easy temptation of starting with a quoted comment:

By Associated Press

WASHINGTON, Dec. 31—Secretary of State John Foster Dulles declared Friday the free world's ability to bounce back from adversity has fostered a unity and strength for dealing with the Communists.
"As a result," he told a news conference, "the danger of general war receded."
Dulles added a word of caution:
"But we must be strong. . . .

Dependent Clause Lead.   Sometimes a story hangs on a choice somebody has made, an uncertainty or other conditional factor. To emphasize it, dependent clause leads, started by conjunctions, are useful. Examples:

> Causal: Because he spent five cents before breakfast, Peter. . . .
> Concessive: Although he dived under his yacht four times, Capt. . . .
> Conditional: If he had known how to spell the word cauterize. . . .
> Temporal: While her husband was asleep in an adjoining room, Mrs. . . .

Noun Clause Lead.   This is simply a lead starting with a clause taking the place of a noun. The opening word is often—too often—"that." "How" and "Why" are also used: How to use a fork properly is a question agitating the Binksville Woman's club. . . .

Prepositional Lead.   Because a preposition is a word that connects a noun or pronoun to some other word and shows a relation between them, it may carry a low-grade note of suspense when utilized at the beginning of a story. Occasionally it can be used to advantage, however, as a device to bring forward a word or a phrase that embodies the feature of a story. Examples:

> At midnight tonight, a cascade of fireworks will boom and crackle—that is, if Sheriff B. C. Jones gets $500 from the county before 5 p.m.

> Off on a perilous mission to Alaska, two Jiggsville boys bid farewell . . .

Special Rhetorical Devices

Every rhetorical trick known to writers is at the command of the newswriter. Examples of several already have been cited; here follow others that, by custom or frequent use, have names derived from their rhetorical forms.

Then-and-Now Lead.   This is a favorite device of the reporter seeking to breathe life into history. It is built on the dramatic contrast, and must move rapidly, as:

> VANCOUVER, B.C., Dec. 20—Twelve years ago a penniless young Englishman left this city for the Yukon. Today he is a wealthy mine owner and his name, John Smith, is revered throughout England as the rebuilder of bombed churches. . . .

Here-and-There Lead.   Contrast in space may be as effective as contrast in time:

> Instead of awakening each morning and going to the office under a clear Arizona sky, in Europe day after day, year after year, one arises under heavy clouds dripping with the threat of war.
> Such a picture was painted verbally here today by. . . .

Anecdote Lead. A popular self-starter for the news-feature writer—and all public speakers—is an anecdote. A swiftly told tale attracts attention and sounds the keynote for what follows. The anecdote lead requires deft handling. Regardless of how interesting the tale may be in itself, it fails as a lead unless it ferries the reader to the body of the story. Occasionally the sheer appropriateness of the anecdote does that by suggestion; more often it requires a steering sentence.

NEW YORK, Nov. 10—Poor old Pat Crowe was picked up—once again—on the Bowery. Soaked with rain. Hat in hand. Begging for pennies. Once he held up trains.

"I'm Pat Crowe," he boasted in the police station.

The young detective did not know who Pat Crowe had been. The old man brought out his thumbed deck of staled clippings to convince them that he had once been a man.

That's New York for you. A tragedy on every corner. No one knows or cares. The other side of it is that the man who has made. . . .

—Herbert Corey in the Chicago *Daily News*

Freak Lead. First cousin of the anecdote lead is the freak lead. It has infinite variations, limited only by the ingenuity and skill of the writer. It may employ alliteration's artful artifice, irony, sarcasm, obvious understatement, "wisecracking," "tearjerking" or any of the multifarious rhetorical devices known to man. Frequently the story is launched with an imaginary tabloid drama of dialogue; sometimes the prelude is a verse; sometimes a significant quotation or a parody on one; sometimes a prose picture, or some other bit of pretentious writing. Overworked, the freak lead becomes tiresome and repellent. Imaginary telephone calls with Santa, for instance, went out with bustles.

> Stephen Vincent Benét
> adores
> Edna St. Vincent Millay
> especially
> on his 39th birthday
> when he's about to write a new
>   epic poem about the Ameri-
>   can frontier, stop, period,
>   end of sentence.

Figurative Lead. An offshoot of the freak lead is the figurative type. Highly imaginative, often it takes the form of a parable.

"Commissioner," the courthouse cat who is caring for five newborn kittens in the Old Frenchman's Well monument, mewed happily today when interviewed by a Press reporter in her maternity ward.

The reporter couldn't dig "cat talk" and an interpreter wasn't available. But the proud mother may well have been saying "Quintuplets! That was really a monumental event, wasn't it?"

Although her ancestry is uncertain and her black and. . . .

—The Fort Worth Press

Epigram Lead.   A staccato tempo marks the epigram lead. It may aptly cite a general truth, moralize, summarize the entire story, or simply catch a glint of human interest. Often the effect is attained by a touch of whimsey or humor, perhaps captured in an unusual combination of archaic words. It is used to introduce both straight news and feature stories:

"Just tell the world with ear rings."

With jade for excitement, cut steel for passion, moonstones for contentment, and pearls for sympathy, milady may express every mood and still go garbed as Fashion dictates in somber black. She can. . . .

—Minneapolis Journal

"Today" Lead.   Most of the illustrative leads invariably contain the "today" angle, but not every lead must have a "today" and, in fact, many stories would read better without it. International News Service, which uses the same wire for press and radio, has dropped the "today" fetish. The day of the week is better than "today."

WASHINGTON (INS)—The federal housing administration has cracked down on 983 home repair dealers and salesmen by putting them on a "precautionary" list used by financial institutions.

Straining for the "today" angle can become ridiculous: Coach John Smith is all smiles today after his Bobcats had won their fifth straight game Saturday by trouncing Manual High 62 to 43.

News should give the main element, not the secondary. In a first-day death story the lead should be on the death, and not: "Services will be held today for John Doe who died Sunday . . ." The city editor's advice is: Let the victim die before you bury him.

Notice how the Associated Press handled the lead of a day-old death story:

BALTIMORE, (AP)—Doubting H. L. Mencken, whose needlesharp pen pricked at civilization for nearly half a century, is dead. And how—as he once literally inquired—shall they stage his "inescapable last act"?

"The Sage of Baltimore"—newsman, author, wit, and critic—died quietly in his sleep early Sunday. He was 75. . . .

Mencken once wrote: "One of the crying needs of the time in this incomparable republic is for a suitable burial service for the admittedly damned. . . ."

Tests for Leads

The foregoing illustrates the great flexibility of leads. There are dozens of ways of starting a story, as every rewriteman knows. Content usually suggests the lead. In the hands of a reporter with imagination, a story reads well from beginning to end. A brief review of the types mentioned yields the following conclusions, for the guidance of both writer and copyeditor:

1. Leads should be simple, brief, compact, vigorous, attractive and should shoot straight as a rifle bullet into the reader's attention.
2. They should be written in a manner appropriate to the subject matter. Not all stories are serious; not all may be treated in a light manner. Leads that are bombastic, exaggerated, weak, inadequate, fantastic or marked by faulty perspective should be edited or rewritten into correct form. Involved leads and lead sentences should be split up and made more forceful and vigorous.
3. They should not carry gratuitous opinion of the writer, unless they are signed.
4. They should fix authority for information lest the reader question the story's authenticity.
5. They should vary in style. The more varied the leads, the more interesting the newspaper.
6. They should avoid beginning with nonessential details, such as "At a meeting of," "Last evening," or "At 2:30 o'clock this afternoon." Details of time and place, unless vitally important, should be made subsidiary.
7. Copyeditors should be alert to detect and bring to the fore "buried" leads—important news mistakenly lost in the body of the story. The lead must have substance; it must justify newsworthiness.
8. Above all, *leads should be accurate.*

Leads that present the essential facts of the news far outnumber those of the types that introduce news-feature and feature stories, which usually take the suspended-interest form.

Beginning reporters and copyeditors would do well to study the styles of writing in the splendid volume by Louis L. Snyder and Richard B. Morris, *A Treasury of Great Reporting* (Simon and Schuster, 1949). In the preface, Herbert Bayard Swope recalls that Matthew Arnold referred to journalism as "literature in a hurry," and quotes Heywood Broun's statement that every good reporter is writing literature for some future historian.

Better newspapers of today are filled with good writing, though not often regarded as literary since the news serves a functional purpose. But they illustrate good story-telling. Invariably, the essential element is a good beginning.

7   Rebuilding the Story

True ease in writing comes from art, not chance,
As those move easiest who have learn'd to dance.
—Alexander Pope (1688–1744), *English poet and essayist.*

It seems like the longer I write the shorter I make my articles. I remember my first newspaper job was on the *Press-Argus* down home. One day one of our senators was in town and the editor sent me over to interview him. When I got back to the office the editor says, "Well, did you interview the senator?" I says "Yes." He says "What did he have to say?" I said "Nothin'." The editor said, "Well, go ahead and write up the interview, but try to hold it down to a column and a half."—Bob Burns (1890–1956), *actor and columnist.*

(© *by Esquire Features, Inc.*)

Keep the Reader Moving

The lead is important. Yet it is only the front porch—there to entice the reader to the doorway whence he is to be escorted room by room through the house. The unseen guide is the reporter.

The reader often is lost between the lead and the body of a story. Perhaps the reporter has so concentrated on the lead the rest of the story is written hastily and lacks unity, coherence or emphasis. Or the lack may simply be a *steering* or *bridge sentence.* Frequently a copyeditor will add a well-chosen word or phrase that supplies the missing link. Note how, in the examples of the preceding chapter, leads are hinged to the paragraphs that follow them.

Coherence, always closely related to unity, may be attained in various ways. Simple stories present little difficulty, but problems of organization arise when one has to select, out of many details, those that are most significant.

The rhetorical principle of emphasis is violated when the body of a story fails to complement details given in its lead. If the feature of a lead is a puppy killed while toddling after a little girl crossing a railroad bridge, every reasonable question the reader might have about the puppy should be answered.

Which Pattern?

Almost the first thing a copyeditor notes, as he reads a new piece of copy, is its structure. Is it planned to fit the common inverted pyramid pattern? Or does it have suspended interest and conform to the upright pyramid?

Here is a simple newsstory, diagrammed.

The summary lead—the whole story in brief.

GRAND CANYON, ARIZ., April 9, —(AP)—On the south rim of Grand Canyon's spectacular mile deep abyss, more than 2,500 worshippers gathered at sunrise today for the fifth annual shrine of ages Easter services.

A major detail— with facts of minor importance following in descending order.

The program, marked by musical presentations by a 50-voice capella choir from Arizona State Teachers college at Flagstaff, was nationally broadcast (NBC).

In his Easter message, the Very Rev. Edwin S. Lane, dean of the Trinity Episcopal cathedral, Phoenix, cited the great chasm of the Grand Canyon as "symbolizing peace to the individual, peace to the world that can come only through greatness of soul."

And here is a simple illustration of a newsstory following the suspended-interest plan.

Details told in straight time sequence.

Thomas F. Flurry, of New Suffolk, L. I., bought a new car yesterday and tried to drive it in the heavy traffic along Jamaica Avenue, Queens. He got nervous when he mixed himself up in a traffic jam at 163d Street and Mounted Patrolman William Searby, of Troop F, tried to help him out of his trouble. Flurry touched something and the car shot ahead so suddenly that it bowled over the horse and Searby was pinned beneath the animal for several minutes.

The details of the affair at the moment —its climax.

Shooter, the horse, was treated by a veterinarian; Searby was treated for injuries of the leg and was excused from duty. Flurry was taken to Jamaica Court, where it was charged that he had no operator's license, and Searby brought a charge of assault against him. Flurry was held in $500 bail for hearing Friday.

—New York *Herald Tribune*

Combinations of these two basic styles are possible:

A summary-style lead.

MANITOU SPRINGS, COLO., Feb. 19—(*P*)—The motorist with any "regard for his future abode" should sing hymns as the speedometer climbs upward, the Rev. L. C. Miller said in a safety sermon at the Mennonite church.

Now a series of details that suspend interest until the final climactic line.

His selections at different speeds:

At 25 miles per hour, "I'm but a Stranger Here, Heaven Is My Home."

At 45 miles, "Nearer, My God, to Thee."

At 55 miles, "I'm Nearing the Port and Will Soon be at Home."

At 65 miles, "When the Roll Is Called up Yonder I'll be There."

At 75 miles, "Lord, I'm Coming Home."

Keeping such diagrams in mind will aid the copyeditor in backstopping the inept or careless reporter. If a story cannot be readily diagrammed, it probably lacks a desirable structural firmness and needs the assistance of a sharp pencil—or a typewriter.

Developing the Story

Various method are used to lure the reader's eye from the introduction into the body of a composition and, withal, to keep the whole composition unified, coherent, emphatic. Rhetoric textbooks discuss such techniques exhaustively, but the following are those most commonly used in newspaper stories: (1) significant details; (2) time sequence; (3) quotations; (4) words and phrases; (5) combinations.

1. Significant Details. The ordinary lead presents the important or striking facts; to expand them in succeeding paragraphs—inverted pyramid style—is a favorite way of writing the rest of the story. This method is comparable to the process in logic known as deduction, proceeding from the general to the particular.

HOUSTON, Tex. (UP)—A New Orleans woman has sued the State of Texas to collect on $46,000 worth of bonds one of her ancestors bought during the Civil War. She said she'd like to have interest, too, from Jan. 1, 1865, to date.

The compounded interest would bring the alleged value of the bonds, authorized by the Texas legislature on April 8, 1861, under the Texas Confederate Constitution, to some $46 million.

Filing of the suit Monday by Atty. Fred W. Moore for Mrs. M. B. Buford of New Orleans was approved by a special act of the Texas legislature last year.

The bonds, which bear the Confederate and Texas flags on their face, were signed by Gov. T. R. Lubbock, Texas Treasurer C. H. Randolph.

The state, represented by Katherine Conti, an assistant attorney general, contends the bonds are no good because they were issued under the Confederate Constitution to get money to fight the Yankees.

2. Time Sequence. Perhaps the simplest method of telling any event is to start "In the beginning—" and then relate the action in chronological order. Ordinarily, it is too slow for a newspaper lead, but some news-feature writers utilize it to suspend interest until the final paragraph.

Several examples have already been given; here is another:

TUCSON, Ariz. (AP)—An injunction suit against four Arivaca miners was being tried in Superior Court.

"What's the name of your mine?" asked Fred W. Fickett, attorney.

"Damned if I know," replied the witness, Claude B. Clays.

Indignant, the attorney repeated his question. He got the same answer. At that point the judge intervened.

Clays explained: "Judge, that is the name of the mine—Damned If I Know."

Frequently an action tangent of the lead becomes the starting point of the next paragraph, with one or more paragraphs thereafter following the events in order of their occurrence.

The lead is a summary— yet has an aspect of suspense that carries the reader on.

Peggy Sweem, 4-year-old dancer, will be denied the thrill of her scheduled dancing debut at a children's party on Christmas eve. Peggy, curly-haired daughter of Mr. and Mrs. Dorwin Sweem, 1530 Ninth st., paid that price to become a heroine in a traffic accident Wednesday afternoon.

An action element from the lead is picked up.

In company with two playmates—Jane Ann Sharp, 3, and Jane's brother, Bobbie, 5—Peggy started across the street in front of her home at 1:30 p.m.

The children were headed for the Sharp home at 1535 Ninth st. with candy for Larry Sharp, 2, a brother of Jane and Bobbie.

The story from here on is simple narration—telling what happened—in the order that it happened.

As the trio, hand in hand, stepped out from in front of a parked car, Peggy heard an automobile approaching. Pushing Bobbie, who was in front of her, to safety, Peggy turned to rescue Jane, who was behind her.

There was a grinding of brakes and the two girls lay prostrate.

—Des Moines (Iowa) *Register*

The second paragraph of the foregoing story illustrates the rhetorical use of the *tie-back,* already noted in second-day leads. It *rehashes* previous events of a related character. While providing a background of understanding for the reader, it arouses and suspends interest to be satisfied only by further details—in this case, narrated in chronological sequence.

To be distinguished from tie-backs are *tie-ins.* These are bits of information about contemporary events which supplement a story. Had parents of the children in the foregoing story been simultaneously doing something of dramatic interest, it could have been tied-in. Another type of tie-in is found in stories which place important contemporary or future events near the beginning of the story because if they were placed near the end, they might be killed in makeup. For example: Announcement of a political candidate speaking during the day might well be interpolated after the lead of a general story about him, even though doing so would interrupt its smooth flow.

3. Quotations.   Quick transition often can be secured by using apt quotations. Observe the word economy as well as the quick-step march of this little yarn:

SALT LAKE CITY, Jan. 25 (AP)—Donald Carl Phillips, a 40-year-old jail inmate, offered an eye today to a 16-year-old Georgia girl who, he heard, is losing her sight.

"I'm not doing this as a publicity stunt, and I'm not doing it as a debt to society," he said. "I want to be able to know that the girl can romp and play like other kids."

Phillips, whose criminal record dates back to 1915, said he learned of the girl's plight from another jail inmate and sent an airmail letter to her father, George Giger of Roberta, Ga., offering the eye.

In some cases the story can best be told with conversation or with long quotations, occasionally relieved by explanations, summaries or description:

BOSTON, Jan. 21.—A dinner at the University club Thursday evening will be the scene of "finals" for the public speaking class of Boston University's evening division, with a generous helping of mid-year exams as the last course. Prof. William G. Hoffman of the English faculty will grade students according to the quality of their after-dinner speeches that evening.

"I can't understand why the students are so eager to spend all the time and trouble to prepare after-dinner speeches," Professor Hoffman said in discussing the examination. "It would be much easier for them to take a written examination. But every year when I ask them to make their choice they all favor a dinner followed by five-minute speeches for their final exam.

"I am, however, in favor of the procedure. It gives the speakers the incentive of a more realistic setting."   —New York *Times*

4. Connecting Words and Phrases. Numerous expressions are little verbal turnstiles passing the reader easily from one paragraph to another. While they should be used sparingly, sometimes they are helpful in unifying long stories. Here are a few:

To stress time: meanwhile, in the end, at length, now that, formerly, at the same time, along with, now.

To point out: here, in this case, at such times, here again, thereby, therein.

To cite: for example, a case in point is, for instance.

To except: irrespective of, with this exception, except for this.

To summarize: on the whole, in a word, as was pointed out, to sum up.

To explain: that is, in other words, this is because, the reason is.

To shift the viewpoint: in point of fact, in general, as things are now; but, in another sense.

To compare: in contrast with, in the same manner, likewise, from another point of view.

To emphasize: especially, above all, most of all, furthermore, in addition.

To infer: consequently, thus, hence, as a result of, this being the case.

To refute: otherwise, else, on the contrary, even so.

To relate: the more, not only, so long as, yet, whereas, to pass to, along with, incidentally, parenthetically, namely, in the first place.

5. Combinations. All methods may be used with good effect in a combination. Montony thus is avoided, but the danger is a loss of unity. The writer should cut his pattern to fit his goods.

Here is an inside-page story from a correspondent. It has been deliberately disarranged to show glaring structural faults. Note how the important facts are scattered throughout the story, thus violating the principles of unity, coherence and emphasis. It is an elementary rule to dispose of one angle of a newsstory before taking up another; this prevents the hopscotch effect that so annoys the newspaper reader. The faulty story:

(1) GREAT BARRINGTON, April 29—This afternoon a strong west wind whipped a fire that endangered a house and totally demolished two large barns, a smaller barn, a sawmill and several outbuildings on the farm of Fred Peck at North Egremont. The total damage is estimated to be in excess of $6,000, of which only a part is covered by insurance.

(2) The Peck farm is just beyond the town limits of Great Barrington on Egremont Plain on route 23, the principal thoroughfare between South Berkshire and Albany, N.Y. A large crowd was attracted by the fire, which is the second hereabouts in recent weeks to consume all of the barns on agricultural property.

The other conflagration took place at the Caron Home on Lake Buel road, when three barns were likewise destroyed a week ago Sunday.

(3) The heroic work of the Egremont and Great Barrington fire companies was all that saved the Peck residence from destruction. Working under handicaps caused by the strong west wind and distance from water, both companies were congratulated by thankful citizens attending the fire for their valorous action in saving the Peck home.

(4) A large quantity of farm machinery, stored and baled hay, tools and miscellaneous equipment was destroyed. One of the large barns was a dairy and completely equipped.

(5) Because of the steady west wind, the fire progressed from the sawmill through a series of sheds, gradually engulfing the three barns. Livestock were removed to safety by passersby and neighbors.

(6) The fire departments of Great Barrington and Egremont were kept busy saving the Peck residence, which became ignited on several occasions because of its proximity to the burning barns. Hose lines were laid 1,450 feet by the Great Barrington fire company to Green River, where pumpers provided pressure, while the North Egremont department laid lines for 1,200 feet to the same stream. A partly constructed pumping engine of the Egremont fire company was rushed to the scene and was utilized in getting water to the fire.

(7) The fire started in the sawmill which is powered by a gasoline motor. Whether sparks from the motor were responsible is not known, but three workmen in the mill saw the entire motor suddenly enveloped in flames. The tinderlike woodwork in the vicinity of the motor blazed up before the workmen could extinguish the burning engine.

Now, the same story edited and rearranged with marginal explanations. Numbers in parentheses refer to paragraphs of the foregoing.

Note the terse and reworded lead. It answers the reader's question, what happened? Here is the gist of the whole story.

GREAT BARRINGTON, April 29—A fire whipped by a strong west wind destroyed three barns, a sawmill and several out-buildings this afternoon on the Fred Peck Farm at North Egremont. The family residence itself was endangered, becoming ignited several times. The damage is estimated at $6,000, partly covered by insurance.

How and why did it start? Here is all that's relevant. Note the use of the time-sequence handling in this and the next paragraph. (7)

The fire started in the sawmill which is powered by a gasoline engine. Three workmen in the mill saw it suddenly enveloped in flames. The tinderlike woodwork nearby blazed up before the workmen could extinguish the engine flames.

The action tows the reader's eye on. Minor details have been grouped. (4 and 5)

Because of the steady wind, the fire progressed from the sawmill through a series of sheds, gradually engulfing the three barns, one of which was a completely equipped dairy. Much farm machinery, stored and baled hay, and miscellaneous equipment was lost. All livestock were removed to safety by passersby and neighbors.

The time-sequence order now gives way to significant-detail development. Here's a minor note of excitement that, unfortunately for the story, didn't expand. The unnecessary praise for the firemen is omitted. (6 and 3)

Now to bolster the story with more details on the where *part. A reference to the other fire supplies a low-grade follow-up element. There's no mystery here—just a coincidence; but the reporter has wrung his facts dry. This paragraph could be dropped without harm to the story. (2)*

Fire departments of Great Barrington and Egremont were kept busy saving the Peck residence nearby which became ignited several times. Hose lines were laid 1,450 feet by Great Barrington firemen to Green river, where pumpers provided pressure. The North Egremont department laid lines for 1,200 feet to the same stream. A partly constructed pumping engine of the latter company helped get water to the fire.

The Peck farm is just beyond the town limits of Great Barrington on Egremont Plain on route 23, the principal thoroughfare between South Berkshire and Albany, N. Y. A large crowd was attracted by the fire, which is the second in recent weeks on an agricultural property in the vicinity. The other fire was at the Caron home on Lake Buel road where three barns were also destroyed a week ago Sunday.

—Springfield (Mass.) *Republican* [adapted]

In the latter version, the lead has been sharpened, sentences have been tightened, and repetition and useless material omitted; but the chief change has been in the arrangement of details. The reader has the essence of the news in the lead. If he is sufficiently interested to read on, he gets a quick picture of the fire moving from the sawmill to the house, where it has halted. Supplementary details round out the story. Then it stops.

To discover the structural faults of the first version, attempt to diagram it. Then note how readily the rearranged story can be patterned. The lead presents matter in order of its importance, hence follows the inverted pyramid plan. The next two paragraphs tell details in the order of their happening—upright pyramid style. The rest of the story reverts to the inverted pyramid.

Teasing Reader Interest

Most news copy is constructed in inverted pyramid style but there is no rule that says a good narrative story cannot withhold its twist or punch to the final paragraph. Saul Pett showed *Associated Press* editors the value of the quiet lead in the following examples (from the *AP Log*):

With one exception John J. Schmigalosa is like millions of other men. At 7:45 every weekday morning, he shaves and complains it's getting tougher every day. At 7:58, he listens to the kids at breakfast and wonders what the younger generation is coming to. Rushing for the 8:08, he vows to take more time tomorrow.

Coming home at night, he pauses wearily before the mirror to notice the new gray hairs, as millions of other men do. For John J. Schmigalosa is like everyone else, with one exception. He has two heads.

John J. Schmigalosa has two heads. He has learned to adjust to the fact and lives a normal life. Every morning, like millions of other men, he. . . .

"Which lead do you like? Personally, I've been waiting for years to write No. 1, but I can't find a guy named Schmigalosa."

Effectiveness of the teaser lead is illustrated in two examples of the same story. Which is the better version?

NEW YORK, Feb. 6 (UP)—Mrs. Ruth Bogen, 26, was reading the morning mail. One letter from the Veterans' Administration read: 'We have learned with regret of the death of your husband.' She was asked to fill out a form to collect the $10,000 life insurance.

Mrs. Bogen, the wife of Harold Bogen, a World War II veteran, looked surprised and then smiled across the breakfast table at her three children . . . and her husband.

NEW YORK, Feb. 6 (AP)—Mrs. Ruth Bogen read the letter from the Veterans' Administration, then glanced at her husband drinking his breakfast coffee. . . .

Theodore Morrison of the English department at Harvard maintains that the competent expository writer follows one simple but absolutely cardinal principle and follows a second principle up to the limits of his skill and his opportunities. The first principle, Morrison wrote in the introduction to the *Nieman Reports* special issue on reading, writing and newspapers [April 1950], is to group related ideas together.

The second principle is to keep the reader reading ahead with a sense of expectancy akin to suspense in fiction. Newsstories frequently violate these two principles because they lack unity and coherence; they do not have transitional phrases that keep the writing from being jerky and often the stories fade out before the final full stop.

Pitfalls in Formula Writing

The newsstory formula itself causes bad writing in newspapers. Wallace Carroll, executive editor of the Winston-Salem *Journal* and *Sentinel,* characterized the writing as juicy as a tootsie roll. "What do you find in a newsstory when you dissect it?" he asked in an article in the July 1955 *Nieman Reports*.

A lead sentence with the back end forward; adverbs stuck in awkward positions ("today" and "tomorrow" are always with us and always ahead of the verb); bits of identification strewn about at random (the defendant swore that he did not murder Bertha Blagg, 36); nouns used as verbs (nobody ever talks to a man when he can *contact* him); clumsy and standardized synonyms used to avoid repetition (it takes a heap o' somethin' to make a house a *structure*— or a flood an *inundation*); archaic words (slay) and tired words from tabloids (probes)—and the whole thing held together with a liberal cement of bromides and clichés.

All this would be bad enough if it were only the aberration of individuals. But this mishmash is a "style" sanctified by the sweat of the copydesk ever since Greeley stayed East and therefore as little subject to improvement as the language of the Psalms.

I have been a newspaperman for more than a quarter of a century, but I find it hard to read many newsstories on relatively simple subjects and still harder to retain what is in them. . . . This situation is not funny. It is dangerous.

It's the Way It Is Written

Former AP writer Don Whitehead insists that people will remember a story that has a beginning, a middle and an end, particularly when it revolves around a person or a small group. Whitehead advises writers to try to let the story tell itself, to condense the news in the first few paragraphs, then go back and put down the story just as it happened. This approach, he says, makes for good newswriting if it is clothed in a conversational style and phrased so that the reader can get a mental picture of what is happening.

O. L. Hall, veteran columnist and editor, once summed this up in giving to student journalists an earful of advice still sound. "Try to keep conscious of a writer's style," he urged. "It is a mark of a good newspaperman. Other people read just for action or plot, to see what happened or is going to happen to Tom or to Ann. Of course the story is important: you must have something to say. But, really, it's not the story that counts so much. *It's the way it is written.*"

8 Making Newspaper Copy
Clear and Precise

The difference between the right word and the almost-right word is the difference between lightning and the lightning bug.—Mark Twain (1835–1910), *American humorist.*

Error is never so difficult to be destroyed as when it has its roots in language. . . . Improper terms are the chains which bind me to unreasonable practices.—Jeremy Bentham (1748–1833), *English writer.*

A word is not a crystal, transparent, and unchanging; it is the skin of a living thought and may vary greatly in color and content according to the circumstances and time in which it is used.—Oliver Wendell Holmes (1841–1935), *Supreme Court Justice.*

Sentences which suggest far more than they say, which have an atmosphere about them; which do not merely report an old, but make a new, impression; sentences which suggest as many things and are as durable as a Roman aqueduct; to frame these, that is the *art* of writing.—Henry David Thoreau (1817–1862), *American author.*

Use Precise Words

"I'm surprised!" exclaimed Mrs. Webster as she came upon Noah kissing the maid.

"Oh, no, I'm surprised; you are astonished," he rejoined.

Newsmen may disagree on latitude to be given reporters with words that have not crashed the gates of popular usage and academic respectability, but on one dictum they are unanimous: use precise words. Copyeditors are always suspicious of a synonym, itself described as "A word you use for the one you can't spell."

"You learn to write by writing and writing and writing," G. K. Chesterton, English essayist, once said, "but you must take each word by itself, examining it as you would a criminal, and avoiding ready-made phrases."

The deskman can do a workmanlike job of editing. With deft strokes he tries to make the copy clear, precise and accurate. He sharpens the reporter's expressions, works in transitions to bring better relation between ideas, or he may have to rearrange paragraphs to get the items in their proper position or perspective. This type of editing demands background, understanding, judgment and perception.

All sorts of material tumbles on the copydesk. Some is without error. Some is honeycombed with mistakes, trivial, absurd, dangerous. Some is a joy, with each sentence glistening like a polished jewel; some is forged in a heavy, clumsy style. One item reports a serious speech; another rings with pathetic or humorous overtones. Knowing when to whack and when to let the copy run is the mark of an experienced deskman.

He tries to make copy precise. It is not what the writer intended but what the words themselves mean; it is not what is implied but what is actually expressed that counts. Exactness sharpens the news and gives the reader a better understanding of what is happening.

What Does It Mean?

The deskman puts himself in the reader's place and asks, "What does this mean?" Lack of precision is emphasized in the following from office bulletins of the *Associated Press* and the New York *Times*:

"The German-American Bund demonstration was attacked in a statement today." How can you attack a demonstration?

"Dewensberry's car collided with Smith's car." The fact is the two cars were in collision, and why should we imply whose fault it was?

"Ellwood faced a murder charge today." Does that mean he was arrested on a charge of murder, or not?

"Brown was convicted of relief chiseling." What, precisely, does that mean? The formal charge cannot possibly be relief chiseling.

"George Edward Grammer . . . was convicted today of deliberately killing his wife . . . so he could marry a pretty New York secretary." Beauty, prettiness and attractiveness are subjective judgments. Why not drop them and stick to objective reporting?

"The three ministers function like a well-drilled basketball or soccer team, passing the ball quickly and surely from hand to hand." Anyone who knows anything about soccer knows it is illegal for any player except the goal keeper to use his hands.

". . . the modernization of the four roads bisecting the big park." *Bisect* means *cut in two,* which is not what four roads do to the park. Make it *crossing.*

"GRAND JUNCTION, Tenn., Feb. 19 (AP)—A smooth-working hound flushed seven bevies of quail in a three-hour trial yesterday for the top performance of the national championship." Said R. F. Paine of the Memphis *Commercial Appeal:* "I imagine that every bird dog owner in the country shuddered in horror at the word HOUND. That would be about the same as saying a cow won the Kentucky Derby. . . . Secondly, the word FLUSH is the exact opposite of the word that should have been used. That would be like saying Babe Ruth won the game by striking out. Flush means to frighten the birds into flying away. The correct word is point."

When a wire service editor comes across a passage that is not clear, he messages to the source, "How pls?" The copyeditor raises the same question. The following example demands a challenge: "The island is warmed by the cool breezes of the Mediterranean."

Help the Reporter to Report

The eyebrow of a trained copyeditor is trained to arch instantly at the sight of loose reporting.

If copy about a labor dispute reads, "Company officials warned today . . . ," the copyeditor should query the reporter with: "Who warned?" If it was the vice president who did the warning, that should be said. Also, what he said.

When the reporter clothes news in anonymity, the reader suspects he is not getting all the facts. The reporter who won't pin down sources resorts to the vague phrases "it is said," "it is reported," "it is believed." There are times, of course, when anonymity cannot be escaped, but the copyeditor should satisfy himself on the point before passing the copy on.

When Senator McCarthy called in reporters to make a statement, he specified that the announcement could not be attributed to him. The wire services started the story: "A person who declined to let his name be used publicly said today. . . ."

Commenting on loose attribution to sources, Alan Gould of the *Associated Press* said:

Many newspaper editors don't like this way of dishing out news. They say a man ought to stand up and be quoted by name if he has anything to say. We are all suckers, they argue, for permitting our wires, news columns and air waves to be used by such people who are sending up trial balloons or manipulating the news to serve their own ends. We don't like it either. If some way could be found to stop this anonymous business or to minimize it, we would welcome it.

Use Adjectives Sparingly

Strong nouns and active verbs seldom need qualifiers. Adjectives are cheap.

"Think twice before you use an adjective," Carl Sandburg admonished fellow craftsmen. "Don't deal in treacherous adjectives; stick to honest nouns and verbs," Carr Van Anda used to lecture the *Times'* staff. "Treat adjectives like garlic—to be used sparingly," advised another writer. Notice how adjectives and adverbs clutter the following from the *AP Log:*

> The couple's *young* 2-year-old son was uninjured.
> The election was a *surprising* upset.
> Mr. and Mrs. Jack Frost are the parents of a seven-pound *baby* girl.
> The 108-year-old veteran planned a quiet birthday. (Isn't that obvious? asks the reader.)
> Hot coffee was served to the disaster workers. (Whoever heard of serving cold coffee?)
> Devout Catholic. (Then why not "devout Presbyterians"?)
> The victim was placed between clean, white sheets. (Naturally he wasn't placed between dirty sheets.)
> The woman was brutally raped and her companion was savagely beaten. (Aren't all rapes brutal and all beatings savage?)

The great misuse of adjectives is their substitution for exact information. "Large audience" is not so effective as "10,000 persons." "Abnormally cold" doesn't conjure up the image that "10 degrees below zero" does. If an audience is "enthusiastic," it is usually better to sketch a visual picture of its enthusiasm by telling what people did to show it. Once "very" was a fresh word, but no longer. Eliminating it and other vacuous words often improves a writer's style by half.

The good copyeditor would do well to heed the advice of Carl E. Lindstrom, executive editor of the Hartford (Conn.) *Times:* "Sometimes by taking the lead out of facts, you can put wings on meaning." Here is an example. Reporting the coronation of Queen Elizabeth, a wire service correspondent wrote:

> The Archbishop of Canterbury placed the five and a half pound crown upon the 24-year-old Queen's head.

Protested Lindstrom, "Now there was a brilliant example of reportorial fact-grubbing: the ascertainable detail of the crown's weight; the age of the Queen and the Archbishop of Canterbury—that answers the question Who.

"The same instant in the drama was described by Rebecca West in the following words in her newsstory, 'They placed the heavy crown upon her young head.'

"That is what I mean by the force of the nonspecific."

Photo by Bill Peery, Denver Rocky Mountain News

TELLING A STORY IN PICTURES. This photograph needs no cutline to let the reader feel its deep impact.

Words That Clutter

Each word in well-written, well-edited newspaper copy carries its full load of meaning and utility. If it does not, the copyeditor should delete it. Clarity is the guide, not any ancient rule of Latin rhetoricians.

That, which, quite are examples of cluttering words. *Which* is a blockader of style and often can be omitted entirely or replaced by the less objectionable *that*. Often *that* is unnecessary. "He said *that* he did not think *that* it would rain." *Quite* becomes a habit word. "He received *quite* a shock from the news."

Needless qualification slows the tempo of the writing. If Jackson is convicted of manslaughter, it is ridiculous to attribute the verdict to the foreman of the jury.

Let one word do the work of several. Note these examples.

all of a sudden (suddenly)
by the name of (named)
consensus of opinion (consensus)

put in an appearance (appeared)
there is no doubt that (doubtless)
in the neighborhood of (about)

Careful writers do not use:

all of the for *all the*
allude for *refer*
amateur for *novice*
answer for *reply*
anxious for *eager*
audience for *spectators*
center about for *center in* or *on*
colored persons for *Negroes*
commence for *begin*
complected for *complexioned*
conclude for *close* (conclude is a mental process)
confession for *admission* (for oral statements)
consummate in referring to marriage
different than for *different from*
donate for *give*
during for *in*
event for *incident, affair, occurrence* or *happening*
exemplary for *excellent*
half mast for *half staff* (ashore)
hung for *hanged* (referring to persons)

inaugurate for *open*
lady for *woman*
leave for *let*
less for *fewer* (referring to number)
liable for *likely*
like for *as* (If you are *like* me, you will do *as* I do.)
loan for *lend*
most for *almost*
onto for *on* or *upon*
over for *more than*
party for *person*
people for *persons*
poisonous for *venomous*
prior to for *before*
providing that for *provided that*
revolver for *pistol* or *automatic*
secure for *obtain*
stated for *said*
unique for *unusual* (there are no degrees of uniqueness)
unknown man for *unidentified* man
unsanitary for *insanitary*
well known for *widely known*

A careful writer never refers to anyone as *the Smith woman, the Snyder child, the Davis girl.*

Redundancies show lack of writing ability: *still persists, controversial issue, old adage, possibly might, regular weekly meeting.*

Use Close-Up Words

Seldom does the copyeditor have to rewrite the story. Usually he can turn badly constructed copy into an acceptable story by careful editing. He allows for variation and originality; if the reporter has made the meaning clear, the deskman need not quibble over minor things. Part of the editing job is mechanical (marking paragraphs, writing directions for the printer). This is copy-fixing. Copyediting calls for bolder strokes.

The trick is to make one strong word do the work of several words, to favor a short, easy word like *farmer* over a long, hard word *agriculturist,* to substitute what Flesch calls a "close-up" word (St. Bernard) for a "far-away" word (animal), to put life and action into slow-moving sentences, variety in monotonous phrases.

Worked-to-Death Words

Unregenerate or crutch words have a tendency to creep into news copy, particularly in reporting public or special affairs. In this category are expressions like *check, target, gap, liquidate, level, operation, spell out.* Such words, William D. Grampp showed in an article for *The Saturday Review,* clutter the vocabulary of the public official. There are *legislative targets, crop targets, charity targets, gross national product targets.* "It is a good word for sharp-shooters and marksmen, but public verbalists rarely hit it. Let them use *objective, end, purpose,* or even *goal.*" Abuse of the word *socialite* forced the Denver *Post* editors to ban use of the term.

To be avoided especially are the platitudes and meaningless phrases we call *bromides* (or *clichés*). Once they were as fresh as mint; now they are stale beer. Such imagery is dulled by constant use, and the copyeditor's pencil should fell them on sight. In *The New Yorker* Frank Sullivan has lampooned them delightfully—"The Cliché Expert Takes the Stand":

Q—Mr. Arbuthnot, you are an expert in the use of the cliché, are you not?

A—Yes sir, I am a certified public cliché expert.

Q—Would you answer a few questions on the uses of the cliché?

A—I should be only too glad to.

Q—Thank you. Now, just for the record—you live in New York?

A—I like to visit New York but I wouldn't live there if you gave me the place.

Q—Then where do you live?

A—Any old place I hang my hat is home sweet home to me.

Q—What is your age?

A—I am fat, fair, and forty.

Q—And your occupation?

A—Well, after burning the midnight oil at an institution of higher learning, I was for a time a tiller of the soil. Then I went down to the sea in ships. I have been a guardian of the law, a poet at heart, a prominent clubman and man about town, an eminent—

Q—Now then, Mr. Arbuthnot, what kind of existence do you lead?

A—A precarious existence.

Q—And what do you do to it?

A—I eke it out.

Q—How do you cliché experts reveal yourselves, Mr. Arbuthnot?

A—In our true colors, of course.

Q—And you expect to live to . . .

A—A ripe old age.

Q—What do you shuffle off?

A—This mortal coil.

Q—What do you thank?

A—My lucky stars.

Q—What do you do to hasty retreats?

A—I beat them.

Q—What kind of dog are you?

A—A gay dog.

Q—And how do you work?

A—Like a dog.

Q—And you lead?

A—A dog's life.

Q—Now, Mr. Arbuthnot, when you are naked, you are . . .

A—Stark naked.

Q—In what kind of daylight?

A—Broad daylight.

Q—What kind of outsider are you?

A—I'm a rank outsider

Q—How right are you?

A—I am dead right.

Q—What meals do you like?

A—Square meals.

Q—What do you do to them?

A—Ample justice.

Q—When you buy things, you buy them for . . .

A—A song.

Q—You are as sober as . . .

A—A judge.

Q—And when you are drunk?

A—I can be as drunk as a coot, or a lord, or an owl, or a fool—

Q—Very good. Now, how brown are you?

A—As brown as a berry.

Q—Ever see a brown berry?

A—Oh, no. Were I to see a brown berry, I should be frightened.

Q—To what extent?

A—Out of my wits.

Q—How fit are you?

A—I'm as fit as a fiddle.

Q—How do you wax?

A—I wax poetic.

Q—How about the fate of Europe?

A—It is hanging in the balance.

Q—What happens to landscapes?

A—Landscapes are dotted.

Q—How are you attired?

A—Faultlessly.

Q—What kind of precision and order are you partial to?

A—Clocklike precision and apple-pie order.

Q—When you travel, what do you combine?

A—I combine business with pleasure.

Q—And you are destined . . .

A—To go far.

Q—And what is it you save?

A—Wear and tear.

Q—What goes with "pure"?

A—Simple.

Q—The word "sundry"?

A—Divers.

Q—What are ranks?

A—Ranks are serried. Structures are imposing. Spectacles are colorful.

Q—Thank you, Mr. Arbuthnot. What kind of beauties do you like?

A—Raving beauties.

Q—How generous are you?

A—I am generous to a fault.

Q—How is corruption these days

A—Oh, rife, as usual.

Q—What time is it?

A—It is high time.

Q—How do you point?

A—I point with pride, I view with alarm, and I yield to no man.

Q—What do you pursue?

A—The even tenor of my way.

Q—What do you throw—and where?

A—I throw caution to the winds

Q—As a cliché-user, have you any pets?

A—Yes, I have pet aversions.

Q—Any tempests?

A—Oh, yes. In teapots. In china shops I have bulls.

Q—What kind of cunning to you affect, Mr. Arbuthnot?

A—Low, animal cunning.

Q—And when you are taken, you are taken . . .

A—Aback.

Q—I see. Well, Mr. Arbuthnot, I think that everyone who has listened to you here today will be a better cliché-user for having heard you. Thank you very, very much.

A—Thank *you*. It's been a pleasure, I assure you, and I was only too glad to oblige.

Troublesome Words

Any old-time deskman has a list of troublesome words. Here are a few:

Alleged. Some writers and copyeditors have the mistaken notion that *alleged* will ward off libel or moral responsibility of the newspaper. The word affords the writer or newspaper absolutely no protection from a libel suit.

Smithy. Writers who confuse smithy for smith should recall Longfellow's lines: "Under a spreading chestnut-tree the village *smithy* stands; the *smith*, a mighty man is he, ..." A *smithy* is a workshop of a *smith*.

Nerve-racking not *nerve-wracking.*

Lambaste not *lambast.*

Borrow pit not *barrow pit.*

Nationals not *natives* (when referring to the citizens of a country).

Insignia not *insigne.*

Miliary tuberculosis not *military.*

Burial not *interment.*

Takeoff is a noun, the verb is *take off.*

An *AWOL* soldier is not a *deserter* until he has been absent at least 30 days.

Presently—means "soon" or "in a little while" but NOT "now."

Biweekly means every two weeks, *semiweekly* means twice a week.

These are meaningless: *nearly all, greater part, large part, considerable part, small part, not much.* The reader wants to know exactly how much.

About, approximately and *some* are estimates and should be used with round numbers: *approximately 300* (not *approximately 312*), *some 1300* (not *some 1342*).

Beware of Technical Jargon

Today's news is hard enough to understand; it becomes almost impossible when the writer brings the specialist's language into the report. Perhaps the readers should know the technical terms used by lawyers, doctors, businessmen and engineers, but they don't. They understand terms like *cuts, bruises, scratches* and *shock,* but not *lacerations, contusions, abrasions* and *trauma.*

"Gobbledygook" is not confined to government reports. It occurs whenever specialists sit down to write or make statements for public consumption.

The following example of "medicalese" appeared in the booklet, *Word Study,* and is used with permission of the G. & C. Merriam Company (Copyright 1950.) It was written by an "editorial secretary to a writing M.D."

The patient, who previous to the onset of his disability obtained his source of livelihood from the manipulation of the exterior keys of the pianoforte so as to form a consistent and harmonious arrangement of musical impressions, suffered a bilateral digital amputation as a result of maljustaposition with a provender bearing vehicle. Resultant from this disability is a diminution of digital dexterity requisite to the execution of his vocational pattern, the end product of same being a severe limitation of the patient's pre-operative ability at livelihood acquisition.

English translation: The patient, who used to be a piano player, lost two fingers after bumping into a grocery truck. Since he can't play the piano as well as he used to, he doesn't make so much money anymore.

Here is another example of gobbledygook:

"Comic books are exercising a vitiating influence on recent progress toward easing racial tension," Dr. Frederic Wertham, psychiatrist, said today.

It means: "Comic books are hampering progress. . . ."

Pity the reader when the reporter puts legal jargon in the news report: "The motions to be argued call for bills of particulars explaining two of the indictments in detail and demurrers filed in all the cases." What does it mean? the reader asks.

The AP anticipated that question when it handled a story about a patent case in which a toy pig was attached to junior's cereal bowl and induced him to eat his cereal. The story quoted the judge of the federal district court in Chicago as saying, "This is more than a toy. It is a device highly utilitarian in character; it has a decided educational and psychological value and its concept is new and inventive." The AP translated for the reader: What the court meant was that it was a clever idea and it worked.

Use Picture-Making Words

Although news is written in a hurry, a reporter with imagination and ability may produce a gem.

W. A. Macdonald created a classic in his description of the funeral of a Negro blues singer: "Harlem Says Bye Bye Honey to Florence Mills." Pat Morin of the AP knew how to achieve color when he started his story:

ABILENE, Kas., June 3 (AP)—A little town put on a party dress today, and began taking its hair out of curl-papers.

Most newsmen strive for color but only the better writers know how to achieve it. Some strive too hard; when they miss, the result can be awful: "Napierville's Bert Haas . . . hard-lucked a line drive foul, and then flew out to deep right."

Charles H. Hamilton of the Richmond *News Leader,* protesting the use of nouns as verbs to achieve color, chided, "I will hiball a couple of times and then I will dinner before I opera."

A Dallas story said FBI agents swarmed a man who was trying to extort $200,000 from a group of Jews, and that the man was bashed over the head as he pulled a barking .38 revolver. Said the reviewer for the *AP Log Supplement on Writing:*

Swarm is all right, but you just can't swarm. You swarm up a pole, or you swarm over a man. Most people say pistol when they really mean revolver. But barking? It couldn't have been barking when he pulled it, or he'd have shot himself. I think the writer really meant that the wild-eyed Jones yanked a revolver and hurriedly fired one wild shot before he was bashed on the head.

When an editor objected to an AP story from Cairo, Egypt, saying that the government had *shuttered* the newspaper *Al Misri,* other editors defended the use of the noun as a verb by pointing out that in Egypt doors are closed by rolling up steel shutters and therefore the word was used accurately.

Improving Newspaper Writing

Carl Sandburg told his readers in an *Atlantic Monthly* article: "At sixty-five I began my first novel, and the five years lacking a month I took to finish it, I was still traveling, still a seeker. I should like to think that as I go on writing there will be sentences truly alive, with verbs quivering, with nouns giving color and echoes."

Editors have never been more conscious of writing style than now. They prescribe books on readable writing for the staff, hire experts to evaluate stories, conduct classes in writing. Twenty-five years ago such practices would have been laughed off as academic. "Learn to write," they would have chortled, "why, man, every soul in the office is a writer." Here is what today's editor says:

Five or six years ago, a lot of us did not recognize the sloppy writing, or if we did, we didn't feel that there was anything we could do about it. Today, we recognize it and do something about it.—William J. Foote, (Hartford *Courant*) in a report for the Associated Press Managing Editors State Studies Committee.

Better writing has resulted from readability studies, principally because the research has motivated an inspection of style. Experts like Rudolf Flesch and Robert Gunning have demonstrated that long, complicated sentences, unfamiliar and Olympian words and lack of personal references make the subject matter hard to read and comprehend. Samples from all types of news copy have been graded according to formula and scaled for readability.

Such investigation is useful for the copyeditor. At least he knows the elements that cause difficulty for readers. By shortening sentences, substituting short, easy words for long, hard words, and by using personal for impersonal words, he can improve the writing style—up to a point.

Sentence Length

Slavish devotion to a writing formula is dangerous. For instance, the length of the sentence is not the all-important consideration. Too much brevity, in fact, makes sentences jerky and monotonous, a characteristic of primer style.

Utility, not a rule, should determine the length of sentences in newspaper copy. Short sentences of under 15 words are preferred, because even children can read them with but a slight movement of the eye, simultaneously comprehending them. They are especially useful at the beginning of a story or a paragraph, or within a paragraph to indicate a transition in thought or to secure emphasis. But that does not mean that long sentences have no place in news copy. They do.

Medium sentences of 15 to 30 words alternating with short ones avoid monotony, and by contrast secure emphasis. Long sentences of 30 or more words can group loosely connected details, such as names. Occasionally, when dignified or impressive thoughts are to be expressed, a deliberate sentence is better than several short and perhaps monotonous ones. The essential point is that the sentence be the servant of the writer.

Good writing style has flow. Edward J. Meeman, editor of the Memphis *Press-Scimitar,* defines flow as "that quality in writing which leads the reader on from word to word, phrase to phrase, sentence to sentence, paragraph to paragraph, to the very end, without break or jump, without work or effort, without puzzlement or boredom. Sometimes a long sentence will be as readable as a short one if it has flow. It is what makes reading not only easy but pleasurable."

No readability formula can make sense of gibberish; too much simplification may rob writing of variety and vitality. And the use of an unfamiliar word isn't necessarily a sin in writing, especially if the writer uses it in a context the reader understands.

Paragraph Length

Newspapers do not follow the old rule that one paragraph should be devoted to one idea. Paragraphs are less units of thought than units of purpose. The contrast of the white space of the indention to the surrounding type tends to catch the eye. Short paragraphs also rest the eye, and make it easier to follow the lines of small type. Information parceled out in small paragraphs is comprehended more quickly. Short paragraphs, furthermore, make for typographical attractiveness of a page and facilitate makeup.

For these sufficient reasons, news copy is usually broken into paragraph blocks of 100 words which make four or five lines.

Quotation marks, like paragraph indention, are a device to catch the eye. They suggest conversation, which may be compared to the riffles of a brook. Although *quotes* have been too much used to start stories, they are frequently of value in starting off a paragraph deeper in the text.

One-Idea Sentences

Seeking comprehensibility as well as clarity and precision, the New York *Times* instituted a practice of limiting each sentence to one idea. It was pointed out, however, that there are instances in which two or more thoughts are inseparable and to devote a sentence to each idea would be absurd as, for example: "The American flag is red. It is also white. It is blue, too."

Testing the theory, the New York *Times* found that reading matter reduced to one-idea sentences could be read faster. When respondents were given questions pertaining to what they had read, the answers indicated that comprehension of one-idea, one-sentence matter invariably increased, sometimes as much as 55 per cent.

Managing Editor Turner Catledge gave impetus to the campaign in a staff memo which read in part:

Brevity, simplicity and clarity are basically what we are striving for. We feel that the main newspoints of any story can be told in simple, short statements. We feel that it is no longer necessary, and maybe never was, to wrap up in one sentence or paragraph all the traditional W's—who, what, when, where and why. I do not wish to lay down any rules. I certainly do not intend to try to fix the length of sentences, since the need varies with each story. . . . I should hope that, in striving for the particular goals of brevity, simplicity and clarity, our writers will develop individual styles which will make their stories more readable and, hence, more attractive to our readers.

As the campaign continued, the New York *Times'* editors began to notice marked improvement in rewrites from edition to edition, such as:

The New York, New Haven and Hartford Railroad is willing to freeze commutation rates at existing levels pending the working out of a plan to put them into the sliding scale of national cost-of-living statistics.—1st edition

Pegging commutation rates to the cost of living is being considered by the New York, New Haven and Hartford Railroad.—final edition

The following passage, taken from a newsstory, would have been clearer to the reader if the writer or copyeditor had reduced each idea to a separate sentence:

He contended the government's finding was unconstitutional and arbitrary and said his union, which represents 600 phone workers here, was planning to file a grievance with the telephone company asking his reinstatement and claiming that the company was not obligated by law to fire him and had taken that responsibility upon itself.

The *Times* has emphasized that "one-idea, one-sentence" is not a rule or established formula. It cautioned against breaking a complex sentence, leaving half an idea instead of one idea. Example: "The commission's 7,000-square-mile estimate (of H-bomb contamination) compared with one of 10,000 square miles." A deskman had lopped off the phrase "advanced last night by Dr. Ralph E. Lapp, atomic scientist," which left the original incomplete. This blooper is typical of what happens when a newsman becomes an unthinking slave to any rule.

Colored Writing and Propaganda

"Society has charged writers with the custody of words," said Bernard DeVoto. "Don't abuse that confidence. Protect the purity of the word to protect the purity of thought." Dr. Henry Seidel Canby admonished, "Strict truth always depends upon the use of specific words, of words which admit of but one interpretation."

Readers use emotions and imagination in transferring things to words. Propagandists know this and deliberately select words that bring a predetermined emotional response. The politician speaks of "mother," "home" and "country" because these are emotion-filled terms and the speaker tries to get the listeners to respond to words. Many advertising messages attempt to overcome us with words. In military dispatches, the enemy always *retreats,* our side *withdraws.* In political handouts, the opponents are the *gang* or the *crowd.*

Loaded words reveal the bias of the writer, but not all readers are able to distinguish between colored and objective writing. Ordinary newsstories can fool the reader or cause him to react emotionally, not to the incident, but to the terms used. Semanticists point out that some writers use synonyms eliciting either favorable or unfavorable response for neutral words for a definite purpose.

Party leader, for instance, is a neutral term. *Leader of the people* brings a favorable response, *rabble rouser* an unfavorable response. If you are sympathetic with those who take part in an uprising you refer to them as *liberators*; if you oppose them you term them *rebels* or *traitors.* Innocent words take on meanings not inherent in the words themselves but as creatures of the times. Thus *Communist* has become libelous in some jurisdictions when applied falsely to a person. The abuse of the expression *fellow-traveler* could put it in the same category as *Communist.*

News should be as original and colorful as the writer can make it but it must not plead or distort. "Do not color the news," said Roy Howard of the United Press, "but give the news its own color. Actually news is not gray, it is full of color, so let your writing show it as it is." If colored words are used to bring either a favorable or an unfavorable response from the reader the story loses its objectivity. That's when the copyeditor should exercise his judgment, substitute neutral terms for the verbal magic and let the reader form his own opinions from the facts presented.

Perhaps some latitude can be allowed in a by-lined story since responsibility for bias can be attributed to a specified individual, but even so, a story displayed as news should contain facts and not the subjective judgment of the writer. Judgment evaluations belong on the editorial pages.

Muddy Thinking Makes Muddy Copy

Producing clear copy is dependent upon clear thinking. For words are simply symbols of thought. Sloppy reporting is invariably traceable to sloppy thinking. A muddy mind cannot turn out clear and brisk copy.

Lincoln, though without benefit of much education, produced prose used even in his day by teachers of rhetoric as models. A reporter asked how he developed his style. Lincoln replied:

I have been putting the question you ask me to myself while you have been talking. I say this, that among my earliest recollections, I remember how when a mere child, I used to get irritated when anybody talked to me in a way I could not understand. I don't think I ever got angry at anything else in my life. But that always disturbed my temper.

I can remember going to my little bedroom, after hearing the neighbors talk of an evening with my father, and spending no small part of the night walking up and down, and trying to make out what was the meaning of their, to me, dark sayings. I could not sleep, though I often tried to, when I got on such a hunt after an idea, until I had caught it; and when I thought I had got it, I was not satisfied until I had repeated it over and over, until I had put it in language plain enough, as I thought, for any boy I knew to comprehend.

This was kind of passion with me, and it has stuck by me, for I am never easy now, when I am handling a thought, till I have bounded it north and bounded it south and bounded it east and bounded it west.

Lincoln would have made a star copyeditor!

9 Various Kinds of Copy

Copyreading [copyediting] is both an art and a science; both critical and creative. The copyreader must have a fine feeling for the drama and color of the news and a high sense of public responsibility. He must have the background of information and the experience and judgment against which to measure the value of the newsstory, so he may emphasize the important, eliminate the trivial, and provide adequate coverage. Above all he must know the meaning of words, so that each does the job required of it and an understanding of the newspaper's mechanics and capacity, including its type style and dress.—Neil MacNeil (1891–   ), in *The Newspaper: Its Making and Its Meaning.*

I. WHERE COPY COMES FROM

Local News

Local news originates in three sources—beat reporters, general (assignment) reporters and volunteers. Beat reporters cover sources like courthouse (including courts), municipal building, state and federal buildings, police and sheriff's offices. Reporters may return to the newspaper to write their stories; they may call in their stories to rewritemen or they may use a *teleprinter* to relay the copy to the news room.

General reporters cover meetings and luncheons, various kinds of exhibitions and special events, obtain news by interviewing, rewrite volunteered copy or rewrite news telephoned by other reporters.

The strength of American newspapers—large and small—lies in the voluntary news—that supplied by dozens or even hundreds of volunteers, many of them unknown to the newspaper. These range from the unknown voice on the telephone with a tip that leads to a page one exclusive to a handout from a private or governmental agency. Government, industry, private business and public and private institutions spend thousands of dollars preparing information for public consumption. Some is special pleading, some is information the reporter should have dug out on his own resources, but much is vital information the newspaper could get from no other source, at least without increasing its staff significantly. Volunteers of all types, from hospital superintendents to club secretaries, help protect the newspaper in its coverage of all kinds of news.

Every day's mail brings a bagful of volunteered copy. A lot is junk—free advertising, promotional matter, "puff" material. Scrounge through the wastebasket of an editor of an average-sized daily. You will find that over a seven-day period more than 200 mailing pieces were rejected, more than half unopened. Among these are "special releases" from industry and business, political action groups, other media, women's affairs, government, educational institutions, health groups and many others.

Suffice to say, the material accepted for publication is judged on the basis of its news worth, for a particular community, on a particular day, for a particular edition. If it doesn't fit these needs, into the wastebasket it goes.

Wire and Wireless.   This category includes radio communication, cables, telegraph and telephone facilities. The first two are used primarily for news from abroad. Newspapers receive news by wire, cable and radio from three major press services (described in a subsequent chapter), from foreign agencies such as Reuters, from other agencies like North American Newspaper Alliance and Scripps-Howard Newspaper Alliance and from six metropolitan dailies that have fulltime staffs abroad and syndicate their foreign news to other domestic newspapers. Radio promises to be used by newspapers more extensively in the future than it is now. News agencies may use radio facsimile to transmit both pictures and text to newspaper clients. Staff automobiles will be equipped with radio telephones. More news may be obtained by monitoring radio newscasts from foreign countries.

Recording Devices.   Recording machines eventually will become standard equipment in newspaper offices. Reporters will carry their own portable recording equipment, thus eliminating much of the note-taking and putting an end to the "I was misquoted" charge. Rewritemen will use playback equipment to transcribe interviews, speeches, news conferences. An editor of a weekly newspaper in Colorado uses a recorder to take down all stories telephoned into the office while he is away.

City News Associations.   In the largest cities, it is customary for newspapers to band together for an economical coverage of local routine news by means of "city news bureaus." Bureau reporters are stationed at the various strategic centers, such as police stations and other public buildings, and the news they gather is phoned, telegraphed or sent out to the bureau's clients in mimeographed form. There is no pretense at putting the story into final shape; the aim is merely to supply facts.

Newspaper Library. The library or editorial filing room (formerly known as *morgue*) theoretically contains clippings, card index records, pictures and often finished engravings of every person who has ever done anything worthy of newspaper note. Whenever a person of any importance figures in a story of the day, the newsroom calls upon the library for all relevant clippings and pictures. Libraries often contain material dating back 50 or more years. It supplies mostly background details.

II. LOCAL AND REGIONAL COPY

Firsthand Copy

Copy that comes from the press associations already has passed over a copydesk; not so the story from the paper's own reporter or correspondent. It is firsthand copy, as yet a stranger to the editing pencil of a copyeditor. Meticulous care must be used on it. Every possible type of error must be watched for.

The local copyeditor concentrates on local affairs. He must be familiar with the topography of his city, its streets, institutions, buildings and peculiarities. He must memorize hundreds of facts, perhaps insignificant to the outsider, but essential to the copyeditor. These include spellings of names and places frequently in the news: Fitzsimons hospital (not Fitzsimmons), Soldier (not Soldiers) Field, Charles Lindbergh (not Lindberg). He must be thoroughly conversant with the policy of his own newspaper on all public questions; he must know local history, and names, and initials, and factions, and dignitaries, and news currents, and likes and dislikes; his judgment on the relative values of local items must be good. If he has been a local reporter, he is in a better position to read copy on local stories; in any event, he must be something of a rewriteman as well as a copyeditor, that he may improve defective stories, recast leads or rewrite an entire story.

On the copyeditor rests the responsibility of making sure the copy is right. He becomes positive by double-checking—by using dictionaries, di-

AMERICA'S OLDEST NEWSPAPER. Established in 1764, the Hartford *Courant* has been in business at the same place and with a continuing ownership from its beginning. It was founded as the weekly Connecticut *Courant*. Hartford came into the title with the beginning of the daily in 1837. The weekly was discontinued during World War I, but the two newspapers are, in effect, a continuous publication with only a few issues missed in the *Courant's* earliest days. The Hartford *Courant* lists itself as "the oldest newspaper of continuous publication in America."

rectories, files, histories, guides, maps and other sources. (*See Appendix.*) By this process he accumulates a storehouse of information that helps him edit copy with confidence. When copy leaves his hands it must be accurate to the last detail.

If the newspaper has a suburban section or edition, the copyeditor assigned to it likewise has a special body of knowledge to acquire. So also has the copyeditor who whips into printable form the often poorly written news manuscripts that come in from correspondents in rural areas, in nearby towns, or in cities scattered throughout the region his newspaper serves.

Another type of firsthand copy is that sent out by the city news bureaus of the large cities. The bulk of this news material consists simply of an unadorned statement of the facts, with no pretense of adroit presentation. Much of it goes to the rewriteman who recasts it into more acceptable shape. However, some goes in its original form to the copydesk to be edited.

How It Will Look

The copyeditor tries to visualize how the copy will appear in print. If the story contains a long list of names, the decision must be made whether the names should be *run-in, i.e.,* contained in paragraphs, or be set in individual lines in smaller (*agate*) type. A change in copy requires only a brief stroke of the copy pencil. A change in type requires the re-setting of one or several lines, and at considerable expense to the newspaper. Part of a copyeditor's job is to prevent costly typographical changes by careful handling of the copy. If the story is slugged "with art" the copyeditor should read the cutlines along with the story, if for no other reason than to make sure the facts in the story and the cutline coincide.

III.   DESK PROBLEMS IN LOCAL COPY HANDLING

Country Correspondence

Copy from community correspondents presents a challenge to the copyeditor. Frequently the copy is in longhand and is hard to read; trivia abound in much of the correspondence with real news often buried; the writers frequently lack training; and contributors sometimes use the columns to play up favorites. Unfortunately, most community correspondence is not edited as closely as it might be, possibly because leeway is given since the material appeals primarily to a particular community.

The copyeditor should go over the material, underscore *u*'s and *w*'s and overscore *n*'s and *m*'s, if the copy is not retyped, tone down the dangerous passages and eliminate the obvious "puffs." If the column contains an item of general news interest, the copyeditor should take out the item and handle it as a separate story.

Although he should edit community correspondence carefully and critically, the copyeditor cannot regard the material as "hogwash." The items may not appeal to the city-bred boy but they do to the readers in the particular community whose activities are newsworthy even though they may be routine. They, too, like to see their names in print, one of the reasons they subscribe to the paper.

Community correspondence usually is scheduled to run on a certain day of the week. The copy can be handled early and sent to the composing room to be set in type during slack periods.

Locals and Personals

A counterpart of the community correspondence is the local or personal item. It simply reports a low-grade news event, usually a slightly more than ordinary happening about an individual who presumably is known personally or by name and reputation to a considerable portion of the people who pay money to read the newspaper.

Columns are devoted to such items in both the small weekly newspaper and the metropolitan daily. The difference is that almost any inhabitant of the community served by the former is sufficiently known to merit news attention, whereas in the latter case the persons singled out for attention are more carefully selected. Thus the Crossroads *News* in its column of local brevities will mention the visit of John Smith to the county seat, and the New York *Times* in its society section will record that Mrs. Geoffrey Gotrox or Lord Bilgwater is wintering at Tucson or Nassau.

The locals are the heart of the small paper. The more names the paper contains, the greater its reader appeal. Small personals not only are useful as news but they are a godsend in justifying a column, infinitely better than a two-line *filler* obtained from the *World Almanac*.

Because of their grass-roots source, the authenticity of village or country personals can be checked by the people who read them. Though the copyeditor may be tolerant of humor or even of opinion expressed by the writer, he will scrupulously edit out elements that may cast the principals in an unsavory light. Newspapers use personals to make friends, not enemies. Gossip columnists—the so-called spies of life—may flourish in cities, but they must be relatively circumspect in smaller communities.

Customarily, locals or personals take the form of a comprehensive lead, but without subsequent paragraphs to elaborate upon details. Here are a few examples, each possessing a fault which a good copyeditor would correct:

Where?   The Desert Camera club will hold its open meeting next Tuesday at 7 p. m., instead of Monday, Roger Burlingame, of Rancho Rillito, announces. Photographs of cacti will be exhibited.

Advertising.   When Miss Vanda Loy, a waitress at the Red Cliff cafe, *where good steaks are available at all hours,* opened a window there this morning, a yellow and black butterfly blew in. It is the first seen in Minnekahta this spring.

Taste.   Allen Jacobi and Miss Ruth Goodnight are spending the weekend with relatives at Castle Rock. They will motor back Monday, in time for Miss Goodnight to resume teaching at Dewey school. (Though the two principals may be known to be step-brother and sister, it is better to say so—or make two items.)

Feature Possibilities.   "Mickey," the wire-haired terrier belonging to the C. N. Beckwith family, was back home today after literally dropping out of sight for several days. He was found in an old well by Boy Scouts of the Prairie Dog Troop.

Births

Additions to families in a large city are not newsworthy, unless they are multiple, some special circumstance lifts them out of the routine—such as a police-aided race to the hospital—or unless the parents are socially prominent. Usually, if a metropolitan newspaper records births, it is done at so much a line in the classified section.

Not so the community paper. It may have a standing head under which to group brief announcements, or it may run a few lines on each such event in a personals column. Questions readers want answered are the name of the parents, their address and the name of the baby—especially if it is unusual; the time of the event and often the place; and the baby's sex and sometimes the weight.

Such bare facts can be embellished with other information, if the paper's policy and space permit. Is the child the first? Do the grandparents live in the community? Was the baby born on a national holiday, a relative's birthday, and so on?

Tips to Copyeditors.   Any newly-born is a baby. Change *a baby girl* to *a girl*. Generally omit whimsical expressions like *Mr. Stork, bouncing boy, strapping youngster, blessed event, bundle of joy,* and attempts at describing the father's condition. Details of the birth, like a Caesarean operation, are unnecessary in the story except under unusual circumstances.

Obituaries

Deaths.   (Often called *obits,* but not to be confused with paid obituary notices supplied by funeral home directors.) Deaths are news in any community.

Sources are news agencies (for deaths of prominent national and regional leaders), staff reporters (including community correspondents) and volunteers (usually funeral home directors).

The best style is one that expresses simplicity and sincerity; maudlin sentimentality, the hearts-and-flowers style, should be avoided: "The spiritual beauty of Christmas became an eternal reality today for Mike Korcheck, 24-year-old star shortstop of the Brooklyn Dodgers' farm team at Fort Worth, Tex."

The death story usually follows this pattern: Name, identification, death, time, place, recapitulation of deceased's career, survivors, funeral arrangements.

Tips to Copyeditors.   Accuracy in names. If the surname appears more than once in the story, make sure the spellings conform. Before releasing the copy, check the name-spelling in the headline with that in the copy.

Use *died,* not *passed away, went to his final reward,* or other euphemisms. If the time element is not included in the headline, the verb should be *dies,* not *died.* Usually omit details about the cause of death, but tell the extent of the illness preceding death. Death may have occurred *following an operation,* but not *as a result of the operation.* Everyone dies of *heart failure,* not to be confused with *heart ailment.* A person is *widely known,* not *well known,* and the adjective should be justified by specific accomplishments. He is survived by his *wife,* not his *widow.* Make it *body,* not *remains* or *corpse.* Use *coffin,* not *casket; funeral services,* not *obsequies; burial* not *interment; body will be taken,* not *shipped.* The burial place is a *cemetery.* Some newspapers permit mention of the funeral home in charge of the arrangements.

The headline should contain the name of the deceased. If the story is an advance biographical sketch, written in expectation of death, make sure the HOLD FOR RELEASE flag is clearly indicated on the copy.

Young, middle-aged and *elderly* are relative terms. The criteria used by *Associated Press* is: young until he's past 35, middle age from 35 to 65 and over 65—elderly.

The following obituary, taken from a small daily, is an example of flowery style and loose editing:

On Monday, February 22nd, at 5:30 in the morning, Mrs. _____, daughter of the late _____, following an operation for a stubborn gallbladder trouble, in New Orleans, La., passed to her eternal reward, at the age of 45 the last day of March.

As a citizen of this city, Mrs. _____ was indeed very popular among all who knew her, being a young lady of very charming personality, active in church and Sunday School work. (then followed survivors).

Members of the _____ family, residing in this state, wanted to bring the body of this noble young woman back to the old home town, for funeral and interment but, after due consideration, she was laid to rest at Greenwood cemetery, New Orleans, February 23rd, and, to use language concerning her: "She was a beautiful corpse and died a peaceful death. Just closed her eyes and went to sleep."

It was our pleasure to know the deceased many years, being a neighbor to her father's family, and, of course, in these hours of such deep sorrow, those surviving her have our most affectionate sympathy.

Social News

On many newspapers, even smaller ones, society is handled by a special society department complete with society editor and society desk. Copy is labeled *soc* and does not go to the general copydesk. The society page's appeal is mostly to women but all readership studies prove that society has a large following among men readers.

Who is society? In the large city it includes mostly the Social Register list; in smaller places it takes in wider areas, usually with one class or section of the community getting major attention. *Time* magazine reported that society page's society for the New York *Times* and *Herald Tribune* are those in the Social Register, but for the *Journal-American* society is a mixture of social registerites, cafe society and stage, screen and other entertainers. In San Francisco, Chicago and many another city, *Time* pointed out, charity is the springboard—anyone who moves up the better party lists. In Atlanta, it is the club you belong to that counts (plus wealth, plus family). In Los Angeles society, it is intertwined with the movie colony.

Most society pages of American newspapers could stand a thorough editing job. Social items are marked by poor writing (an abundance of adjectives and clichés), are too detailed and frequently miss the essential news.

Tips to Copyeditors.   Women are married to men, not men to women, matrimony means as much to most readers as holy matrimony, noon is as specific as high noon. *Bridegroom* is preferred to *groom,* though some papers tolerate the latter. The copyeditor will be expected to conform to his paper's policy in regard to euphemisms and adjectives, but he should exercise caution to see that "fine writing" is not carried to the point that copy either drips with sentimentality or freezes with snobbishness.

Business and Professional News

Activities of the business community have a legitimate place as news in the newspaper. These activities include changes in plant location, remodeling and expansion, staff changes and promotions, financial statements, labor-management relationships, bankruptcies and activities and opinions of business leaders.

Business provides straight news (markets, expansion), feature stories (opening of new businesses), interpretives (business trends) and promotional (stories intended to boost local economy). News sources are wire services, local reporters and public relations firms serving the particular business activity.

Pitfalls abound in the business story. Here is one example: Under the headline, Culinary Artists Serve Dishes Fit for Kings, a newspaper described in glowing details a local restaurant just reopened. In the course of the story the reporter wrote:

> During the first year, the restaurant suffered from its former reputation as a haven of drunks whose taste for food, whenever they felt like eating, ran to a glass of milk and a few crackers.

The copyeditor let the paragraph stand. The former owner, who meanwhile had opened another restaurant, filed a damage suit against the newspaper, asserting that the paragraph was inaccurate and injurious. The newspaper had to run a correction and retraction to appease the former owner.

Tips to Copyeditors. No hard and fast rules can be laid down about when and when not to use the names of business or professional firms in newsstories. If a man is arrested in a hotel on a confidence charge, the name of the hotel need not be mentioned unless circumstances require it. If police state that the hotel was used as the headquarters for a ring of confidence men, the detail is newsworthy. On some smaller papers, the name of a hospital may or may not be specified in a death story, unless, of course, the victim is prominent or there are special circumstances requiring the naming of the hospital. In an accident story involving drivers of two automobiles, it is not necessary to give the makes of the automobiles, but in a car theft story, description of the car could help recover the vehicle.

Some scientists observe a time-honored practice of avoiding personal publicity. The embargo does not apply to newsstories concerning nonprofessional activities, to professional activities like medical association work or to public health pronouncements. Nor does it apply in instances where agreements have been reached between professional groups and the press whereby a spokesman is designated who may be quoted by name in medical matters of public interest. In cases of illness of prominent persons like the president or a prime minister the name of the attending physician usually is used.

Deskmen can save a lot of headaches for doctors and the newspaper by making a distinction between *cure* and *treatment*. The warning applies to all scientific terms, but copyeditors should be especially careful to see that medical expressions are used accurately.

A memo from the general office of *United Press* to all bureau managers cautioned:

> Beware of new "cures." No treatment or drug is a "cure" for anything until it has been tested repeatedly and exhaustively over a long period and certified by an authoritative medical group. No reputable scientist will claim a cure under any other circumstances. Most drugs publicized as "cures" are merely new treatments and should be so described. One of the worst crimes a news service can commit is to raise false hopes of a cure for the incurably ill.

"Puffing" is not good journalism, whether the gratuitous words are used to boost an advertiser's product or service or to promote the newspaper itself. The point is illustrated in an article picked up by the Wall Street *Journal* and reprinted by newspapers all over the country:

Newspaper editors of half a century ago never neglected the minutest detail of local activities, but, above all, they always remembered on which side their bread was buttered.

Witness this account of a wedding:

"Miss Jennie Jones and Bob Henry were married at the Jones mansion last night. The bride is the daughter of Constable Jones who has made a good officer and will doubtless be reelected this year. He offers a fine horse for sale in another column of this issue. The groom runs a grocery on Main Street and is a steady patron of our advertising columns. He has a good line of bargains in his ad this week. All summer he paid two cents more for butter than any other store in town. They were married by Rev. Josiah Butterworth who last week called at this office and gave a nice order for printing. He is also going in business and will write fire insurance. So say the business cards we recently printed for him. Jennie and Bob left on the 10 o'clock train for Milwaukee to visit with the bride's uncle, who, we understand, has lots of money and cancer."

Weather Stories

A major topic of conversation in all communities in all seasons is the weather; thus, weather is a prime newsstory whether it be a long story on the front page giving details of a blizzard, or a weather box giving the forecast and the temperature variation.

Readers want to know the extent of destruction caused by the weather, the causes of unusual storms and the probable duration.

Copyeditors should note the difference between *cyclone* and *tornado,* and should use the proper descriptive term for wind. The following has been recommended by the *Associated Press:*

Wind	Miles Per Hour
light	up to 7
gentle	8 to 12
moderate	13 to 18
fresh	19 to 24
strong	25 to 38
gale	39 to 54
whole gale	55 to 75
hurricane	above 75

Tips to Copyeditors. The weather may be unchanging, but the headline can do better than announce, day after day, *Little Change in Weather.* Here is an opportunity for the copyeditor to try a headline in rhyme, in alliteration or any other device that will let the reader know he is reading a fresh newspaper.

We Can Cheer-O While Midwest's Far Below Zero

Our weather's at a standstill,
The kind betwixt between;
We've plenty of warm sunshine
But our snowy days are lean.
—Ella A. Christal.

Thursday night and Friday will be fair and mild in Denver with an early morning low of 25 to 30 degrees and an afternoon high near 45, the U. S. weather bureau predicts.

A rush of intensely cold air

Avoid the expression *Jupiter Pluvius* or any variation of it.

The alert copyeditor will lift an eyebrow at stories emphasizing threats of storms that may not materialize. Probably no one knows for sure where a hurricane will strike. When a reporter expands a warning into a prediction, he does an injustice to his readers. Many property-owners have been hurt financially because of "hurricanes" that never materialized.

Speech Stories

A speech provides good copy if the speaker has said something worthwhile or if the occasion was a memorable one.

Sometimes the speaker tells the reporter during an interview before or after the talk more than he tells the audience. In such cases, the reporter should make the differentiation clear. Some readers will have heard the talk and will believe the paper is faking if the story reports more than what the reader heard.

The speech story should quote the speaker accurately and fairly, but it need not be a verbatim account nor must it stress what the speaker emphasized. A speaker who, in the course of a talk on business conditions, deviates to accuse state university officials of permitting excessive drinking at football games should have no quarrel with the reporter who capitalizes on that part of the talk for his story. The reporter would lose his job if he did otherwise.

Tips to Copyeditors.   A reporter doesn't know what another thinks or believes. He knows only what the speaker said he believes or thinks. Don't be afraid to use the word *said*; it is infinitely better than *smiled* or *laughed*. The reporter should use correct grammar in quoting a speaker, even though the speaker did not speak flawlessly. The exception, of course, is the quotation from a speaker who is expected to employ inelegant style.

Estimates of crowds vary, depending upon the impression the estimator wishes to create. If the reporter writes that a hall was filled to capacity, he should indicate, somewhere in his copy, how many the hall seats. The reader would have more confidence in his newspaper if the reporter would reveal who made the estimate of the size of the crowd. Most estimates are just that. When a church group staged a protest in Liege, Belgium, INS reported: "Ten thousand Roman Catholics marched . . ."; the AP said, "Fifteen thousand Catholics paraded . . ." and UP told readers, "Some 30,000 Catholics marched. . . ."

Sports

Time was when sportswriters wallowed in jargon unintelligible to any but their followers. They considered it smart to toss around such clichés as "sock" and "looms in the field" and "sent to the showers" and "scintillating sophomore with the apparent abandon, if not the skill, of a juggler."

Then America became, as not even ancient Athens was, sports-conscious. And sportswriters have had to learn how to tell their stories in ways that will appeal to the broadened base of their public. The old verve and the nimble use of words are still there, but good sportswriters today use words to report what happened and not for verbal exhibitionism. They are accorded a wider latitude for free and elastic expression than any other newswriters, and there are those who think that the briskest writing found in the American newspaper today is on the sports pages.

The copyeditor, assigned to the sports desk, seeks to preserve the color and the flavor of the copy but he never forgets he is there to backstop the reporter. He must know sports of all kinds: their records, the great men, and above all, their rules. If in the haste and excitement of a game a reporter makes a bobble about any point not pertaining to the action he has witnessed, the informed man on the desk should catch it. Fortunate is the copyeditor who can in a flash recall big league records, batting averages, epic plays in college football and other minute details of sporting history.

But if his memory is lame, scores of books and booklets offer a ready crutch. (*See Appendix.*)

Sports pages have the most critical readers of any section of a newspaper. Fans are legion. They delight to wrangle one with another about games, heroes and records. And a reputation for accuracy on its sports pages is a cash asset for any newspaper.

Tips to Copyeditors.   Many sports stories are complete except for one little detail—the writer forgot to mention what type sport was described. Of course it should be obvious the writer is reporting, say, a basketball game but the story should say so. "Cagemen" or "quintet" or "hoopsters" will be understood by most fans, but some readers like to know specifically what they are reading about.

An example is: "San Francisco led the *United Press* ratings yesterday for the third straight week," but the story never disclosed what sport was involved, nor, for that matter, what San Francisco was—a university, a pro team or just a city.

A story with pictures about the "great international pancake derby," held each year on Shrove Tuesday, gave no background or explanation of the custom.

Tone down harsh criticisms and alibis, especially in stories dealing with amateur sports. Also, keep the reporter from going overboard in building up heroes, especially in school and sandlot activities.

An alert deskman can help de-emphasize the gambling side of sports by burying references to odds and by using a feature other than betting odds in the headline.

Sports editors look for an *angle,* a *feature* and *humor.* If the copy accents any of these, let the headline carry the same emphasis.

It's wise to tally figures in the box scores and to compare names in statistical summaries with those given in the main story.

Ten tiredest sports clichés—

cager	gridder	outclassed but game
circuit clout	inked pact	pay dirt
clobber	mentor	roared back from behind
gonfalon		

Accidents and Disasters

It's an unusual day that doesn't produce an accident or disaster story. On most days from 3 to 5 per cent of the front-page news is devoted to this category. The stories range from the banner disaster story to the two-paragraph freak accident feature.

Style patterns vary, but usually the lead tells what happened ("Two men were killed when . . . ," "Fire destroyed . . .") with succeeding paragraphs describing how it happened and the consequences.

The accident or disaster story, despite the fact it is often written in a hurry, lends itself to good writing. The big story is a straight account with each detail newsworthy. Too gruesome and unpleasant details may have to be toned down, but generally the reader wants a complete description. Deaths and injuries usually are the lead aspects of the story, with a separate line devoted to each name in a casualty list.

If it is a big or late-breaking story it is likely to come to the desk in "takes" and probably will have new leads, additions, inserts, side-bars and precedes. Methods of handling sectional stories will be discussed later.

Tips to Copyeditors.   An injury is *received,* not *sustained.* A person doesn't *have* his leg broken. Accidents *happen* and explosions *occur* (weddings *take place*).

A fire may *damage, destroy, gut,* or *raze* a house; it does not *partially destroy* the house (or *burn it to the ground*).

Damage figures usually are estimates and should be given as such. Better still, let the story tell who made the estimate.

It is safer, because there is no implication of responsibility, to say "cars driven by x and z collided at Fifth and Vine" rather than "a car driven by x collided with a car driven by z. . . ." ("corner of" is redundant.)

Airplanes may collide on the ground or in the air (not midair).

Most passenger trains are fast. "Crack streamliner" is no better than merely "streamliner."

Worth repeating is a warning by the New York *Times*: Don't deal lightly with personal afflictions and don't try to be funny or featurish in cases where death or serious injury is involved.

Crime and Court News

A symposium in *Publishers' Auxiliary* on handling crime news proved what many editors already know—that practices vary from paper to paper. Typical of the hypothetical situation presented to the editors was this: Jimmy Jones, 13, son of a widow, is caught by the night policeman while stealing the tires off an automobile. This is Jimmy's first offense. His mother is a respected citizen of the community. How would you handle this story? Would you mention the boy's name?

Some editors said they would use the story without mentioning the name. Some said they would omit the story altogether. Some pointed to state laws forbidding use of juvenile names in crime stories.

When can a juvenile's name be used in a crime story? State statutes vary, but usually juvenile names are omitted in all cases before the juvenile court. Many juvenile authorities do not regard minors as criminals and would like to see statutes amended so that all juvenile matters are placed before a juvenile court and not be left to the discretion of the prosecuting official.

"Suppose," said the *Auxiliary,* "the same Jimmy Jones, having been placed on probation, is arrested a year later on another theft charge and is sent to the state reform school. How would you handle this story?"

Again the responses varied. Some said they would use the story but omit the name; some replied they would use the name but would not dramatize the story; some said they would omit the story entirely.

The point of this is that the deskman should be familiar with the paper's policy regarding the handling of juvenile crime news; he should also be acquainted with his state's statutory provisions. Questions as to whether to use the story or leave it out, to use the names or leave them out are for the newspaper executive to answer. There is no hard and fast rule; each case is judged on its merits.

Describing a decision he had to make on withholding a name in a crime story, Ralph McGill, editor of the Atlanta *Constitution,* wrote in his column:

A short time ago a poor kid who worked in a textile mill near Atlanta was seduced and when she found she was to have a child, she killed herself. It came to me and I said, "Print it merely that she died." Her family had already suffered enough. I have done that many times. On many occasions I have hurt families by refusing to do this because the suicide was otherwise involved. Maybe I am inconsistent, but I don't think so.

So we come to the present story. The girl, it seemed to me, had paid and paid in full. Her name wasn't important. When I made the decision about her I didn't know if her family was worth 10 cents or 10 million. I still don't know their financial worth. They are not advertisers. It was just a kid who had had a lot of trouble. The man was different. He was 11 years older. If he had seduced a girl his was the responsibility to protect her. He hadn't. So, he was news. If it turns out the girl is named in a murder warrant she will become news. But now, in my book, she isn't. Nor is anyone else—of her age and in similar straits.

Now come four letters from jerks whose sires were ghouls and whose dams were vampires. They whine to know the girl's name. They say we were paid money to withhold the name. They invoke the petty lie and the little would-be-blackmail phrase that if it had been someone on the wrong side of the tracks their names would have been used. My answer to them is to go somewhere else to find bloody bones to gnaw. I am not yet in the abattoir business. Any kids in trouble for the first time, and not involved in and associated with law violation that's important, will get a break here whenever it is humanly possible, regardless of who they are or where they are from. And if that isn't good journalism and doesn't provide enough bones for the ghouls to mumble then I am not even sorry. I like to be able to sleep at night.

The Legal Process

Law is a trap for unwary newsmen, no less than wayward citizens. The "compleat copyeditor" will not pass a crime or court story unless it is written in English understandable to the layman and is technically correct. He should keep in mind a basic American tenet: that every person is innocent until he is proved guilty—and the burden of proof is on the accuser. A law dictionary will aid in understanding legal expressions so they may be translated into simpler terms. But basic to intelligent handling of crime and court copy is a fairly comprehensive knowledge of the processes whereby justice is dispensed.

Courts are of three types: *inquiry, trial* and *appellate*. The routine of criminal procedure is as follows (names of courts vary in different states):

An arrest is made upon the issuance of a *criminal warrant* (or *bench warrant*) by a judge of the lower court upon the sworn allegation that a crime has been committed by a particular individual. The warrant is served and the accused is brought before the *committing magistrate*. (No warrant is needed when the offense is committed in the presence of the arresting officer or if a felony has been committed and the accused is attempting to escape.)

If the accused waives his right to a preliminary hearing before a committing magistrate, the case can be carried directly to the trial court. If he doesn't waive the preliminary hearing, he is taken before the committing magistrate or judge who in many instances will be a justice of the peace. If there is sufficient evidence against him, he is *bound over* for trial. Except in *capital cases,* the accused may gain *release on bail* awaiting trial.

In the case of a *misdemeanor* (minor crime), the accused may be charged by the prosecuting officer of the court without an *indictment* or formal *presentment*.

Accusation of a felony is heard by a *grand jury* which may issue a *no bill* (indicating there is insufficient evidence for prosecution) or a *true bill* (indicating there is sufficient evidence for prosecution). A true bill or *indictment* is not a trial verdict, merely a formal accusation. A grand jury may return a presentment on its own initiative if it wishes. In many states, the accused may be brought to trial on an *information* filed by the district attorney.

The case is then *docketed* by the clerk of the court. The county in which the trial is held (*venue*) is determined by the place where the crime was committed; a *change in venue* may be granted by the court where there is reason to believe the accused cannot get a fair trial in the place where the crime was committed. The trial judge may *disqualify himself* if he feels he has a prejudice in the case.

If the *defendant* feels there is some irregularity in the indictment, he may file a *demurrer,* or objection. If the demurrer is sustained, another indictment may be obtained, or the prosecution may be dropped. Another maneuver to end prosecution is a move to *quash the indictment.* If the defendant has been tried before for the same offense, he enters a *plea of former jeopardy,* and if the motion is sustained, the case is dropped.

The defendant may plead *guilty* or *not guilty.* If he pleads guilty, he is called before the trial judge who listens to his statements and passes *sentence.* If he pleads innnocent, his trial is before a jury, unless he waives jury trial. The trial is heard by a *petit jury,* whose verdict is guilty or not guilty.

The attorneys *examine* and *cross-examine* the witnesses. After the evidence is in, the counsel for the prosecution and then counsel for the defendant make their *summation* or *argument,* with the prosecutor having the right to make the *closing plea.* The jury, after receiving instructions from the judge as to possible verdicts, retires and sooner or later, unless it fails to agree, returns its *verdict.* If the judge feels the jury has disregarded the court's instructions, he may ignore the verdict and find for the other party.

The defense may charge some irregularity, offering a motion for *arrest of judgment.* If granted, the court discharges the prisoner subject to prosecution under another indictment. The court may *suspend sentence* (relieve the convicted defendant of compliance with the sentence during a period of good behavior) or it may place him on *probation* (require him to report periodically for a specified period to a probation officer).

If the sentence is *indeterminate* (in which the court imposes a sentence of imprisonment, for example, from three to five years), the exact time of the incarceration depends upon the good behavior of the prisoner. The person found guilty on more than one *count,* each of which provides for imprisonment, may be ordered to serve the terms *concurrently* (for the longest terms with the other terms being absorbed therein) or he may be required to be imprisoned for the total time under a *cumulative* sentence.

If a verdict is unsatisfactory to the defendant, his attorney may ask for a *new trial* immediately after the jury's verdict is announced. If the judge refuses a new trial, the case may be taken to a higher (or *appellate*) court on a *writ of error.*

Civil Suits

There are filed when the *complainant* or *plaintiff* seeks (because of such causes as breach of contract, libel, slander, negligence, breach of promise or divorce) to recover money or property from the *defendant.* In most cases, either party may demand and is entitled to have the suit tried by a jury. In the absence of a demand for jury trial, the case is tried by the judge. *Answering the complaint,* he may sometimes file *counter charges* in a *cross-claim* or *counterclaim.* An additional party alleged in a complaint also to be guilty is termed a *co-respondent* or *co-defendant,* depending upon the practice set forth by law in the various states.

In some jurisdictions, after a jury has reported its findings in the form of a verdict, the judge enters a judgment upon the verdict in the amount of the judgment and *decrees* that the losing party is judicially indebted to the prevailing party for that amount. If the judgment debtor will not pay the amount of the judgment voluntarily, his goods may be sold under a *writ of execution* issued upon the judgment.

The decree of a judge in an *equity* suit (forcing or prohibiting a certain action) is final unless it is in the form of a *decree nisi* or *interlocutory* order. Such interlocutory decree expires at the close of the suit unless the plaintiff establishes a right to permanent relief. If contending parties reach an agreement outside the court, the judge may approve it with a *consent decree.*

Probate Court.   An *executor* of an estate makes application to the judge of the *probate* court to admit to probate the will of a deceased person. When a person dies without a will, *intestate,* the court on application of an interested party appoints an *administrator* who is charged with the responsibility of settling the estate as provided by law. Where a person has died *testate,* leaving a will, the court on application for probate of the document and a showing that the person or institution named in the will as executor or trustee has died, or is incapable of acting, will appoint a person *executor cum testamento annexo—C.T.A.,* that is, executor with the will annexed. An executor or trustee C.T.A. is really an administrator of the estate who distributes and administers the same according to the terms of the will rather than as required by a state statute setting forth the method of distribution where a person dies intestate.

Tips to Copyeditors.   A person is arrested on a *charge* of *robbery* or is being held *in connection with* a *robbery.* He is not arrested *for* the robbery (which implies guilt). In the headline, the word "in" is understood to mean "in connection with." *Indictment for robbery* is permissible since indictment implies mere accusation.

Drop the racial tab in reports of crime, both in the story and in the headline unless the use of race is absolutely essential. The reason is obvious. The headline "Negroes Face Trial on Murder Count" indicts a whole race.

Mistaken identity can be costly to the newspaper. Unless the identity is positive, it is wise to use a phrase such as "police identified the man as. . . ." or "a card carried by the man bore the name of . . ." The name, of course, must be accurate. If a cut is used, make sure the name in the cutline corresponds to that in the story and be positive it is the correct picture. When gangster "Baby Face" Nelson was named slayer of an F.B.I. agent, a Minneapolis paper—to its embarrassment—ran a picture of the wrong Nelson.

Robbery, theft and *burglary* usually fall into the same crime classification but a distinction should be made in use of the terms. A *robber* (or *bandit*) steals by force, a *thief* steals without duress (*pickpockets* and *shoplifters* are thieves), a *burglar* steals after breaking into a building. A person who breaks into a building, overpowers the night watchman and takes money from the safe is a robber (since he uses force) not a burglar. Many papers frown upon use of the word *'burglarize'* (to commit burglary).

The copyeditor, as well as the reporter, should get the principals straight. Notice in the following story the copyeditor misread the story and thereby misinformed the readers.

Denver Man Is
Killed By Detective

A 25-year-old Denver man was shot and killed early Wednesday, Detective Sgt. Blank said, while attempting to force his way into the home of his estranged wife.

Blank quoted Charlene M_____ as saying she fired two shots at her husband, Ezekiel M_____, after he broke a window in her home. M_____, fatally wounded, ran from the scene and dropped dead on a nearby street.

The detective sergeant said the woman told him the shooting followed an earlier quarrel and arose out of her intention to institute divorce proceedings against M_____.

No charges have been filed.

Summing Up

Enough examples have been given to indicate the special problems arising with various types of news. The deskman can't select the copy he wants to edit; he must take whatever is assigned. Gradually he becomes familiar with the technical aspects of all types of stories so that he may handle a business story with as much ease and confidence as he handles a fire story. From reading well-constructed stories written by good reporters and foreign correspondents, he knows what to do with copy not so expertly handled.

General principles underlie all types of news copy. The copyeditor looks for what Carl E. Lindstrom of the Hartford *Times,* in a talk before an Associated Press Managing Editors conference, called the "seven sins of news writing." He listed them as follows:

1. Muddy thinking. The reporter hasn't been able to write clearly because he has an insecure grasp on what he wants to say. . . .
2. Passive reporting. The writer may have been satisfied with half the story. Even if he has nine-tenths of it, that is not enough. . . .
3. Poor story organization, often the result of an awkward lead. . . .
4. Forgetting the reader. Sometimes the writer is so full of his subject that he suffers a mental block in getting the facts out. . . .
5. Letting mere accuracy substitute for truth. Literal accuracy is not enough. . . .
6. Misused words. And I don't mean misused long words. Short ones are just as frequently misused. . . .
7. That horrible word bias. I suppose we shrink from the word because it is supposed to indicate malice. But there are several kinds of bias—at least three. There is the bias of selection. . . . There is the bias of organization. . . . Then there is the bias of disproportion.

10 Editing the Wire

The blackest of fluids is used to enlighten the world—Douglas Jerrold (1803–1857), *English humorist and editor.*

If you think the editor sometimes makes a mistake in what he gives you to read, you ought to see the mass of stuff from which he saves you.—Karl A. Bickel (1882–   ), *former president of the United Press Associations.*

There are correspondents in the press gallery at Washington who have more influence in the nation than any one of 90 senators out of a total of 96.—Arthur Capper (1865–1951), *former United States Senator, publisher.*

I. NEWS FROM THE WIRE SERVICE

The News Agencies

The three major wholesalers of news in the United States are the Associated Press, the United Press Associations and the International News Service. Largest and oldest of the three is the AP, a cooperative news-gathering agency owned by the member newspapers. Reorganized in its present form in 1900, the AP traces its origin to the New York Associated Press (1848). The United Press Associations, organized in 1907, is a private agency controlled by the Scripps-Howard interests. Youngest of the three, the International News Service, was founded by William Randolph Hearst in 1909 and is part of the Hearst enterprises.

Each of the services has its own facilities for gathering and distributing regional, national and international news. Further, each has exchange agreements with agencies of other countries and thus can provide a comprehensive report on world events. Seventy-five per cent of the foreign news appearing in newspapers in the United States is supplied by these three agencies.

AP, UP and INS serve newspapers, magazines, radio and television stations and—in the case of UP—even ships at sea. The service includes not

GALVESTON COMMUNITY COLLEGE LIBRARY

only news, but features, pictures and special coverage as well. Before smaller papers were served by *leased wires,* the agencies provided condensed *pony* copy, sometimes by telegraph, more often by telephone. If weeklies requested wire service, they could obtain condensed *bulletins* on press days.

Wire services serve newspapers and radio stations with one or more circuits—a *state* wire, a *regional* wire, a *sports* wire, a *general* wire, a *special* service for *markets* and *race* results, *features, pictures* and *mats* and *facsimile* photos for newspapers and television stations. AP and UP will sell a newspaper the radio wire and radio stations the newspaper wire if that is what clients want. They offer services the newspapers can't provide for themselves without great expense. For instance, few newspapers, other than large metropolitan dailies, can afford to maintain their own correspondents in Washington, D.C., or their state capitals; they rely upon wire services to supply news of state and federal government.

Although they must serve a common general interest of their clients, the wire services are alert to individual client needs. If the Chicago *Tribune* requests coverage of a trial of an Illinois man in an Atlanta court, the Atlanta AP office is prepared to supply the story to the *Tribune.*

Because they serve clients with a variety of political and economic interests, the three agencies have established a reputation for impartiality in news. Because they are competitive, speed in delivering the news is highly important. A one-minute advantage in breaking a story is hailed as an accomplishment. The goal of each of the agencies is to deliver the report first and in such a manner that it will be chosen over the competitor's report. Accuracy is attained by employing competent newsmen to cover the news and by backstopping the report. News passes over one or several editorial desks before it reaches the newspaper. When errors occur in the delivered report, they are frequently caught by clients' editors who call attention to the inaccuracy so that corrections can be made.

Agencies Make Errors

These attributes (accuracy, impartiality, speed), plus the fact that news from the wire service is uniform in type and style, should not tempt the copyeditor to be caught off-guard in handling wire copy. The wire services have a reputation for accuracy; they also have been guilty of some of the worst bobbles in American journalism. Examples are the premature announcement of the armistice ending World War I and the premature story on the invasion of Normandy in World War II. Even the court sentence for Bruno Richard Hauptmann, kidnaper and slayer of the Lindbergh baby, was reported incorrectly by one of the wire services.

In the following excerpts from the same story reported by rival press associations, notice the discrepancies in matters of fact.

DANVILLE, Va., July 27—A mysterious triple shooting in which a 25-year-old housewife, her husband and his aged stepfather were slain, was discovered at the trio's small farmhouse near here today.

The bodies, already badly decomposed, were identified as those of John Kizee, Sr., 55-year-old Danville-Martinsville bus driver and former taxicab operator; Beatrice Kizee, 25, his wife, and George Johnson, 70, Kizee's stepfather.

The coroner . . . reported he was unable to determine the exact time of the deaths, but neighbors said they had not seen members of the family since Wednesday. Kizee had not been at work this week.

Johnson, in his underwear, was lying across the feet of Kizee, who was fully clothed, and on the latter's chest rested a 38-calibre revolver. Police took the weapon to Danville police headquarters for identification and to determine if there were any fingerprints but no report was available immediately.

The blond woman was wearing slacks and a blouse, which had been ripped open. Morticians at the funeral home to which the bodies were removed said the torn clothing may have resulted from the tremendous swelling of the body.

DANVILLE, Va., July 27—The bloated bodies of a beautiful 25-year-old brunette, her husband and her stepfather-in-law were found shot to death in their home Saturday and police said the three apparently had been slain by a sex killer.

The victims were identified as Beatrice Allen Kizee, 25; her husband, John Kizee, 55, bus driver for the Danville-Martinsville Line; and his stepfather, George Johnson, 80. They had been dead since Monday, police believed.

The three bodies, which had begun to decompose, were found in the Kizee home on the outskirts of Danville Saturday afternoon by Mrs. Kizee's aunt, Mrs. J. C. Hankins. She had gone to the Kizee home for help in making a dress.

A 32:20 caliber Colt revolver lay in the lap of Kizee, who had been shot twice.

Clad in a blouse and slacks, which had been ripped up the front by her assailant, the body of Mrs. Kizee was sprawled on the floor. Nearby lay the body of her husband, still wearing his bus driver's uniform and cap. Johnson's body, clad in pajamas, was across the room.

Neighbors had seen no signs of life about the house since last Monday morning, and police theorized that the crime occurred Monday night.

The wire services frequently have higher standards, in regard to accuracy, writing style, good taste and libel-free copy than the clients they serve, but the responsibility for the stories they deliver rests with the user rather than with the supplier. For instance, a wire service may send a story which, in some states, is libelous. In such cases, a cautionary note usually is tagged to the story, but the responsibility as to use rests with the newspaper editor. Court decisions would indicate that privilege cannot be pleaded in defense of libel occurring in a wire story. A newspaper is responsible for what it publishes, from whatever source.

Copy from a wire service should be *challenged* as vigorously as copy from any other source. There is nothing in a contract between a news agency and a newspaper to prevent the copyeditor from deleting portions of a wire story or rewriting it altogether, if the story is faulty. The following lead, from a wire service story which appeared in newspapers from coast to coast, clearly called for a rewrite:

NEW YORK—All hands were safe Thursday aboard a Coast Guard cutter which raced to a radio-guided rendezvous with a military plane forced to ditch into the stormy Atlantic more than 800 miles east of Bermuda. . . .

What the lead meant was that the crewmen who abandoned a military plane forced down at sea were safe aboard a Coast Guard cutter.

Mistakes in transmission (*traffic errors*) occur frequently enough to keep the copyeditor constantly on guard. The general wire of one of the services sent out a story which mentioned that "the fishing trawler Lorella was nicknamed Lucy because of her big catches." The story got by relay editors, breezed by member copydesks and appeared in print. Apparently few thought to question the relationship between Lucy and big catches. It turned out that the trawler was nicknamed Lucky, not Lucy.

Another tendency in handling wire copy is to assume that, since the story originates with a big news agency, it is of prime importance. Trivia abounds in wire copy, as it does in copy from other sources. An example from a wire service:

MOSCOW, May 22—The weather is hot and Muscovites are gobbling up two million portions of ice cream daily, the official news agency reported today A common sight is children buying chocolate-coated ice cream on a stick from little street wagons.

How the System Works

Heart of the wire service is the main office which collects news from worldwide correspondents, foreign agencies and domestic bureaus. News is screened, routed to a bureau which then relays the news over smaller regional and state wires to individual clients. The bureau's function is to provide an assortment of good international, national, regional, sports and state stories. It may furnish state news over a state wire or it may split a wire to handle state news. In either case, the client does not have to wait until the last line of national copy is delivered to get important regional and state news.

The genius of the wire service is the correspondent or *stringer* system which provides coverage of news from all parts of the country. The relay system keeps points protected both on news of general interest and news primarily of interest to one city or area.

A stringer in a remote part of Colorado covers the story, say, of a triple murder. He telegraphs or telephones (*overheads*) the story to the *Associated Press* bureau in Denver which files it directly on the A, or general news wire, for national distribution. If the story has world interest, it is cabled or radioed from New York to foreign offices for distribution to overseas clients and may be supplied to one or more foreign news agencies for redistribution.

Less important stories reaching Denver go to the Kansas City bureau whose news editor decides whether the story has sufficient interest to be relayed to the East. If the Denver bureau gets a story about the awarding of a contract to a Phoenix, Ariz., firm, the story goes directly to Phoenix.

In the event a story filed to New York does not get on all the trunk wires, the main office relays the story on a regional wire. During certain hours of the day the *A* wire is hooked together so that a story filed in Denver goes without relay to Atlanta, San Francisco, Boston, New York, everywhere there are big cities taking that wire.

Filing editors must be alert to the news interests of the region. A cotton story may be prime news in Atlanta or Dallas, but not in San Francisco or Seattle. Uranium mining is big news in Denver, worth less space in Providence. A small news feature of general interest, on the other hand, can earn a place on the national wire.

Cap and Lower Case

At one time wire copy came to the newspaper in *all-cap* letters. The copyeditor assumed the letters were lower-case and marked letters requiring caps accordingly. Today the copyeditor seldom sees all-cap wire copy unless he works for a big city paper, a radio station or a news service. All AP state wires have been converted to *TTS* or *teletypesetter* (which delivers copy in caps and lower case) and even newspapers on state circuits which do not use tape get cap and lower-case copy.

Each item transmitted by the wire service is headed by a *book number* indicating the wire designation and the file number. For instance, SD16 means that the story is from the Denver state wire, the 16th item dispatched over that wire. The copyeditor should not obliterate this number because reference may be made to it later. A correction, for example, refers to the book number for the story in which the error appeared. The wire story also contains a time designation, showing when the item was filed. This information can be useful to the copyeditor, especially if he has two stories on the same topic and he wishes to know which is the later version. On teletypesetter copy the day of the month is carried at the top of each item.

Datelines

Wire copy is either datelined or undated. A dateline includes place of origin, date, credit: CHICAGO, May 22 (UP)—. In practice, wire agencies no longer include the date, especially in copy for afternoon papers. The day of the week usually is preferred to "today," "yesterday," "tomorrow." If the paper carries a date in the credit line, "today" refers to the dateline date and not the date of publication. "Here," of course, refers to the place listed in the dateline. Wire service designation is set on a single slug, or ligature.

In an undated story the wire credit is carried as a byline:

By the Associated Press

Undated stories are used for *roundups* involving more than one place of origin for the news. Instances are stories describing weather throughout the nation or election forecasts from several states.

Bylines are included on some wire stories, usually features, exclusives and interpretive or explanatory matter. Papers are not required to retain the byline, but many do, especially on *interpretives* and on columns by widely known writers.

News Budgets

Wire service bureaus usually provide clients with a *news budget* at the start of the news transmission showing the half dozen or so main stories to be included in the day's news. Sometimes the budget not only describes the expected story (in a sentence or phrase), but may also include the length of each story. Later, when these stories arrive, they carry the notation BUDGET along with the book number. The budget is useful to the news or makeup editor since it enables him to plan his page makeup before the stories are delivered.

Not all the matter coming over the wire is intended for publication. Messages, notes, queries and *FYI* (for your information) take up part of the wire's transmission time.

Urgent News

When big news breaks, the wire services call attention of the clients to the urgency of the message. At one time, the warning bell on the teleprinter caused the office force to rush to the machine to ascertain the latest *FLASH*. This method is now rarely used. The *Associated Press* calls attention to a major news break with a brief *bulletin*. United Press slugs the item *Urgent*. *BUN* is the INS symbol for bulletin.

Having alerted editors to a major story, the service then prepares as comprehensive a report as possible on the big story. If the news breaks just before press time, the paper uses whatever is available, even though it be only a brief bulletin. Some newspapers use on the front page a part of a column labeled "Late News Bulletins." These may not be bulletins in the sense just described but rather are leads or full stories received by the newspaper just before press time. Abuse of the word *bulletin* by radio stations, newspapers and even the wire services themselves has tended to reduce the original significance of the word, *i.e.,* news of transcendent importance.

A story of more than ordinary general interest or of especial interest to a single point may carry the designation 95—a reminder of the days when the Morse code was used.

II.   EDITING SECTIONAL STORIES

'Wrapping Up' the News

Newspaper editors want the news as rapidly as they can get it but they prefer to have a complete story (*wrap up*) rather than a flood of bulletins, new leads, adds, inserts and precedes. The day of the newspaper extra is disappearing because of instantaneous broadcasting by radio and television.

A complete story, even if it arrives late, can be handled more easily and more economically than piecemeal stories.

Sectional stories, however, are still unavoidable if there are new developments that alter the news picture. This applies to local as well as to wire copy. On wire copy the telegraph editor can piece out the story as it is received or he can collect the sections and eventually put them together into a comprehensive story before sending it along to the composing room. The telegraph editor must have news judgment to tell him what to hold back and what to let go.

No need to rush along the first story about a sea disaster, for example, because the wire editor knows there is likely to be a later development (rescue, survivors). The president's news conference story, on the other hand, can be edited immediately because all the facts are available at the time the story is sent over the wires.

Sluglines Identify and Guide

One key element in a sectional story is the *guideline* (also known as *slugline* or *slug*). It identifies the story for everyone handling the story—from managing editor to printer—and it is the code word for a piece of copy that may have to undergo changes after it has left the desk. The same guideline must be followed throughout on a story. If the copyeditor sends along the lead marked "Riot—#1," then follows it with "Add 1 Fight," "Add 2 Labor," "Add 3 Riot," "Add 4 Fight" and "Labor—#1" trouble will ensue.

Use of guidelines extends even to such pictures, maps, diagrams, boxes and tabulations as may accompany a story. If the story marked "Riot" is accompanied by art, the slug reads something like this: "Riot—#1 with art." A sidebar story intended to be used alongside the main Riot story is slugged "with Riot."

Handling a Local Story in 'Takes'

Usually a story is complete and in its final form before it comes to the desk. The reporter's name and the guide are on the first and subsequent sheets: *Fire—Browne; 2 Fire—Browne; 3 Fire—Browne*. In the composing room the longer stories are cut into sections by a *copycutter* and lettered and numbered: L-1, L-2, L-3, etc., and distributed to compositors. The purpose is to get the story into type as fast as possible.

If a story breaks near press time it is handled in *takes,* or sections. The first take is the lead which is rushed to the copydesk, edited, slugged— *Lead Fire #1* (signifying the head size) and sent to the composing room. Often, the copyeditor gives the lead a cursory reading, slugs it—*Lead Fire—HTK* (hed to kum), and sends it along. Then he writes the headline, meanwhile handling subsequent takes.

The second take is slugged *Add 1—Fire,* the second *Add 2—Fire,* and so on. At the bottom of each sheet appears the word *more.* The last take on the story is slugged *Fifth and Last Add—Fire* or simply *Last Add— Fire.* It closes with the end mark. The copyeditor remembers to keep track of the takes, to write in subheads and to keep a tally on the story's length.

Handling the Sectional Wire Story

Suppose the wire service sends a budget story slugged *Congress,* then later comes along with a new development. It will carry a notation like· A96 FIRST LEAD CONGRESS.

The end of this lead will be marked: SENATOR JONES SAID X X X THIRD GRAPH A74. This means the copyeditor is to substitute the new lead for the first two paragraphs of the original story. The remainder of the original story remains intact.

Then later comes another development, slugged SECOND LEAD CONGRESS. It, too, will close with a phrase telling the copyeditor where to resume the previously sent material.

If more material is to be added to the second lead, it is marked FIRST ADD SECOND LEAD CONGRESS X X X PRESIDENT SAID. This shows that the new matter follows the second lead ending with the words "president said."

A subsequent addition to the second lead is marked SECOND ADD SECOND LEAD CONGRESS and so on. If the notation calls for a FIRST ADD CONGRESS, the deskman remembers that this material is simply added to the bottom of the original *Congress* story.

Now comes an insertion to be placed in the second add of the second lead. This slugline reads: EDITORS: TO COVER DEVELOPMENTS THE FOLLOWING MAY BE INSERTED IN THE SECOND ADD SECOND LEAD CONGRESS AFTER SECOND GRAPH STARTING "THE NATION FACES X X X" AND ENDING X X X MEANS TOTAL WAR. A notation at the end of the inserted matter tells the editor where to resume the story: THE SENATE APPROVED, ETC., THIRD GRAPH.

After the *Congress* story apparently is completed, a new development breaks. Instead of making a new lead, the service can send a BULLETIN PRECEDE. This usually is set in boldface type or in larger type than the original *Congress* story and, of course, leads off the story.

Unless a deadline is pressing, the telegraph editor does not rush along each section as it is received over the wire. Instead, he folds a sheet of copy paper, marks it *Congress* and inserts all the sections. The copyeditor then has the job of putting the pieces together in their proper order. It is easier to make changes in the copy than to kill and reset type. And a copyeditor can take much precious time recasting headlines to fit new developments. That is why copy arriving in sections is held to the last possible moment before it is edited and sent to the composing room.

Insertions Are Troublesome

An insertion to be made in either local or wire copy after the copy has cleared the desk presents a problem. If the copy can be retrieved from the composing room before it has been handed to the typesetter, the insertion can be made in the copy. If the copy already has been set into type, the insertion is indicated on a galley proof. This is called *fixing* or *marking* (the galley proof is sometimes called a *marker*).

The copyeditor writes on the proof at the place where the insertion is to go: *tr* (turn rule) *for insert A*. This instructs the composing room to turn a type-slug in the story upside down so that when the inserted material has been set into type the makeup man will know where to place it in the story.

A second insert in the same story is termed insert B, a third insert C. Each insert ends with the notation: End Insert A (or B, C, D, etc.). In each case a proof or marker must be obtained and the point indicated where the insertion is to go.

A marker also is required when the story gets a new lead. The old lead is crossed out on the proof and a notation in the margin tells the printer: *Kill for new lead*. The remainder of the type is marked *pickup,* meaning that it is to remain. The new lead copy (whether local or wire) is slugged *New Lead*—(name of story, *e.g.,* Fire or Congress). But instead of ending with the notation "more" or "end new lead" it says, instead, *Get Pickup*— telling the makeup man to pick up the rest of the story in type.

The following chart provides a handy reference until the copyeditor gets used to handling sectional stories.

EDITING RUNNING STORIES

Section	Use	Page 1 Slug or Guideline	P. 2 (3, 4, etc.) Slug	End Mark	Marks on Proof
Adds	When story comes to copydesk, or is sent to compositor, in sections called "takes."	*Lead Fire—#3 Jones (i.e.,* guideline, number of head and reporter).	*Add 1 (2, 3, etc.) Fire— Jones*	# *or More,* if more copy is known to be coming	None
Inserts	When later information is to be inserted in story already sent to compositor.	*Insert A (B, C, etc.) Fire— Jones*	*Add 1 (2, 3, etc.) Insert A Fire— Jones*	*End insert A Fire*	Indicate place for insertion on proof with: *Turn rule for insert A.*
New Leads	When new or corrected information necessitates a fresh lead on a story already sent to the compositor.	*New lead Fire —Jones*	*Add 1 new lead Fire— Jones*	*End new lead Fire— Jones. Turn rule to pick up story as corrected.*	Kill old lead on the proof, and edit rest of story to follow the new lead. Mark on proof: *Turn rule for new lead.*
Precedes or Bulletins	When new information (usually short and set up boxed or bold face) is to be run ahead of the main story.	*Lead All Fire* or *Precede Fire*	*Add 1 lead all* (or *precede* or *bulletin*) *Fire*	*End lead all* (or *precede* or *bulletin*) *Fire*	None
Letters (or Matter)	When a part of a story other than the lead is sent to the compositor first— usually compiled from data supplied by the "morgue."	*Letter A (B, C, etc.) Fire— Jones* (or *A Matter Fire— Jones*), *Lead to come*	*Add 1 letter A Fire* (or *Add 1 A Matter Fire*)	*End letter A Fire* (or *End A Matter Fire*)	None

In case of an insert in a precede or bulletin, slug it: *Insert A Fire bulletin.* Then indicate place of insertion, in the usual way, on the proof.

To avoid confusion, when you have an insert for letters, slug it: *Insert X (Y, Z, etc.) Letter A Fire.*

When a story is sent along without a head, it may be slugged: *Fire H.T.K. (Hed to Kum)* or, of course, *H.T.C.,* or one may write it out: *Head to Come.*

It is always advisable to "ring" slugs and directions to the printer, thereby avoiding any possibility of their inclusion in the body of the story.

Corrections and 'Kills'

When wire services send erroneous material, they follow up with a correction as soon as possible.

CORRECTION

FOURTH LEAD CONGRESS (A 128) SECOND GRAF BEGIN-
NING SENATOR JONES ETC., READ SENATOR JONES SAID HE
WOULD N-O-T FAVOR X X X INSTEAD OF WOULD FAVOR
AS SENT.

If the desk still has the story, the correction is made in the copy and
the message from the wire can be discarded. If the story has gone to the
composing room, a proof is obtained and the correction is made.

Sometimes the service orders a story or part of a story previously sent to
be deleted. This is called a MANDATORY KILL, a warning to the client
not to use the material under any circumstance. The copy should be discarded. If it has been sent to the composing room, a proof should be
obtained and the matter killed. A mandatory kill carries even to the extent
of stopping the press.

Release Dates Should Be Respected

If the president of the United States is scheduled to speak, the wire
services usually have the text of the prepared talk before it is delivered.
This copy is sent to the newspaper as an advance, giving the specific
release time expected. (Any story, of course, can be sent as an advance.)
The copy may be edited and headlined and sent to the composing room with
the notation: *Hold for Release*. When the talk has been delivered, a release
is signaled. Deviations from the prepared text also are given. Regular
advances usually are transmitted when there is a lull in news transmission.
Newspapers are expected to respect release dates on advance material,
using the story only on the date indicated for release.

III.   EDITING COPY FOR TTS

TTS Becoming Universal

The teletypesetter (TTS), using perforated paper tape to operate line-
casting machines automatically, was tried out by the Gannett newspapers
as early as 1928. The Associated Press opened a TTS circuit in North
Carolina in 1951 and within two years had converted every state single
wire service to TTS. By the end of 1954 the International Typographical
Union counted 759 daily newspapers using tape for typesetting.

The obvious advantage of automatic typesetting is in reducing composition costs (as much as 40 per cent). Whether an advantage or not, TTS has tended to invite greater use of wire copy, sometimes at the expense of local copy. Some editors feel that TTS, by producing more "live" copy (400 to 600 lines an hour), has improved the quality of *filler* or *plug* copy. If editors require a greater volume of wire copy (and are willing to bear the expense) TTS has the answer since high-speed transmission, operating at a speed of 600 words a minute—or 10 times faster than ordinary transmission—is available.

TTS has forged another link in the standardization of newspapers. Papers using tape for automatic composition are forced to accept the *style* of the service transmitting the copy by TTS, or make numerous proof corrections. What has happened generally is that newspapers have revised their *stylebook* to conform with the wire service. Type styles also have to conform to the pattern of the TTS. If the editor wants the lead set double-column, he has to have the lead matter reset by manual operation. Furthermore, use of TTS copy tends to discourage revisions in wire stories since each change requires duplicate composition. Newspapers traditionally refrain from ordering changes once a story is in type—unless, of course, the story is in error. Thus choice of wording, style, arrangement of sentences and paragraphs and even type styles are standardized by the news agency, leaving little flexibility for the newspaper client.

How TTS Operates

Teletype is actuated by a five-unit code perforation, TTS by a six-unit code. Transmission by the latter is slower (54 instead of 60 words a minute) but TTS has upper and lower case shift, teletype only upper case. TTS *justifies* the copy, *i.e.,* copy is sent line for line as it will appear in type.

The code combinations for TTS are obtained by perforating a maximum of six holes in the tape in predetermined locations. With the code, 64 combinations are possible. Two of these combinations are used for shifting and unshifting to upper and lower-case characters respectively so that actually 124 selections are possible from the tape. The tape is fed directly into a line-casting machine equipped with a TTS operating unit, thus eliminating manual operation.

The client using the TTS circuit has *reperforator* machines to receive tape, and *monitor* printers. Editing is done on the monitor copy rather than on the tape. Corrections, revisions, subheads and the like are marked

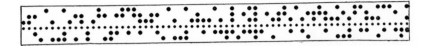

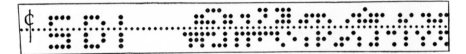

Two types of tapes are used in news transmission. The top tape is a five-unit teletype tape used to send news by wire from one bureau to another. This type actuates an automatic typewriter (teleprinter).

The bottom tape is a six-unit perforation used to transmit news over a teletypesetter circuit. At the receiving end are two machines, one to perforate the tape, the other to print the monitor copy. Teletypesetter tape (bottom) is fed into a typesetting machine and thus causes type to be set automatically.

on the monitor copy and sent to the proofreader who makes the revisions on the galley proofs.

Book numbers and sluglines are punched visibly in the tape so that an editor can recognize the tape's contents without referring to the code. If the transmitting operator wishes to have the word "NOTE" appear visibly on the tape, he refers to the visible code, punches the combinations listed for N-O-T-E.

1	Un	**A**	Un S S Un	**N**	Un A Sp O Un
2	L B Y L	**B**	Un Y Y R	**O**	C Z Z C
3	Z Y Y Un	**C**	C Z Z	**P**	Un S S U
		D	Un Z Z C	**Q**	Un Z Z Un T
4	U Sp V	**E**	Un Y Z	**R**	Un S R T
5	W Y Y F	**F**	Un S E	**S**	Q Y Y X
6	Un Y Y X	**G**	Un Z B	**T**	E Un E
		H	Un Sp Un	**U**	UN T T Un
7	E E Un	**I**	Un	**V**	K T K
8	R Y Y R	**J**	N T T K	**W**	Un T C T Un
9	Q Y Y Un	**K**	Un Sp R Z	**X**	Z C Z
0	C Z Z C	**L**	Un T T	**Y**	E V E
		M	Un E C E Un	**Z**	Z B Y W

Teletypesetter visible code is used to guide operators in making perforated outlines of letters and numbers on the tape. To make an outline of the figure 8, for instance, the operator depresses the keys RYYR. The Un refers to unshift.

Photos by the Associated Press and the Boulder (*Colo.*) Daily Camera

TELETYPESETTER SENDING AND RECEIVING EQUIPMENT is shown in these photos. In the top photo, the machine with the keyboard in the center foreground is a TTS perforator. It produces a six-unit tape which is fed into the transmitter at left. In the background are the TTS monitor and a reperforator. Bottom photo shows a newspaper wire editor marking the monitor copy. Machines at the left are the monitor and reperforator.

158

Tape for ordinary matter is designed for 8-point type, 11- or 12-pica width. If type size transmission is changed, a warning is given visibly on the tape, as "SWAP TO AGATE." Agate matter on the monitor copy will appear under the slug: *ag*.

Identification slugs appear on all items. An example:

d 3   zzczyy   h510ams   20
   BOZEMAN, Mont. (AP)—Montana State college will be trying

In the above, d 3 (Denver wire, third item) is printable; zzczyy is the garble representing the d 3, punched visibly in the tape; h510ams is the operator's signature and time, 20 is the day of the month. Datelines are capitalized and, except for major cities or generally known cities, also carry the state or country. Since this report is for an afternoon paper the date is omitted.

Tapes containing unpublishable material should not be fed into a typesetting machine, especially if the message copy is *unjustified* (uneven). Unjustified tape "fouls up" the operating unit, causing mats to spill on the floor. If the message material is *justified* and the tape goes to the composing room, the kill can be made on the proof. Unpublishable matter includes editors' notes, messages, photo advisories and the like. Bureau corrections are marked on the monitor copy which is given to the proofreader. If the correction runs through the operating unit, the proofreader will have a double notice to make the correction.

Parenthetical matter poses a slight problem because the monitor printers lack the parenthesis character. In its place is a blank space on the copy. The punctuation can be supplied by manual operation.

Identifying addresses often are sent in separate paragraphs so that points which do not care to use the specific address may discard the unwanted material.

Tape Handling Varies

Editors have devised their own systems for speedy, efficient handling of TTS tape. Some editors send all the tape to the composing room to be set into type. Others select tape corresponding to the monitor copy they intend to use, attaching the tape to the monitor copy and sending both to the composing room. Still others file all the tape in the composing room but use only the pieces required for the day's paper.

One simple system involves use of a series of hooks numbered from 1 through 10. Hook 1 is for tapes containing book numbers 1, 11, 21, 31, 41; hook 2 contains book numbers 2, 22, 32, 42 and so on. A special hook is reserved for agate type size tapes.

Photo courtesy Boulder (*Colo.*) Daily Camera

MANUAL OPERATION OF A TYPESETTING MACHINE is eliminated by the teletypesetter. The operator simply feeds a perforated tape into a linecasting machine equipped with a TTS operating unit and the type is set automatically. Tapes on the wall in the rear are arranged according to book numbers designated by the wire service. The first spike is for tapes numbered 1, 11; the second for 2, 22, etc.

When the edited monitor copy reaches the composing room, the operator selects the tape with a corresponding book number and feeds it into the linotype. Unused tapes remaining on the hook after deadline are discarded.

If the copydesk is behind schedule, the editor can release tapes on stories he intends to use. By the time the monitor copy is edited, the story

Edited TTS Monitor Copy

Ins *Driver Killed* – 1-14-2

sd 4 qyyxzzcu v r 821ams 18

LAMAR Mi — Esaw Jimenez, 24, of Syracuse, Kan., was killed Sunday when the pickup truck in which he was riding went out of control and overturned four miles east of here on U. S. Highway 50.

The death raised Colorado's 1955 traffic toll to 88, compared with 85 on this date last year.

The State Patrol said the driver of the pickup, Manuel Guerrero apparently wanttreated for a cut on the left leg. Jimenez died of a crushed chest and broken spine.

The State Patrol said the driver of the pickup, Manuel Guerrero of Granada, apparently went to sleep at the wheel. He was treated for a cut on the left leg. Jimenez died of a crushed chest and broken spine.

EDITED TTS MONITOR COPY. The tape (sd 4) is fed into the operating unit of a linotype. The monitor copy first goes to a manual operator who sets the slugline—Driver Killed 1–14–2. *Ins* directs the makeup man to put the story on an inside page. After the operator has set the slugline (and subheads if they are indicated), the monitor copy goes to the proofreader who deletes the paragraph indicated on the monitor copy.

is in type and needs only the proofreader's corrections. Thus the desk need never hold up the composing room, nor must copy be "railroaded." The story can be set in type while it is being edited.

Roughly eight lines of double-spaced monitor copy equal an inch of type. Instead of counting lines, some copyeditors use a ruler to measure depth of copy. Copy 12 inches deep corresponds roughly to five inches of type.

Following is typical content of a TTS state wire, operating from 5 a.m. to 3 p.m.—

Type	Number of Items
National news	26
International news	12
Regional news	23
National sports	11
Regional sports	7
Interpretives (including advances)	2
Agate sports	2
Agate markets	11
Messages (including corrections)	16

Agate material includes items such as scores, boxing results, stock and grain markets. Some messages (news budgets, corrections) are intended for all editors; some are intended for one point only:

HL

NY asking for avble closeups of Montana candidates to go with Bell's piece for Thurs AMS. Apc let us know prospects, where pix be sent for fastest handling. Tnx.

DX

This is a message from Denver to Helena, Mont., requesting pictures of political candidates. *Apc* is an abbreviation for appreciate, *tnx* for thanks.

Syndicated Copy

Presenting but few problems to the copyeditor is copy from syndicates. Usually a hasty reading is all that is required. The *columns* have *standing heads,* and often heads are suggested for other material. Should space not permit using all the copy, paragraphs can usually be lopped off, starting from the bottom and working up.

Small newspapers in varying degrees make use of syndicated material in *mat* or *stereotype* form. Here, there is no opportunity to read copy, but the person responsible for the paper's contents does well to scrutinize a proof before letting it go through. Embarrassing situations have arisen when this precaution was neglected.

Syndicated material often provides a newspaper with *time copy* (also called *filler* or *plug* copy), to be used especially on days when the edition is larger than usual. This copy can be edited, sent to the composing room and be put into type during spare time. Then, when large gaps have to be filled when the paper is larger than usual and the composing room is working to capacity on current material, the plug copy can be used to fill the holes. Papers with more than one edition use time copy for early editions until fresh matter can be put into type to replace filler copy for home editions. Smaller dailies find time copy useful to lighten the burden on days when the paper runs heavier than usual.

Since time copy may be used any day of the week, the date in the dateline (if any) should be removed. Care should be taken to edit out time designations that would date the story.

Early editions of large metropolitan newspapers often use some of the type used in later editions of the day before. This enables newspapers to meet an early deadline, gives compositors a chance to set fresh material and gives readers of early editions a chance to read stories appearing only in late city editions of the previous day. Galley proofs of these stories come to the desk where the copyeditor updates the dateline and changes "today" to "yesterday" or the day of the week. Much of the syndicated copy is used under a *stet* (or *standing*) head: *Hollywood Today, Stamp News, Your Horoscope,* etc.

The amount of wire and syndicated copy used varies with each newspaper. Some surveys indicate that the small daily uses a greater percentage of its wire copy than does a metropolitan paper with the latter using a greater proportion of syndicated material than the smaller daily. On some small dailies as much as 45 per cent of the news is wire copy, suggesting that local news is not being covered adequately.

11 The Copyeditor on Guard

Let me commend the copyreader [copyeditor] to you. His work is no less essential to the paper than that of the reporter. A first-rate copyreader can make a first rate newspaper out of third-rate copy. On the other hand a poor copyreader can spoil the work of the best reporter. . . . He must possess keen literary appreciation. If he cannot write brilliantly he must write well enough to convert bad copy into good. He must be able to apply sandpaper to the bodily excrescences of an article, but not to its soul. His range of information must be wide and at instant command. He must know where to lay his hands on the facts he cannot draw from his memory.—Carr Van Anda (1864–1945), *former managing editor,* New York *Times.*

I. LITTLE THINGS THAT COUNT

Confidence Is Vital

For generations, Englishmen have believed, "If it's in *The Times* it is right." So highly have *The Times'* editors esteemed that reputation that once its presses were stopped to insert a missing comma. Another time, when the name of a small town in Panama was misspelled, an editorial conference was convened to discuss what should be done. Should the error be admitted, ignored, or should *The Times* thereafter cling to its spelling? The latter course was adopted, and occasions were made to use the misspelled word. Eventually, so the well-authenticated anecdote runs, the prestige of *The Times* forced gazetteers and lexicons to adopt the new spelling.

The moral is plain. A newspaper's most treasured asset is the confidence of its readers. Little but obvious errors that slip by careless copyeditors can corrode and corrupt it more than erroneous subtleties. A newspaper that is laughed at is slipping.

Commas Can Be Costly

Scores of lawsuits have hung on a comma. An engrossing clerk inserted an unwanted comma in this phrase of a tariff act, "all foreign fruit, plants," admitting all foreign fruits free of duty until Congress could remedy the blunder months later. That comma cost Uncle Sam some $2,000,000.

Note what a comma—or its lack—does in these examples:

"There is a destiny that shapes our ends rough, hew them as we may."
"Woman is pretty generally speaking."

Spelling Is Important

A favorite parlor pastime of Victor Heiser, the celebrated physician, was to ask friends to spell correctly a pet list of 10 words. A president of Harvard missed three, a Wall street magnate failed on four, and even editors have pulled a cropper on as many as six. The words are: inoculate, embarrass, harass, supersede, innuendo, rarefy, vilify, plaguy, desiccate, picnicking.

Copyeditors should cultivate the dictionary habit, looking up every suspect word. Here is a list to work on:

accommodation	biplane	clamor
acknowledgment	blond (adj.)	clue (to a crime)
advantageously	blonde (female)	colossal
adviser	bluing	connoisseur
aggregate	boulder	consensus
aid-de-camp	bouquet	consul
anemia	bric-a-brac	council
antitoxin	Buenos Aires	counsel
anyone	cannot	cozy
aperture	canceled	criticize
assistance	cantaloupe	defense
ax	canvas (cloth)	definitely
backward	canvass (for votes)	demagogy
baptize	capital (chief; governing	desperate
barricade	city)	develop
baseball	capitol (building)	dietitian
bas-relief	caress	dilettante
battalion	catalog	diphtheria
bazaar	chaperon	dishabille
benefited	chauffeur	downstairs
benefiting	chiffonier	downward
bettor	cigarette	employe

endorsee
enforce
Eskimo
eyewitness
facsimile
fiancé (man)
fiancée (woman)
fictitious
fiery
flies
forceps
forward
fulfill
fusillade
gaiety
gaily
gauge
gelatin
glamorous
glycerin
goodby
gray
gruesome
guerrilla
gypsy
halloween
horsepower
hosiery
imposter
inasmuch
incurable
incredible
indispensable
innocuous
intolerable
jiu-jitsu
judgment
kaleidoscope
kidnaped
kidnaper
kimono

laundered
leggings
liaison
likable
lily
mantel (shelf)
mantle (covering)
marshal
mass meeting
medieval
midweek
moneys
monoplane
mustache
naphtha
nickel
nitroglycerin
occurred
oculist
offense
oneself
paraffin
parallel
parquet
part-time
pastime
payee
pedagogy
percentage
permissible
persistent
Philippines
Pittsburg, Kan.
Pittsburgh, Pa.
playwright
portiere
post office
practice
procedure
program
propeller

prophecy (noun)
prophesy (verb)
quartet
questionnaire
quintet
raisin
renaissance
repentance
restaurant
restaurateur
sauerkraut
seize
separate
sextet
sheriff
siege
sizable
skillful
sobriquet
soccer (football)
soluble
stanch
strait-laced
sirup
tariff
thrash (to whip)
thresh (grain)
toward
typify
under way
vender
vengeance
vermilion
vitreous
weird
whimsical
whir
whisky
willful
woeful
zeppelin

The following words end in -ise. All others rhyming with them end in -ize.

advertise
advise

appraise
apprise

arise
chastise

comprise	enfranchise	premise
compromise	enterprise	reprise
demise	exercise	revise
devise	franchise	rise
disfranchise	improvise	supervise
disguise	incise	surmise
emprise	merchandise	surprise

More Tremendous Trifles

Every error of diction, thought and writing to which the human mind is heir creeps into newspaper copy. Here are a few special cautions for the copyeditor:

AGES ARE PITFALLS. Tony Belmont, *240 years old,* a watchman, was killed yesterday when he was struck by a train on the Chicago and Western Indiana railroad tracks at Taylor street and Plymouth court.

BE SUSPICIOUS OF ALL FIGURES. *Fifty* persons ended their lives during the month of September in Fall River county, the coroner's office reported yesterday. Seventeen persons turned on the gas, four shot themselves, 16 took poison, two leaped into the lake and two jumped from windows.

WATCH FOR "TYPOS." The bull started to run and Schmidt was hurled under the fence, barely escaping being *bored.*

BE SURE OF FOREIGN EXPESSIONS. Vive la France! Vive *la* Zateau. This famed French general is Washington's guest today.

BE SURE OF YOUR ALLUSIONS. Even *Medusa's dragon's teeth* could not have made more trouble, the speaker declared, and there was no *David to lead* them unharmed from the *lion's den.*

VERIFY REFERENCES. Ernest Hemingway, whose *"Bridge of San Luis Ray,"* was a best seller a few years ago, spoke briefly.

CHECK ON ALL NAMES. The W.C.T.U. presented a program in observance of *Francis* E. Willard Day.

WATCH FOR CONTRADICTIONS. Tokio.—Zenjiro Yasuda, 23, *for nearly 60 years* an influential banker of Tokio, was stabbed to death at his home here yesterday. His assassin, a lawyer, committed suicide with the same sword with which he killed the *young* banker.

CHECK TOTALS. *One boy was killed and two others were injured* when a toy express wagon in which they were coasting was hit by an automobile. The dead boy is Edward Lenahan, 8 years old, West Fishers lane. The other boys are Struthers Lester, 9 years old, Potter Alexander, 10 years old, and William Russell, 4 years old.

BEWARE OF RACIAL NICKNAMES. Mrs. Bronco Danguivich, 40 Euclid street, was taken to a hospital suffering from a fractured skull last night as the result of an attempted robbery and beating with a blackjack. Peter Torrentino, 26, a *dago,* of 300 Addie street, is held by the police.

SILVER OR GOLDEN? Fifty years ago Mr. and Mrs. Arthur S. Mann, 24 East Center street, were married in Boston. They will make a renewal of their marriage vows at the First Baptist church at 11 o'clock today. The Rev. Karl Barfield will officiate at the ceremony, and a *silver anniversary* reception will follow at the family residence.

ELIMINATE TRIVIALITIES.   David Walsh Jr., 18 years old, of 951 Cedar street was probably fatally shot last night by James Scala, an *Italian* watchman for the Scala State bank, because he with other boys laughed and ran away when *the Italian* tried to question them. The watchman fired several shots, one striking Walsh in the back. Police held *the foreigner. Walsh is a Methodist and belongs to the Mystic Workers of the World. He is a small man, only 4 feet 2 inches tall.*

WANTED: A COMMA.   Yeager left the engine running and jumping into the puddle rescued the half-drowned dog.

KNOW WHAT WORDS MEAN.   Highly modernized, thoroughly *reenervated,* the TIMES brings to serious-minded readers a responsible newspaper that prizes accuracy above ballyhoo or self-exploitation, fairness above personal bias, and straight, clean reporting above grandstand scoops.

GUARD AGAINST INCONGRUITIES.   The Rev. Frederic Knipe's chief hobby is fishing, which he does *religiously* every day during his month's vacation spent on Long Island Sound.

LOOK OUT FOR UNCONSCIOUS HUMOR.   Mr. Randall is still suffering greatly from injuries received when he protected the boy and is writing his dispatches, which messengers bring to me, on *scraps of paper in great pain.* He fell from the roof of a house, *striking himself on the back porch.*

ERROR COMPOUNDED.   By an unfortunate typographical error, we were made to say the departing Mr. Blank was a member of the defective branch of the police force. Of course this should have read: the detective branch of the police farce.

—Holyrood (Kan.) *Gazette*

KNOTTY NAUTICALS.   The vessel's speed is 30 knots *per hour.*

UNCOMPLIMENTARY REFERENCES.   A party was given for the author, who autographed his *last* book. (Note: Make it *last* few years, not *past* few years.)

KNOW YOUR ANIMALS.   He raises *purebred* horses, *pedigreed* cattle and *thoroughbred* dogs.

The late Lincoln Steffens, who has been called "America's best reporter," once advised a young writer that "Memory is the best editor." Few things aid a copyeditor new to a job more than a deliberate committing to memory of names of streets, suburbs and townships; hotels, hospitals and other important buildings; prominent local men; city, county, state and, of course, outstanding national officials.

Copyeditor's Friends

When in doubt, there is always some place to get correct information. Sometimes it is the office stylebook. More often it is reference books, such as the dictionary, almanac and atlas, found in the office. (A selected list of standard references useful to the newsman is found in the *Appendix IV*.)

Even the old hands around the rim often have their own handy reference sources like a pocket dictionary, a thesaurus or a map. If the copyeditor has his own desk drawer, he invariably keeps a few guidebooks.

Most newspaper offices, unfortunately, are poorly equipped with books. The larger papers have libraries but often this room is apart from the city room where copy is read. More books would result in more and closer checking of newspaper content.

II. COLORS, TRUE AND FALSE, IN THE NEWS

On Propaganda

Propagatus is an old Latin word meaning to cause or to continue or multiply by generation. When Pope Urban VIII in 1627 set up a school to educate missionaries it was quite logically called the College of The Propaganda. To it the modern meaning of the word traces: any organization or plan for spreading a particular doctrine or system, or the doctrine or principles themselves.

The essence of propaganda is selection and spread of ideas to produce the desired belief or action. It is transmission of opinion to influence people. Whether it advances their welfare or serves selfish ends is beside the point. It is propaganda in either case. Whether a newspaper is to be a vehicle for good propaganda or bad is a choice each must make.

Propaganda Devices

Techniques for influencing opinion are numerous and devious, as students of social psychology can attest. But seven devices commonly employed—either for or against public weal—have been aptly labeled by Prof. Clyde R. Miller of Columbia University, as follows:

1. THE NAME-CALLING DEVICE. This simply provides a label having emotional overtones. A few examples:

Political henchman, hireling, czar, dictator, red, so-called liberal, fifth-amendment Communist, conservative, radical, sons of wild jackasses, brain-truster, tory, yankee, damnyankee, scab, bureaucracy, kept press, capitalist, the so-called roll of honor, nuisance tax, red tape, un-American, labor, power trust, plumed knight, copperhead, pre-Pearl Harbor, fascist, communist.

2. THE GLITTERING-GENERALITY DEVICE. Also a substitute for thinking is the uncritical use of good words or phrases or sentences. A few frequently so employed are:

Truth, justice, service, the best, the worst, freedom of the press, pax Brittanica, kept press, entangling alliances, feet-on-the-ground, roll of honor, Hollywood star, on good authority, beautiful blonde, showgirl, faith of our fathers, the founding fathers.

3. THE TRANSFER DEVICE. This is used to carry over the authority, sanction or prestige from something revered and respected to something somebody wants revered and respected. Robber barons of the Middle Ages camouflaged their selfish motives by insisting they were extending the influence of religion and civilization. Word symbols such as the flag, the cross, Uncle Sam, John Bull, Washington and Lincoln are frequently employed in our day.

4. THE TESTIMONIAL DEVICE. A Hollywood star does it; therefore, if you do it, won't you be glamorous, too? Atlas the Strong Man eats it; so should you—if you would be strong. This former president of the United States says all good citizens support this cause, so—.

5. THE BAND-WAGON DEVICE. Symbols, colors, music and slogans are used to prove everybody's doing it. And who wants to be left out of the crowd, off the band wagon?

6. THE CARD-STACKING DEVICE. The magician's object is to mystify his audience. With studied skill he gives to his spectators selected stimuli so that they think what he wants them to think. The newswriter also selects details to be presented. His object should be to give a clearly focused picture of the event he reports. If he withholds certain details and gives prominence to others in order to direct a reader to his own opinion—regardless of whether it is good or bad for society—he is card stacking.

7. CONSPIRACY-OF-SILENCE DEVICE. "That," say editors, "is news—and that is not!" Principles governing such decisions are fairly well defined. But if the person seeking headlines for himself is ignored, his plaint often is a *conspiracy of silence* resulting, he asserts, from pique or prejudice of the editor. Many a politician has failed because he has been ignored by the press. Barnum even went so far as to declare that he didn't care what the papers said about him as long as they said something.

Propaganda devices are *a*moral, like any tool. They can be used to promote or to oppose vice, juvenile delinquency, loan sharks, gambling, graft, highway carelessness or strawberry socials.

With Eyes Open

The copyeditor is the watchdog of the news columns. He sniffs everything submitted for publication. His nose for news is allergic to opinionated writing, no matter how skillfully it may be dressed up.

His sophisticated alertness may prevent his paper being roped in by hoaxes that would make it appear foolish as well as by insidious forces. If the propaganda is harmless or helpful and measures up to his paper's policies and professional standards, he will allow it to pass. But it is severely edited or discarded if he deems it subversive of the five responsibilities of journalism. They are: (1) self preservation; (2) to present adequate, authentic and acceptable information; (3) to give wise guidance; (4) to entertain; (5) to give public service.

On Guard

"Who supplied this information?" and "Why is it offered?" are tests for copy suspected of being propaganda. Here are a few of the many forms in which it may come to the copydesk:

HANDOUTS. Avowedly to protect their clients from time-taking interviewers, but sometimes to cover up information, public relations men give inquiring reporters prepared statements called *handouts*. These often are useful —but do not give the more inclusive and exclusive story a reporter might obtain if given a free hand.

MADE NEWS. Reporters as well as publicity men often manufacture circumstances that make news. There seems to be no truth in the report that Krueger, ill-fated Swedish match magnate, originated the superstition that it is unlucky to be the third to light a cigarette from one match; that belief is a tribute to the marksmanship of the Afrikanders in the Boer War. But Edward L. Bernays, public relations counsel, is credited with popularizing if not inventing soap sculpture—to increase the sales of a soapmaking client. Another publicity expert was not too successful, however, with an innocuous-appearing proposal issued through a "National Patriotic League" to wash the Statue of Liberty— with "super suds."

And then there is the case of Anna Held, a famous stage figure of her day, who got bales of clippings because her publicity man persuaded her to take milk baths. Hollywood, need it be added, has made a fine art of made news.

HOAXED NEWS. Newspapers may be tolerant of whimsicalities of actresses, but they dislike to be "taken in" by palpably faked news. So does the public.

Leo, a 350-pound lion, left San Diego by airplane, and more than 2,000 people awaited his arrival in New York where he was to lap up five gallons of milk. No Leo arrived. For 50 hours the lion hunt went on. Then, at a remote Arizona point, the pilot and Leo emerged from the desert. Newspapers told how cowboys had presented Leo with a live steer. Story followed story. Even the New York *Times* gave Leo five stories and an editorial, totaling 28 valuable column inches. Then the balloon burst. A Hollywood film corporation took paid advertising space in motion picture magazines to tell how the whole thing had been staged—and swallowed by gullible newspapers and their public—under the caption "Pardon me while I laugh." Needless to add, the press wasn't violently pleased.

CAMOUFLAGED PUBLIC SERVICE. Frequently the most innocent-appearing publicity release hides the subtlest propaganda. A national "Hygiene Bureau" sent out a pretentious symposium of medical opinion, summed up in the point that the caffeine in a morning cup of coffee is harmful to health. The bureau, of course, was not a creature of a coffee roasters' association. Scores of hastily edited community papers have been glad to get gratis a "home page" service from an apparently legitimate feature syndicate. Careful copyediting would have detected the naming of a particular brand of baking powder in each instalment.

POLLUTED NEWS. Public opinion has a cash and a political value. Honest as well as dishonest men know that.

Comes a story giving a factual account of a public utility company improving its properties—with a phrase suggesting dissatisfaction with the local municipal electric plant. That phrase may or may not be propaganda; it will bear scrutiny. Statements from either employer or striking union are to be handled with caution—and fairness. Something more than patriotism may be behind a prepared statement from an industrialist praising a new alloy. Most dispatches coming through a government-sponsored news agency may be expected to be "inspired"—for a purpose not always visible to the naked eye. Always to be regarded with an uplifted brow are dispatches from foreign countries in time of war, especially if they discredit a rival.

The 'Free Publicity' Problem

Even the smallest weekly newspaper is bombarded daily by requests or demands that its readers be propagandized with *publicity, plugs, puffs, boosts, blurbs, readers, fillers.* These range in form from releases and handouts skillfully prepared by ex-newspapermen to reports of a ladies' club meeting scrawled on perfumed note paper.

Shall it be printed? There is but one real answer to that question. If it is legitimate *news* and space is available, use it; otherwise, into the big basket it goes.

Some publicity merits space with hardly a scratch of the copyeditor's pencil. Other pieces are usable with the *poison*—editorial-room argot for the publicity element—carefully extracted or counteracted. In one classic instance, a newspaper whimsically noted that a skywriter had made "an unlucky strike" by landing in a tree while "advertising a popular cigarette." Frequently a publicity story, as in that case, can be rewritten into acceptable copy or will yield a tip for a reporter to follow up.

Behind efforts of commercial interests to *break into* news columns is their tacit admission that the public expects newspapers to present unbiased news. It has been suggested, therefore, that one way to reduce pressure back of handouts is to publish them, but with identification of sponsor and source.

News or Advertising?

Obviously, the chariness with which newspapers regard publicity is based not less upon their feeling of responsibility to readers than upon the more elemental responsibility, which is to survive. If advertisers could tell their stories adequately through the news columns without cost, there would be little incentive for them to buy space.

It is difficult for the newsman to draw a rigid line. Should a lost wedding ring be seen as a news item or a classified ad?

Necessitous facts sometimes must overrule finely drawn theories, especially in cases where it is tacitly understood that aid given in newsgathering will be repaid by such favors. Newspapers vary in practice, but each has its rules, written or otherwise, and copyeditors will be expected to govern themselves accordingly.

A few newspapers lean backward. They refuse to publish any publicity material that will react to the advantage of interests supplying it. But this is a doubtful service to readers for, as the *Publishers' Auxiliary* has editorially observed:

> The editor all too frequently overlooks the fact that when he prints the item about the women's club dinner, he is being paid for that space. His subscribers are paying for it. When he fails to print, is he double-crossing his most valuable customer, his subscriber, for the fact that such a dinner is to be given is a part of the news of his community. . . . The editor who has an iron-clad rule against the use of any free publicity frequently cheats his reader. The editor who uses any and all such material sent to him does the same thing.

This principle has long been recognized in the liberal space accorded sports, stage and movie shows and other events run for private profit. Identification of radio and television programs by their sponsors has been questioned, yet also appears to be justified on grounds of news interest. But quite obviously, "news" that canned peaches can be bought at the Buy Itkwik store for ridiculously small prices is a matter to be recorded in paid advertising space.

'Line for Line'

To be resisted are the requests of advertisers for free publicity *because* of paid advertising space taken. New automobile models are news, and a newspaper is justified in running stories about them. But to give publicity only to cars that advertise is to start a dangerous practice.

Especially insidious is the development of public relations divisions within advertising agencies. Not infrequently, their releases carry a broad hint—even a note from Mr. Soandso, "chief space buyer." Some advertising agencies, encouraged by response of ad-hungry newspapers, demand a "line-for-line" reciprocity between advertising and news columns—and contribute, as the practice becomes generally known, to the undermining of public confidence in the editorial independence of newspapers.

Any organized attempt to influence a newspaper's policy through the big stick of advertising, whether done by advertising agency, political party, church, money-lender or what, strikes at the vitals of the American press. It should be openly rebuked.

III.   TASTE, DECENCY, FAIR PLAY

Taste Is a Variable

Blasphemy and salacious words and situations are much more common in books and plays than in newspapers. The novel-reading and play-going publics are relatively small groups, and self-selected. Like the movies, the newspaper is produced for consumption by all classes and is properly wary of that which may offend public decency or contribute to moral delinquency.

Newspapers follow the mores of their place and time. Tabloids often deal more frankly with sexual aberrations than do even their metropolitan compeers. The word "damn" is allowed in direct quotation in most papers of whatever size, but "God damn" and other blasphemy falls under the copyeditor's pencil.

Most community newspapers still consider it is in bad taste to announce that a woman is to have a baby. Some even insist that a child has been born to "Mr. and Mrs."—which, however, may reflect, not so much prudishness as a concern for male prestige in a world rapidly being feminized. It has been the fashion, doubtless dating from the Victorian era, to use genteel synonyms for simpler expressions of common speech. Here are a few:

powder room *for* toilet	stomach *for* belly
purchase *for* buy	nude *for* naked
pass on *for* die	odor *for* smell
casket *for* coffin	perspire *for* sweat
retire *for* go to bed	expectorate *for* spit

A reaction is under way, however, in favor of the homespun terms. They may not be so "nice," but they are forceful, and there are those who believe they make for fresher, more zestful copy.

Fair Reporting

The passing of the "personal journalism" of Horace Greeley's day is greatly lamented by emotional critics of modern journalism, who are all too forgetful that newspapers of a few generations ago were often marked by prejudice and vindictiveness of their editors. One exhibit will suffice. It is from the San Francisco *Chronicle,* for Sunday, April 14, 1889:

PERFIDIOUS ALBION.

HER GALLANT SON SEEKS A
DIVORCE.

An English Swell Who Has a Wife in England and Wants a California Divorce.

John A. Barton is a man of tone, dignity and position. Even though Mr. Barton were a person less distinguished by nature in mustache and carriage, his birth, accent and apparent affluence would insure him a position in San Francisco society.

It may perhaps have been thought by the fond mammas of California Street that the dashing gentleman who succeeded so well in entwining his mustaches around the affections of their daughters was an unmarried man, like the multitude of Britishers who "endure this blasted climate" for a spell. The aforesaid fond mammas may even have looked with favor upon the smiles and dignified attentions of this courteous son of Albion, all ignorant of the fact that the gentleman with the mustaches and the smiles has a wife already; still his wife, though very far away.

The truth is that John A. Barton has begun an action for divorce against his wife, Annie S. Barton, alleging that she has wrongfully and without cause or provocation deserted him.

It is not likely that Mrs. Barton will soon file her answer to this complaint, inasmuch as she is in Sheffield, England. Mr. and Mrs. Barton did not travel together to San Francisco. She remained behind, and, taking advantage of her absence, the husband sues for divorce. The basis of Barton's claim of desertion is that she will not join him, even though he has written her to come to him and has offered her enough money to pay her passage out. She refused to cross the Atlantic and the continent alone in order that she might join a husband who had left her on another hemisphere, and he thinks that this now justifies a divorce, and seeks it by the grace of the caoutchouc divorce laws of California.

Is a 'Scandal' News?

Reputable newspapers, which are in the majority, act on the principle that implicit in the *quasi* public utility character of the press is a responsibility to inform the public on public matters. When a scandal reaches the public through the courts, or otherwise comes in contact with the law, they believe a newspaper is justified in treating it as routine news. When a scandal does not come in contact with the law, and when publication would only injure the persons involved and furnish improper reading for the public as well, the average newspaper does not feel called upon to publish the story.

Newspapers are expected to take the initiative in exposing unsavory social conditions, but they are not called upon to snoop, or to invade the personal affairs of the average citizen. However, with the following, lifted from instructions of a news service to its correspondents, few newsmen would find fault:

Faithful portrayal of day-by-day history of the world and its people precludes writing only of pleasant things. So long as human nature is what it always has been, much that is sordid and mean will need to be included. The highlights must have contrasting shadows else the picture will be flat. In this ungrateful task, strive to be decent. Decency is not attained solely by the use of inoffensive words; some of the most salacious tales are told in "purest English undefiled." It is the thought behind the printed word that is important. Prudishness is equally to be avoided. Tell your story without emphasis upon the vicious, and without vulgarity, but tell it with proper clarity.

Do not glorify crime nor heroize criminals by giving a false glamour and thus exciting sympathy for a criminal or for crime. Coupling an incident possessing only regional interest with a crime that has attracted general attention gives the lesser incident a factitious news value. Transmission of crime news cannot be avoided, but each case must be held to its individual worth.

Crime stories or other dispatches in which ex-service men are concerned should not gratuitously bring in the fact that a man has been a soldier.

In reporting trips of the president by train, the name of the road over which he is traveling or is to travel should not be mentioned, nor should any hour of departure or arrival be given beforehand. A policy of keeping this information in confidence is followed by the government as a measure of safety to the president.

It is bad practice to mention the age of a woman unless age is essential to the story. Keep out of the report stories of unimportant young women who may have become involved in trivial escapades. Never bring in the names of young girls under circumstances that they may be bandied about by persons who do not realize that such thoughtlessness may reflect permanently upon the reputations of these girls, or affect their future happiness.

Where the fact is not essential to the news of a story, avoid the statement that one or the other of parties to an action for divorce obtained the decree. Refer only to the fact that the person in question "had been divorced" from so-and-so. "Statutory grounds" means nothing. If the divorce is granted because of infidelity, say so, but do not lug it in unnecessarily.

On Forcing Interviews

A fine point in newspaper ethics arises when a man from whom a statement is sought declines to speak. Pique and even revenge of the reporter may creep into his copy. It may be in the overtones of such words as, "He refused to talk to reporters, and drove them from the room with a curse." It may be a magnification and distortion of a hapless remark such as "The public be damned."

The Rev. Charles M. Sheldon, in his extraordinary best seller, *In His Steps,* published in 1896, observed that it was fortunate there were no newspapers in the time of Christ. Had there been, he declared, no accurate and unbiased account of His life would have been preserved. Further:

If there had been dailies and reporters in Jesus' time, of the sort we have now, everything He did and said would have been made the basis of a sensational "story." If He had refused to be interviewed, the reporter would have made up something. If He had said something new in the way of teaching, as He did, the newspapers would have made the headlines make him say something different.

It is a harsh criticism. To avoid justification for such comment on today's paper is an important function of the copyeditor on guard.

Controversial Issues

The newspaper that claims to present news fairly will be particularly careful in handling issues on which opinion is divided.

Many newspapers take pride in publishing syndicated columns of writers opposed to their policies, as visual evidence of their fairness. Such papers will also give equal prominence to statements of political candidates during a campaign, even seeking an expression from one when it has not been forthcoming.

Such a policy manifestly redounds to the reputation of a paper for fair play and justifies the respect and confidence of its readers. "The masses," says Dean Carl W. Ackerman, of the Columbia University School of

Journalism, "as well as organized minorities, military leaders, politicians, and men and women in public affairs, know that there is such a force as the power of suggestion and that this force springs from information. . . . The use as well as the misuse of information has made the power of suggestion the decisive force in world affairs. It can cause or prevent a war. It can strengthen or destroy a democracy. It can build or wreck a nation."

12   The Newspaper and the Law

A lie will travel around the world and back again while truth is lacing its boots.—*Old Proverb.*

> Who steals my purse steals trash; 'tis something, nothing;
> 'Twas mine, 'tis his, and has been slave to thousands;
> But he that filches from me my good name
> Robs me of that which not enriches him
> And makes me poor indeed.
>   —William Shakespeare (1564–1616) in *Othello,* Act III, Sc. 3.

Papers Are Legally Responsible

A newspaper is legally responsible for whatever it publishes. The copydesk is the backstop against possible legal action. The best defense against embarrassment and legal action is thoroughness. A little textbook knowledge of libel can stifle good writing, especially if the copyeditor tries to make the safe safer. "It is quite difficult to avoid being libelous in a daily newspaper, but it isn't difficult to avoid getting into a libel suit," according to William German, head of the copydesk of the San Francisco *Chronicle.*

The copyeditor's job, of course, is to tone down or eliminate the obvious defamation and to question or challenge any statement that could possibly invite legal action. He must know when to whack and when to lay off.

Defamation Is Dangerous

Libel is a published statement that tends to harm the reputation of another by lowering him in the estimation of the community or by deterring other persons from associating or dealing with him. Or better, "It is libelous of any person if its effect is to make its readers think worse of that person." A published statement may be defamatory if it is false, if it is damaging and

179

if it has the effect of injuring the victim in the minds of others. A statement is damaging if:

1. It accuses a living person of a crime or imputes a crime to him.

2. It states or insinuates that a person has insanity or a loathsome or contagious disease.

3. It tends in any way to subject the victim to public hatred, contempt or ridicule.

4. It asserts a want of capacity to conduct one's business, occupation or profession.

Libel may be contained in a story, a headline, picture, cartoon, caption (*cutline*), editorial, signed column, letter to the editor or any type of advertisement. The liability of the newspaper is not necessarily for originating slander but for speading it by publication.

Some expressions, normally innocent in themselves, may become libelous when special circumstances are shown. For instance, a false statement that a person died is not damaging since it is no disgrace to die. But if the plaintiff offers proof of specific damages he suffered as a result of the publication, he may collect. A false statement that a doctor died could cause him to lose hundreds of dollars in business. He can collect by offering proof of the actual damage he has suffered as a result of the publication.

Malice and Intent

Malice is presumed in all defamatory stories.

The newspaper is responsible even though no defamation was intended and even though no specific identify was intended. The test is not who the story intended to name but who readers may think is named. The newspaper takes a risk even when it attempts to avoid liability by omitting names, by abbreviating or by giving fictitious names.

A libel directed at a group may form the foundation of an action by an individual if the group is small enough so that a person reading the article may readily identify the person as one of the group; *e.g.*, a city council.

Criminal Libel

Criminal libel actions are rare. They do not involve collection of damages. They are brought by and prosecuted by the state. The gist of criminal libel is the tendency of a malicious defamatory publication to cause a breach of the peace. Punishment for criminal libel is a fine or imprisonment or both.

Colorado Statutes, which are typical, define criminal libel as follows:

A libel is a malicious defamation expressed either by printing, or by signs, or pictures or the like, tending to blacken the memory of one who is dead, or to impeach the honesty, integrity, virtue or reputation, or publish the natural defects of one who is alive, and thereby expose him or her to public hatred, contempt, or ridicule. . . . In all prosecutions for a libel the truth thereof may be given in evidence in justification, except libels tending to blacken the memory of the dead or expose the natural defects of the living.

Libels of federal, state and municipal governments and their subdivisions are not recognized in the United States. Publications which advocate a violent overthrow of the government or tend to instigate a breach of peace or law may be punished under criminal law.

Trade Libel

A corporation, partnership or trust or other business may be damaged if untrue statements tend to prejudice such entity in the conduct of its trade or business, or to deter others from dealings with it. Nonprofit organizations likewise may collect damages resulting from a publication which tends to prejudice them in the public estimation and thereby interferes with the conduct of their activities.

Some Causes of Libel Suits

As it is the copyeditor's business—a responsibility shared, of course, by all editorial workers—to challenge all libelous statements and guard against their publication, the following compilation of some actual cases of libel actions is worthy of study:

A man who was called a crook sued the newspaper for $25,000.

An advertising solicitor seeking matter for a program was called a swindler and accused of not turning over his receipts; he sued for $50,000.

A man who sold insurance by lending patrons money to pay the premium was called a loan shark. He sued for $50,000.

The picture of the wrong woman was used in a scandal story. She was awarded a judgment.

Two men were called anarchists; both got judgments, although one was for only six cents.

A famous art critic called the works of Whistler "willful imposture." Whistler sued and recovered one farthing in the English courts.

The wrong picture in an advertisement won a jury verdict of damages for the woman who charged her reputation had been damaged.

A mayor who was called "the rankest of socialists" in favor "of blowing up tenement houses," won his suit.

Humorous stories ridiculing a corset model led to libel suits against two newspapers.

Each of the following expressions, or errors, according to *Editor & Publisher,* has figured in a libel suit won by the plaintiff:

Anarchist, bankrupt, black-leg, black-sheep, brainstorm, briber, crook, crooked, damaged-goods chap, destitute and extreme poverty;

Felon, fraud, frozen snake, gambler, henchman of a notorious character, humbug, hypocrite, impending insanity, impostor;

Infernal villain, insane, insolvent, insulting to ladies, ironical praise (such as to call an attorney "an honest lawyer" when the opposite is implied), itchy old toad, liar, mere man of straw and an obituary of a living person;

Packing a jury, pseudo-scientist, rascal, rogue, scoundrel, slacker, suicide fiend, syphilis, thief, tool of profiteers and unfit to be trusted.

Dangerous Statements

Here are a few types of dangerous statements that should be avoided or at least closely examined before they are permitted to get into print:

Unequivocal charges of crime—"a notorious swindler," "the swindler," "the bigamist," "the thief," "the crook," etc.

Ex-parte statements—"neighbors said."

Racial terms that may be considered discreditable by the persons involved; also racial nicknames and underworld names.

Malicious expressions—"the lily-white war hero was a thorough-paced scoundrel."

Harsh terms where milder ones are possible. It may be advisable to use "slayer" instead of "murderer" and "killer" in some cases.

Anonymous matter—"It is said he has murdered several other wives."

Not all these expressions are always libelous. Some are simply provocative of needless trouble. Many law suits against newspapers arise from trivial items which would never have been missed if they had been omitted.

Defenses Against Libel

Truth is the best defense against libel, though in some states it is only a qualified defense. In Nebraska, for instance, truth is a sufficient defense provided it is published "with good motives and for justifiable ends."

But if truth is offered as evidence, it must be substantial truth, not hearsay or secondary proof. Mere repetition of what someone else said is not admissable evidence of truth. The truth must be as broad and complete as the publication upon which the charge was made. If the newspaper quotes Brown as saying Smith is a liar, the burden of proof must be that Smith actually is a liar, not that Brown made the statement.

Truth offered in evidence need not mean the literal accuracy of the published charge but rather the substance or gist of the charge.

What Is Privileged?

The official conduct of governmental bodies, agents and officers can be safely reported "under privilege" provided the publication is:

1. Fair and substantially accurate and complete;
2. Non-malicious;
3. Without comment;
4. Of matters constituting or being relevant to official action or performance of such public bodies or officers.

Privilege is accorded to reports of official, judicial, legislative, executive or administrative proceedings, federal, state, or municipal, but not to public meetings of churches, chambers of commerce, cultural organizations and other such nongovernmental bodies.

Furthermore, it is only the official conduct of governmental bodies, agents and officers that can be reported under privilege. If the police say something which is not within the scope of their duty to make public, no privilege is accorded, and it is not made legally safe by prefacing it with the phrase "police say" or "police reported." Statements by police about the guilt or innocence of a prisoner are not privileged.

No privilege arises until official action begins. The safe rule is to report only acts and statements occurring in the presence of the court. The mere filing of a complaint, petition, affidavit or other document with the clerk of the court does not in itself make the contents privileged. Anyone can go into the court house and file a complaint containing false, scandalous and damaging statements about another merely upon payment of a small docket fee. Proof of the fact that libelous statements were contained in the complaint is no defense. The defendant must prove the truth of the allegations contained in the complaint and affidavits.

If a story is used when the complaint or other document is first filed and before any judicial action is taken, at least the specific defamatory allegations should be omitted or toned down.

Malice can be rebutted by publishing both sides of lawsuits, criminal prosecutions, proceedings before commissions and regulatory bodies and the like. Even where the accused person or litigant or proponent or antagonist refuses to state his side, reporting that such an opportunity was given and refused, will serve the same purpose.

Confessions usually have no legal standing until they are introduced as evidence and accepted by the court. Reporting a confession is dangerous, particularly if the defendant later is acquitted, if the court refuses to admit the confession into evidence or if the confession implicates others. In dubious cases, the copy of the confession should be photographed and filed.

Courts generally have held that an article received from a press service and published in a newspaper does not make the publication privileged.

An individual has a right to reply in a newspaper to an attack upon him made in a newspaper. Even though the reply is defamatory, it will be privileged for the individual and the newspaper provided the defamatory matter is essential to support a contention that the original attack was not true.

Fair Comment and Criticism

Newspapers are privileged to criticize and comment adversely upon candidates for public office, public officials, public institutions, scientific artistic, literary and dramatic productions and exhibitions, sporting events catering to the public and all goods and products offered to the public for use and consumption. This privilege, however, is conditioned by the following:

    1. The comment must be found upon facts or the result of honest opinion.
    2. The comment must not be malicious.
    3. The comment must not involve the private life or moral character of a person, except where such has a direct bearing upon his qualifications or work.

Courts allow considerable leeway to newspaper comments upon subjects possessing public interest. The right to criticize government or public officials is one of the precious ingredients of freedom of the press. But this freedom does not give the newspaper the right to assassinate a character simply because the victim happens to hold public office. A newspaper has the right to comment freely upon the fitness of those seeking or holding public office, but this does not constitute a license to injure one's reputation in his private capacity. The comment must confine itself to the candidate's qualification for office and must not reflect upon his personal or professional career except as it may affect his qualification for holding public office.

Correction and Retraction

Some states have a retraction law which limits claims to actual damages provided the publication has used a correction and retraction upon request. Newspapers published in states lacking a retraction provision often condition a retraction (technically an admission of libel and often impossible if the justification is truth) upon a written release from the injured party.

Publication of a retraction often helps refute the claim of malice, which is the damaging ingredient in all libels and the basis for the award of substantial damages. A refusal to retract may be used by the plaintiff to show malice. The retraction, if published, should be full and frank and used as conspicuously as the article complained of.

Few newspapers today have the stiff spine of the Springfield (Mass.) *Republican* in the days of its most famous editor, Samuel Bowles. Confronted with the complaint of a man whose death had been announced, he is said to have consented to correct the mistake only by giving him a birth notice. Today, it is considered good editorial policy to admit error when it has been committed.

Some newspapers have a small department under some such head as "Beg Your Pardon" in which to publish corrections, retractions, and such added facts as seem advisable to present. Readers respect a paper not above admission of its mistakes—provided they are not made too often.

Four Things to Do

It is obvious that a newspaper, if it is to have any character whatever, cannot retreat every time a person involved in a story roars out an indignant protest at the prospect of getting into print. Nor can it continually suppress stories simply because the persons affected raise a threatening cry of "libel."

There is a clear-cut path to the news that is reasonably safe: first, the story must be investigated and its truth and its freedom from malice established; next, it must be written dispassionately and impersonally; then, it must undergo scrutiny from the standpoints of malice, libel and credibility—a duty that falls to the news executive and the copyeditor. Finally, if an error occurred, a correction should be published.

The reporter and writer cannot investigate too thoroughly; the editor and copyeditor cannot scrutinize too carefully. But once the credibility of a news item is thoroughly established, only a cowardly newspaper will withhold it from readers. No newspaper need fear to tell the truth if it speaks impartially and with the detached attitude of the observer.

Identifications Are Important

Make sure of correct identifications. Check or verify all names appearing in libel-laden copy. Mistaken identity has been one of the major sources of embarrassment and legal action. It is safer to have it read "a man who gave his name as John Doakes was arrested" than "John Doakes was arrested." Take similar precaution with addresses.

Restrictions on Publication

Governmental prohibitions as regards the newspapers are extremely few, but they do exist and they are dictated by commonsense, governmental necessity and the public welfare. These few federal regulations, combined with the strict newspaper policing of news columns that is enforced by the libel laws of the various states, constitute virtually the only formal peacetime curbs on the American press.

In addition to the universally applicable provisions of the United States Penal Code regarding treason and sedition, newspapermen, like other citizens, are forbidden to print:

Counterfeit weather forecasts or warnings fraudently credited to government sources (*Penal Code, Sec. 61*).

Reproductions of certificates of citizenship (*Penal Code, Sec. 75*).

Reproductions of any kind of paper money, or even of a semblance; this applies to the paper money of foreign countries as well. Possession of even the plates or engravings to make such reproductions is regarded as *prima facie* evidence of guilt. Illustrations of coins may be used in "numismatic and historical books and journals and the circulars of legitimate publishers and dealers in the same" (*Penal Code, Sec. 147 to 178; also Sec. 172*).

Obscene, lewd, or lascivious text, pictures, or advertisements (*Penal Code, Sec. 211*).

Indecent, lewd, lascivious, obscene, libelous, scurrilous, defamatory or threatening matter on outside cover or wrapper (*Penal Code, Sec. 212*).

Text, pictures, or advertising matter referring to lotteries, gift enterprises, or similar schemes offering prizes dependent in whole or in part upon lot or chance (*Penal Code, Sec. 213*). This section also in effect prohibits any news, pictures, or advertisements concerning raffles, or concerning card parties at which admission is charged and prizes are competed for. There are special laws and regulations regarding the conduct of newspaper prize contests and competitions, which are not affected by this section and are legitimate enterprises.

A lottery is a scheme containing three elements: a consideration paid, a prize or award and determination of the winner by chance. This includes all drawings for prizes and raffles and games such as Bingo, Bunco, Keno. It is immaterial who sponsors the scheme, whether it be a church group, a philanthropic or patriotic organization or a private agency.

All matter intended to aid and abet mail frauds of any sort, such as the "green goods" game and others (*Penal Code, Sec. 215*).

Copyeditors should have a working knowledge of all these points, because a single false step may result in barring an entire edition of a newspaper from the United States mails.

Certain states also have measures regulating or prohibiting the advertising of intoxicating liquor.

Postal regulations prohibit the mailing of the following:

Obscene, lewd, lascivious or filthy publications or writings. . . .

Anything intended to prevent conception or produce abortion. . . .

Any matter of a character tending to incite arson, murder or assassination.

Any matter otherwise mailable which has upon its outside wrapper . . . any libelous, scurrilous, defamatory or threatening language. . . .

Any newspaper . . . or publication of any kind containing any advertisement of a lottery or similar enterprise.

Any . . . publication . . . containing any matter advocating or urging treason, insurrection or forcible resistance to any law of the United States.

Any . . . matter containing any threat to take the life of, or to inflict bodily harm upon, the President of the United States.

Publications which violate copyrights granted by the United States.

—(*Sections 124: 31 through 72*).

Stories which are *solely* about lotteries cannot be used in mail editions. If the lottery factor is incidental, the story is mailable. An example is the story of a housewife who said her husband ran away with another woman after winning $139,285 in the Irish Sweepstakes.

An extreme application was an order by the post office solicitor to a newspaper to refrain from using the word *pari-mutuel* in print.

Protection of Children

In some states, juvenile court judges request newspapers to refrain from publishing names, photographs and identification in juvenile cases (a juvenile is generally considered to be under 18 years old). Such laws are aimed primarily at delinquency, dependency and adoption, but often they can apply to any case before the juvenile court.

This restriction does not usually apply to juvenile cases brought before criminal courts although among juvenile authorities it is considered most important that the minor should not be considered a criminal, and that his transgressions should not be made public.

Two Canadian parents won damages totaling $2,250 and costs for defamatory libel in connection with the publication of their child's picture provided by the community chest to spark a fund-raising campaign. The parents contended that an article accompanying the picture gave the impression the child was delinquent and neglected.

Statute of Limitations

Usually actions for libel must be started within one year after the publication of the article complained of. But republication of the offending article starts another period of one year within which an action upon the article as republished can be begun.

Contempt of Court

Actions which disregard the authority and the dignity of the court or which tend to impede the administration of justice may result in a contempt of court citation. Courts may cite stories which tend to produce an atmosphere of prejudice where a pending case is being or is to be tried, to delay or interfere with the administration of justice or to cause justice to miscarry. Truth is no defense against a citation for contempt of court.

Courts and judges, however, are not immune from criticism. Comments on a case that tends to hinder the administration of justice might result in contempt proceedings. A criticism of a judge that could affect a pending case might also subject the writer and the newspaper to contempt of court proceedings.

Right of Privacy

It is generally safe to publish anything which has news value and is true. The doctrine of privacy usually relates more to advertising than to news. A person has a right of action if a firm uses his name in a testimonial without his consent. But use of pictures and names without consent is permitted in current news items, educational, informative and entertaining features.

A safe procedure to follow in the use of live illustrations for advertisements, magazine and feature sections is to hire professional models or get written consent from persons whose pictures are used.

Be Wary of Photographs of Patients

Use of unauthorized photographs of patients in private hospitals may invite trouble for the newspaper.

In 1930, a Georgia court ruled that it was an invasion of the right of privacy of the parents to publish a nude photograph of their deceased deformed child without their permission. The hospital allowed a photographer to take a picture of the child. The photographer then gave a copy of the picture to the local newspaper, which published it with a story about the deformed child. The parents brought action against the hospital, the photographer and the newspaper, asking $20,000 damages, plus an injunction against further use of the photograph.

Medical and Hospital Stories

Today several states have a code of cooperation between the press and the medical profession and hospitals. Following are some of the general provisions that affect the reporter and the copyeditor:

In matters of private practice, the wishes of the attending physician or surgeon shall be respected as to use of his name or direct quotation. He shall give to the press, where it does not jeopardize the doctor-patient relationship or violate the confidence, privacy or legal rights of the patients—

1. In cases of accident or other emergency: the nature of injuries when ascertained, the degree of seriousness, probable prognosis.

2. In cases of illness of a personality in whom the public has a rightful interest: the nature of the illness, its gravity and the current condition.

3. In cases of unusual injury, illness or treatment the above information and any scientific information which will lead to a better public understanding of the progress of medical science. Any physician becoming aware of such a case is urged to notify the designated spokesman of his local medical society at once for immediate communication of appropriate information to the press.

Hospitals. Each hospital shall designate spokesmen who shall be competent, in the absence or non-availability of the attending physician, to give authentic information to the press in emergency cases at any time of the day or night without the necessity of clearing with higher authority, except information which shall jeopardize the hospital-patient relation, or which violates the confidence, privacy or legal rights of the patient.

In return, it is provided that representatives of the press shall cooperate by refraining from any action or demands that might jeopardize the patient's life or health.

When a physician or hospital authority is quoted directly and by name, the press shall make certain to the best of its ability that the quotation is accurate both in content and in context.

Representatives of the press shall exercise editorial judgment to avoid publishing material designed solely to exploit the patient, and doctor or the hospital.

On all matters of health or medical news, representatives of the press shall make all reasonable effort to obtain authentic information from qualified sources before proceeding to publication.

Copyright Protects the Author

Copyright is legal protection for literary or artistic work. Ideas cannot be copyrighted—only the expression or illustration of ideas. If use of copyrighted material deprives the owner of credit or profit, it is an infringement. Paraphrasing or copying with evasion is an infringement, even though there may be little or no conceivable identity between the two. Copying must be done to an unfair extent to constitute infringement.

Facts that are available to anyone cannot be copyrighted. Any reporter may do his own investigation and on the same subject. Quotations may be made from historical and public documents even though such documents are quoted in full in copyrighted works. Copyright covers only material that is copyrightable and not in the public domain. Copyright lasts for 28 years and may be renewed for an additional 28 years.

Copyright is secured by publication of the original work with a notice of copyright. The notice must consist of: *Copyright, (date), (by whom)*. After publication, two complete copies of the edition must be deposited with the Register of Copyrights, Washington, D.C., and payment made for the registration fee.

PART IV

Understanding Typography,
Perfecting Headlines
and Handling Photos

13   An Introduction to Typography

Nothing which won't be read is worth printing, and to get things read under the present pressure on readers' time and attention, printing must be superlatively legible.—Douglas C. McMurtrie (1888–1944), *typographer, historian.*

Much progress is being made in printing. Metal type is on the way out, although it will take some time for it to disappear completely.

We are approaching national newspapers, and magazines that are nearly current exert a profound influence on the public's understanding, or perhaps at times on its misunderstanding. We can confidently expect better methods of printing, and better methods of distributing what is printed.—Dr. Vannevar Bush (1890–   ), *educator, electrical engineer.*

I.   TYPOGRAPHICAL FUNDAMENTALS

Points on Typography

Although the copyeditor need not have an elaborate knowledge of typography, he will be a better deskman if he knows some of the elementary fundamentals of the subject. Certainly he should know something about the mechanical operation of the plant that produces his newspaper. If he hopes to advance to the position of news editor or managing editor he will have to acquire a rather extensive knowledge and appreciation of typography.

He will learn to regard typography as an expression of art. He will find delight and inspiration in discovering the contributions of master craftsmen like Nicolas Jenson, Aldus Manutius, Claude Garamond, Giambattista Bodoni, William Caslon and Frederic Goudy. The more he understands typography, the better equipped he will be to use printing types intelligently.

The ability to identify faces of type is the least important of the benefits the copyeditor will get from a study of typography. But it has to be learned because it is the starting point.

Type Classifications

Almost all type faces fall into five easily remembered major classifications—Roman, Italic, Cursive, Script and Text or Blackletter—each having common characteristics.[1]

1. Roman. In this classification fall the common types: Old Style, Modern, Transitional, Blockletter (including Sansserif) and Flatserif—five easily distinguished subclassifications, the characteristics of which will be described.

Old Style types were designed to follow the lettering of medieval scribes who lettered with a broad pen held at an angle to the line of lettering. The strokes vary somewhat in weight, but are not extreme in their contrasts. Serifs are club shaped or wedge shaped, as can readily be observed in the lower case, b, d, h, i, j, k, l, m, n, p, s and z. Another Old Style characteristic is the fact that the ball *finials* of the letters are not perfectly round but more oval, noticeable in the a, c, f, g, r and y. Caslon, Garamond, Cloister (or Eusebius) and Old Style No. 1 are Old Style types. The line below is Eusebius Bold.

Eusebius Bold, An Old Style Letter Design

The name, Modern, is confusing, since it is not modern in our sense of the word, but a descriptive term applied years ago to differentiate between what was then new and the Old Style types. The chief characteristic of Modern is its strictly geometrical contour, its contrasting strokes and its straight, unbracketed serifs. These types were drawn with a pen held at right angles to the line of lettering and the serifs do not curve into the body of the letter. The ball finials are rounded—not oval. The line shown below is Bodoni, which is typically Modern and is the best known representative of this classification. Bodoni was originally designed by Giambattista Bodoni, an Italian, about 1788.

Bodoni is still a Favorite of Typographers

Transitional types fuse elements of Old Style and Modern together into a new design, such as Baskerville and Sotch Roman.

Blockletter is today used in headlines more than any other class of

[1] To prevent confusion, type designations in this chapter are capitalized. In practice, they often are not.

types. In this classification are all those devoid of serifs, including the recent and better designed Sansserif types (meaning without serif). Blockletter is available in the widest range of color and widths. Shown below is a common Blockletter usually referred to as *Gothic,* and a line of one of the newer Sansserifs, Tempo Bold:

Franklin Gothic, a Blockletter
Tempo Bold, a Sansserif Type Design

The term, "Gothic," in this connection is a misnomer, and should actually be applied only to types derived from the German Fraktur. The Sansserif types, or *Modern Gothics,* are geometrical in design, being made up of straight lines and arcs of circles. Representatives of this subclassification are: Futura, Kabel, Tempo, Vogue, Metro and Twentieth Century.

The Flatserif types, another subclassification, are really geometrically designed Sansserifs, with the addition of straight-line bar serifs. All strokes in both the Flatserifs and Sansserifs are of uniform weight, which accounts for their being described as "monotone" faces. Their modern vogue is quite recent and they are available in a wide range of weights and widths. Karnak, Memphis, Cairo, Stymie and Beton are Flatserifs. Here is a line of Karnak Medium:

Karnak Medium, a flatserif Type

The newest kind of type face in the Sansserif classification combines the simplicity and modern feeling of a Sansserif letter with the increased style and superior legibility of a letter with varying weight strokes. Combining as it does the advantages of both features, this new departure in designing has resulted in a family of type faces destined to become increasingly popular. The Radiant family, available in several weights and widths, is the result. It is shown here in the bold weight:

Sansserif with varied weight strokes

2. Italic. Based originally on the rapid, angular handwriting of certain scribes, Italic types have a flowing quality. They are used chiefly for differentiation, emphasis or a change of pace in typography. *Oblique,* which is a subdivision of Italic, is a Roman letter, drawn on a slant without attempt to revise the design of the Roman. The Obliques are found almost exclusively in the Sansserif group. Examples of a Roman type with its companion Italic, and a Sansserif with its companion Oblique, as shown below:

Caslon Roman with *Caslon Italic*

Sansserif Shown here and its *Oblique*

3. Cursive. Cursive types, based on the exceedingly rapid writing of "chancery" clerks, partake of both an Italic and a Script. The capitals for Cursive types are freely drawn and often quite ornamental. By substituting Cursive capitals, which are often available with Italic types, the latter can be converted into Cursives. Many so-called Scripts are really Cursives, inasmuch as the letters do not actually join or give the impression of a connected line.

Mayfair, a Cursive Typeface

4. Script. In recent years there have been many additions to this classification. Scripts are especially effective for advertising and for special newspaper headlines. They are available in a wide variety of *faces* and are characterized by their free design and their impression of flowing together, being either actually connected or with the connecting strokes slightly apart.

Mandate, a Connected Script

5. Text or Blackletter. In this classification will be found those types whose design originated in the German style of lettering known as Fraktur —the true Gothic types. Their use is largely limited to printing with an ecclesiastical background and printing at Christmastime. Representatives of this classification are Old English, Cloister Black and Goudy Text.

Old English is a Type Difficult to Read

In addition to the foregoing, there are purely ornamental types, decorative in character, and "freak" types which do not fall into any of the above five classifications. Their use is naturally limited and of a special nature.

Taste in Type

Pages pleasing to the eye result from subtle harmonies and brilliant contrasts achieved by the proper use of type faces. Generally speaking, good typographers avoid mixing Old Style and Modern. The safest and most satisfying procedure is to rely on one major family, introducing variations by using different weights and widths of letters.

Too many type faces result in a hodgepodge which is neither effective nor esthetically pleasing. At least as much attention should be given to selection of type faces as is given to the choice of office furniture; far more people are influenced by the former.

II. TYPE FOR NEWSPAPERS

Body Type

The prime requirement for newspaper text type is the highest possible degree of legibility consistent with the least demands on space. Great progress has been made in recent years by type composing machine manufacturers in developing faces that are easy to read and yet get a surprisingly large number of words into the column inch. Among the type faces designed for high legibility are *Ionic, Excelsior, Textype, Ideal News, Regal, Corona, Paragon.*

Ideal News (Intertype) 7 on 8

WASHINGTON — (AP) — Did you ever squeeze a toothpaste tube and find everything going backward instead of out the nozzle?

Herman J. Poock of West Milton, O., apparently has done it more than once.

But instead of grumbling, he decided that something should be done and that he'd do it.

He did. He studied a bit and came up with a gadget that he says will assure a smooth flow of toothpaste or any other tube-packed material at all times.

Corona (Linotype) 8 solid

WASHINGTON—(AP)—Did you ever squeeze a toothpaste tube and find everything going backward instead of out the nozzle?

Herman J. Poock of West Milton, O., apparently has done it more than once.

But instead of grumbling, he decided that something should be done and that he'd do it.

He did. He studied a bit and came up with a gadget that he says will assure a smooth flow of toothpaste or any other tube-packed material at all times.

Regal (Intertype) 8 on 9

WASHINGTON—(AP)—Did you ever squeeze a toothpaste tube and find everything going backward instead of out of the nozzle?

Herman J. Poock of West Milton, O., apparently has done it more than once.

But instead of grumbling, he decided that something should be done and that he'd do it.

He did. He studied a bit and came up with a gadget that he says will assure a smooth flow of toothpaste or any other tube-packed material at all times.

Paragon (Linotype) 9 on 10

WASHINGTON—(AP)—Did you ever squeeze a toothpaste tube and find everything going backward instead of out the nozzle?

Herman J. Poock of West Milton, O., apparently has done it more than once.

But instead of grumbling, he decided that something should be done and that he'd do it.

He did. He studied a bit and came up with a gadget that he says will assure a smooth flow of tooth-

Eight-point usually is considered the standard size for body type on daily papers (especially those using TTS), although smaller sizes down to the agate may be used for certain purposes, as will be explained later in this chapter. To improve readability, some dailies have shifted to 9-point on a 10-point slug.

Headline Type

Not many years ago, choice of headline type was practically limited to two families: Cheltenham and what was known as Gothic but should be called Blockletter. They were available in wide varieties of size and degree of condensation and, being simple in design, were unobjectionable generally.

Here is an assortment of Cheltenham faces:

Cheltenham Oldstyle	**Cheltenham Bold Extended**
Cheltenham Italic	**Cheltenham Extrabold**
Cheltenham Oldstyle Condensed	**Cheltenham Bold Condensed**
Cheltenham Medium	*Cheltenham Bold Condensed Italic*
Cheltenham Medium Italic	Cheltenham Bold Extra Condensed
Cheltenham Medium Condensed	CHELTENHAM BOLD EXTRA CONDENSED TITLE
Cheltenham Medium Expanded	Cheltenham Bold Outline
Cheltenham Wide	Cheltenham Bold Shaded
Cheltenham Bold	*Cheltenham Bold Italic Shaded*
Cheltenham Bold Italic	**Cheltenham Extrabold Shaded**

The very simplicity of Blockletter—straight *strokes* of approximately equal weight, combined in the most elementary manner—has given it wide popularity for the workaday function of news heads. A few typical faces:

Medium Gothic of Square Design

Heavy Gothic in Upper & Lower

Condensed Heavy Gothic for Narrow Heads

Condensed Gothic, Lighter Form and More Compressed

The simplicity and beauty of the better designed Sansserifs or "Modern Gothics," which have been growing in popularity since their introduction in the United States about 1925, are responsible for their being preferred for news and feature heads. Four weights—light, medium, bold and heavy —are available for most Sansserif faces, and in addition, there are many other variations, such as Italic (Oblique) and condensed letters in various weights.

Here is a typical Sansserif series favored for newspaper headlines, shown in various versions:

Tempo Light and the *Tempo Light Italic*
Tempo Medium, an intermediate sansserif
Tempo Bold, a strong new sansserif
Tempo Bold Condensed, a compressed sansserif
Tempo Heavy Condensed, shown here with *Italic*
Tempo Heavy, the boldest version

These faces are monotone in character, with almost no differences in the weight of strokes of letters, but some Sansserifs have marked contrasts and varying weight strokes. For example:

Ultra-Modern and *Ultra-Modern Italic*
Ultra-Modern Bold is very forceful
Radiant Bold is a New Type Design

Popular for headlines have been four old-type families which should be familiar to the copyeditor. They are Caslon, Bodoni, Goudy and Garamond.

Caslon. There is more contrast between the weight of the light and heavy strokes in Caslon than in Cheltenham. Caslon, an Old Style family, has established itself as the standard type of the Anglo-Saxon world, especially among discriminating advertisers. Its Italic is one of the most beautiful ever designed, and a bold face in several degrees of condensation and expansion is also available.

Caslon, an old style type design of popularity
Caslon Italic is the companion to the roman
Caslon Bold for Display Ad Work
Caslon Bold Condensed for Tight Lines

Bodoni. The series making up this Modern family represents the ultimate in contrast between light and heavy strokes. Observe that the serifs, which are flat and straight, are reduced to *hairlines*.

Bodoni Modern with *Bodoni Modern Italic*
Bodoni Bold and the *Bodoni Bold Italic*
Heavier Bodoni *with its italic*

Goudy. This type was designed by an American. It is made in a light and bold face—the latter and its Italic being used widely for heads two or more columns wide.

Goudy Oldstyle and *Goudy Italic are two*

Goudy Bold and *Goudy Bold Italic*

Garamond. The bold and bold italics of this Old Style family are standbys of composing rooms for headlines:

Garamond Oldstyle shown *with Garamond Italic*
Garamond Bold and *Garamond Bold Italic*

Type of varying weights and widths, but with the same general design, is said to belong to a *family*—for instance, Caslon, Garamond, Goudy, Bodoni and so on. In these names have been frozen interesting typographic history, for often they recall the artist who designed the types, or the place of their origin. Contrary to common opinion, type faces are still being designed, and numerous examples are put on the market every year.

Printer Arithmetic

Type size is measured in *points,* each point being approximately $\frac{1}{72}$ of an inch. Measurement is made from the top to the bottom of the *body* of the printed type itself, and thus is equivalent to the space occupied by a line. Here are examples in the Tempo family, showing only the size range in medium weight from 8- to 42-point.

Eight Point Tempo Medium Shown Here

Ten Point Tempo Medium Shown

Twelve Point Tempo Medium

Fourteen Point Tempo Me

Eighteen Point Temp

Twenty-four Po

Thirty Point T

Thirty-six t

42 Point

Common headline type sizes (in points) are: 14, 18, 24, 30, 36, 48, 60, 72, 84 and 96 and larger. A headline set 72 points is one-inch deep, 36-point type is ½-inch deep. Two lines of 36-point type should occupy an inch of space but the space used above, below and between type lines gives the headline more room than the size of the face itself would indicate.

The point system also is used to express the alphabet measurement of any given size of type, that is, the total (in points) of the lower case letters of the alphabet. The teletypesetter service, for instance, uses an alphabet measurement of 118.1 points for body type and 94 points for agate and a 12-pica column width.

The dimensions of the body of the type, or actual piece of metal on which the character appears, determine the depth. Nine lines of 8-point type occupy one inch of space. If 8-point type is set on a 9-point slug, it takes eight lines to fill an

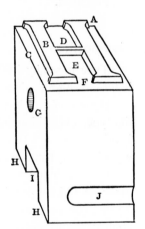

THE PARTS of foundry type: A, serif; B, stem or stroke; C, neck; D, hairline; E, counter; F, shoulder; G, pinmark; H, foot; I, groove; J, the nick.

inch. Extra white space between lines of type is accomplished by leading (*ledding*). A lead measures two points in depth; thus 7-point type leaded occupies the same space as 9-point type set solid.

Pica Measurement

The unit for determining the length of type lines, the widths of columns and the depths of columns is the *pica,* which is 12 points or $\frac{1}{6}$ of an inch. Most newspaper columns are two inches (12 picas) wide. A line of type or a column of type that measures three inches across is an 18-pica column.

Since a newspaper uses a standard size for its body type, some printers refer to picas as *ems.* An em is the square of any piece of type; thus an 8-point em is 8 points deep and 8 points wide. Half an em equals an *en.* To keep from confusing the two, some printers apply nicknames such as "mutton" for em, "nut" for en.

Agate, $5\frac{1}{2}$- or 6-point type, is used in a newspaper for tabular matter (markets, box-scores). The term also refers to the agate scale used to measure depth of advertising. Since the agate point size has a fraction, advertising men arbitrarily select 14 agate lines to represent an inch. An ad two columns wide and five inches deep is 10 column inches or 140 (agate) lines.

Composition

Type is set by hand, by manual and automatically-operated line- and letter-casting machines and by photographic processes.

Hand composition is as old as printing itself. Until the invention of the linotype, everything in a newspaper—text and display lines—was set by hand, a letter at a time. Hand composition is still used in newspaper shops, especially for some headlines and advertising display lines.

Ottmar Mergenthaler obtained a patent on an automatic line-casting machine (Linotype) in 1885 but the machine was not in operation until 1886. The line-caster was followed by other automatic typesetting machines: the monotype, a machine actuated by a perforated paper ribbon which casts single letters; the Ludlow typograph which casts handset matrices into a slug line; the teletypesetter, a mechanism attached to a line-casting machine which permits typesetting from a perforated tape.

Each of these principles has been adapted by the new process of typesetting—*photocomposition.* The *Photon* machine (Graphic Arts Research Foundation) consists of an electric typewriter, a telephone relay system and a photographic unit. Different fonts of type are arranged on a disc which rotates within the machine. A memory or storage system does the line justification. Each letter and space is photographed on a sensitized film which can then be developed and made into a plate.

The *Fotosetter* machine (Intertype Corporation) sets type photographically on film or photographic paper in one direct process. In appearance and operation, the *Fotosetter* is similar to the slug-casting machine. When the type line is justified it is photographed and the matrices are then distributed as in regular Intertype operation. The film or photographic paper is developed and made into a line engraving.

The *Linofilm* (Mergenthaler Lintoype company) is a two-unit machine. The keyboard unit produces regular typewritten copy and a perforated tape. The tape is then fed into a photographic unit which operates automatically to set type to be filmed.

The *Monophoto* (Lanston Monotype Machine company) is similar to the Monotype except that a photographic unit replaces the metal melting pot, the pump and the mold and the letters are made on film rather than in type.

The ATF-Hadego *Photocompositor* (American Type Founders Inc.) is designed for handset display composition. The handset matrix is a plastic block with a negative image of the letter on the face. The line is then reproduced on film.

Photocomposition is not yet in general use but it promises to be as revolutionary as the linotype was when it made its appearance near the close of the 19th century. It could end the career of the old "hot metal" process of typecasting.

Applying Some Fundamentals

The deskman can save himself trouble, and the newspaper money, by acquiring a few facts about his newspaper's operation. For example, he should know which headline faces and sizes are available on the line-casting machines, which have to be set by hand. He should limit himself to as few handsets and type faces as possible. If the plant has a Ludlow, the deskman might hold his handset orders to Ludlow matrices wherever possible. If he insists on using handset, he should try to limit orders to headlines of more than one column wide and to sizes larger than 24-point. The reason is obvious. Machines usually have all the variety needed for one-column heads. Handsetting a line of type smaller than 24-point is tedious and time-consuming.

The copyeditor should know the potentialities and the limitations of the typesetting machines. For instance, an operator who is setting straight matter can switch to an italic face or to boldface, but he can't do both unless he shifts magazines or has the line set on another machine. It is a good editing practice not to use italics or boldface for emphasis. It is sometimes easier to put quotes around a word or phrase than to use italic type. Boldface is properly used to call attention to names, especially in listings.

If the copyeditor yens for an unusual type combination, he would be wise to consult the composing-room foreman, explain what he wants and seek the cooperation of printers. It flatters a printer to get his opinion or judgment on typographical arrangement.

If there is a choice between an all-cap head and caps and lower case, the copyeditor takes the latter because it is easier to read. Before ordering a small cap head he finds out if the type is available on the machines.

Headline type smaller than 14-point offers little, if any, display. Even 14-point will look buried unless the face is extrabold. The width of the line should help determine the size of type to be used. Eighteen-point is readable in a two-column head, but perhaps 24-point is a better size; 18-point in three columns is tiresome. Large type sizes can be used in one-column heads, but above 36-point there won't be space to say anything unless condensed or extra-condensed type is used. Type for streamers ranges all the way from 36-point, which is quite small, to letters 180 points or more in height. Letters above 120 points are generally referred to as so-many-line letters, a line being 12 points. Thus, a 180-point letter would be a 15-liner.

Too many italic heads on a page tend to deemphasize rather than emphasize, which is the function of display type.

A good rule-of-thumb for bank sizes is to keep *banks* to a minimum of half the size of the main head. A bank for a 48-point main head would be 24 points according to this principle. A bank on a 24-point head probably would be 14 points instead of 12 points because the latter is too small and the size might not be available.

III. LEGIBILITY FACTORS

Type Size

Big type is easier to see than small type but not always easier to read. With the eye physically unable to get a sharp focus upon more than four or five letters of 7-point type, obviously there is a natural limit upon the size of type that should be used. The eye will jump along to read a banner head-line without rebelling, but 12-point is the optimum of practicability for body type in the standard 12-pica column. Experiments show a 14 per cent increase in visibility as type is raised from 7- to 9-point. The law of diminishing returns operates thereafter. Increasing from 8- to 10-point brings a gain of only 12 per cent.

What, then, is the ideal size type for newspapers? That depends upon the length of the type line, the legibility of the type and the white space surrounding type. Prior to World War II newspaper designers pleaded for wider columns, larger type and more white space. The *Linotype News* advocated a 16-pica column and Typographic Counselor Gilbert Farrar predicted a 24-pica column for newspapers.

Actually, the trend has been in the opposite direction, mainly because of the demands for economy due to the enormous increase in cost of news-print (from $46 to $130 a ton). The standard eight-column paper uses 12-pica widths and 6-point rules. Now that has been reduced, on many papers, to eight 11¼-pica columns with 3-point rules or eight 11½-pica columns with 4-point rules.

Many papers have adopted nine columns for classified advertising pages and some have gone to nine columns for general news pages and 10 columns for classified advertising pages. These use a larger page size, 11½-pica columns and 3-point rules. Some managers maintain that the nine-column page is only ⅝ inch wider than when they were using eight columns, 12-picas with 6-point rules. The trick has been to use high shrinkage page mats.

Of course, there is a limit to the compression. When excess shrinkage begins to tell on circulation and advertising, some means will have to be found to open the pages to allow more "breath." The Indianapolis *News* has gone to a six-column front page on its final markets edition. Each column is 15 picas and is set in 10-point type.

Selecting Line Lengths

Printers have a rule-of-thumb governing type size and line length. It is that the length of a line should be no longer than an alphabet and a half of lower case of the type face used. The narrower column can thus accommodate smaller type.

Newspapers sacrifice legibility and readability by adopting small type. Compensating factors are leading and better type designs.

Leading of the text type is important. Tests have proved that the addition of even ½-point space between lines of text on an 8-point slug is more legible than 8-point type set solid. As the size of type increases, more leading is needed. When text type is set two or more columns wide, generous leading enhances its legibility.

Readability Is Vital

The essential function of typography is to enable the reader to read with ease, speed and understanding. Newspapers are read by persons with defective vision and by those with normal vision. They are read under ideal lighting conditions and under poor lighting conditions. High standards sought by readers must be weighed against the economics of newspaper publishing.

But publishers will have to decide whether it is more economical to save newsprint than to save readers' eyes. It should be apparent that if a newspaper becomes easier to read it will be read by more persons—and when it becomes too hard to read the customers will turn to other media for information and entertainment.

Tabloid Sizes

Tabloid pages generally are about half the size of conventional newspapers, that is, about 15 inches deep and five (12-pica) columns wide. But the styles vary even more sharply than do those of standard-size newspapers. The New York *Daily News* uses a five (12-pica) column page. The Chicago *Sun-Times* has six (10½ picas) columns to a page, seven columns for classified ad pages. The Long Island *Newsday* presents a combination of two, three, four and six columns, with widths ranging from 10 to 29 picas.

14   Mastering the Headline Art

Some persons can pack a world of meaning into a few lines of type, but have no sense of form. Others can build a well-balanced, excellent-appearing head which, however, says nothing. The person who can do both is a good head-writer.—M. V. Atwood (1886–　　), *newspaper editor.*

I. WHY AND HOW HEADLINES CAME TO BE

There's History in Headlines

Headlines in American newspapers have recorded the history of the times. The form, or style, of the headline likewise has reflected the conditions of the country.

The first American newspapers, following English models, had no headlines. Often the only *display* the story got was a large initial capital letter starting the main story on the page. Later, some variety was achieved by keeping the first line the width of the column and indenting succeeeding lines of the opening paragraph—and all in slightly larger type than that in succeeding paragraphs.

As newspapers became vehicles for more exciting news, a technique was needed to call attention to big events. Hence, came the crossline or centered display line such as:

"NEWS FROM EUROPE"

For greater emphasis or if there were too many words for a single line, a second line was used. By centering the second line the editors devised a design known as the *inverted pyramid:*

FURTHER DETAILS OF THE
GREAT CRIME

207

A combination of crosslines and inverted pyramid lines (usually in descending type sizes) produced headlines of several *decks*. An example is found at the right.

Headlines grew vertically instead of horizontally because of mechanical restrictions (forms had to be locked tightly, especially on type-revolving presses). When the single crossline gave way to the double line, editors tried to achieve more symmetry by keeping both lines approximately the same length and indenting the second line. This resulted in the *stepped* (or *drop*) head, a design that was long to prove a strait-jacket to copyeditors because of the necessity of keeping the unit count of each line uniform.

QUEEN VICTORIA
DEAD AT OSBORNE

Then came multiple-column headlines, first two columns, then headlines stretching across the page. (See illustration, page 209.)

By World War I, newspapers were using type so large on major stories they had to fashion letters from wood because metal type of the size desired was not available. The number of decks increased so that in some cases they were telling practically the whole story. The Boston *Transcript,* for example, used 24 decks to a headline, occupying 16 inches of space for the headline alone.

MULTIPLE-DECK headline from the New York *Sun* (1865).

IMPORTANT.

——

ASSASSINATION

OF

PRESIDENT LINCOLN

——

The President Shot at the Theatre Last Evening.

——

SECRETARY SEWARD

DAGGERED IN HIS BED

BUT

NOT MORTALLY WOUNDED.

——

Clarence and Frederick Seward Badly Hurt.

——

ESCAPE OF THE ASSASSINS.

——

Intense Excitement In Washington.

——

SCENE AT THE DEATHBED OF MR. LINCOLN.

——

J. Wilkes Booth, the Actor, the Alleged Assassin of the President,

&c.,   &c.,   &c.

——

THE OFFICIAL DISPATCH.

——

1898-----DEFEAT OF SPAIN BRINGS U.S. TO FRONT AS WORLD POWER

SAN JOSE MERCURY.

VOL. LIII. SAN JOSE, CALIFORNIA: MONDAY MORNING, JULY 4, 1898.—EIGHT-PAGE EDITION. NO. 185.

GLORIOUS NEWS FOR
DAY WE CELEBRATE

Bold Sampson Utterly Destroys the Spanish Fleet Under Cervera in the Harbor of Santiago.

STARS AND STRIPES WILL CERTAINLY WAVE OVER THE CITY TO-DAY.

WASHINGTON, July 3.--The following dispatch was received at the War Department: "Playa del Este, July 3.--Siboney office confirms the statement that all the Spanish fleet except one warship was destroyed and that the ships are burning on the beach. The sight was witnessed by Captain Smith, who told the opera tor. No doubt of its correctness. ALLEN, Signal Officer."
WASHINGTON, July 3.--The fol lowing cable dispatch was given out at the White House: "Playa del Este, July 3.--The destruction of Cervera's fleet is confirmed. "ALLEN, Lieutenant-Colonel."

Newspapers Become Streamlined

After World War I came moderation in headline styles. In 1918, Benjamin Sherbow of the New York *Tribune* discarded all-capital headlines in favor of caps and lower case and lopped off some of the decks. The Chicago *Tribune* also discarded most of its decks.

Streamlining captured the imagination of America and newspapers followed suit by simplifying makeup and adopting a flush-left style for headlines that allowed more white space around the heads. In September 1928, the *Linotype News* (trade publication) presented sample pages showing new headline styles. One of the first newspapers to adopt the new streamlined makeup with simplified headlines was the New York *Morning Telegraph* in December 1928, its makeup designed by Heyworth Campbell of New York. The new pattern caught on quickly. In less than a year after the streamlined style had been introduced, at least 75 weekly newspapers and school publications had begun to revamp their makeup.

Decks Are Disappearing

Decks are still being used on some newspapers, especially for top of page headlines (a multiple-column or *banner* headline at the top usually requires a drop or *read-out* deck), but most papers, even foreign periodicals, now use no more than the main headline to summarize the story.

Readership studies indicate that readers do not read the decks. Today's informal headline often has resulted in much careless headline writing but the unit count is not so meticulous and today's headlines doubtless make more sense than did those of the "old days."

If a deck is used, it usually amplifies the information already given and, if possible, adds a new detail. If the top deck does not give the subject, the second deck is compelled to carry it. Decks should be counted so that words do not break from one line to another. The deck should not repeat words used in the main head.

Experimentation Goes On

Most editors and copyeditors are of a restless breed, never satisfied with the old, always trying something new. If they weren't that way, journalism would lack the dynamics that have brought progress in summarizing and organizing the news, luring the reader into the text quickly and brightening the pages.

Mother, 3 Children Killed

Princeton, Ind.,

Feb. 12 (AP)

Kerosene thrown on an open coal fire exploded tonight and a young mother and her three small daughters burned to death.

—Decatur (Ill.) Sunday *Herald and Review*

MIAMI GRADS

Are To Be Invited

To Cooperate With University Of Cincinnati Alumni In Interest Of Charity Grid Game.

—Cincinnati *Enquirer*

TO SURGERY 50 TIMES

MORE OPERATIONS AHEAD FOR A KANSAS GIRL.

Margie Jean Orton, 10, Victim of Odd Accident, Attends School Regularly Between Trips to Hospital.

—Kansas City *Star*

The Wisconsin *State-Journal* once had a trial run with a "spotlight" edition, devoting the front page to headlines and indexes. Tabloids frequently experiment with heads set up almost like display advertisements. The Decatur (Ill.) Sunday *Herald and Review* sometimes emphasizes time and place by playing them up in separate lines. The Cincinnati *Enquirer* reads from one deck to another. The Kansas City *Star* has an individual head style. (*See page 210.*)

Students should watch for variants from the norms of headline forms, then study them. What was the *idea* in the mind of the creator? Maybe he was groping for a way to save the typesetter's time and cut costs. Maybe he was fumbling for a technique to speed reading. He might have been searching for a new device to suggest to readers the relative importance of news-stories. Maybe his motive was esthetic—or simply a desire to be different.

Whether new ideas should change old ways-of-doing is, of course, a question for a newspaper's policy makers. There's an understandable tendency to cling to practices that have proved successful and are accepted by readers. But the sharp elbow of competition has nudged many an American newspaper in recent years to restyle its headline schedule.

II. THE MECHANICS OF HEADLINE MAKING

How Size Is Decided

All newspapers, from the smallest weekly to the largest daily, want to display their news wares effectively. They do it chiefly through headlines— some in light type and multiple decks, some in extrabold type and no decks. Their purpose is to call attention to the news loudly or mildly.

Headlines come in all widths—from one column to eight columns— with type sizes ranging from body type (usually 8-point) up to 120-point and even larger. The head size usually depends upon the significance of the story and its placement on the page (*makeup*). The main story of the day gets the largest headline above the fold. A long story usually gets a bigger headline than a short story because a long story has to break over to two or more columns.

Makeup of the page helps determine the size headlines to be used. The front page must have a variety of single and multicolumn heads, headlines in large type and fillers with small type. A story at the top of the page may get a one-column head, but below the fold the same story may be put in a single-line, six-column head. On inside pages, newsstories have to be displayed boldly enough to compete with the large type and illustrations in advertisements.

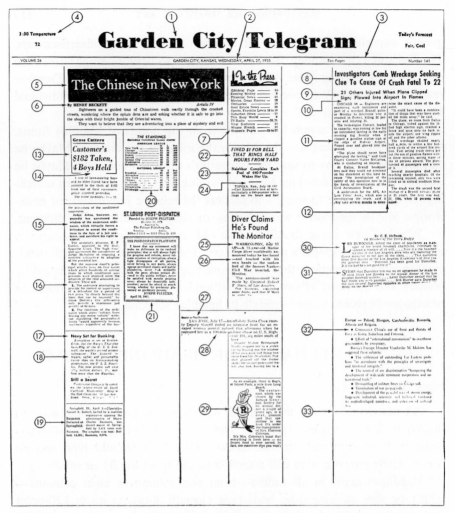

NEWSPAPER PAGE ANATOMY

1. nameplate, 2. newspaper dateline, 3. folio (or top of page rule), 4. ear, 5. reversed plate, 6. boldface byline, 7, index, 8. flush-left head in 24-point Spartan condensed, 9. flush-left deck in 14-point Spartan heavy, 10. six-point lead (or slug), 11. body type (8-point Corona on 9-point slug), 12. column rule (hairline on 6-point slug), 13. Bodoni italic head with overline (or kicker), 14. broken box, 15. boldface paragraph, 16. numbered paragraphs, 17. subhead (boldface), 18. paragraph in italics, 19. marginal (or thumbnail) head, 20. agate sports table, 21. editorial page masthead, 22. all-cap head (stepped), 23. inverted pyramid deck, 24. jim (3-em) dash, 25. dateline, 26. ten-point boldface single column lead, 27. credit line, 28. ten-point double column lead, 29. thumbnail sketch (type set 6 picas), 30. four-line initial capital, 31. two-line initial capital, 32. marker dot, 33. cutoff rule.

There is no single criterion for determining a headline size. A banner head can be used on a two-paragraph story; a mediocre story can justify a four-column headline on the inside if it is used to fill a hole between an advertisement and the folio line. A headline is relative to the news of the moment. A story may earn a banner head in the first edition, drop to a two-column head in the second edition and wind up under a one-column head on the inside in the final edition. When the day's news is big, the headlines are big. But on some newspapers when the news is light, big headlines are used to eat up space. Headline sizes depend upon newspaper policy. Some carry a banner every day, no matter what the news; some seldom carry a banner (cynics say the conservative Kansas City *Star* is saving its banner type for the second coming). If paper A plays up a story in big display lines, rival paper B is likely to play down the same story (unless, of course, a smash play is unavoidable).

Many beginners have a tendency to be too modest in displaying the news. They overwork one-column heads in 14-, 18- and 24-point type and neglect headlines two columns and larger in 24-point or larger.

A page without multiple column heads is monotonous and inevitably results in a vertical appearance, a violation of today's trend in makeup.

More on Headline Schedules

That most newspapers have *hed skeds* (headline schedules) to designate each style and size of type was noted in Chapter 5. But beginning copyeditors should know American journalistic practice is not uniform in this field. There are at least four systems:

1. *Numbering.* Each head, from the smallest to the largest, is assigned a number—which the copyeditor must indicate on his headline copy. Thus he may call for "No. 1" (or "line"), "No. 5" or whatever. Some papers reserve numbers from 1 up to 10 for one-column heads, numbers from 20 to 30 for two-column heads, and so on.

2. *Letters.* This follows a similar pattern, but with letters instead of numbers. Often the column width is also indicated, *e.g.,* "2-A" (a two-column "A" head), "4-F" (four-column "F"), etc.

3. *Type Style.* Here the name of the type to be used is stated. A notation "2–36–2– Metro" would mean two lines, in 36-point size of the typeface known as "Metro," set two columns wide.

4. *Special Names.* Individual papers sometimes sanction by custom their own names for certain types. "Railroad," for example, might mean a bold arrangement of type that some forgotten copyeditor in an imaginative moment

thought looked like a locomotive. And "Peanut" might be the smallest type used.

Head Copy for the Printer

When the head is to be in small type that can be conveniently set by the same machine that composes the story, it need not be written on a separate sheet and for obvious reasons requires no guideline. It is simply written above the newsstory, with a notation on the size and style in which it is to be set.

All major heads are written on a separate sheet. Usually they are folded on the outside of the story copy and sent to the printer.

Copyeditors must be mindful always not only of the editorial-department deadlines but also the need to cut time and save costs in the composing room. That's why it's important to draw guiding lines on head copy so the printer will instantly know which head is flush, dropline, inverted pyramid or whatever it may be. Special instructions should be clearly indicated: *e.g.,* 'bc" (boldface caps), "bf" (boldface) "clc" (caps and lower case). Ringing these instructions is advisable.

Running the Story Over

Many readers are lost when stories *jump* (continue) to another page— hence the zeal of newspapers to develop jump heads that will recapture attention.

If the story calls for a jump (or *runover*) the head-writer writes the jump line on a separate sheet and at the same time he prepares copy for the major headline. If the jump repeats the original headline, the compositor is directed to reset the original. Here are two styles:

Just Things

(Continued from Page One)

Giant Press Makes Real Diamonds

Continued from First Page

least—give you gems for rings or necklaces or affect prices or values of diamonds used as gems. They will very likely go to

Boxing the Head

Almost any kind of headline can be boxed. Boxes range from two heavy lines, one above and one below, to complete enclosures with a plain or fancy rule or a three-way box.

The simplest box is formed by placing a column-width rule above the headline and below the story and indenting the body type:

Coon Is Dying to Put in Plug for New Raceway

DETROIT, MICH. — (*AP*) — The untimely death of a raccoon will delay the opening of a new auto speedway at suburban Flat Rock for a week.

The unfortunate coon crawled into the main drain tile at the newly completed speedway. Torrential rains fell, filling the tile and drowning it.

The animal's body plugged the tile, and when the rain ended, two feet of water stood in the speedway bowl.

STORY AND HEAD RULED TOP AND BOTTOM WITH TYPE INDENTED

City to Honor Washington; Not Meters

Banks, courts, the postoffice and all city, state and federal offices in metropolitan Denver will be closed T u e s d a y—Washington's birthday.

Retail firms generally will be open for business as usual. So will Denver parking meters. Washington's birthday is not one of the six yearly meter holidays.

Postmaster F r a n k A. Pomponio said only special delivery mail will be handled Tuesday. Windows at the main Denver postoffice and all branches and stations will be closed.

BEN DAY FULL BOX

U.S. Weather Bureau Says:

Providence and vicinity— Cloudy, warm and humid this afternoon and tonight with scattered showers and thunderstorms this afternoon and early tonight and highest temperature in the low 80s; lowest tonight in the low 70s.

Sunday partly cloudy warm

highest temperature in the middle 80s.

Southerly winds 20 to 25 miles per hour and gusty to 40 miles per hour in thunderstorms this afternoon and early tonight. Diminishing southwesterly winds, becoming 10 to 15 later tonight. Gentle to

FULL BOX WITH HEADLINE ON REVERSED PLATE

SECOND GUESS

Martinez' 'Big Test' Due Monday Night

By Jack Carberry

BROKEN BOX

Timely Reply
To Sexy Error

WASHINGTON, (UP)—A mother
in California wrote her congressman to ask if the government had

THREE-WAY BOX

In Today's Post

RULED HEAD

Handy Headline Words

Out of necessity for concision has come a special vocabulary used in headlines. Often these words are overused, even abused. Some newspapers taboo certain ones. Because they occupy so little space, some words are worked to death in headlines. Head-writers need good judgment.

Probe, Quiz, Grill, Study are headline words—all serving to replace the long verb *Investigate. Senator* frequently appears in a headline, *Representative* almost never because it is too long, especially for a one-column head. So, enter *Solon,* an overworked word referring to a legislator or congressman, both representative and senator.

Words like *criticize, attack, condemn, upbraid, castigate* are seldom good headline words because of their length. *Hit,* on the other hand, takes up little space; consequently, it abounds in newspaper headlines.

If *hit* becomes too monotonous, *rap* might be substituted, or *flay* or *slap. Predict, report, advise, speculate* are good words, but useless in a headline if space is limited. So readers come to understand that *see* and *eye* express another's opinion.

A national leader with a name Taft is a joy to the copyeditor. Certainly it is easier to fit that name into a headline than Roosevelt or Eisenhower. The head-writer must grab a short identification—*F. D. R., Ike* or *Chief. Reds* is overworked in headlines, but it has to be because *Commu-*

nists is a space-eater. The copyeditor doesn't think in terms of airplanes; he uses *planes, ships, jets.*

Shortened forms, inappropriate in the story, are permissible in headlines: *Thai* for Thailand, *Muny* league for Municipal league, *Gotham* for New York City, *Amvets* for American Veterans of World War II, *Dems* for Democrats and, occasionally, *Grads* for Graduates. Use *Pct.* instead of the % sign because some line-casting machines do not have the % character.

III. HOW TO WORD HEADLINES

A Facile Vocabulary

Mechanical transmission of copy edited at a central point tends to reduce the copyeditor's "copy fixing" load. But all copy, whether TTS or locally produced, needs headlines. And the beginning copyeditor should give specialized attention not only to the techniques and mechanics of the art but to the development of the mental equipment needed to extract the vital elements from a story and to compress them to vivid phrases.

This starts and ends with words. A copyeditor needs a broad vocabulary and a facile skill to use it. All that has been said on this point earlier applies with special force to the headline-writing art. Synonyms are especially valuable and a dictionary of synonyms should be in every copyeditor's kit of tools. Fortunately, English is rich in substitute words, but even among synonyms there are shadings of meaning and overtones of connotation that every copyeditor should know.

More Handy Headline Words

Here are some more words—and their more ponderous synonyms. Every copyeditor should be sufficiently familiar with them to know when they should not be used.

Accord—agreement	Boost—increase	Fake—counterfeit
Agog—astonished		Fight—campaign
Aid—assist	Chief—president	Flaunt—display
Aide—assistant	Cite—honor	Flout—insult
	Clash—controversy	
Bare—reveal		Grab—acquire
Bid—invitation	Dick—detective	Group—committee
Body—group	Dip—pickpocket	
Bolt—desert	Dope—predict	Hike—increase

Hold—arrest   Parley—conference   Shun—abandon
Hold—retain   Pennsy—Penn. R.R.   Slate—schedule
Hurt—injure   Peril—danger   Slay—murder
                               Plot—conspire   Spur—encourage
Laud—praise   Prod—instigate   Step—progess

Mate—husband (or wife) Quit—resign   Take—arrest

Nab—arrest   Raid—search   Unit—committee
Named—elected,   Rip—denounce   Urge—promote
    appointed
                               Scout—doubt
Oust—expel   Scrap—contend   Vow—pledge
                               Set—arrange
Pair—couple   Shakeup—reorganize   Win—victory

Such Interesting People

Mythology, literature and slang have reinforced the tension copyeditors maintain to "type" news-making people in headline words. Here's a veritable gallery of such celebrities:

Adonis   Dr. Jekyll   John Bull   Paul Bunyan
Amazon   Dr. Watson   John Doe   Portia
Ananias   Don Juan   Juliet
                                                  Romeo
Bluebeard   Enoch Arden   Lothario   Samaritan
                                  Mars   Sherlock Holmes
Cinderella   Fagin   Mr. Hyde   Simon Legree
Croesus   Munchhausen   Svengali
Cupid   Hercules
                                  Neptune   Thespian
David Harum   Izaak Walton   Nimrod   Uncle Sam
Davy Jones
Diana   John Barleycorn   Old Sol   Venus

Headlines 'Play' the Story

By the time the professional copyeditor has run his pencil through a newsstory he has, as a general rule, formulated a headline and needs only to transfer it to paper. But the beginner faces difficulties.

His entire training has been in the direction of expanding his thought, yet now he is under the necessity of contracting it; there is no alternative. This process must not be allowed to become purely mechanical if the best results are to be attained. The importance of writing ideas into headlines, and of writing them coherently and intelligibly so that any average reader may understand what is meant without first reading the story and then reverting to the headline, cannot be overemphasized.

The task takes on understandable form when it is remembered that the cue for the headline is usually found in the lead and that the lead is built on the pattern of *what happened*. If it is a summary lead, the probabilities are that the headline should also summarize; if it is a lead that plays up some outstanding feature, it is likely that the headline should do the same.

The writer has written his story in the hope that it will attract attention and will be read; *i.e., that it will get the play.* The news editor assigns the story to a position on the page and designates a type that will get play. All this is wasted, however, if the copyeditor creates nothing but a dull, lifeless, uninteresting, insignificant headline. He might as well go back to the early days of newspapering when news was lumped under the leaden headline: *Interesting News.*

Four Important Questions. . . .

The experienced copyeditor, confronted with a story, will ask himself, perhaps unconsciously, these questions:

1. What is its *action*? This is by far the most important idea to be carried up into the headline, for it is this element that reflects the most interesting phase of this little drama of human life. It is action or movement that makes the most elemental bid for eye attention so the first rule is to put a verb in the headline, one that shouts action—specific action. "Man attacked by animal" won't do. What animal? What kind of attack? "Dog *Bites* Man" is the headline phrase.

2. What is its *feature*? Does it have one dominating, graphic fact that gives significance, amuses or entertains? Almost certainly it should go into the head. "Foggy Weather" won't grab the reader's attention, but this will:

Hudson Valley Fog Puts
Drivers in Shadowland

3. What is its *essential fact*? It may be one or more of the question-answering elements, but without it the headline would be vague, wobbly, perhaps meaningless. When the president of a state university fired his new son-in-law, as comptroller of the university, because of a law prohibiting

relatives from serving on the same staff, newspapers over the nation played the one essential element of the story in the headline: **Gets Wife, Loses Job.**

4. What is its *time element*? When did it happen? If it is today, the present tense may carry that idea, but if the report is a second-day chapter, the second-day or follow-up ideas must be worked in. Headlines use the present, not the past, tense even if the action in the story happened in the past. Yesterday's headline said a plane was missing; today's must tell the progress of the search: A key word orients the reader, in this case "missing DC6":

**Nightfall Cuts
Search for
Missing DC6**

There are several combinations of these four basic ideas. Most stories have many phases of action and many features. Many carry all four basic ideas in their text. Some have only a single motivating idea to justify their use, or a single feature. The headline writer exercises fine discrimination in selecting what is to be played up and the success of the reporter's effort largely depends upon his skill.

Try Fresh Start

Words and phrases in the copy usually clue the headline writer. Sometimes the wording is appropriate and dynamic, but the composition just won't fit the space limitations. The trick then is to try to find shorter synonyms to substitute for longer words. If that doesn't work, the headwriter should try juggling the lines and if the result still isn't right the only solution is to start all over, probably with a different slant.

The headline need not tell the obvious. The president is the only person authorized to sign a bill passed by congress. **New GI Education Bill Signed** has as much meaning as **President Signs New GI Bill.**

Nor should the headline writer struggle to get grand jury in a headline describing an indictment. Since only a grand jury can return an indictment, the phrase "jury indicts" is sufficient, or "man indicted" implies action by the grand jury.

A copyeditor is expected to find a headline to fit the specifications assigned; rarely does he confess he can't write the headline and ask for a longer head count. Of course he can't do the impossible. He can't fit a name like Esterbrookshire into a one-column 24-point all-cap head no matter how adept he is in composing headlines. If the name has to go in the headline, the copyeditor will have to have a headline specification that will accommodate the long name.

If the headwriter gets stuck, he can get help from the slotman. He should not bother a fellow deskman to write the headline for him.

Improving Headlines

Heads must convey not merely the news, but its quintessence. If they are to be effective, they should shoot fast and straight without a surplus word. A headline that does not conform to these requirements will harm a story instead of helping to "sell" it; if it is stupid, the reader is warranted in assuming the story may likewise be stupid; it tells nothing, possibly the story also is a vacuum.

Experienced copyeditors rarely have any trouble in formulating the one headline that fits the story in hand; it is a matter of habit with them to pick the graphic, dynamic words and phrases. But the beginner is likely to accept the first headline that meets space requirements and let it go at that.

He need not do this. He can take his crude, commonplace and awkward headline and, by more picturesque words and more apt constructions, transform it. He needs but a good vocabulary, a thorough understanding of the story and the alchemy of the imagination. If he makes use of these to work over his headline he will be surprised to see his baser language transmuted into a species of verbal gold.

This is the whole secret of improving headlines.

Writing develops with practice. By training himself to visualize stories in terms of headline phrases, the copyeditor soon develops a knack for writing compact, meaningful headlines.

Sports Present Special Problems

The headline over the sports story should be as colorful as the story itself, but the sports deskman should use restraint to prevent headlines from becoming top-heavy with slang. Allowances are expected because less formality exists on the sports pages than on other pages. Most sports followers recognize the more familiar titles of the star performers.

Football, basketball, baseball, ice hockey, swimming are long-unit words, especially for the heavy type found on the sports page. The head-writer has to have a lot of space to fit Utah State Agricultural College into a headline. He reaches for a shorter form, in this case *Utags.* Basketball players become *cagers,* ice hockey players *icers,* swimmers *mermen* or *tankers,* football players *gridders.* Philadelphia Athletics becomes *A's,* St. Louis Cardinals becomes simply *Cards,* a team representing the University of California at Los Angeles becomes *Uclans.*

Prep in a sports headline means high school; *Parok* means parochial school; *Army* means United States Military Academy; *Flag Chase* means pennant race; *Five* means basketball team; *Pro* means professional; *Go* means bout or contest.

Sports page readers are lost unless they understand the following: *Demons, Eagles, Cubs, Bears, Bruins, Buffs, Blues, Mackmen, Blue Devils, Engineers, Trotters, Frogs, Hilltoppers.*

Many of the headline verbs are colorful although they are anything but literal: *spanks, romps, snags, pelts, trounces, jars, dumps, drops, smears, takes, downs, measures, ices, cops, spurts, belts, upsets.* If the headline reads: **Frisco Tops In Defense,** the reader is to understand that the University of San Francisco has the best defensive record among major collegiate basketball teams.

In one generation, *Babe* in a headline referred to George Herman Ruth, in a later generation *Babe* referred to Mildred Didrikson Zaharias.

The sports page has become a specialized section. But that does not mean that sports editors should not use English that nonexperts can understand.

More care can be given to prevent misuse and abuse of the language. Here is an example: **Lakewood Can Cinch Title Tonight.** The verb, of course, should be *clinch* which means to make conclusive. Cinch is a strong girth for a pack or saddle.

IV.   A HEADLINE WRITER'S GUIDE

Other Do's and Don't's

On some newspapers, anything goes in headwriting as long as the headline fits. On others, the editor insists that headlines have style and precision. The top line, in particular, should carry as much of the meaning of the story as possible. That means the top line should not end with a preposition, a hyphenated word or a verb part. Try to write each line in such fashion that it will stand alone and make complete sense.

1. *The first requirement is that the headline be accurate.* Here are examples of sleepy editing:

1000 Students Register at CU

BOULDER, Feb. 12—Nearly 1000 more students registered for the spring semester at the University of Colorado than were enrolled last spring.

But the school's total enroll-

MENACE ALLEGED BY PROTESTANTS

Petitions asking the board of supervisors to refuse approval of a plat for a cemetery in Emery Park were filed with the board of supervisors yesterday by Victor H. Verity, attorney for the petitioners.

The petitions bear 55 names. They argue that the proposed establish-

On some days everything seems to go wrong:

Freedom Crusade Sky Drop At Noon On Tuesday

The "Freedom Sky-Drop" is to occur in Boulder at noon Friday, as the article in Saturday's Camera stated. The head, however, gave the date as noon Monday.

2. *Write headlines that can have only one interpretation.* Fixations on the part of copyeditors result in *two-faced* and sometimes absurd headlines.

Free Trips to Europe Await Girl Sewers

Two Colorado girls between the ages of 14 and 22 who are nimble with a needle may win free trips to Europe, cash and prizes.

The awards will be given to winners of "Make It Yourself With

Winners of the Colorado championships will be sent to Ft. Worth by the F. W. Woolworth Co. to compete in the national contest in January 1956.

State prizes will include travel,

Conscious Trouble Nets SF Man Year

SIOUX FALLS (Æ)— Richard Tolliver, 23, Sioux Falls, was sentenced to one year in the state penitentiary by Circuit Judge Roy D. Burns today, but a suspension of the sentence appears certain.

Other examples of *two-faced heads* (susceptible of two different readings):

Fencers Club Victor

Fly to Attend Venice Art Show

Attorney Says He'll Have Baby in Court

Pair Held in Watch Case

Barrier to Press Ends

India Cuts Water, Pakistani Says

Holland Visits Mexico

Policeman Shot on S. Side

Anna Russell Hit as Opera's Witch

Steers of Teenage Girls are Champs

Two-faced heads can be easily avoided. After writing a headline, read it twice: first for the meaning you intended, then for the meaning someone *might* get out of it. If it's two-faced, better chuck it.

3. *Avoid label heads.* Make your headline say something. A dull, wooden headline, without life and motion, has killed many a good story. It is called a label head because it has no more character than the label of a tomato can. In this category are the dull standing heads (sometimes called *stet heds*) like **Club Notes** or **Police News** and over-generalized phrases like **Local Man Dies**. Also avoid dead heads: **Scholar Wins Award.**

4. *Don't write a book in the headline.* Avoid packing the headline so tightly that it is so overcrowded with facts as to become nearly meaningless: **Prison to Take Boy Girl Wed to Save. Jews Score Bard Fete on Play** (story of protest over including the Merchant of Venice in Shakespearean festival). **Calmness, Brightness Regained by Nativity Scene Despite Truant.**

5. *Avoid awkward verbal breaks.* Ease of reading is a headline goal; you lose it when you turn out copy like this:

Biggest West River Calf
Show In History Coming Up

Shirtsleeve
Weather Good
For Few Days

Hill City
Shooting Up
To Attorneys

Pioneer Devils
Lake Woman Dies

6. *Don't jump to conclusions.* The story said a physician apparently chose suicide to a federal morals charge trial, his body was found in his apartment, a .45 caliber pistol was found near the body and there was one bullet hole behind the victim's right ear. Here are headlines from two newspapers carrying the story:

Doctor, Indicted	**Doctor Accused**
On Morals Charges,	**In Morals Case**
Commits Suicide	**Shot to Death**

The first headline presumes evidence to be fact. The police chief said in his opinion the doctor committed suicide, but there still had been no inquest or official determination of suicide. Until there is, the headline writer should stick to the known facts in describing the story to the reader.

Another instance: Police arrest two boys and charge them with committing theft of tools from a garage. The headline writer convicts the boys, even before they have been brought to trial, when he writes: **Two Boys Arrested for Theft of Tools.**

Actually, they were arrested on a charge of committing theft, or in connection with the theft of tools. These qualifying words usually cannot go into a headline because of space limitation, but if the head-writer uses "in" instead of "for" he implies, at least, that the arrest is in connection with a tool theft.

The story says the United States has issued a strongly-worded protest to Russia. That can mean only one thing to the unthinking copyeditor who writes: **US Issues Ultimatum to Soviets.**

In diplomatic parlance, there is a difference between a strong protest and an ultimatum. Ultimatum is the final warning or proposition. If it is ignored, the result is war. But protests, even strongly-worded ones, have been defied and no war has resulted.

The story says the Senate agricultural committee has passed a new parity bill. The careless copyeditor writes **Senate Passes Parity Bill** instead of **Senate Group OKs Parity Bill.**

7. *Don't editorialize or propagandize.* Avoid expressing an opinion or drawing a conclusion of your own in a headline; opinions of others, if ascribed to their source, may be used. Notice the editorializing in these headlines: **Molotov Sneers at Proposal; Congress Urged to Curb Menace of Comics; Labor Chieftain Bellows Denial He Is Union Czar; CIO Mob Attacks Police; Police Thugs Slug Pickets.**

In the same category because it often has the effect of editorializing is the imperative head: **Overlook Traffic Tickets.**

Question heads frequently have the effect of editorializing: **Ike Has New Trick Up His Sleeve?** There are times, of course, when a question head is justified, but they should be used sparingly. Newspapers are supposed to answer questions, not ask them.

8. *Use dramatic, image-filled words.* But avoid overworked and slang expressions.

Blast is a powerful headline verb but if the head-writer lets the mayor blast council members and students blast Greek-letter fraternities, the word *blast* is no longer appropriate when the writer wishes to show that army *x* delivered a stunning blow to army *z*. *Car crash* carries more impact than car wreck. Note some other combinations: *plunges,* falls; *tabs,* terms; *gears,* prepares; *jolts,* shakes; *pact,* agreement.

Although the headline should be as colorful and dramatic as the head-writer can make it, the headline must not distort or exaggerate. A headline must promise no more than the story offers, but it should never present less.

Some headline words are abused because they are inexact or overworked—an example: *clobber.* The head-writer soon finds that he must overwork some words for the sake of brevity; an example is *set* or *slated* for scheduled.

9. *Avoid negative headlines.* Sometimes, of course, the news is the negation. Note these examples:

New Storm Not	**No Federal**
Due to Be as	**Law Covers**
Severe as Last	**Baby Selling**

The first is a poor headline but can easily be turned into a positive statement: **New Storm Due, but Blizzard Held Unlikely.** The second example is justified because it tells the news—that a federal law is lacking to curb illegal adoptions.

10. *Be wary of names.* Names or nicknames of prominent persons may be used in headlines, but not those of relatively unknown persons. *Eden* is better (and shorter) than British Prime Minister. Names that recur frequently in the news may be used in the headline because the reader recognizes them. Examples are heads of states (Nehru), industrialists (Ford), scientists (Salk).

11. *Never use the past tense.* Use the historical present to get the tone of immediacy. There is lack action in this: **Rally Day Was Marked by Baptist Church Sunday.** Of course, a present tense verb should never be used with a statement of a past or future event, such as "dies yesterday." Just "dies" is sufficient.

12. *Use passive voice when needed.* In most writing the active voice is preferred, but in the headline the passive is sometimes better when the subject is implied and you get the feature of the story in the first line.

Poor	*Better*
POLICE NAB 12	**12 SEIZED**
IN CAFE RAID	**IN CAFE RAID**

13. *Avoid starting a headline with a verb.* **Claims Man She Wed Already Had One Spouse** is an example. If it is necessary to start a headline with a verb, the next deck should start with the subject. Likewise, avoid starting a headline with an infinitive: **To Wage Battle on High Taxes, Landlords Say.**

14. *Don't repeat words in the headline.* If the headline has a lower deck,

also avoid repeating words used in the top lines. Get synonyms, unless repetition adds flavor:

Fake Detectives
Give Fake Gem
For Fake Reward

15. *Catch the spirit of the story.* If it is a feature, either humorous or pathetic, that depends upon its climax for effectiveness, don't destroy it in the head. Arouse the curiosity of the reader but don't give away the writer's surprise. Some headline classics follow:

Call Army's Ban
On Diet of Beans
Half Baked Idea
—Chicago *Tribune*

Gridiron Club Serves Up
A Prime Rib to Politicians
—Detroit *News*

Science to Take Drunk Apart
To Find What Makes Him Hic
—Dallas *Morning News*

Hives Give Heaves
To Aging Queens
—Longview (Wash.) *Daily News*

Economy Wave
Washes Many
Out of Jobs
—Seattle *Post-Intelligencer*

Sh! Don't Look
But Emily Post
Spilled a Berry
—Chicago *Daily News*

Milkman Wants
Soured Love Put
Thru Separator
—Chicago *Tribune*

Teapot Tempest
Rages in Britain
As Prices Soar
—Richmond *Times-Dispatch*

To Valley Forge
Again, By George
—Chicago *Daily News*

'Plumber's' Pause
For Poodles' Paws
Proves Profitable
—Detroit *Free Press*

16. *Use appropriate humor.* Don't write heads so fanciful, so loaded with metaphor and allegory, that none but yourself will understand what you are trying to say. Fanciful heads that are easily understood are to be encouraged, however, for they lend zest to the newspaper's columns. In the west a cowboy is a *cow-puncher* or a *cowpoke,* thus *'Poke* is an acceptable headline word to western readers, doubtless meaningless to eastern readers.

A generation or so ago editing was a more leisurely process and not a few papers regularly regaled readers with fanciful heads. Typical labels over the columns of births, marriages and deaths: **Hatched, Matched, Dispatched.** Some turned to rhyme:

SHE WAS A WIDOW

Fat and Fair; He Was
A Lover in Despair
He Wooed and Married and
Then He Forsook Her
He Sighed for Her Love—Now
She Sues for His Lucre.

Today's headlines likewise frequently turn up in rhyme:

Convention Parley
Called by Farley
—Atlanta *Constitution*

Never Saw a Purple Cow, Never Even
Hoped;
Sees Purple, Sees Cow; Bossy Had
Been Doped
—Dallas *Morning News*

Better a straight head than a feature head if the humor is misplaced. The classic example of a head that offended taste is **"Jerked to Jesus,"** said to have appeared over a story of a hanging. Puns, rhyme, alliteration and repetition when used with skill and good judgment give sparkle to a page.

(NEVER use an obscene or off-color slugline because as sure as you do that will be the one time the printer will forget to remove the slug before he matches headline and story. Printers are fine friends but don't tempt them.)

17. *Make headlines symmetrical.* Write headline copy line for line as you wish it to appear in print. Even the greater freedom allowed by flush-left headlines should not be abused:

Boy's Cat
Wins Fight with
Dog

Man
Fatally Dies
Today

The flush-left headline is intended to provide white space, but too-ragged lines are displeasing to the eye. A one-line crossline should fill out two-thirds of the column width, unless the paper has a style that specifies otherwise.

Subheads need not be counted if the copyeditor uses no more than three medium-length words. If copy is set double-column measure, the subheads will be larger than usual. These should be written on a separate sheet and slugged the same as the headline copy.

18. *Use correct capitalization, punctuation.* When headlines are set in cap and lower case, the customary style is to start each line and every important word (not prepositions under five letters) with capital letters. The first word of each line is capitalized.

Figures are usually preferred to spelled-out numbers in headlines unless the number contains numerous digits: **$100 Billion Road Fund** not **$100,000,-000,000 Road Fund.** Lump sums should be spelled out: **Thousands Join Easter Parade.** Some newspapers frown upon the practice of starting the top line with a figure though the usage enables you to pack more news and essential news into the head.

A half quote is preferred to a full quote (because of appearance and because half quotes occupy less space than full quotes). A comma in a headline replaces *and,* serves as a semicolon and frequently carries the weight of a full stop.

Plane Lost,
16 Aboard

Use a dash in the middle of a line, a colon or comma at the end of a line:

School May Go   **Tabbert Unique:**
Coed—Gals Agog   **Shuns Publicity**

19. *Abbreviate when necessary* but do it only when abbreviation is unmistakable as to meaning. Some accepted headline abbreviations: *D. A.* for District Attorney, *A-Test* for Atomic Test, *Jaycees* for Junior Chamber of Commerce, *GI* for serviceman, *Tram* for Tramway, and all recognized abbreviations. US and UN are abbreviated in headlines whether used as adjectives or nouns. Occasionally, an apostrophe can be used to indicate omission of a letter: *M'Carthy*. Certain local abbreviations are acceptable. *GI* to Nebraska readers means Grand Island, *CDA* in Idaho means Coeur d'Alene.

20. *Make heads fit.* Write headlines to fit the line without crowding. Sometimes it is a good practice on a close-counting headline to provide an optional word, thus giving the typesetter an opportunity to make the headline fit. Here is an example:

21. *Use correct grammar.* Although headlines condense, omit articles and parts of the "to be" verb, they should be grammatically correct. Note this example: **Five Running but None Are Officially 'In' Top Race.** Not only did the writer pad the headline with "Are" but he used the wrong verb.

22. *Use paper's style on spelling.* Headline writers follow the same style of spelling as reporters and each newspaper has only one style; unless simplified spelling is authorized, do not employ it.

15 When Cameras Make Copy

One picture is worth ten thousand words.—CHINESE PROVERB.

Do you remember the first sentence of any news lead?—Edward Stanley (1903–   ) *former executive editor, AP News Photo Service.*.

After all, suppose you have a staff of writers as great as Thomas Mann and Ernest Hemingway. All that they can do for you on an event is to give you a picture which can never be as faithful as the picture made by the camera.— W. W. Waymack (1888–   ) *former editor,* Des Moines *Register and Tribune.*

Cameramen who use their heads as well as their legs are rare. Rarer still are camera editors. . . . And almost nowhere is there an attempt to edit pictures into a coherent story—to make an effective mosaic out of the fragmentary documents which pictures, past and present, are.—*First prospectus for* Life *magazine.*

I. GETTING AND SELECTING PHOTOS

Pictures Are Short Cuts

Most of us are incurably picture-minded. Talking, we try to use words that get our friends "to see" as we do. Listening, we manipulate new ideas into familiar mental images. Reading, we unconsciously visualize words and phrases as pictures that flit across our mental screens.

There is something psychologically elemental about pictures. They recall the use of the ideograph in the development of the written language. A Sioux who drew on a deerskin the figures of mounted warriors and soldiers was endeavoring to tell others not of an idea, but of an actual battle. The photographer does the same thing, only better. An actual photograph brings us one step closer to reality than do words. Pictures short-circuit mental processes by appealing directly to the senses and become a substitute for the physical sensation of an actual experience.

230

Photo courtesy of Bill Wilson

"HERE COMES THEIR P.O.W." depicting a family's welcome for a son returning from Korea won for Photographer Bill Wilson of the Atlanta *Journal* and *Constitution* a Sigma Delta Chi award for the year's best news-picture. Said the judges, "He shot at the climactic moment. The technical results are superb. This picture perpetuates the happy agony of relief so inherent in this great story." This dramatic shot is an example of a photograph that "clicked."

The Age of Pictures Is Here

No longer are pictures a luxury for newspapers. Thanks to syndicated mat services and plastic engravings, even small newspapers can have lively news-picture pages. Newspapers produced by offset are picture-hungry since pictures are no more expensive to reproduce than type lines.

Metropolitan newspapers are extremely sensitive to shifting news values. Starting the day with feature pictures, these pages are made over for each edition with new photos synchronized to the day's events. Roto and color-gravure sections are now frequent features in Sunday editions and are even being syndicated for smaller papers. *Run of paper* (ROP) color process permits large dailies to run natural color on ordinary newsprint and also permits a paper to make changes on pages containing color.

Photos That 'Click'

Hundreds of photographs cascade into large newspaper offices each day. Assuming all are good prints, why are the chosen few selected?

Watch the picture editor at work. His fingers flip through a stack so rapidly he gives each picture but a glance. Study the few he lays aside for a second look and you will note a common characteristic; each has one striking element thrust forward. It may be the expression on a face or a truck hanging at a precarious angle over a bridge—or anything that instantaneously catches the eye. Now study the discards. Most of them are without that single, quick bid for attention. They are like overloaded comprehensive leads with details which should be subordinate, vociferously clamoring for attention.

A good news photographer is more than a shutter-clicker. He is a pictorial reporter. He has techniques of his own, similar to, but not identical with, those of the newsman who writes copy.

Tell a Story!

A fortune was made by a patent medicine manufacturer whose advertising consisted of pictures of people with their backs bent in pain, captioned "Every picture tells a story." That slogan suggests a motto to go over the desk of every newsman who handles photographs: "Every news picture *must* tell a story."

What is a story? Reduced to essentials, it is a relationship expressed between two or more elements. Given a Person and Fate, for example, a story tells of their interaction. A single news photograph seldom relates action in detail, but ideally it should catch some phase of the relationship which is so dramatic that, with but few words of explanation, the reader's imagination automatically supplies the missing element. Candid photos do just this. With a scene or a face in action, they project the reader's mind further into what has happened. *Before and after* pictures are an extension of this principle. So are *sequence shots*—a series of pictures tied together by a common theme. Characteristically they depict successive phases of an event, with a minimum of explanatory text being required.

Photo Limitations

But even seeing an event does not entirely satisfy the spectator; picture reporting can never completely displace text. *Life* magazine discovered this in its early days. Pages upon pages of pictures did not suffice; subscribers wanted along with them what the late Col. William Rockhill Nelson, of the Kansas City *Star,* liked to call "readin' matter." Furthermore, advertisers demanded a longer "time exposure" of their copy to the reader's eye than a glance at pictures afforded.

Words are needed to bring out the news or human-interest colors even of news photos. The more complex the idea presented, the greater the need for explanation. Scientific discoveries can be illuminated by a photograph, but frequently it doesn't justify the space it takes if it has no interpretive text, which may range from a brief *caption* to an extended story. A skillful use of photos and text in the right proportions is a mark of the discriminating and successful editor. Expert photo editing is a job that requires quick decisions based on knowledge and experience.

Taste and Decency

Because people resent the sight of a corpse or other unpleasant reminders of their own mortality, newspapers long refused to publish such pictures. Instead of showing the actual body when reproducing the scene of a murder, the stock phase was used, "X marks the spot." But with the spread of candid camera reporting the question has been raised recurrently whether death pictures might properly be published.

The matter came to a focus in a classic case in 1928. A photographer for a New York tabloid, the *News,* by means of a miniature hidden camera strapped to his ankle, snapped Ruth Snyder, a murderess, while she was being electrocuted in the Sing Sing death house. The blurred but grisly photograph was distributed by an agency to 250 newspapers: many printed it.

If a reporter can cover a court trial with his pencil, why can't a news photographer cover it with his camera? The reason is that some lawyer groups believe that the dignity and prestige of the court are lowered if photographs are permitted. Canon 35, a rule of the American Bar association, was appropriate in the days of flash powder, but today's courtroom pictures can be taken without the knowledge of the judge, the attorneys or the witnesses and cause no disturbance. Pictorial reporting is a function of the press. Banning news photographers from the courtroom is an abridgment of press freedom. Courts today, however, are becoming more lenient in permitting courtroom photographs. At least one state has opened its courts to cameramen.

Photo by New York Daily Mirror, *from International* News Photos

SOME DON'T LIKE to have their picture taken. A prisoner, his face ablaze with fury, is restrained by a policeman as he tries to lunge at an unidentified news cameraman who tried to take his picture at a metropolitan police station.

News Photos

Timeliness is the prime factor in news, whether it be reported by the writer or the photographer. And just as it was used to differentiate newsstories from feature stories, with an in-between hybrid called news-feature stories, so there are *news* and *feature* and *news-feature photos*.

A news picture is one that illustrates news of the day or, in case of events at distant points, provides the first available illustration. There are three kinds:

1. The picture that shows the news *happening*.

2. The picture of the *agency* or *site* or *result* of the event.

3. The *personality* shot, preferably with a spot news peg.

The most frequently used news pictures are of persons. Often these are stock portraits, dug out of the office morgue because some news event has catapulted the personality back into front-page prominence. Sometimes these have been made into cuts from which *matrices,* more commonly called *mats,* are made and supplied to client newspapers. Editors of small and medium-sized papers, with limited budgets for illustrations, are ingenious in the ways they utilize mats—especially those of maps, drawings and diagrams.

Feature Photos

A feature picture purports to show lighter and less urgent phases of the human drama. The news picture has the quality of immediacy; it demands to be published; if it is not published on receipt by one paper, a competitor will use it, which means its value is spoiled for the tardy one. The feature picture has no such urgency. Here are some typical examples of the latter type—good for any day, any week, almost any year.

A platypus—the Australian believe-it-or-not called the duckbill; it is furred, has webbed feet, lays eggs and suckles its young.

California nymphs disporting themselves on the beach alongside the shattered hulk of an old-time sailing vessel.

A "publicity shot" of a new way for apartment dwellers to dry their washing in a device controlled by a thermostat.

News-Feature Photos

A photograph rich in human interest but with only a minor reliance for its importance upon the news is to be classed as a news-feature picture. It tells no important news, yet if not used quite promptly, is of no value. Examples:

The lettuce-gowned maiden crowned as the "lettuce queen" at an early spring fiesta in an Arkansas community famed for its "rabbit food."

A picture of Florida palm trees—and overcoated natives—frosted by unseasonable weather.

The president of the United States on a fishing cruise registering glee over a string he and companions have caught.

Appraising Photos

Some photos, like some newsstories, simply grade low because of uninteresting subject matter. But while a clever rewrite man may do a scintillating piece out of unpromising material, not much can be done to help along a photo poor in interest. An automobile shot, for example, has no chance of making a newspaper without a something to lift it out of the ordinary. It might be a winged automobile that flies, of course, or one used by a notorious bandit, or one that figured in an accident.

The crop of bathing beauties knows no season, and apparently the public's capacity to consume is infinite. And for the slightest reason at all, newspapers will use pictures of charming co-eds. Striking photographs of animals have their special and perennial appeal. But scenery must be surpassingly beautiful or freakish to have a chance, unless it can be hung on a news peg.

When the picture editor studies the usability of photos, he calls into play all of the factors that govern news values. For, as is now clear, pictures like words are but devices to convey ideas to the newspaper reader and the same principles apply to both.

How to Select Photos

Given a photo, here are some of the questions that will be answered by the picture editor in the decision he makes.

1. *How does the photograph classify?* Is it a feature or a news picture? If it will "save" for a month or two, it is probably a feature picture. If it synchronizes with the day's news, it is a news picture. There are newspapers that specialize in news pictures and there are others that concentrate on features; editorial judgment is governed accordingly.

2. *What elements give the picture news or feature value?* How unusual is the news event that is pictured? There may be news in a posture, facial expression, a crowd, a grin, the fatigue of the athlete, the debris of a wreck—all action or the symbols of action. How great is the local significance or the general interest and appeal? Is it worth more than the reading matter that it will displace? What is its degree of timeliness—does its spot news value alone demand that it be used? Does it tell its story adequately? Or, if it is a feature picture, does its beauty, oddity, general attraction or appeal warrant its use? Was it extremely difficult to obtain? Is it exclusive?

3. *Is it forbidden matter, such as a lottery or raffle?* Is it salacious or otherwise improper for public display?

4. *Does the picture simply illustrate—or does it tell a story?* Is it a stiff, old-fashioned portrait without character? A stupid and solemn posed group, than which there is nothing more uninteresting? Is the *idea* so old and hackneyed

that pictures of the kind have ceased to hold any interest to the public? For example, the conventional "wedding picture"; the picture of the college man arrayed as a woman for the college play; the picture of the child wonder who dances; the picture of the town band or the city council in its Sunday best, posed on the steps of the court house or in front of the fire station.

5. *Examine the print itself with a critical eye.* Is it blurry, furred, out of focus and not printable? Some pictures that are slightly out of focus may be *retouched* into usability by the artist. Is the print blurred by the rapidity of action alone? If it is, and the blurring is not too great, the picture has an added news element. Is it clear, with sharply defined details? Does it have decided blacks and whites to make clear-cut contrasts? Does it have the middle tones between black and white? One expert avers that every really good print should have a gray scale in five tones; black and white, gray, the middle color, a tone between white and gray and a tone between gray and black.

6. *How large a cut should be made of the picture?* Are there parts that could and should be eliminated? Is there too much sky, surplus background, much bare floor area, much superfluous scenery and decoration? Can the news or feature element be brought out more forcefully by enlargement or reduction? Does it need retouching to bring out the contrasts and values more sharply?

7. *What shall be its position and setting in the paper?* On what page and at the top of what columns shall it be placed? What kind of caption and text does it require to show off its advantages?

Naturally, no such long and deliberate process as these questions infer takes place in the editorial mind when pictures are selected; but though selection is a matter of automatic habit and instantaneous judgment, principles underlying these questions prevail.

Photo Sources

Newspapers obtain their pictures in several different ways:

Reporters and correspondents gather portraits to be used in connection with newsstories.

Each newspaper of any size has its staff photographer or photographers. One large newspaper has a force of 15 and a number of especially equipped automobiles, including a motorized darkroom.

News services supply pictures to their clients or members. Such pictures may be *positives* (direct from wirephoto or telephoto receivers), *prints* made from negatives received at the regional bureau and delivered to clients, *mats* (usually mailed to clients), *negatives* (for color pictures) or *facsimiles*. Engravings can be made from pictures transcribed by facsimile, thus eliminating the necessity of waiting for prints from negatives. Facsimile is especially geared to newspapers that do not have wirephoto or telephoto receivers.

Private individuals offer pictures for publication.

Press agents working for various enterprises, private and public, have pictures to give out.

Commercial photographers take assignments to obtain photographs.

There are several agencies, most of them having headquarters in New York, whose cameramen scour the world for pictures to sell to newspapers and magazines.

A fee is charged for each picture used, and it is customary to give the agency a credit line, set in small type beneath the picture. If a newspaper desires a picture for exclusive publication, the cost is greatly increased. Copyrighted pictures carry the symbol © in the credit line, or the word may be spelled out, depending on the newspaper's style.

Color Photography

Newspapers no longer need color press units or special stock to reproduce color. They can use standard press units and can print color on ordinary newpaper (run of paper or ROP process).

The St. Louis *Post-Dispatch* prints its daily comic page in full color. The Milwaukee *Journal* carried 1,082,540 advertising lines in ROP and devoted 520 page units of ROP to editorial color in 1950. In 1951 the *Journal* published more than 900 pages of newsprint color, an average of nearly 20 pages weekly. Today more than 500 dailies are equipped to print color.

Tinted stock and blocks of color ink were used as early as the 1890s by newspapers such as the Milwaukee *Journal,* New York *Recorder,* New York *Herald,* New York *World,* New York *Journal* and Chicago *Tribune.* Many of the first attempts at color reproduction were stunts. The Milwaukee *Journal,* for example, used a series of red and blue horizontal bars on the front page to give a banner effect on the occasion of the inaugural of Governor Peck. Blocks of color were added to the Sunday comic pages during the hectic race for newspaper circulation. Then came Sunday comic sections in full color and rotogravure and special magazine sections in four color.

Although color has been a tool primarily for advertising, it has been used in various editorial features and will be used to even greater extent on news photos. *Pre-madeready* color mats are processed for advertising; *color separations* or bromides for editorial features already are on the market. The news agencies, of course, transmit separation negatives (red, yellow, blue) by wire. From these, the newspaper clients make color prints.

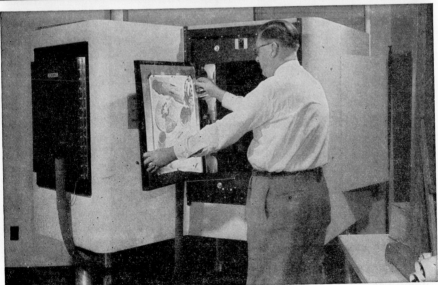

REPRODUCING COLOR PICTURES is relatively easy with the color analyst. After the subject is photographed, negatives are made from each of the three color separations. Enlarged bromide prints are then made from the negatives and masks (top photo). Register marks are placed on the prints so that the color in the engraved plate will correspond with the colors in the original picture. The color analyst (bottom photo) tells the artist if prints are in color register.

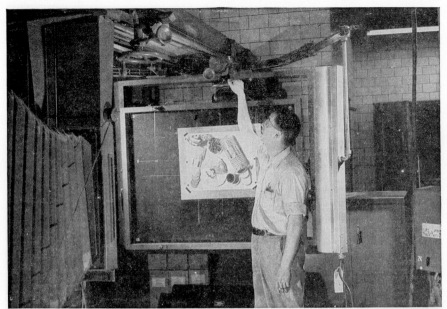

Photos courtesy of the Milwaukee Journal

WHEN LOCAL AREA CORRECTIONS are made to obtain correct color correspondence, the bromide prints are given to an engraver who photographs the black and white prints (top photo). Since the prints are handled as black-and-white photos, no filters or prism are needed to make engravings. Each of the engraver's screened negatives are printed on metal. Plates are then etched and proofed. Each plate is put into page form and the stereotype press plates are nickeled (bottom photo). Then the plates are placed on color press units.

One-Shot Color Camera

Process color owes much of its advance to the *one-shot color camera* which separates colors by an arrangement of mirrors and filters and produces, in one shot, yellow, red and blue negatives. The camera is used in the studio for still life subjects or it can make excellent action shots, especially with the aid of *stroboscopic* light.

The three negatives can be made into color prints by a dye-transfer process and turned over to the engraver for separations and engraving. If the newspaper has a *color analyst,* the negatives are enlarged into black and white bromide prints. The color analyst is an optical device also employing filters and mirrors that reassembles the separations into a full-color image and shows the operator whether the prints are correct for color printing.

After corrections have been made on the prints, they are sent to the engraver who reproduces each print as he would black and white halftones. Color balance is again checked by the color analyst before the plates are put into the form and stereotyped. Press plates are run in sequence so that through the combination of yellow, magenta and cyan pigments the natural color of the original subject is reproduced. (See illustrations pages 239 and 240.)

Combinations of color ink produce a variety of hues. Sixteen basic ink colors, for instance, will permit 650 variations in hues.

II. PICTURES AND THE COPYEDITOR

Copyeditor's Opportunity

Only occasionally does a news photographer give his paper a scoop. Most of the pictures that come in are from syndicates and are pictures equally available to rival publications. The possibility for pictorial distinction, therefore, arises chiefly in (a) selection of photos to be used, (b) the way they are laid out—both these jobs are for the art editor on large newspapers—and (c) their captioning. The last is the copyeditor's opportunity.

A paper's own photographers are expected to supply data for the captions, commonly called *cutlines.* Writing them is a task usually devolving upon the man at the copydesk. Even though they are done by a reporter, they must be copyedited. The copyeditor is expected also to transform the wooden, factual information usually typed on slips attached to agency photos into bright and brisk cutlines that charm and interest the reader. If the cutline forms part of the picture, it (the cutline) should be trimmed off the picture and rewritten.

Most smaller dailies insist that cutlines on picture mats should be rewritten or, at least, reset in the paper's typeface. In the latter case, the deskman rings the cutline on the proofsheet and sends it to the composing room. He marks through the line copy on the mat and leaves it to the stereotyper to remove the cutline before the mat is cast or to saw off the cutline after the mat has been cast.

Writing Cutline Copy

The mechanics of the job are simple. The copy is preferably typewritten on a sheet of paper; should it be written in longhand, special care must be taken to make it legible.

The picture goes to the engraving department; the cutlines go to the composing room. A guideline serves to match the two after the plate has been returned from the engraver. A tab pasted to the back of the pictures specifies: the guideline, size of the desired plate, edition for which the picture is intended and department ordering the cut.

The cutline copy must contain: the guideline, size and (sometimes) the page and edition. Some copyeditors draw a rectangle on a piece of copypaper, write the overline or caption above the rectangle, the underline or cutline beneath the rectangle. Inside the rectangle they specify the column width and the guideline. The guideline should be marked on the proofsheet of the engraving and, as a further precaution against getting the plates mixed up, the guideline is written in red crayon on the back of the plate.

Practices and Styles Vary

Cutline-writing practices vary from paper to paper. Some use both *overlines* and *underlines,* some prefer to use only underlines. The caption, like the headline, should do all in its power to attract the reader and give him some essentials of the subject. The caption should suggest action and should do more than tell the reader what he obviously can see for himself by glancing at the picture. The caption writer should keep in mind the width of the cut and write a line that will take up most of the space over the picture.

Cutline styles also vary. Some start with a phrase or short sentence in boldface or bold caps. Some use the first word of the cutline like an initial cap. Some start the cutline text without any special typographical treatment. Copy for a one-column cut is set one column wide; for two columns, two columns wide; for three columns, two columns, each 1½ columns wide or all in three columns; for four columns, two columns, each two columns wide; for five columns, two columns, each 2½ columns wide. The writer must provide enough copy to fill the lines extending under pictures more than one column wide.

Some newspapers like to have the last line of the cutline fill the full line. The writer can fill the line by using the unit count for the cutline or he can justify the lines by editing a proof of the cutlines.

Special Points to Remember

The copyeditor usually marks the cutlines to be indented one *em* on both sides so that the lines will be even with the face of the cut. The photo credit line may be pasted on the picture before it is engraved or it may be included in the cutline. Some papers require that the dateline of a syndicated picture be worked in the text of the cutline rather than starting the cutline with the dateline.

Writing a cutline from the engraved plate will give the writer trouble unless he remembers that the plate is reversed. The figure shown on the right will appear on the left when the cut is printed. The figures are in the correct position in the original picture, the mat and the proof.

If the picture appears on one page and the accompanying story on another page, the cutline should key the picture to the story: (*Story page 12*). If a half-column (*thumbnail*) cut is to be used in the story, the copyeditor should indicate to the compositor that part of the story is to be set in half-column measure. Bracket off several lines on either side of the copy and write in the margin: Indent for 6-em cut (giving the subject's name). Since a newspaper usually has a standard depth for thumbnail cuts, the compositor will know how many lines of type to indent to accommodate the cut.

Tell the feature as well as the news—subtly and clearly if you can. Make the lines vigorous—give them punch. A picture showing the president of the United States milking a cow would hardly carry a caption starting: **Milks Cow. . . .** A better beginning: **So-o-o Bossy. . . .**

In writing captions for a picture layout, make sure the pictures are identified correctly. If the cutline tells readers the picture on the left shows the president concentrating on his favorite hobby, the reader will howl if the picture printed on the left shows a beautiful blonde instead of the president playing golf.

Study the picture carefully before writing the caption. This caution was emphasized in the *AP Log:*

1. Too often we try, without justification, to ascribe a mood or an attitude to a picture subject. Captions say a person "looks amused" or "was shocked" when the picture shows no such thing. Also, the fewer adjectives, the better.

2. There is frequent failure to call a spade a spade in describing a situation. If a picture is posed, don't hesitate to say the people are posing. And when a politician is holding a child, let's NOT say, as a Detroit caption did, that Mr. Truman is holding "an admirer." That's a double error. It's editorial, and it's untrue.

Working with News Mats

Cutline handling can be illustrated by showing the steps in getting a *news mat* ready for publication. A half-dozen or so mats come in each mailing. These include spot news, feature and sports pictures. Each picture on the mat is lettered. An accompanying cutline sheet keys the cutline to the mat letter. Here, for instance, is a typical listing from an *Associated Press* Telemat:

B—three cols x 3½″

JOURNEY INTERRUPTED BY TRIPLETS

Mrs. Ruth Keith, whose transatlantic passenger flight was interrupted by the imminent arrival of children, rests in a Gander, Newfoundland, hospital after the birth of triplet daughters. With her are her two older children, Tordis, 3, and Bruce Eric, 1. The transatlantic plane bringing her home from Norway made an unscheduled stop at Gander for her benefit. (AP Wirephoto.)

The editor writes a slugline (*e.g.,* Journey), on the back of the mat and sends the mat to the stereotype room to be made into a cast. The cutline is written and sent to the composing room. Here are three methods of handling the cutline.

1. Caption and cutline:

Triplets Interrupt Journey

3-Col. Journey

A transatlantic passenger flight, etc.

2. Displayed cutline:

> 3-Col. Journey

Journey Interrupted—Mrs. Ruth Keith, whose transatlantic, etc.

3. Capitalized line:

> 3-Col. Journey

TRIP HALTED   Mrs. Ruth Keith, whose transatlantic flight was halted, etc.

The edited cutline:

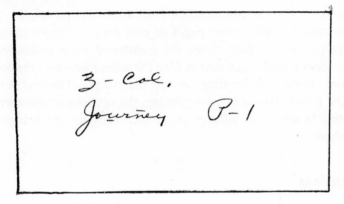

Journey Interrupted--Mrs. Ruth Keith, whose transatlantic passenger flight was interrupted by the imminent arrival of children, rests in a Gander, Newfoundland, hospital after the birth of triplet daughters. With her are two older children, Tordis, 3, and Bruce Eric, 1. The transatlantic plane bringing her home from Norway made an unscheduled stop at Gander for her benefit.

III. REPRODUCTION AND LAYOUT

Picture Copy

To the art editor and the photoengraver, all *art* and *pix* to be reproduced are copy. The foregoing discussion has dealt exclusively with photographs, but here it should be noted that drawings, diagrams, maps and other graphic representations also are copy.

Various methods of reproduction are in use, but with only three need the newspaperman be familiar. They are:

1. *Photoengraving.* This produces two kinds of cuts—line engraving and halftones—which will be discussed in detail.
2. *Rotogravure.*
3. *Offset.*

Roto printing is to be distinguished from *letterpress* process by which ordinary printing is done. Entire pages of roto copy—pictures and printing—are prepared at a time. They are transferred by a photochemical process to copper cylinders, an acid etching the copper wherever the original copy showed up black. In printing, ink fills these depressions and is transferred to the paper. This is *intaglio* printing, the opposite of letterpress or relief printing in which ink adheres to the high surfaces and is impressed upon the sheet.

Line Engravings

Cheapest and simplest form of photoengraving is the *line engraving,* or line etching, done on zinc. It is used only for picture copy consisting of solid blacks, such as maps and printing and diagrams. The process is not used for wash drawings or photographs because it cannot reproduce tones. However, it is possible to give a shaded effect to a line etching by two methods.

One is the use of *Ross board,* if the copy is a drawing. Ross board is simply a special cardboard with an uneven surface. Penciled lines on it have a mottled appearance, not unlike those of a lithograph. Skilled artists attain very attractive results with Ross board—but, of course, relatively few newspapers have such artists or a need for such drawings.

The second method of getting a shaded effect on line engravings is employed by the photoengraver when he uses a patented process of stippling solid blacks in various patterns, known as *Ben Day* or *Tintograph.* Details are unimportant to the newspaper editor, but he should know of the results obtainable—and that the cost is somewhat more than that of the regular line etching.

Halftones

Considerably more expensive but possessing a far wider range of possibilities for newspaper use is the *halftone*.

Put a picture reproduced by halftone under a microscope, and it will be seen as patterns of tiny dots. That is because, in the photomechanical process by which halftones are made, the image on the copy is photographically strained through a *screen*. Think of it as a window screen, with the squares ever so much smaller. The photoengraver's screen is a sheet of glass with opaque screenlines which, when the picture copy is "photographed" on the copper plate, cuts the image into thousands of tiny dots of various sizes. These dots survive their acid bath and when the cut is put on the press catch the ink and transfer it to the paper.

It is important for anyone handling halftones to understand the screening process, for it supplies the word that distinguishes cuts used on a coarse newsprint from those that print best on heavy, coated magazine paper. If there are 100 *screenlines* to an inch, the cut is said to be 100-screen. The higher the screen, the finer the dots.

When cuts give bleary and smeary reproductions, the probability is that they are cut too fine-screened for the paper used. Newspapers ordinarily use cuts with a 65- to 85-line screen; slick-paper magazines take them up to 150. Newspapers that print directly from type (on a flatbed press) generally get better results from a fine cut than those printed from stereotyped plates. In fact, it is all but impossible to make usable mats from fine-screen cuts, as small-city editors frequently must explain to club women who want speakers' cuts from programs or yearbooks printed in the newspaper.

Magnesium Plates

Magnesium is replacing both zinc and copper as engraving metal. A magnesium alloy (produced by Dow Chemical company under the trade-name *Zomag*) not only has clean, uniform etching qualities but has a press life equal to copper. Its producers say the plate can stand a press run of a million before it shows wear and that as many as 3,000 mats have been pulled from one plate.

TINY RAISED DOTS, etched on a copper plate by acid, make the printing surface of a halftone. The top cut is 110 screen; note how the engraving dots show up when the marked rectangle is magnified (to the equivalent of a 20 screen).

Since it is only one-fifth as heavy as copper, the magnesium plate can easily be filed in a newspaper library. Magnesium does not stretch or warp and is not distorted by temperature changes, thus allowing for close register on both original and subsequent press runs. Screens as fine as 200-line have been produced on this metal.

Along with the development of magnesium for plate-making have come improved processes of etching that produce engravings more quickly and more efficiently than the older methods. A completed "flat" takes about 75 minutes by conventional engraving methods; by the rapid dry process, the time has been cut to 32 minutes.

Plastic Plate Engraving

The engraving methods, described in the foregoing, use a chemical process to etch the metal. Another process is mechanical or photoelectric engraving which is used with *plastics*. One system, the *Fairchild engraver,*

Fairchild Camera and Instrument photo

LETTING THE MACHINE do all the work. This young lady is at "work" making a plastic halftone engraving. Using the Fairchild Cadet Scan-A-Graver, which produces the plates electronically, she has opportunity to carry on other work.

uses the same principle as a wirephoto transmitter, that is, a scanner to record the density of reflected light.

The picture is attached to a cylinder. As it rotates, a scanning eye records the amount of light reflected. On another rotating cylinder is attached the plastic to be engraved. A cutting head responds to the impulses from the scanner, burning craters in the surface as it moves along the cylinder. Depth of the cutting depends upon the picture's tones; the darker the area on the picture the lighter the burn or cut. Raised dots produce the screen effect. Current model machines are adapted for 65-, 85-, 100- and 120-line screen halftones. (The *Fairchild Cadet Scan-A-Graver* makes an 85-screen, four-column plastic halftone in 24 minutes.)

The plate can be mounted on a base and used on a flatbed press or it can be taped on the stereo plate of a rotary press.

Offset Process

Use of *pictures in the offset* process of newspaper reproduction is limited only by the space and the pictures available. It costs no more to use pictures than line copy in the offset process since no engraving is involved. The pictures may be glossy prints or printed pictures clipped from published sources.

This process derives its name from the fact that the image is transferred from a photographic plate to a rubber-blanketed cylinder which, in turn, offsets the impression upon paper.

Preparation of a page for offset printing is essentially an editing and layout job. Everything to appear on the page is pasted on a layout sheet. This includes all text matter (including headlines) and drawings. Pictures are photographed through a screen and then *stripped* on the page. The entire page is then photographed and the negative is imposed on a finely-grained plate coated with a light-sensitive emulsion. The plate is exposed to an arc light. The chemicals harden and become insoluble in water wherever the light penetrates the film.

During the printing process, the face of the plate is brushed by a wet roller. The printing area repels the water, but it adheres to the non-printing area. When ink rollers press against the plate, the water-covered (non-printing) areas repel the ink while the sensitized areas accept it. The inked plate is pressed against a rubber blanket which transfers the image to paper.

A variation of this offset production is the dry offset process which uses a thin, flexible plate on which the image is photoengraved to positive relief, then etched. Magnesium can be used for making dry offset plates.

It has been demonstrated that by a direct-image offset process a newspaper can be put to press within less than 15 minutes from closing of pages to press run. After the page is locked and inked, an impression is taken on the surface of a disposable offset plate. This plate is treated with a solution to protect and strengthen both the printing and the non-printing areas. After it is run through a debossing machine for final leveling, the plate is placed on a special press whose normal speed is 12,000 completed papers an hour. This production requires neither stereotyping equipment nor photo-mechanical methods.

The Enlarging-Reducing Formula

A picture can be blown-up or reduced to any size the editor desires. The size depends in part upon space available and cost, but above all upon the editorial purpose in using the picture. It must be large enough to tell the story it is intended to tell and it must emphasize its feature. If its interest is its beauty or detail, such as faces in a group, obviously the reproduction must be large enough to bring out these values. Enlargement or reduction is governed by the laws of proportion. The width of the photograph is to the width of cut (in inches) as the depth of the photograph is to the depth of the cut. On larger papers the artists handling the retouching use a slide-rule to give the picture editor the exact depth for the cut. But any novice can scale a picture.

The picture, let us say, is a small one to be enlarged to a two-column width. Carefully place it in the upper lefthand corner of a blank sheet of paper ruled off into columns (or use a layout sheet which has been printed with rules on it). Now lay a ruler diagonally to the right, across the photo so that the ruler touches the upper left and the lower right corners. The ruler will cross the boundary of your second column at the exact depth your pictorial copy will take when enlarged to the desired two-column width.

A similar operation, reversed, will of course enable one to reduce a photograph in scale.

No difficulty need be experienced in enlarging or reducing odd-shaped picture copy if it is squared up. Here, the outside limits of the image are defined by lines making a rectangle, which is then enlarged or reduced as described above.

Some picture page editors work with regular-sized cuts rather than trying to fit halftones of various sizes on the pages. On the Milwaukee *Journal,* two basic cut depths are used: 3⅛ inches and 4⅝ inches. These produce 10 standard depth combinations.

Cropping

The foregoing explanation is based on the assumption that all of a given piece of picture copy is to be used. In practice it seldom is. Frequently the photo includes a *static* area or unimportant details which had better be omitted. Or it may be that the feature of a picture is a face which should be enlarged tremendously and used alone to achieve the desired editorial purpose. "Pants," say photo editors, "are all alike."

In all such cases, photos are *cropped*; that is, the person handling them indicates to the photoengravers just which portion of the picture is to be used. He probably will have squared off the desired section and by applying the enlarging-reducing formula will have eliminated all guesswork as to the size of the halftone.

Two methods of cropping are employed. The first is to indicate the corner marks of the desired section on the margin of the picture copy with light strokes of a crayon called a *grease pencil.* These can be removed by a finger without harm to the photo. Marking across the picture is to be avoided, for an impression made by the pencil pressure may damage the emulsion and preclude using the picture later for another purpose. The other method of cropping is to hold the emulsion side of the picture against a window pane, or an illuminated *ground glass,* and with an ordinary lead pencil to mark on the reverse side the section from which the cut is to be made.

In cropping, the art editor always bears in mind the possibility of *flopping.* Without extra expense, a picture can be *reversed* as the halftone is being made. Not infrequently, it is desirable to flop or reverse a portrait to avoid having it "look" off the page, but in all such cases it is important to watch for details that would make it look lefthanded. Lapel badges, for example, look queer on the right side, and a picture of a man made to milk a cow on the wrong side would create derision among rural subscribers.

Ordinarily, on newspapers, size instructions for the photoengraver are indicated by column widths—with the depth coming as it will in proportion. Usual sizes are ⅓, ½, ⅔, 1, 2, 3, 4, 5, and 6 columns, very seldom larger.

A PROSAIC PHOTO, prosaically handled. Now observe (below) what skillful cropping does. Just enough of the bank at the right has been left to carry out the suggestion of a curve. Static areas on the other side have been excised—thus moving the steam forward. The straightened telegraph pole tilts the locomotive slightly. Now the picture shouts to the reader "Look out."

Photo from New York Central Line

253

Retouching

The retoucher is a person with more or less special art training who *retouches* picture copy to give it a desired effect. His tools are a brush and black and white water paint, various pencils, and an *airbrush*. The latter might be described as a combination of a fountain pen and an atomizer. It sprays a water paint evenly, and is especially useful in *graying out* unwanted details or *blowing back* a too prominent background.

Retouching requires skill. If lines are too heavy, they show up even though they have been softened by the halftone screen. The work must be done with an especially deft and light touch if the photo is to be blown up for flaws in retouching become more evident as the picture is enlarged. If the photo is to be enlarged and needs much retouching—and time permits—it is advisable to have the print enlarged beyond the size of the desired halftone, and then retouched. The reduction will make the work less conspicuous. In fact, it is always desirable to reduce photos for halftones, and the best cuts result when the reduction has been approximately one-half.

Ornaments on the Wane

It used to be the fashion to redeem a poor photograph by *painting up* its subject and by crowning the masterpiece with a decoration of scrolls, arabesques, rosettes and fanciful sketches at top, bottom and along the sides. Those were the days when every man whose pictures passed through the artist's hands appeared in the newspaper as a Prince Charming and every woman became a raving beauty. Society leaders remained perpetually young as far as photographers were concerned and men of prominence wondered "whether they really looked like that" when they saw themselves in the papers.

As the art of photography improved, and as it became increasingly easy to get plenty of excellent photographs, higher standards began to prevail. Today there is comparatively little ornamentation, only absolutely necessary retouching is done and the pictures are allowed to speak for themselves. Where ornamentation is used it is of a simple, dignified type and does not trespass on the photographic verities.

Photoengraving processes have kept pace with the progress made in photography and the results now achieved on ordinary print paper often excel those obtained years ago by use of the more costly coated and glazed papers.

Layouts

Besides the single cut dealing with a single subject or person, a combination of pictures may be made. This is called a *layout*.

It is economical to make layouts which can be reproduced as a single cut. However, a method growing in use and known as the *unit system,* calls for each picture to be made in separate cuts. These, for obvious reasons, are said to *float* in white space and one or more can be dropped from the layout as space requires.

The single-cut layout frequently is adorned by art including hand-lettered words. By a special process, type can be introduced into such a layout and reproduced with white letters on a dark background, that is, *reversed lettering.* Or when the background is light, type can be photographically reproduced in black and then is said to be *overprinted.*

Often it is possible to *mortise* out certain portions of the cut and fill the openings with type. Picture a two-column cut with extra space half a column wide at one side; the half column of extra metal can be sawed off, and in the space thus left the entire news caption can be set—say in 8- or 10-point type, each line centered or ragged down the side of the picture.

Mortises may be of any width or depth, depending on the layout, and in nearly any marginal position. It is not usual to mortise a one-column cut, but even this can be done.

Photomontage

When time permits, effective illustrations can be worked out by blending portions of several photographs to be reproduced as one. The best and most expensive way of doing this is by rephotographing sections wanted so that they *overprint* lightly, after which retouching can be done as desired.

PHOTOMONTAGE. An expert can obtain striking effects by bringing together parts of several photos to illustrate a topic. Amateurs seldom succeed.

But in newspaper practice these *photomontages* are made by cutting up various photos, pasting them on cardboard, then retouching the lines where they join—or perhaps *blowing in* with the airbrush the desired airy effects.

Photomontages are especially useful for feature treatment. They bring various pictorial elements together in striking ways and can often be used to advantage when an impressionistic concept of several ideas is sought.

The danger to guard against in making montages is giving a confused impression—a danger that even expert layout men do not always avoid. Photomontages are good or bad, with few gradations between.

PART V

Making Up the Pages

16 Makeup: Principles and Mechanics

We didn't have display back in 1776 or in any of our pioneer newspapers because everybody read everything. Display, as I take it, is an indexing device which, in effect, grants that everybody can't read everything.—Douglas C. McMurtrie.

Personalities for Papers

Newspapers have personalities no less than human beings. Some are sensational and flamboyant, even vulgar; others are quiet, modest, thoughtful. Editorial content and policy play a large part in creating a newspaper's reputation, but so does appearance.

Only the weakest paper, handicapped by lack of skilled help or unworried by competition, is "thrown together." All others give deliberate attention to arranging and displaying their contents. Each detail of position and effect on every page is thought out in advance; nothing is left to chance. The process and the result of this effort is called *makeup*.

Makeup is a term borrowed from the stage. Just as an actor uses grease paint and costumes to "take a character," so the newspaper employs type, illustrations and other devices. The success of a play is recorded at the box office; one index of a newspaper's success is its circulation. Newspaper makeup, therefore, is not the result of an editor's whim or fancy. It is a studied effort of trained men to present their product in a form that will please readers, give a "break" to advertisers and sell papers.

Makeup: Ends and Means

More specifically, makeup has four distinct purposes. They are:

1. *To enhance readability.* Makeup is the final step in the process, initiated by the reporter, of getting the gist of the news to the reader in the shortest possible time.

2. *To grade news.* Readers expect big stories to be played up, both by position and by typographic emphasis.

3. *To make pages attractive and interesting.* Good makeup does not offend the eye by unesthetic typography, or the mind by a lack of variety.

4. *To create favorable recognition values.* This reader reaction is sought: "I can recognize the *Bugle* as far away as I can see it—and I want it!"

Makeup is one of the graphic arts. It calls for a working knowledge of typography, some feeling for esthetics and a practical understanding of how the newspaper's graphic elements—body type, headlines and illustrations—can be juggled to catch, please and hold the reader's roving eye. Makeup men use two principles to emphasize, or de-emphasize, stories and make attractive pages: *contrast* and *position.*

Emphasis by Contrast

Contrast is a common concept—but in makeup it has special importance relying on three factors:

1. Size.   Large headlines, contrasting with adjacent smaller heads, instantly suggest the superior significance or interest of the stories they adorn only when they are adjacent to smaller heads over less important items. Two-column heads likewise are contrasted with one-column heads. And long newsstories can be relieved by short ones.

2. Density of Color.   This refers to actual "colors"—red, yellow, blue and so on—or the blackness of illustrations and headlines. They contrast with *gray* body type and *white space.* White space is usually underrated: it's as welcome to the reader as light at the end of a long tunnel is to the weary motorist. "Open" headlines—droplines, hanging indents and flush lefts—and subheads help to *break up* a sea of gray type.

3. Style.   Headline in italics contrast with bold heads set in a roman face, and capital letters with lower case. Cartoons contrast with halftones. Halftones of different shapes or subjects contrast with each other.

Special friends of the makeup editor are short *fillers*—usually little news-feature stories—cartoons, comic strips, photos and advertisements. When ads are set up artistically and well illustrated, they tend to liven the makeup. The full page devoted to stories, even when *spotted* with cuts, often is not one-half so attractive as the page graced by display advertising.

Men Who Make Up the Pages

Makeup is a simple matter on the one-man newspaper. Here the reporter-copyeditor-editor-compositor-printer merely puts the type where he wants it. But divisions of labor and specialization become progressively necessary as newspapers increase in size and complexity.

On small- to medium-sized papers a news executive will plan the first page, at least, along with his other duties. *Floormen* in the mechanical department then take over, relying chiefly on their own knack effectively to fill the holes with type.

Seldom does the deskman on the larger papers have occasion to dirty his hands in the mechanical department. His part in the process of making up the pages is remote. He rewrites headlines ordered by the makeup editor, occasionally gets a proof with instructions to trim a certain number of lines or rushes through a batch of short fillers required by the makeup editor.

Larger papers have at least one man who devotes all his time to planning the pages. He's the *makeup* (or *news*) editor. He works closely with the managing editor and is the liaison between the editorial department and the composing room.

The makeup editor starts where the reporter and the copyeditor leave off. *Galley proofs* of stories and headlines come to him. Subject to a veto from a superior, he can lop off paragraphs at the ends of stories when space is limited, drop decks and subheads or request different headlines that will be better adapted to his plans.

What the Makeup Man Does

Regardless of what system he employs, each day, the makeup editor must:

1. Ascertain how many pages are available for a given edition and what space can be used for editorial matter.
2. Allocate this space to news, sports, society, coming events and other departments and features.
3. Specify where leading newsstories and illustrations are to be placed.
4. Follow a system of keying stories and their headlines with sluglines so that the right head will go over the proper story.
5. Exercise some degree of judgment in fitting stories to space.
6. Follow through to see that his instructions are carried out.

The news or makeup editor has two tools. One is a schedule of stories for the day commonly called a *slugsheet*; the other is a diagram of the newspaper's pages, the *dummy*.

How Many Pages?

Advertising (both display and classified) determines the size of the newspaper. Normally, on Monday, Tuesday and Wednesday the paper is medium-sized, on Thursday and Friday it is heavy and on Saturday it is light. On metropolitan papers the largest issue of the week is the Sunday edition. Light, medium and heavy are determined by the amount of advertising space sold. The average is 60 per cent advertising, 40 per cent editorial. If advertising amounts to the equivalent of 14 pages and the ratio is 70 per cent advertising and 30 per cent news, the total will be 20 pages. Twenty-six pages of advertising with a ratio of 65:35 produces a 40-page paper, 14 of which will be news and features (including comics, radio and TV columns, crossword puzzle, bridge columns, stamp news, patterns, recipes and the like). Average space devoted to editorial content in the American daily is 12½ pages; in the Sunday paper, 42 pages.

Allotting the Pages

As soon as the number of pages is determined, the advertising director makes a dummy showing the position of the day's advertising. The news-editorial departments fill in the space remaining.

The makeup editor allots certain pages to society, sports and other departments and features. Next, he compares the total remaining space with the space the city, telegraph and other editors think they will need. Possibly they are asking for too much, or not enough. At any rate he informs them of the conditions and they make the necessary adjustments in their plans. If space is tight, the heads of the various copydesks instruct copyeditors to trim and cut.

Only so many metal slugs can go into a column. When the forms are filled, the remaining type (*overset*) has to be junked or held over (if possible) for the next day. Oversetting is expensive and editors do not look kindly upon a departmental editor who cannot keep within his allotted space.

But the system isn't as rigid as it would appear. Newspapers deal with intangibles. A big story is breaking and the city editor requests a column to handle text, headlines and art. But if the story is bigger than was expected or the art is particularly good, the layout may require 1½ columns. The city editor will get the space he needs to display the story properly. Sometimes the story proves mediocre and can be wrapped up in half a column. Again, a last-minute adjustment can be made.

The composing room is the real gauge of the flow of copy. When the holes left for news start filling up and copy is still cascading from the tubes, the makeup editor gives the order to hold down copy. The flow immediately slows to a trickle, each department trimming sharply and sending along only the "must" copy. When the banks become vacant and the copy hooks thin out, the composing room demands more copy. Then the departments pull out stories they have been holding back and the flow swells until the composing room again cries enough.

The size of the staff of each department is geared to the size of the paper—a full staff on days the paper is heavy, a skeleton staff on days the paper is light. On smaller papers, the city editor and society editor send to the composing room all the copy they can handle. The sports editor trims the wire sports copy in relation to the amount of local sports he has available. The wire editor knows from experience how much copy he should process and how many pictures he should have engraved or stereotyped. If other departments report a heavier or a lighter flow than they expected, he adjusts the wire output accordingly.

Using the Slugsheet

Before an editor learns to estimate copy by the "feel," he'd do well to keep a copy schedule, commonly called the slugsheet.

The simplest type is a sheet of copy paper containing the cumulative lengths of the stories handled. The length can be in terms of copy line totals or column inches or column percentages. Suppose an editor knows he has 14 columns to fill. That is roughly 280 column inches. If it takes five lines of copy to make an inch of type, he has available 1400 lines including art and headlines. He makes sure the schedule includes a generous number of shorts or fillers to aid the makeup man in justifying the columns of type.

Data for the slugsheet are obtained from the various news executives. The city editor, for example, will have made an entry in his *assignment book* every time a reporter has informed him a certain story has made good or is likely to do so. Its probable length is noted, usually in the percentage of a column it will take, and this estimate is scaled down or expanded according to its merit when finally edited. Other copydesks—telegraph, cable, state, and so on—keep similar records, basing their calculations on copy *in hand* and on stories ordered from correspondents.

The makeup editor is kept posted. If a story expands or collapses or a new one comes in, he is notified at once and alters his record accordingly. Here is a section of a makeup editor's typical slugsheet or space schedule:

LOCAL

Rob	.70
Milk	.40
Storm	1.75

TELEGRAPH

Feud	.30
Fire	.50
Autos	.30

CABLE

Irish	.40
Paris	.25

CUT

Cartoon	100 × 3

This illustrates one slugsheet system. Another one widely used departs from this procedure and the story identification system described earlier at one important point: a slugline or guideline, instead of being constant throughout the life of a story, will include the first few words of the story's headline and will vary as the headline is changed. For example: a story slugged "#2 Turks Rampage" might for a later edition become "#5 Istanbul Riots." In such cases, the slug on the proof is also changed so the printer will not be confused as he matches the story with its head.

MIDTOWN NEWS SLUGSHEET

Head Number	Story Length	Slugline	Source and Comment	Copyeditor	Time Cleared
1	10″	Blizzard Rages	AP	Roseen	9 30
6	7″	Eat Eggs	Interview - Pete	Joe	9 35
3	8″	CIO Opens	Soft Coal Scrap	Roseen	9 42
8 or 5	4″	Goat Chews	Univ. Release	Smith	9 45

SLUGSHEETS, also called space schedules, vary in form and completeness, depending on the complexity of the news organization. This style can be used when the slug or guideline consists of the first few words of the head.

A slugsheet not only helps the desk keep track of stories but it also shows the slotman and makeup editor the range of headlines sent to the composing room. Where a slugsheet is not in force, some editors keep a record of headlines used. The tendency, for beginners at least, is to write too many heads of the same size. A variety of head sizes is essential if the makeup editor is to build an effective page and fit type into the page holes.

The Page Dummy

Now the makeup editor is ready to plan his pages, designating the position for each important story and picture. This is done on a printed diagram so useful that it can hardly be dispensed with even on the smallest paper. It is the *page dummy*—also referred to as the *page schedule*. Usually it is a sheet the size of an ordinary page for typewriter use, ruled for columns. Examples, somewhat reduced, will be shown later.

On this form the makeup editor scribbles in the sluglines of the stories and other directions for the guidance of the *makeup man* (a printer, not to be confused with the makeup editor) in the composing room. Frequently the managing editor will supervise the front page, but the makeup editor will *lay out* the rest of the newspaper.

Here is a simple dummy page, utilizing the items listed in the foregoing section of a slugsheet. It calls for an eight-column streamer in 96-point type. Three stories have a No. 1 headline, two have No. 5, two have No. 4, and one has a No. 3. The cartoon is three columns wide and 100 agate lines deep. "Turn" at the bottom of the last column simply means the "storm" story is to *turn* or *break over* without a jumphead to the first column of page 2.

The slugsheet indicated that the "Rob" story will require 70 per cent of a column. This will fill the column allotted to it, for all columns on this front page are shortened greatly by the newspaper's nameplate, the streamer line and the large headlines. That fact must always be considered in scheduling front-page stories.

It also will be observed that several stories are shorter than the "Rob" story; in these cases filler items will absorb the surplus space. No notation is necessary on the page schedules when these are to be used, as it is understood that they will fill the small *holes* left on all pages after the *top heads* are placed. Vigilant news executives endorse "Page 1" on the proofs of the liveliest items in order to be sure that they get the position they deserve.

```
┌─────────────────────────────────────────────────────────────┐
│                    96 pt — STORM                            │
├──────┬───────┬──────┬─────┬─────┬─────┬──────┬──────────────┤
│  1   │   5   │  1   │     │     │     │  3   │   1          │
│ ROB  │ IRISH │ FIRE │     │     │     │ MILK │ STORM        │
│      │       │      │   Cartoon        │      │             │
│      │       │      │     100          │      │             │
│      │       │      │      X           │      │             │
│      │       │      │      3           │      │             │
│      │       │      │  4   │  5  │  4  │      │             │
│      │       │      │ FEUD │AUTOS│PARIS│      │             │
│      │       │      │     │     │     │      │             │
│      │       │      │     │     │     │      │       Turn   │
└──────┴───────┴──────┴─────┴─────┴─────┴──────┴──────────────┘
```

Perfecting the Pages

It is customary for each story to pass through the makeup editor's hands on its journey to the composing room. He looks over it quickly for content, then jots down on his space schedule its headline designation. As the paper takes shape and form, he may decide that different headlines are needed, whereupon he requests them from the appropriate copydesk executive. If a story has not yet been delivered to him, he may specify the kind of headline he wants to carry out his makeup plans.

Final Steps

The completed page schedules go to the composing room where the type has been set. No changes may be made there without consulting the makeup editor.

Often the makeup editor will accompany each instalment of his schedules to the composing room where he and the superintendent or foreman will collaborate in the solution of such incidental problems as arise. Customarily, they send galley proofs back to copydesks for desired trims, cuts or rewriting headlines to the desired style.

When the printer is ready to make up a page, he places a heavy metal frame or *chase* of proper size upon a composing *stone* or upon a metal *table*. Then he assembles the advertisements in proper position, puts in the dateline and *folio* (page) numbers, places the cuts, column rules, and cutoffs and *packs in* the news type and headlines. When the chase is filled, it is *locked up* with metal clamps or with *quoins* and sent to the stereotyper.

The makeup editor is a strategist. He must be a master of organization and acutely time-conscious. He synchronizes editorial and mechanical work—staggering his page schedules to the composing room so that the madeup pages of type can be delivered in time to meet the deadline for each edition.

Presses Don't Stop

On the one-edition paper the last pages to go on the press are the front and jump pages. Once the presses start rolling, it takes an unusually big story to force an editor to break open page 1, insert a bulletin, replate and stop the press long enough to substitute the new page 1 plate. High-speed presses complete a pressrun in a matter of minutes. (On the Chicago *Tribune* the paper travels 1,300 feet a minute.) Once the presses are running at top speed a late story, unless it is spectacular, just doesn't have a chance of getting into the day's paper. The Hollywood notion that a minor editor dashes into the composing room and yells "Stop the press" is purely fiction. The country is full of managing editors who have never experienced that exhilaration.

17   Making Up Page One

Our first Papers made a quite different Appearance from any before in the Province, a better Type and better printed . . . Bradford still printed the Votes and Laws and other Publick Business. He had printed an Address of the House to the Governor in a coarse blundering manner; We reprinted it elegantly and correctly, and sent one to every Member. They were sensible of the Difference, it strengthen'd the Hands of our Friends in the House, and they voted us their Printers for the Year ensuing.—Benjamin Franklin (1706–1790), *American statesman, journalist,* from the *Autobiography.*

Styles Do Change

The old-fashioned newspaper page, like the Victorian house, was dominated by curlicues and dingbats—layer-cake headlines, fancy boxes, odd little *ears* on either side of the nameplate, adorned cuts and other frills and furbelows of the gingerbread era.

Today's front page stresses utility, simplicity and harmony. The page is designed to be read hurriedly. By placing accents on certain stories, the editor is able to maneuver the reader about the page.

Today's page 1 is a more complete unit than in the past because of the weight placed on the page below the fold. Stories are shorter and therefore are complete on the page, thus saving the reader from having to flip pages to read continuations. All these changes have been made so gradually that many readers are not aware that the newspaper they read today looks entirely different from that of former years.

Good makeup involves three considerations: (1) importance of the news; (2) pictures available; (3) variety.

The News Is Boss

News determines the page makeup, not vice versa. Every day's page is planned according to the importance of the news available. Or, perhaps it is more accurate to say that display is conditioned by the relative importance of the news offerings of the day. Even on light news days the biggest stories are adequately displayed. When big news breaks it gets a smash play.

Pictures are used to emphasize the main story and to offset the heavy type on the lead story. Pictures give the makeup editor an opportunity to build display around focal points. Pictures also enable him to present a variety of patterns of makeup.

As news changes, so must makeup. Even though a banner headline is used on page 1 every day, the overall effect should not repeat the previous day's pattern. The reader expects something different every day. Yet the change cannot be so radical that the newspaper loses its identity.

The makeup editor has a variety of patterns, some of which he uses more than others. But he does not say, "Today being Monday I'll use makeup A." Again, news determines the pattern. The makeup editor has patterns to use when the news is big, when it is mediocre and when it is light. Seldom does he come out with exactly the same arrangement he has used previously.

Why Makeup Varies

Makeup reflects the tradition of the paper, the whims of the publisher, the times and, in many cases, the nature of the community the paper serves. The Kansas City *Star* by tradition is conservative in appearance. Its readers have grown accustomed to its period-piece makeup. The Denver *Post* by tradition is extravagant in makeup, using large heads and red ink to display its wares. After Palmer Hoyt became publisher of the *Post,* the paper gradually toned down until one day its largest display on page one was a two-column head. The management became convinced that readers preferred the former style and ordered the more flamboyant makeup restored. Although the *Star* and the *Post* are opposites in appearance, there is little difference in the type of contents used by the two papers.

Use Some System

Two general systems are found in current practice. One strives for balance; the other deliberately avoids it. Both types are patterned into numerous variations, some of them difficult to classify as will be noted.

Which system a newspaper shall follow is a problem to be solved only through study of its general appropriateness with respect to editorial policy as well as typographical esthetics and such practical considerations as ready adaptation to equipment available and the exigencies of news.

To be avoided is any form of makeup so extreme and so noisy typographically as to offer no chance whatever for adequate display when there is a story of supreme importance to be handled. Thus front pages that shriek daily are likely to find themselves impotent when the news offers something real to shriek about. On the other hand, it is a mistake to establish and enforce a system so conservative and hidebound that it will not give way before the emergency of a newsstory demanding special display to bring out its importance.

Use of a definite plan for every page of a newspaper, no matter how small, has an unquestioned value. The well-dressed newspaper always commands respect; the slovenly one forfeits it.

Balance and Symmetry

Nature may be said to abhor lopsidedness almost as much as it does a vacuum. Branches grow on all sides of trees, animals have two eyes and normal human beings have feet of comparable weight and size. It is literally natural, therefore, that a basic principle of art should be balance and symmetry, which is the balance of all parts with reference to the center of the whole.

Ordinarily when a balance is mentioned, one thinks of weights in equipoise. And a useful concept in newspaper makeup can be visualized by a simple experiment in physics. Two pounds of, say, butter perched on both ends of a yardstick can be balanced on a single point of support, or fulcrum, at the 18-inch mark. Add another pound to one end, and a balance can still be struck if the fulcrum is moved toward it. Thus, disproportionate weights can be balanced by an off-center fulcrum.

If *color—i.e.,* the degree of blackness of typographic elements—be thought of as weight, the two kinds of balanced makeup become understandable. One is balanced on an optical fulcrum in the center of the page, establishing an equipoise between headlines and cuts on either side. The other has an off-center balance, with an optical fulcrum near the heavier unit. And thus we have named the two general systems of balanced makeup, the *center balance* and the *off-center balance.*

Center-Balance Makeup. Under this heading fall two common patterns. One is often called *balance makeup,* but, to avoid confusion in terms, might well be designated *true-balance.* The other is *inverted-pyramid makeup.*

Both strive for symmetry and typographic beauty through an orderly balanced use of headlines, boxed heads and cuts.

In true-balance makeup, a large headline placed in the last column of the front page calls for a correspondingly large one in the first column. Other headlines are arranged in an orderly sequence to carry out the impression of equipoise.

If there are headlines below the fold of the paper, they also are balanced. If there is a one-column cut at the top of column 2, it is balanced by a cut of like size at the top of the next to the last column.

Conservative newspapers, especially, favor true-balance makeup, or some variant of it. However, there are but few that preserve a strict hair's-breadth balance, as this is likely to become monotonous to readers. The most familiar variation is to place a three-column cartoon at the tops of columns 3, 4 and 5, or 4, 5 and 6, and run major headlines in columns 1, 6 and 8, or 1, 3 and 8, with subsidiary headlines in the remaining columns and beneath the cartoon. Carefully selected fillers take up the remaining space. Another variation is the use of unusually large headlines in columns 1 and 8, or in column 8 only. In other cases there may be two-column headlines toward the bottom of columns 2 and 3 and 6 and 7.

In pyramid makeup, similar practices are followed, but with one difference. An optical fulcrum is established in the page's center near the fold, and heads or cuts are so arranged that they create lines of an inverted pyramid. Using a crayon to connect color elements on a page will help the student in locating the optical fulcrum and classifying the makeup system employed.

Off-Center-Balance Makeup. The two makeup patterns just described have an obvious balance; more subtle is the balanced effect secured by the *brace* and the *broken-column* methods which use the off-center principle.

First, the brace pattern. It developed because of the common need to give to one outstanding story a maximum display. Once streamer lines were accepted, it was easy to give one to the big story, then drop into a large headline at the top of the righthand columns. The typographic weight was thus concentrated in the upper right quarter of the page, roughly suggesting the pattern of a brace or wall bracket, hence the name.

Variants of brace makeup include the occasional reversing of the plan— that is, leading from the streamer into the columns at the left. Brace makeup is especially useful for papers that use three- or four-column heads instead of streamers.

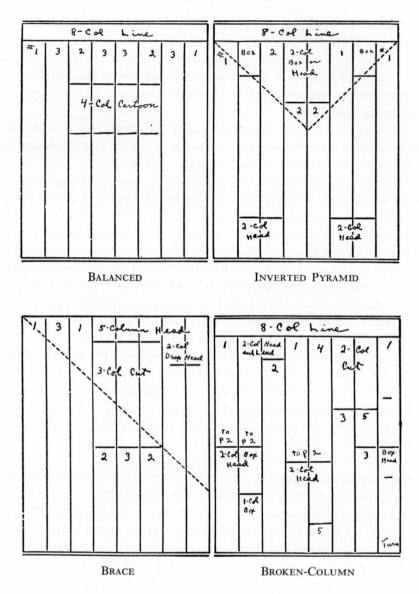

BALANCED   INVERTED PYRAMID

BRACE   BROKEN-COLUMN

There is no rule for achieving balance in brace makeup. Various devices, such as two-column heads, boxes and cuts, are spotted elsewhere on the page to offset the concentrated weight. It is in solving such problems that new headlines and new ways of displaying news values are evolved and editorial acumen and ingenuity are shown at their best.

BRACE MAKEUP of the Washington Post gives the page an off-center balance. Two-column headlines on the left are used to offset the weight at the right of the page. The two pictures and the banner headlines give the page its brace effect. The two display stories at the bottom of the page keep the page from becoming top-heavy. One problem in this double banner arrangement is that the reader has to hunt for the story accompanying the second banner headline.

273

Broken-Column Makeup. This calls for typographic skill and a nice sense of symmetry and proportion. Otherwise the page may look like something assembled by a printer's apprentice assisted by the office boy. It can be done expertly, however, giving the news display an effervescent quality.

If a news index is run on the front page, the tendency is to run fairly long stories so as to reduce the necessity for trailing jumps through other pages. But broken-column makeup was developed primarily to get as many short stories on page 1 as possible.

An impression of symmetry on a page cut up by many headlines, boxes and cuts is difficult to secure. But it can be done by carefully arranging all elements so that they do not cancel each other out by propinquity and by spotting the large ones where they tend to give a pleasing pattern to the whole page.

Unbalanced Makeup. Just as flush headlines mark a reaction against the carefully organized headlines that stress symmetry and design, so some newspapers refuse to be cabin'd and confined by the limitations upon freedom imposed by balanced makeups. When freed of arbitrary restraint, makeup takes multitudinous forms, but two general trends are discernible and can be given the labels *circus* and *panel*.

THE STRUCTURE of a typical panel page, featuring a news summary.

Balance will suggest poise and equanimity—which are precisely what certain newspapers do not want. Symmetrical niceties, they theorize, make for uneventful reading, do not jolt the reader along from one sensation to another. So, carrying the broken-column technique to its ultimate, they have produced the circus type of makeup.

In this, the page is broken up with no thought to regularity, symmetry or apparent order. Many headlines, of all sizes, and boxes and cuts are used, each a circus barker for the reader's attention. It is not a makeup favored by conservative papers.

Whereas the circus style is sensational and brusque, the second unbalanced makeup seeks to be quietly forceful. It is characterized by a panel or block effect on the front page, whence it gets its name.

The panel pattern usually is set by a news summary or an expanded index in two-column measure, or by a vertical tier of pictures of the same width. This panel may fall in the center of the page, but practice favors columns 1 and 2, though occasionally it is to be found in columns 7 and 8. Horizontal panel units, consisting of three-, four-, five-, or six-column heads or cuts, may branch from it. Such an element at the bottom of the page gives the whole an "L" pattern. Or the "L" can be reversed and upset by running it near the top.

Panel makeup is sometimes called *streamline* makeup, for it commonly is associated with flush headlines and other earmarks of modern typography. It often omits column rules and otherwise strives for contrast of gray or black areas with white spots known as *airholes*. The style lends itself to departmentalization of the news, with the summary or index panel quickly giving the reader the gist of the day's happenings. The rest of the front page may handle news in somewhat the orthodox fashion, or it may swing at once into news departments, each carrying its general head.

Advocates of this style hold that it offers a refreshing relief from traditional makeup and is functional because it aids the reader effortlessly to organize his reading. They maintain that the summary gives a concentrated overall view of the news, which makes it possible to scatter even important stories under appropriate departmental designations through the inside pages—which, incidentally, raises their value to the advertiser.

The Upper-Right Fetish

Some editors hold that since readers read from left to right, the number one news position is the top right of the page with the text in column 8, or where the headline leaves off. Typical is a spread head occupying columns 4, 5, 6, 7 and 8 with a two-column bank in columns 7 and 8, and the body of the story in column 8.

Although the preference for the top right position for the lead story is still strong, many papers have demonstrated that emphasis can be shifted to other parts of the page. The Atlanta *Journal,* for instance, frequently places a picture at the top of columns 6, 7 and 8. This arrangement gives emphasis to the headlines next to the cut and below the cut. In the Cleveland *Press* the *readout* (or drop) from the major head is likely to be in the middle of the page (columns 4 and 5). In the New York *Times* columns 1 and 8 often claim equal emphasis.

Actually, a makeup editor can draw attention to a story no matter where he places it on the page. The top-right dominance could be the result of newspaper habit rather than reader preference.

Makeup Should Be Fexible

Makeup must be flexible enough to permit last-minute changes without disturbing the whole pattern.

Suppose a late-breaking big story comes in, demanding the number one position on the page, after the dummy has been completed. Quickly the makeup editor shifts the earlier lead story to number two position, moves the number two story to the bottom of the page, forcing its predecessor to the inside. Such shifts are possible if the makeup editor prepares for the eventuality of a last-minute switch.

He has many choices: usually he selects the easiest regrouping. If the page is tight and the makeup editor does not want to increase the number of jump stories, he can pull out a picture and replace it with a story. Or he can make the late story a bulletin, put it in boldface type and squeeze it in somewhere on the page. He doesn't worry too much about the page as an art form; he is interested in giving the reader the latest possible news and in helping the composing room meet the all-important deadline.

Makeup for Big News

The biggest *spread story* of all is the story of the quadrennial national election, the telling of which requires many pages. Usually, a great deal of appropriate material—pictorial layouts, tabulations, headlines and even text matter—will have been prepared in advance. To this is added the growing body of information, either as divisional stories with separate headlines, or in the form of new leads, precedes, inserts and bulletins.

The makeup editor must be quick to adapt his plans to obtain a maximum degree of display value for the latest or most significant information. The problem is complicated, of course, if other important news happens to break at the same time. Usually it will be relegated to a minor spot on the front or some inside page, although occasionally it will be of enough interest to merit a small line. In case of presidential elections, two or more streamers will be set up, the appropriate one being used when the final *flash* comes.

Such news naturally divides itself into a succession of stories, beginning with a general lead that summarizes every important feature and gravitating into a series of subsidiary stories that take up specific angles. Pictures, diagrams, tables, boxes, other features, may accompany such a story, and it may begin on page 1, turn into and fill page 2, and even extend to other pages.

Here are page diagrams, starting with a front page built on the brace pattern, showing the play on it and pages 2 and 3 that might be given big

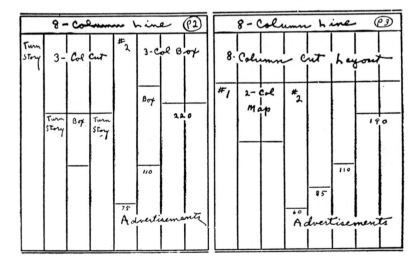

news. To simplify them for study purposes, indications of other stories, boxes, and cuts have been omitted.

Double Front Pages

Every news editor in the country would rather play local news than wire news but in the cities most local stories simply cannot compete with tense news from the state, the nation or from abroad. Some papers retain page 1 for the major news of the day and use a second page (usually the back page) to display local or regional news.

The Minneapolis *Star* and the San Diego *Union* have two main news pages—page 1 and the first page of the second section, the latter stressing local news. The Denver *Post* uses the back page to present regional news. In this instance, the second main page is a treat for readers who insist upon reading the back page first.

Departmentalization Can Be Helpful

All newspapers departmentalize the news to some extent. That is, they group related stories together on the page, reserve special sections for departments like sports and society, and usually try to have the editorial page appear in the same position every day (*e.g.*, left side, right side, back page).

Even more departmentalization of the news doubtless would be used if news arrived in compartments. But it doesn't. There may be a gap of several hours between stories bearing foreign datelines. In the interval are undated roundups, state and national items. News from the state capital might lead off the report, then disappear completely until late morning and pour in with a flourish in early afternoon. Pages cannot be held open to wait for news of a particular variety.

Some papers, however, try to package news into boxes under standing heads like *Washington, The Human Side, Local News, Weather, Business, Over the State, Labor, Births.*

Departmentalization helps readers select the types of news they want to read. Furthermore, readers can find related items in one place and do not have to hunt through the paper for certain stories. Its disadvantages are lack of variety and flexibility in makeup and particularly lack of effective display.

University of Colorado
Journalism Department
Boulder, Colo.

The OURAY COUNTY HERALD

OURAY — RIDGWAY

Volume LXX — No. 41 — COLORADO — Friday, November 4, 1955

AL FEDEL CHOICE FOR MAYOR IN OURAY ELECTION TUESDAY

Al Fedel, Ouray's own native son will be the chief city dad for the next two years, being chosen by a majority of 60 votes over incumbent A. F. Nickel. Total votes cast, Fedel 186, Nickel 126.

All new members of the council were elected with the exception of Frank Rice, who was recently appointed to fill a vacancy.

Mike Driscoll (Citizens Party) led with a total of 175 votes. Clair Chamberlain (Citizens Party) was elected with 120, Frank Rice (Progressive Party) 57 and Samuel L. Fellin (Citizens Party) 56.

Defeated candidates were Marvin Gregory (Progressive Party) 26, Kenneth R. Moorehead (Citizens Party) 42, Tom Osborne (Progressive Party) 88, H. B. Flora (Progressive Party) 37.

Marie Gilbert, unopposed for city clerk, received 288 votes, and 241 to fill vacancy which will occur on Nov. 15 following the resignation of Drois Clark, present city clerk.

LaVaughn Merling, unopposed for city treasurer, received 299 votes.

SCOTTS SEE GREAT FUTURE FOR OURAY

Following is a letter received by Willard Croft, president of the local Chamber of Commerce. The Scotts have vacationed in Ouray for the past two years staying at the Croft Courts.

Mr. Scott is associated with the Scott Rug Cleaning Co. in Fort Worth, Texas, an old firm established in 1892 and it is quite a boost to the town to have him advertising it:

Fort Worth 3, Texas
Oct. 26, 1955

Dear Mr. Croft:

We are happy to enclose our check in the amount of $5.00 for the Community Raffle. If by some remote chance our number is drawn, you have our permission to donate same to the city of Ouray to the best advantage. We wish we were there now and look forward to our early return. We definitely feel that Ouray and the Western Slope are on the rise and wish we could be there to grow with it. Best regards to Mrs. Croft and you.

Mr. and Mrs. Derrell R. Scott and Norma

RELATIVES KILLED IN AUTO ACCIDENT

Mrs. Jennie Ernesberger of Hempstead, Texas and daughter, Miss Gertrude Ernesberger, were killed in an auto accident about ten days ago. Mrs. Ernesberger was a sister of J. P. Carney, who is now in Evanston, Ill. with his son and family.

THANKS

I wish to thank all my friends for the lovely flowers and cards sent during my stay in the hospital.

Ruth Hutter

Save this date, Thanksgiving Eve, and attend the Fireman's annual dance.

URANIUM BOWL FOOTBALL GAME AT DELTA NOV. 11

Western State college at Gunnison and Colorado School of Mines at Golden will clash Nov. 11 at Delta in the annual Uranium bowl football game. It will be the only college tussle of the year on the Western Slope.

Sponsored by the Delta Quarterback club, the traditional game is expected to attract gridiron fans from all over the Western Slope. Last year State won a thriller from Mines, 21-12, in a contest highlighted by 100 yard kickoff return by Mines' Bill Westhoff.

State and Mines have played once this year—at Golden—resulting in the closest contest in State's colorful season. Winning 18-12, State was hardpressed thruout the game. If the early season meeting is any indication, the second go-round in the Uranium bowl should prove the Big Game for both teams.

Reserved seat and general admission tickets are now on sale and may be obtained by writing the Comet Drug, 407 Main street, Delta, or by contacting any Quarterback club member.

BOB MEARS is star quarterback for the Western State college Mountaineers and will be calling the signals in the Uranium Bowl game Nov. 11 in Delta.

MRS. O. N. WESTON PASSES ON TUESDAY NIGHT, OCTOBER 25TH

Mrs. O. N. Weston passed away Tuesday night, October 25th at 11 p. m. at the Memorial hospital in Montrose, just two weeks after entering the hospital. She had suffered many years with diabetes, and suffered a paralytic stroke during her two weeks illness.

Mrs. Weston was born, October 12, 1888 at Geneva, Nebraska. She, with her husband and son came to Colorado in the middle 1930's, and lived on ranches at Mayfield until this summer, when they bought property and moved into Ridgway.

Alma Weston was a willing and ardent worker in the Rebekah Branch of Odd Fellowship, having transferred to Ridgway Rebekah No. 12 in March of 1938 from Sidney Rebekah No. 66 at Sidney, Nebraska. She was a Past Noble Grand, having served three terms and was the holder of The Decoration of Chivalry, the highest award bestowed upon any Rebekah. She was also a member of the Booster Club, ladies order of the Canton, and Ladies Auxiliary, Patriarchs Militant, branches of Odd Fellowship, at Montrose, and a member of the Ridgway M. E. Church.

She leaves to mourn her passing, her husband, a son, Byron and his wife and a grandson, Bobby Lee Weston.

Funeral services were held from the M. E. Church, Saturday afternoon, Reverend Bowden, officiating. Flor Funeral Home, of Ouray, had charge of arrangements. She was laid to rest in Cedar Hill cemetery. Ridgway Rebekah Lodge No. 12 in charge of graveside services.

The large attendance and vast profusion of floral offerings attested to her standing in the community.

Pallbearers were: Buel Adams, W. M. Carmichael, Kenneth Kelly, Wm. H. Kettle, Leonard Kinzick and George R. Stoner.

Another link is severed from the Golden Chain of Love and Sister Alma will be missed by all who knew her.

WOMAN'S CLUB HAS INTERESTING MEETING

Only twelve members were present at the regular meeting of the Woman's Club Tuesday due to the election and stormy weather.

President Elsie Sonza presided at the meeting with Mrs. Harold Leicester acting as secretary due to the absence of Mrs. Hal Hall.

A card was read from Margaret M. Porter asking that the report of any international activities be reported to her office before February 1st.

Details were discussed pertaining to the sale of the building. Mrs. Dorys Muffingle gave a report on past legal transactions having to do with past sales on the building. Mrs. Howard Hammond was appointed by the president to investigate the situation further with Mrs. Eva Moule to assist. Mrs. Willard Croft also volunteered to help in any way she could.

Mrs. Maude Soderburg and Mrs. Maltzburger were reported ill.

Mrs. Fran Johnson, chairman of the Mary Hill concert, gave a report on ticket sales.

Mrs. H. B. Flora asked for volunteers to help with the addressing of T. B. seals at her home Friday. Mrs. Anderson, Mrs. Sonza, Mrs. Zadra, Mrs. Hammond, Mrs. Staley and Mrs. Croft volunteered to help.

The president, Mrs. Sonza, gave a report on a child welfare program attended in Montrose by herself, Mrs. Sherbino and Mrs. Soderburg.

Mrs. Croft, program chairman, announced that Mrs. Fitch of Albuquerque would be present next meeting to show her slides on the Navajos.

Following the business meeting, Mrs. Croft introduced Mrs. Marvin Gregory who was in charge of the program.

100 per cent member participation followed when Mrs. Gregory placed all sorts of shells, sequins, plants, feathers, etc. on a table and announced "Everyone do it yourself." The results were outstanding and we found we had several artists who had been keeping their talents a secret.

CHARGES FILED IN WRECK

A charge of making an improper left turn was filed in Justice of Peace court in Montrose against Larry Anderson of Montrose as a result of an accident on U. S. 550 north of Ouray last weekend.

According to state Patrolman Dick Tappan, Anderson was driving north on the highway, and just as Jack Hayes, of Grand Junction started to pass him, he attempted to make a left hand turn causing a collision.

Damage to the Hays car was estimated at $150 and to Anderson's $100.

FUNERAL SERVICES FOR SAM J. PHILLIPS SUNDAY

Funeral services for Sam J. Phillips of Ridgway will be held at the Ridgway Community Church Sunday afternoon Nov. 6th at 2:00 o'clock. Rev. Foster of Montrose will officiate.

Mr. Phillips was born Feb. 2, 1880 at Piedmont, Colo. and passed away at the Montrose Memorial Hospital Nov. 3rd, 1955.

Burial will be at the Cedar cemetery in Montrose with the Flor Funeral Home in charge.

REMEMBER THIS—

Your Volunteer Fire Dept. protects all our homes and property. They only ask help from you once a year, so when you are solicited to buy a ticket for the Thanksgiving dance, give to them cheerfully.

DON COMFORT, ACCORDIONIST, AT SCHOOL NOVEMBER 10

The first National Assembly program of this school year will be presented by Don Comfort, accordionist, on Thursday, November 10 at 9:00 a. m. The public is invited.

Don started to study the accordion at the age of eight, and he majored in music in high school. He holds an Associate of Arts Degree in music and he did further study at the University of Redlands, California. Much of his serious training and study of the classics was with Anthony Galla-Rini, world famous concert accordion artist.

Mr. Comfort has done television work and has appeared coast to coast over the National Broadcasting Company on several occasions. For the past four years he has been under contract to National School Assemblies and has given programs before more than eight million people.

On his return tour he is featuring a very rare electronic accordion which is the only known such instrument west of Chicago. It was manufactured in Philadelphia and is worth approximately $2,000. Mr. Comfort also uses two other accordions to bring to his audiences a well-rounded program of music ranging from classical to a musical visit through Disney Land, to the very latest in popular music.

MILLION DOLLAR HIWAY TO BE WIDENED

According to the 1956-57 Highway program for Western Colorado as proposed and approved by members of Club 20 there will be construction of approximately five miles on Lime Creek south of Silverton. This will complete pavement of entire length of 789 from Canada to Mexico.

Also stabilization and re-oiling from Uncompahgre to Ouray and widening of road between Ouray and Silverton—particularly narrow stretch on so-called Million Dollar Highway.

NEW GRANDDAUGHTER FOR THE DRISCOLLS

Mr. and Mrs. Mike Driscoll are rejoicing over the safe arrival of a new granddaughter at the home of Mr. and Mrs. Richard S. Driscoll of La Grande, Oregon. The young miss arrived October 29th weighing 5 lbs. 8 ounces. She has been named Vicki Lynn.

Beautiful Ford Club Coupe given away at the Firemans annual dance Thanksgiving Eve.

FIRST SNOW IN CITY LAST THURSDAY

A light rain started falling in the night last Wednesday and by the time daylight descended had turned to the first snow of the season.

Skies were cloudy most of Thursday, Friday and part of Saturday morning and a light snow fell part of the time.

Surrounding mountain peaks of the San Juan ranges have been topped with snow noticeably for the past week, earlier in the month they were covered with snow, which later melted, but they are now sporting a fresh covering.

It was reported to have snowed hard on the Million Dollar Highway between Ouray and Silverton and we hear the local garages and service stations received rush calls for more than a dozen pair of chains to be delivered to motorists stranded on the loop.

CALENDAR

November 10—National Assembly, 9:00 o'clock.

ANNUAL FALL BAZAAR AT ST. DANIEL'S CHURCH NOVEMBER 12

The Annual Fall Bazaar for St. Daniels Church will be held on Saturday, November 12th in the St. Daniels Hall. Fish pond, cake booth, fancy work and game booths as well as refreshments will be part of the evenings entertainment. Three main awards will be given in the course of the evening. A large hooked rug, an electric shaver and a fine Thanksgiving turkey. All are invited to take in this community event.

MRS. SCALA ENTERTAINS FRIENDSHIP CLUB

Mrs. Mike Driscoll and Mrs. Frank Fedel were guests last Wednesday night when Mrs. Tullio Scala entertained the Friendship bridge club at her home. Delicious refreshments were served by the hostess. Mrs. W. E. Davis will be the hostess when the club meets November 16.

COMBINING TABLOID and standard format, this weekly newspaper uses tabloid size for front and back pages. But when the paper is opened and turned, three pages become standard eight-column pages. This paper thus has five pages.

Making Up the Tabloid

Front pages of tabloids vary widely. Some tabloids, especially those of small towns, are conservative in their makeup, often following conventional patterns. Tabloids in large cities tend to be more sensational, some resembling their predecessor, the *Illustrated Daily News* of New York. A front page may consist of as large a headline as possible, perhaps in two lines, with a line of small type referring to the page on which the story is found. The rest of the page may be taken up with one or more pictures.

The tabloid format has won favor with many weeklies, college newspapers and especially with newspapers produced by offset where pictures are used liberally.

The tabloid size is ideal for emphasizing a few elements. A three-column picture, for instance, dominates the page. A one-line head, which struggles for attention in a standard paper, stands out on a tabloid page. Because of its size (usually five columns wide and 15 to 17 inches deep) the tabloid lends itself to magazine-type display. It also provides greater opportunities than the standard newspaper for departmentalization.

Ten Makeup Tips

Caution is needed in the use of any system of makeup. Some general observations:

1. *Avoid huddling the headlines at the top of the page.* One will cancel the effectiveness of another and all are nullified as to news values. There should be even no momentary doubt in the reader's mind as to which columns of type follow multiple streamers.

2. *Don't huddle at the bottom of the page, either.* This section is more frequently underused than overused, however.

3. *Avoid tombstoning.* Headlines of the same size side by side in more than two columns will bury each newsstory and make the headline its tombstone. Study the tricks makeup editors use to avoid tombstoning—such as placing boxes and cuts at the heads of columns, thereby forcing headlines under them so far down they won't fight with those in the next column.

4. *Avoid monotonous arrangements.* If all headlines scattered on page 1 are large, black and of the same size or nearly so, again they cancel one another. None stands out and the makeup becomes monotonous.

5. *Use a variety of types.* One of the most noticeable shortcomings of the small paper is the lack of appropriate display type in all sizes of the same family. The headlines are too small (10-, 12-, 14-point) thereby giving no display at all, or a few heavy handset heads are scattered about the page, thereby killing the smaller, lighter heads. Or faces from various families of type are used together,

giving the page an ugly appearance. An assortment of machine type ranging from 14- to 60-point in the same family would do wonders in improving many small papers.

6. *Play up big stories.* There should be a distinctive headline for the two or three most important page 1 stories, a headline that will give these "stories of the day" the prominence they deserve, so that the reader is guided to them. Though he manipulates cold metal, the makeup editor is a practical psychologist, constantly studying the reaction of people to the ways in which the day's news is served up.

7. *Don't waste your shots.* This big lead headline, which of course should be the largest that is used by the newspaper, should be confined to the first page. It is a good plan to use the next largest headline for the most important stories to be run on the inside pages. The other subsidiary headlines also should be used here as well as on page 1. If color headlines are used, or patches of color typing, be sure they are placed so as not to dominate the entire page, unless this effect is desired.

8. *Respect the fold.* Avoid breaking either headline or picture on the fold; place face pictures so that the subject is not looking off the page.

9. *Think of quarter pages.* Visualize the page as being divided into quarter sections, then see that each section has at least one emphatic attraction.

10. *Be courageous!* Don't be afraid to experiment with a makeup pattern that will give the paper a fresh, appealing appearance.

18 Making Up Inside Pages and Special Sections

Apart from the question of making the advertisements in a newspaper more effective, there is a responsibility on the part of editors to make certain that every page is attractively and interestingly made-up, and in such a manner as to get the maximum reader traffic below the fold as well as above the fold.—Dr. George Gallup (1901–   ), *public opinion statistician.*

I.   INSIDE NEWS PAGES

News Versus the Ads

An attractive window display beckons to a prospective customer. But if the store's interior is drab and "junky," the customer is likely to forget all about the appealing items he saw in the window. He'll do his shopping elsewhere.

Many newspapers have passable, even good, front pages but the inside pages are dull. Headline type faces are too small to grab the reader. Long, unbroken columns of type tell the reader the page is hard to read. Poor news display on an inside page puts its advertiser, who has spent money to make his message attractive, at a disadvantage with advertisers on livelier pages. When any page of a newspaper fails to attract and hold the reader it does damage to the whole paper.

Most inside news pages contain advertising ranging in size from nearly full page to a few inches in size. Usually it is arranged in pyramid fashion with the larger ads in the larger part of the pyramid. The pyramid may extend from the upper right to the lower left, on both sides of the page (double pyramid), or in double-page pyramid—on the left side on one page, the right side on the facing page.

Advertising employs borders, heavy or distinctive type faces, illustrations, color and white space to attract the maximum attention. Some ads appear in newsstory form (but labeled advertisement).

In the space not occupied by advertising the makeup editor has to fit news text, headlines and pictures and arrange these to balance the advertising. If advertising dominates the lower-right corner of the page, the makeup editor utilizes the top-left position for major news emphasis. Some editors prefer to spot a picture in this corner position. If the makeup editor has art available for the page he tries to avoid placing the cut too near advertising containing illustration.

A makeup editor should have at his disposal a variety of headline sizes, stories of different lengths and plenty of fillers if he is to fill the gaps and give adequate display to the news. The old rule was to allow a minimum of one display head for each open column at the top of the page, that is, any column not filled by an ad. On a page in which advertising is light, the minimum will have to be increased considerably.

Avoid 'Dutch' Breaks

Display advertising salesmen seem to have an unfortunate facility in selling ads 19 inches deep. Further, the advertising layout department, for some reason, insists on stacking ads to within two inches of the folio. In both cases the page has a hole two inches deep into which the makeup editor must fit a newsstory.

Suppose the gap is four columns wide. The makeup editor has a story long enough to wrap over the four columns but it has a one-column headline. If he starts the story in column 5 and breaks the type over in the remaining three columns he produces a *raw wrap* or a *dutch break*. He prefers to have every column headed by display type. He can use a four-column head which will leave hardly any space for the text; a three-column and a one-column head; two two-column heads; or one two-column head and two single-column heads.

That's when he has to start lopping sentences or full paragraphs from stories, or change headlines. He may convert a two-line single-column head into a double-column single liner and flank it with smaller heads. He will try various combinations to avoid the raw wrap and *tombstoning*.

A single-line head stretching across four or more columns (called a *binder*) is used to top a longer story that has to be wrapped over several columns. A binder may be used with or without a bank.

A *blanket head* is one of two or more columns that brackets two or more stories. It is used if the makeup editor gets stories alike or directly opposite. For instance, three short items describe the illness of the heads of three governments. Here is a chance to blanket the three stories under a common headline.

A *type wrap* has to go to the right. If the story goes from one column to another, the wrapped portion should not go above the headline.

Good makeup practices sometimes have to be abandoned if the page is especially *tight, i.e.,* crowded with advertisements. Appearance may be sacrificed, but type should never be arranged so that the reader has trouble following the story.

II. SPECIAL INSIDE PAGES

Some Are Dull, Some Lively

There is no excuse for any page of a newspaper to be dull. Even the classified ad page can be dressed up with bold headings to break the monotony of type. Good makeup cannot save poor content but poor makeup lessens the appeal of a good story or advertisement.

Advertising has done its part to bring color and variety to the newspaper. Furthermore, it has finally conceded that white space lends emphasis, tone, dignity to the message. Editorial makeup, unfortunately, has not always kept pace with advertising makeup.

No editor can plead ignorance for poor makeup. Even the smallest paper can be attractive throughout if the editor will pay attention to makeup and invest in enough equipment to give his paper the materials for good display. The techniques used by the big-city papers give him all the models he needs to make every page attractive.

Women's Pages

Compare the society (or women's) pages of today with those of a decade or so ago. Bolder headings have replaced the light type faces that made the page vapid. Pictures no longer are confined to actionless *face* or *mug shots.* Today's pictures show club women doing something—teenagers at play, models dressed in latest fashions. Short fillers are topped with heads, longer stories get spread heads, names stand out in boldface,

WOMEN'S ACTIVITIES, ranging from society to cooking and gardening, get attention in the women's department of the Chicago *Daily News*. Heavy display type has replaced vapid italics in headlines. Banner headlines are common. Numerous photos, in a variety of sizes and shapes, give the page eye-appeal. The page generally reflects good writing and good editing.

285

boxes call attention to sparkling features, regular columns contain headlines intended to arouse curiosity, departmental headings are illustrated.

Change in content has been accompanied by a change in presentation. Weddings, engagements, meetings and parties now share space with items devoted to food, health, gardening, travel, hobbies, fashions, rearing children, manners and education. Layouts like *Paris in the Spring, Outdoor Play Center, New Hairstyle Changes* have given the *soc* page a new look. The page no longer is confined to the activities of the 400. It reflects, rather, the widening interests and activities of women.

Sports Pages

The sports page, unlike the society page, has a tradition of bold, forceful makeup. Heavy type, action-packed photos, sports columns and other features combine to give the sports page the greatest appeal in the paper next to page 1. In fact, the sports editor has to battle the news side to keep the latter from stealing the sports lead for page 1.

The sports editor has the advantage over other departmental editors in that usually he has at least one open page on which he can display his material properly. When he gets to the jump sports page he, too, finds a makeup problem. The page containing stories jumped from the sports page should come after, not before, the main sports page.

Art work is the main reason sports pages are well-displayed. This includes large, detailed cuts, sequence pictures, cartoons, sketches and panels, thumbnail face shots and mortised cuts.

Sequence shots give the reader the impression of movement. In a football series, for instance, the halfback starts around right end in the first photo, in the second the blockers have cleared the way for the runner and in the third the ball-carrier is sprinting across the goal.

Occasionally a static picture (*e.g.,* a team lined up for a group shot) appears on the sports page, but usually even the posed pictures indicate action or represent an unusual angle (huddle pictures, for example).

Other methods used to attract attention to the sports page include heavy binder heads, boldfaced paragraphs interspersed in the text, double-column boxes, illustrated departmental headings, sketches within the text.

Detracting elements are too much agate type, headlines that conflict, too many typographical stunts. Most box-scores are now set half-column measure so they can be doubled over and thus consume less space. Still lacking on most sports pages are stories and pictures of sports activities of

ACTION PHOTOS and big display type put spirit into the main sports page of the Madison (Wis.) *Capital Times.* Notice the effective use of boxed heads and "kicker" lines. Statistical matter is set in agate type to save space. Ads and additional sports items are carried on succeeding pages.

women. The page, with all its devices for appealing makeup, caters mainly to avid male fans of spectator sports.

Editorial Pages

More than any other page in the newspaper, the editorial page has lacked bold experimentation in makeup. Little wonder, then, that readership studies show the editorial page to be one of the least-read sections of the newspaper. It need not be unattractive, as many newspapers are now proving.

Dominant position for editorials is the left page although some papers use the back page and a few the righthand page. Some newspapers use two pages for editorial material—a main editorial page containing editorials, cartoons, columns and an opposite (*op ed*) page containing various types of editorial features.

Widths for editorial columns vary—one column, one and a half columns, two columns. Some papers use column rules, others do not.

Among changes that have improved the editorial page are the following:

1. *Art work.* This includes the editorial cartoon (usually three columns), panels, drawings and sketches both in the editorials and in the columns (including letters to the editor), news photos and thumbnail cuts.

2. *More and larger headlines.* This includes larger heads over editorials (the Cleveland *Press* uses a large double-column head for its lead editorial, two-line heads for longer editorials and one-line display heads for shorter editorials), headings over each letter in the letters column, descriptive headlines over syndicated columns.

3. *More white space.* This has been achieved by shorter paragraphs, shorter editorials, more space for gutters, eliminating column rules, more horizontal makeup.

4. *Color.* Pictures, cartoons and other drawings appear in color to give the page eye-appeal and interest.

Other typographical devices found on today's editorial page are initial capital letters, underscored headings and kicker lines, stars or marker dots in place of "30" dashes and three-way boxes.

Most of the innovations mentioned above have been made without loss of dignity to the page. The pages have a variety of material and all displayed in a manner calculated to appeal even to the casual reader. Contrast makes the page exciting and inviting, something that could not be said of the editorial section of yesteryear.

SPRIGHTLY MAKEUP on the editorial page of the Cleveland *Press* is achieved by type arrangement, drawings, cartoons, pictures, boxes and variety in length of editorials. Generally, one or several elements dominate the page.

289

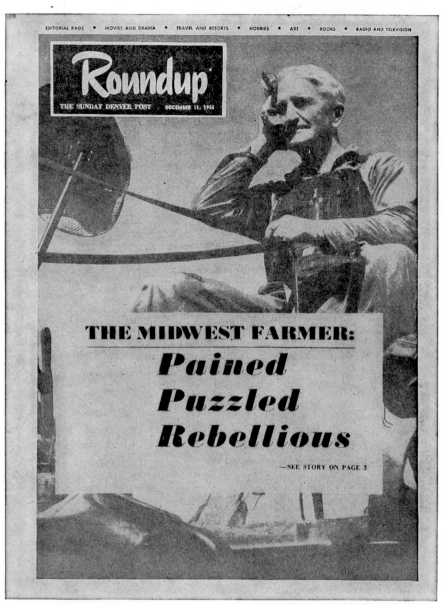

Roundup

THE SUNDAY DENVER POST   DECEMBER 11, 1955

THE MIDWEST FARMER:
Pained
Puzzled
Rebellious

—SEE STORY ON PAGE 3

TABLOID FORMAT is used by the Denver *Post* for its Sunday editorial section. The section contains letters, editorials and columns, editorial features, book reviews and various other features like travel notes, stamp news, crossword puzzles.

290

Editing of editorial page matter usually is done by an editorial page staffman and not by copyeditors on the main desk. All the diligence in editing news copy must be applied to editing editorial page matter. Editorial writers, especially on metropolitan newspapers, have time for research and writing, but even they are not infallible. On occasion, they obscure ideas with words, misquote well-known passages, and get careless with facts or figures. Their copy needs to be checked—and edited.

Enough editorials are prepared so that the editorial page makeup editor can select those that will fit the space available (exceptions are the lead editorial and those marked for a specific date). Short paragraphs, called by one editor "spitballs lovingly fired out of a rubber band," are invaluable in justifying the column.

III.   SPECIAL EDITIONS

Editions Change Content

An edition consists of the entire number of copies printed and published at one time by a newspaper.

Small and medium papers cover their circulation field with one edition or printing each day (or week), and occasionally come out with a whopper special edition of 80 or more pages.

A special edition is the result of long planning and preparation. Weeks in advance of the special edition publication the entire staff starts putting in overtime, writing and editing material for the special. As soon as a section is completed it is run off the press and stacked away. The last section to be printed is the regular paper which is then combined with the preprinted sections.

Special editions are built around themes like progress, anniversary, vacation, Christmas, Easter, automobiles, fall fashions, convention, harvest, school.

Larger newspapers have three or more editions daily in addition to specials like *pre-date* and Sunday. Each edition is intended for a certain class of readers or certain geographical areas. These bear characteristic names like *City, Final, Home, Sports Extra,* descriptive titles like *Bluestreak* and sometimes distinctive colors. Some editions are intended for *street sales,* some for *mail distribution,* some for *home delivery.*

For an afternoon paper to reach the edges of its primary circulation territory by afternoon, the paper has to be printed early. First edition of some metropolitan afternoon dailies comes off the press by mid-morning or late-morning. Final edition times vary, but the trend is to move up edition times so that the subscriber has his paper when he comes home from work so he can read it before he sits down to dinner. For areas several hundred miles away, some dailies print a pre-date edition containing material prepared in advance of the paper's dateline. For instance, a paper edited and printed Saturday carries Monday datelines and is intended for Monday delivery. Sometimes country readers have an advantage over big city cousins because they can read the Sunday comics on Friday.

Actually, the bulk of the paper remains the same throughout the various editions. Editorials, editorial and magazine-page features, cartoons, comics, fiction, women's pages and all other departments that are not sensitive to news changes, together with a variable quantity of advertising, appear in all editions and furnish the solid foundation for each.

On some papers, certain pages are reserved for stories that are not likely to change from edition to edition. The name *sticker* or *frozen* is used for such a page, meaning that no changes are to be made in stories on that page once it has been locked up. Copy designated for such a page usually carries the "sticker" or "frozen" slug. Typical is a page containing color. If the page has to be "sweated in" to retain color register, changes in the page's makeup become expensive and time-consuming.

Makeover or replating is done on page 1, sports, market, jump pages and sometimes classified advertising pages if the paper permits a late deadline for classified advertising insertions.

Early editions usually carry major stories that broke late and appeared only in the final editions of the previous day, thus protecting readers on all news of major importance. These stories, together with fresh material the composing room has had time to set, plus *plug* or *time copy* go into early editions. Each edition sees more new or fresh material and less plug copy. But even with these changes, the number of replates is relatively low. On some editions, the replates may affect no more than two or three pages.

IV.   THE SUNDAY EDITION

A Newspaper Plus Features

Sunday newspapers are merely daily newspapers with feature supplements added to them. The news section of such papers is produced by the same staff that is responsible for the weekday paper.

To this are added the characteristic *Sunday sections,* produced by a separate staff called the *Sunday staff,* which is headed by a *Sunday editor.* This staff limits its activities to the production and handling of entertaining and instructive articles and stories of various kinds and to the characteristic Sunday-paper photographs and drawings, including the funnies. The only news or newslike features for which it is responsible are departments dealing with society and club news, the churches, books, art, the drama, motion pictures, real estate and fashions.

Syndicates Supply Much Copy

Analysis of the contents of Sunday newspapers as a whole makes it obvious that each one must originate its departments dealing with society, clubs, books, the drama, motion pictures and the churches. They must be grown in home ground if they are to have the greatest home value.

With the other departments it is different; there is nothing local about style, beauty, cooking, advice in love affairs, fiction, comic drawings and most photographs. Therefore the departments dealing with these matters may either originate in the office of the newspaper that publishes them or may be purchased from some other newspaper agency. Agencies that deal in these features are known as *syndicates.* There are some 50 of these in the United States that are widely known, and 100 smaller ones often offering but one or two features.

The great producing newspapers that originate all the features used in their pages in most cases have syndicates that sell these features to other papers outside the competitive field. There are other syndicates that have no connection with any newspaper, although they deal in newspaper features. Originally the syndicate was made up of a group of newspapers banded together to buy collectively articles, novels, stories and art work that they did not feel they could afford singly. According to the present system, one great newspaper will buy an unusually attractive feature outright and then resell it to clients. The bulk of the trade of the syndicates, of course, consists in sales of comic drawings and departments devoted to women's interests, but all manner of material is marketed for both daily and Sunday paper use, including news.

Working Ahead Helps

Few, if any, of the Sunday features are perishable in the sense that news is perishable. Fiction, for instance, does not "spoil" on the hands of the editor by ceasing to be timely. If a newspaper buys a serial story, there is nothing to prevent it from setting up the story in type several weeks before the first installment appears and syndicating it to papers outside its own sphere of influence. It can go further; it can assemble an entire fiction magazine and syndicate it. The same process is applicable to the many other distinctive Sunday features.

Meantime, the paper in which the features originate reaps certain advantages: The artist has plenty of time for his illustrations, the makeup man is enabled to do extra good work and the color printer is given leeway in which to produce his best effects. Most important of all, the newspaper can send several of its Sunday sections to press in advance of the date of publication—a vital and necessary step when the huge size of the modern Sunday newspaper is considered.

Generally the comics are sent to press first of all; the rotogravure sections follow; then come the picture sections, the sections devoted to women's activities and the sections devoted to movies, the drama, books and like subjects. Last of all the news section is added, and the Sunday paper is complete. The whole process, from beginning to end, may require from three to four weeks, and while one Sunday paper is being sold on the streets another is in the process of making.

19 Editing and Producing the Small Magazine Supplement

PRINTING

In me all human knowledge dwells;
The oracle of oracles,
Past, present, future, I reveal,
Or in oblivious silence seal;
What I preserve can perish never—
What I forego is lost forever.
I speak all languages; by me
The deaf may hear, blind may see,
The dumb converse, the dead of old
Communion with the living hold.
All hands are one beneath my rule,
All nations learners in my school.
Men of all ages, everywhere,
Become contemporaries there.
—James Montgomery (1771–1854), *British poet.*

I. SUNDAY ROTO MAGAZINES

An Expanding Market

The Sunday magazine supplement has become a common appendage to newspaper dailies, large and small. Once confined almost exclusively to the major market dailies, the syndicated magazine now is available to the smaller market papers as well.

Some papers buy syndicated magazines like *Parade, This Week, American Weekly, Family Weekly,* with the name of the local newspaper printed on the cover. Some newspapers produce their own local magazines; a few have both a syndicated supplement and a home magazine. And still others have a Sunday rotogravure magazine of their own (printed locally or elsewhere), a local feature magazine produced in the newspaper's plant and a syndicated magazine.

A magazine differs from a newspaper not only in format but in purpose and design. Because it must serve a national area, the syndicated magazine carries features of general interest. The distinction of the local magazine is that it is devoted exclusively (or nearly so) to regional interests.

Placing pictures and feature stories in a magazine format doesn't necessarily create a magazine. A magazine differs from a newspaper feature supplement primarily in the manner in which the pages are displayed. Content is important but appearance is the distinctive element of the magazine supplement.

Newspaper magazines have an impressive readership (frequently the highest for any part of the paper) because of the studied appeal to all classes and ages. Here story-telling, whether in text or pictures or a combination of both, reaches its highest art. Lacking the appeal of spot news, the features find their mark with good writing and attention-grabbing pictures or sketches.

Home-Made Magazines Can Do Well

In both content and appearance some of the locally edited newspaper magazines equal, often excel, the best of the syndicated magazines. And in almost every case these are directed by a skilled magazine editor rather than by a longtime staffer who is retired to the magazine staff because he can no longer pull his weight on the regular staff.

To produce a local weekly magazine a newspaper must have a plant capable of handling a magazine (or hire the printing to be done elsewhere) and an adequate production staff—usually consisting of an editor, artists, writers and photographers. The editor has to be a combination executive, writer, copyeditor, makeup editor, public relations and promotion expert. Unless he also is an artist, he will need the services of a first-class art director. The latter, in fact, can make the difference between a mediocre and an outstanding magazine.

Material for the Magazine

News shapes the newspaper, but in the magazine the editor selects the contents to fit a specific pattern. Articles must be appropriate in regard to other contents, the time of publication and the readers to whom the publication is directed.

SUNDAY MAGAZINES have become standard sections for newspapers, large and small. At the top are covers of two outstanding locally edited magazines produced by the Denver *Post* and the Atlanta *Journal* and *Constitution*. At the bottom is an inside double-spread from *Family Weekly,* a syndicated publication serving a large family of non-metropolitan dailies. Among syndicated magazines for larger dailies are *This Week, Parade* and *The American Weekly.*

297

News is published while it is still current. Material for the magazine must be projected to publication date which may be weeks after the material has been prepared. Production period for a magazine is usually four weeks at the minimum, the planning period even longer. Sometimes editors gather and prepare articles one season for use the following year.

Of course, anything can happen in the interval between story development and publication. One Sunday magazine editor ordered a story telling how it feels to be the wife of a varsity football coach. Pictures were taken and the text was written—all for use the following fall. But at the close of the football season the coach packed up and left the state after receiving a contract to coach at another university.

Advertising Calls the Tune

The amount of advertising sold for the magazine determines the number of pages in the magazine. The *breaking point, i.e.,* number of lines of advertising, provides a ratio varying from 50 to 65 per cent advertising. If the advertising is in large segments (*double spreads, full pages*), the editor has an *open* publication. That is, he has opportunity to use full pages and double pages for story layouts. If the advertising consists of smaller-sized units scattered throughout the magazine, the editor has fewer full pages and more *partial* pages to fill.

Color in advertising helps determine the amount of color for the editorial matter. If color is used on one page in an eight-page form the other seven pages also can accommodate color.

Advertising in the magazine occupies standard segments of the page, like double-page, full page, half page (either vertical or horizontal), third of a page and so on. Often a minimum is placed on the size ad sold for the magazine. Advertising is not pyramided on a page, as it is in the newspaper, but instead occupies the outer half or third of the page, the bottom half, or it may appear on both sides of the page, leaving a well in the center for editorial matter. If there is a last-minute cancellation by a client, the editor has to plug the space previously occupied by the ad or make a new page layout. Invariably, he'll do the latter.

Front, Back Positions

As soon as the editor receives the dummy showing placement of advertising, he is ready to lay out the magazine. He selects major or lead articles to go in the front of the book, secondary material for the back of the magazine. Regular departments such as recipes, hobbies, poetry, occupy the same space and are placed in relatively the same position each issue.

The editor must determine not only what he wants to use in the front of the magazine but also how he wants to display the main articles. Sometimes, the layout is adjusted to the text; other times, the text is adjusted to the picture layout. If the text is dominant, it gets the emphasis; if not, the text is submerged in favor of art. Either the layout is arranged so that the art enforces the text or the art carries most of the emphasis.

Since magazine-editing involves long-range planning, many editors have layouts in reserve—to be used anytime, especially if late changes demand revisions. Such reserve usually is secondary—and timeless. It can be used, however, only if it can fit into the page (assuming advertising will occupy part of the page) and if it is appropriate for the other editorial matter in the book. Some reserve material stays in the files for months before it can be used; sometimes it gathers so much age it is finally discarded.

Copy Must Be Fitted

Rough estimates of copy length based on a copy-line count won't work in the magazine where copy must be measured precisely. Some magazine editors use the character count system of measuring length of copy. This is done by placing a character gauge on lines of typewritten copy, one measurement for elite type, another for pica type. Comparing the character count of the manuscript with the space available tells the editor how much to trim the manuscript or how much to increase the space if the manuscript cannot be cut.

By consulting a type measurement scale, the editor knows, for example, that 10-point Linotype Bodoni allows 49 characters for a type line 18 picas wide. If the type is set on a 12-point slug, six lines of type occupy a column inch, or 294 characters. Dividing the total characters of the manuscript by 294 gives the space (in column inches of type) the manuscript will occupy.

If the space is fixed, the editor determines how many characters can be accommodated, then trims the manuscript accordingly.

If the manuscript is to occupy a certain space and column width, on one page, then jump to another page in another column width, the editor has to determine the character count for each page and fit the copy accordingly.

All this, of course, assumes that the copy needs little, if any, editorial revision or editing. Such copy is rare. If the copy has undergone major repairs, the editor might have to get it retyped before he starts fitting it into a layout.

Constant handling of copy soon gives the editor the "feel" for judging the length of a manuscript. If he decides to let the text run in its entirety, he can have it set into type, then make minor trims, if necessary. For instance, he can delete *widows* (one-line sentences standing by themselves), or even short paragraphs. If trims cannot be made without doing injustice to the story, the editor has no choice but to jump the story to another page, or revise the page layout.

Copy produced in the office can be written to size by setting the type-writer stops to correspond with the type-line length. If the column contains 100 type lines, the writer simply writes 100 lines, each line corresponding to a type line. The character count system is almost a "must" in writing picture cutlines so that the last line is a full line and not a straggler. For all headlines, of course, an exact unit count must be used.

Laying Out the Magazine

A magazine page is designed to attract and hold the reader, to call attention to particular elements, to help the reader find his way through the story and, often, to complement the facing page. Generally, the newspaper magazine uses a dramatic layout.

Normally the reader's eye focuses at a point on the page slightly above the center of the page rectangle. But the page can be designed so that the focal point is anywhere on the page. Then other elements are added to get the reader's eye to move along a definite route. If there are too many high-spots on the page they tend to clash, causing the reader to flip the page to escape the confusion. The design or layout attracts the reader to the contents and helps whet his curiosity and interest.

The primary element of layout is the subject matter. A layout is a method of showing a story to the reader. The end is not a pretty page, but an arrangement that does justice to the story and is appropriate to the tone and character of the book. Layout helps the reader get the story. The techniques are many and varied.

Art (picture, sketch, drawing) attracts attention, tells part of the story itself, and provides the reader with an image of the subject as he goes through the text. Illustrations play a heavy role in the newspaper Sunday magazine because the magazine is designed for all members of the family,

Orin A. Sealy photo for Empire Magazine

ART DIRECTOR H. Ray Baker lays out *Empire Magazine* (Denver *Post*), two facing pages at a time to achieve a pleasing unified effect. Where the spread is primarily devoted to a photo story, layout favors the pictures and Baker allots an area for the text which will be written later to fit the space exactly. Where the story is more important than the illustrations, he estimates the wordage, determines what width the article should be set in type to insure an attractive page, and then lays out the material as necessary. By this tissue-layout method, an inviting and handsome consistency is thus assured throughout the "magazine."

and all classes of readers, many of whom prefer to get a message from pictures rather than from the text.

Articles and Illustrations

The magazine editor gets hundreds of manuscripts from free-lance writers (one editor of a local magazine counted 2,000 contributed articles in a nine-month period exclusive of 800 pieces of fiction and poetry). Sometimes the story is acceptable but the illustrations are poor. Occasionally the illustrations are worth more than the text.

If the story is good and the illustrations poor, the editor buys the story, assigns a staff or an outside photographer to get appropriate pictures, or uses sketches for illustration. If the story is mediocre but the illustrations are exceptional, the editor will buy the story for the illustrations—and usually rewrite the story to fit the illustrations.

To get the pictures he wants, either to illustrate a story or to be used as a photo story, the editor and art director might *script* the story, instructing the photographer precisely as to what shots to obtain.

A good photo story, it will be recalled, is not simply a collection of pictures relating to the subject. A photo story, like a newsstory, must have a lead and continuity. The sequences should tell the story so clearly that the cutlines are needed only for identification and some details.

Usually the editor or the art director can read a story and tell immediately how the article should be illustrated for the particular issue. Once the illustrations are obtained, the art director can proceed with a page layout.

Color is a powerful attention factor, provided it is used with discretion. Using color simply because it is available is as likely to distract as to lure the reader. A little color often is more effective than too much color. The editor wouldn't think of using red ink for the text, yet he often sets off the initial capital in red ink. Some black-and-white pictures can tell a story more effectively than color pictures. If so, the editor would be foolish to order color simply for the sake of adding color to the page. Let him use another device to attract attention to the page.

Magazine Headlines Are Different

The headline for the magazine article is more likely to arouse readers' curiosity than to summarize or grade the article. It gives enough to hint at the contents of the article but it does not necessarily denote action. In the magazine the headline usually has supporting elements such as illustrations, *teasers* or *blurbs*. An article recalling a meeting between Churchill and Roosevelt might be headed simply **Tea for Two**. The same story in a newspaper proper would carry a headline something like: **Winnie's 'Austerity Tea' for Roosevelt Recounted.**

Here is a story of a Georgia farmer who produces cane from which he manufactures sorghum. The topic has about as little appeal, especially for the city reader, as a sewing bee would have. Occupying the top half of the left page of a two-page spread, the headline beckons the reader with: **He Cooks All the Sorghum in Nacoochee Valley.** Beneath the heading is a half-page color photo showing the farmer checking the color of sorghum flowing in golden streams from the scoop.

An entire page is devoted exclusively to the headline and one picture, but the layout is purposeful; it is designed to attract the reader's eye, give the reader some information and lure him to the facing page which contains four photos showing the sorghum-making process. Thirty-some lines of text get the reader into the story. If his interest is aroused, more than likely he will turn the page to get the details in three columns of text illustrated by a single-column black-and-white photo showing a tot chewing a juicy stalk of sorghum.

Type Tricks

Another device used to gain variety on the page is an initial capital letter. It is used on the lead paragraph and sometimes on other paragraphs throughout the text to break the monotony of body type. The capital may extend above or drop below the line. A three-line initial cap is the equivalent of three lines of body type in depth. If the initial cap extends above the line, extra space must be allowed between paragraphs.

Different families of type may be employed throughout the book provided harmony is maintained. This is especially true of type on facing pages where a clash of type disturbs the eye no matter how effective the layout may be.

Editing the Magazine

A newspaper's plant is geared to the production of a daily newspaper. Production of a special section like the Sunday magazine must be staggered so that the plant can handle the extra work as efficiently and economically as possible. Such production is possible by placing the magazine on a strict schedule for advertising, art and copy.

The editor follows a schedule showing when the copy and art must be delivered to the appropriate production departments. He keeps a slugsheet showing when the item was handled, the form for which the layout is intended (four color, two color or monotone), the page number and the publication date.

Armed with proofs and rough sketches, the editor proceeds to make a complete layout of the magazine, showing location of stories, art and the regular departments. When this has been set up, the editor receives page proofs, usually on slick paper. Then a final *pasteup* is made exactly as the layout is to appear in the book. The pasteup contains the text (in type), art work (color transparencies are attached to the layout), cutlines, headlines. The pasteup is mounted on stiff paper and becomes the master copy for the roto department.

EMPIRE MAGAZINE	ISSUE _August 21_	PAGES _32_		
FORM	PAGE	SLUG	TO ROTO	TIME
①	1	Fire — Paul Gregg Painting	7-29	8⁰⁵
	2	Letters	8-5	12⁰⁰
①	3	Lux Soap 9g 4 C.		✕
	4	Fast Time	8-16	11⁰⁰
①	5	Fire in Dinwoody Canyon	7-28	8⁰⁵
	6	Small Fry Fishing Party	7-28	1²⁵
	7			
	8			
	9			
	10			
	11			
	12			

SLUGSHEET FOR NEWSPAPER SUNDAY MAGAZINE

Both photographs and text are engraved on huge copper cylinders, forming intaglios in distinction to the usual cameo form of metal type. If color is employed (called *coloroto* or *colorgravure*), the color plates are etched upon the various cylinders, a separate cylinder for each color. The cylinders are automatically inked as they revolve. The paper receives an impression from the cylinders, following which it runs through an elaborate drying apparatus and emerges from the press folded and cut and ready for delivery.

Filling the Magazine's Pages

The editor's job involves much more than selecting and preparing material for publication. He must cultivate goodwill for the publication through promotion, answering letters, dealing tactfully with contributors and, most important, by making the publication fresh, varied and appealing to a wide variety of readers. Primarily, he is interested in exploiting all the feature possibilities within the area of the newspaper's Sunday circulation.

All the locally edited newspaper magazines use about the same types of articles, adapting them to regional topics. These broad classifications include: agriculture, animals, art, automobiles, children and youth, fashions, entertainment, groups and organizations, health, history, hobbies, house and home, how-to-do-it, personalities, places, quizzes and contests, religion, social problems, sports. As would be expected, articles devoted to personalities dominate the local magazine.

II. MAGAZINES PRODUCED BY LETTERPRESS

Production Elements

Most of the techniques used in preparing copy for and arranging the contents of the roto magazine apply as well to the smaller magazine produced by the letterpress process. If the magazine is printed by a commercial letterpress firm, the editor should be familiar with the production steps, particularly if he has to account for costs.

Usually the editor draws up the specifications for the publication—format, number of pages, circulation, illustrations—then submits the specifications for bids. Production costs are based on the following:

Stock.   The first element in cost is paper (or *stock*), both for the inside and the cover. Stock ranges from newsprint to enamel-coated paper. If the magazine contains halftones, the editor may select a *machine finish* paper; if he wants a hard, glossy surface he picks *super-calendered* paper.

Weight of paper is measured in terms of pounds per ream, specifically the weight of a ream (500 sheets) of book paper 25 by 38 inches (17 x 22 inches for bond paper, 20 x 26 for cover stock). Thus, 100-pound book paper means the weight of 500 (25 by 38 inches) sheeets. Weights go from 30 to 120 pounds for inside stock, higher for cover stock.

Stock need not be ordered in sheets measuring 25 by 38 inches. Nearly 20 sizes are available, ranging from 22 by 32 inches to 44 to 64 inches. Dimensions of the magazine page determine the size stock. Ideally, stock sheets allow a certain number of pages with a minimum of stock trim.

Suppose the specification calls for a 9 by 12 magazine, 32 pages in addition to cover, 2,000 copies. The paper desired is 70-pound enamel finish. A stock sheet 25 by 38 inches allows 16 pages without excessive trim.

If eight sheets (16 pages) can be cut from each sheet of stock, a ream will provide 8,000 pages. Total needed (32 x 2,000) is 64,000 pages, so eight reams of stock are required (64,000 ÷ 8,000).

Composition.   Typesetting costs are determined by the amount of type needed to fill the magazine. Usual rate for composition is estimated by the number of ems of type to be composed. Ems are determined by multiplying the length of the type line, in picas, by 12 and dividing the product by the size of type.

Suppose the page has three columns, each 14 picas wide and 10½ inches deep. The type size is 8-point on a 9-point slug. To determine the ems per page:

$$14 \times 12 = \frac{168}{8 \text{ (size of type)}} = 21 \text{ (ems per line)}$$

$$\frac{72 \text{ (points per inch)}}{9 \text{ (size of type slug)}} = 8 \text{ (lines per inch)} \times 10\frac{1}{2} = 84 \text{ type lines}$$

$$84 \times 21 \times 3 \text{ (3 columns to page)} = 5,292 \text{ ems per page}$$

Composition is one of the major items in the cost of producing a magazine. If the type is small and the pages are in solid type, the composition cost will be considerable. If the type is larger and the pages are liberally illustrated, the composition cost decreases.

Imposition.   After type has been composed it has to be placed into page forms. This process is called makeup or *imposition*. Pages are made up into forms which may contain several pages, depending upon the size of the magazine page and the size of the press. Suppose that four pages can be placed into each form. Then eight forms will be required for a 32-page magazine. Another form will be used for the cover.

Pages in the form are not in 1–2–3–4 sequence, but rather 1–32–16–17; 2–31–15–18 and so on. An easy method to determine the page sequence in the forms is to fold a sheet of paper into a book form with four folds, then number the pages. When the sheet is opened the numbers will be arranged the way the pages are to appear in the forms. If color can be used on four pages in the magazine, the editor would be wise to use the pages in one form rather than putting color on pages appearing in four different forms. The reason is the cost factor. A new makeup is required for each color in each form in which the color is to be used.

Lockup and Makeready.   After type and blocks have been placed in page forms, the forms have to be lined up so that each column is justified and will be locked tightly into the form. The form will not print evenly unless all the elements are type-high. If a halftone, or block, is not type-high, it has to be built up so that it will receive as much ink as the type. This is done by placing paper (*makeready*) under the cut. If the cut is too high, causing the type to be under-printed, it must be *planed down*. The process of making the printing areas of the form even is called makeready.

The Press Run.   After the form has been locked on the press, the run starts. In our case 2,000 impressions are made. Then the paper is turned over, another form is placed on the press, and the sheets are *backed up,* *i.e.,* run through the press again. On this run the pages are cut and folded, making two *signatures* of four pages each.

Gathering and Stitching.   When all the forms for the inside pages and the cover have been run, the signatures are assembled into complete magazines. These have to be *stapled* or *stitched,* then trimmed to make the edges even.

To the unit costs for stock, composition, imposition, makeup, lockup, makeready, press run, ink, folding, stitching and trimming, the printer adds his profit based on a percentage of the total production cost. Color increases the production cost because for each color is needed a separate form, make-up, makeready, lockup, press run and an additional expense of color ink.

The production cost does not include art work and engraving or etching.

Cutting Costs

The editor can reduce production costs, and have a better publication, if he submits neat, legible copy, follows a stylesheet, measures copy accurately, uses a minimum of handset headlines and prepares an accurate dummy.

He should request duplicate galley proofs of all material. One is to be proofread and returned to the printer. If the editor has had to mark numerous typographical errors he should request a corrected galley proof. The duplicate proofs are used to make a *pasteup dummy*. This shows the position of the contents on the page, including text type, headings, art, advertising.

The dummy guides the printer in making up the pages. Page proofs are sent to the editor for his final approval before the pages are placed on the press. Since new errors frequently appear in reset lines, the editor should go over the page proofs carefully for typographical errors. Unless he has had long experience in reading proof, he is likely to miss errors, all of which will become only too apparent to him when the pages come off the press.

If the editor has not prepared enough material, the magazine pages will have gaping holes. If he has to rush through last-minute filler copy, he is likely to delay production. Furthermore, the magazine will instantly reveal the improvisations. If he sends too much copy, he delays composition and causes oversetting. He requests a proof of the overset copy and tries to use the type in the next issue, if possible. If he has to discard the type, the printer is likely to place the extra type on the scales and add an overset charge based on the weight of the unused type.

It will pay the copyeditor to devote some attention to the various editing techniques used in magazines. The rapid growth of magazines, especially industrial publications, presents an opportunity to anyone who has learned the fundamentals of editing.

PART VI

'Sitting In' at the Editor's Desk

20   What People Read

I may not stick to my text, but I will try to stick to my audience.—Sam Jones (1847–1906), *popular evangelist.*

> O wad some power the giftie gie us
> To see oursel's as ithers see us!
> It wad frae monie a blunder free us.
> —Robert Burns (1759–1796), *Scotch poet,* in To a Louse.

What is the newspaper's job if not to discover and report what people know, think, and are doing about the happenings of the day? What they think and do and how they react determines to a great degree what tomorrow's news will be. —Gideon Seymour (1901–1954) *former executive editor,* Minneapolis *Star* and *Tribune.*

Facts Versus Guesses

A great dispute is said to have raged among medieval scholastics. Why, it was asked, does a dead fish dropped into a vessel level-full of water cause it to overflow while a live fish does not? Theories were spawned in abundance until one man, unafraid to soil his hands or perhaps lacking in academic dignity, experimented. He discovered that any fish, dead or alive, displaced its volume of water. The discussion ended at once.

What do people read in newspapers? That's a top question for copy-editors who *sit in,* occasionally at least, as editor and must decide what is to be printed and how it is to be played. Fortunately, the answer no longer need be entirely a guess; the science of measuring news-reader tastes and habits, even opinions, is making it more and more a matter of ascertainable fact. But before looking into it, let's review less formal systems.

The I-Like-It Method

This is the oldest, simplest and least scientific system of all. It takes no account of opinions of others. It's based on this line of reasoning: I am a typical literate person; I am interested in this; therefore, other literate persons will be too. The celebrated "personal journalism" of Dana and Greeley, of Pulitzer and Northcliffe, followed this formula.

The I-like-it method is the father of brilliant hunches, which have made many excellent stories and successful newspapers. No newsman will entirely discard it. But obviously it has limitations. The swivel-chair news dispenser may lose touch with humanity on the street; he may think of his subscribers as he wants them to be instead of as they are.

The Catch-As-Catch-Can Method

This is marked by quick judgments shaped by reader reaction channeled to the editor in various ways.

It may come through fellow newsmen or "letters to the editor" or from reports of the circulation department. It may be theorized from a remark overheard at the bridge table or any informal experience that gives an inkling of what currently interests people.

Imitation falls within this pattern. Editor Hansen of the *Post* "picks the brains" of Editor Jensen of the *Star*—and in the *Post* appears a *Star*-like feature.

The Harun Method

Harun-al-Raschid (hä-rōōn'-är-rà-shēd'), the fabled Caliph of Bagdad (786–809), won the title of The Just because his subjects applauded his decisions. Spurning counsel of court sycophants and advisers, he donned disguises and mingled incognito with the people to learn what they were thinking.

A modern disciple of his method was Joseph Medill Patterson, who within four years brought to the New York *Daily News* the largest daily circulation in America. Patterson often mingled with the crowds at Coney Island to catch the pulse of their interests. He even panhandled to see life from the beggar's viewpoint. Not infrequently, he took his editors on tours to measure public taste at firsthand. Loitering near newsstands, they would note how poor or well dressed, how stupid or intelligent, were those who bought the *News*.

"You can't publish a successful paper by ear," Patterson is quoted as having given as his formula.

It is an excellent one for any journalist, regardless of what staff position he may hold, or whether his paper caters to brows high or low, rural folk or city cliff dwellers. He who edits can kill a paper. Not outright—but by himself sleepily freezing to death on his swivel chair.

The Gallup Method

The old-time, I-like-it editor would have scorned the scientific system given form, name and popularity by Dr. George H. Gallup. While a young newspaperman seeking a doctorate in psychology at the University of Iowa, he came across a statement made in 1891 by Lord Bryce. The English statesman asserted that the final stage in democracy's evolution would be reached "if the will of the majority of citizens were to become ascertainable at all times."

Straw votes were not new, of course. The old *Literary Digest* (since then absorbed by *Time*) had been conducting quadrennial polls prior to presidential elections. Advertising agencies had been testing public preferences through *consumer research* studies. Gallup brought the science of statistics to bear on the problem, taking his cue from experiments carried out in laboratories under known or controlled conditions. His system takes the realistic approach and is based on the following.

Parts for Wholes

When the poet Edwin Markham described *The Man with the Hoe* as having "the emptiness of ages in his face," he was speaking of all men who bear "the burden of the world." He used the common rhetorical device known as *synechdoche,* taking a typical part to characterize the whole. Those who make *surveys* or *studies* or *polls* do the same.

Their part is a *sample*. Their whole is a *public* or an *audience* or a *market*. Individuals who answer questions are *respondents*. When additional reactions from respondents would produce no significant new information, a *norm* has been reached. Then the *returns* may be *blown-up* mathematically and yield conclusions reasonably valid for the entire group being studied.

What's the Purpose?

Surveying is functional: that is, the information sought determines the methods used.

If a consensus on a "yes or no" question is desired from a limited public, visits to every tenth person listed on every tenth page in a telephone directory may suffice. Street-corner polls have some validity but only for the public on the street at a certain time of day. Mail *questionnaires,* or those printed in newspapers, may suffice to indicate popular preference, but they gain in reliability if *weighted* to *compensate* for such factors as sex, age, income, occupation, standard of living, education, social status, racial background or geographical distribution.

But conclusions based on questionnaires published in newspapers or sent out by mail are of dubious value. Only a small percentage of persons exposed to them usually respond. They may do so because of a partisan interest or because they have little else to do. In any case, the danger is acute that returns will not be representative of the larger group who do not answer.

Best results are obtained by interviewers trained to extract information even from the *DK*—the respondent who answers, "Don't Know." Questions most fruitful are specific. "Do you agree with last night's editorial on the city hall?," for example, will get an answer as to whether it was read. "Do you read the sports page before the society column?" also will elicit more information than the respondent realizes.

Newspapers are increasingly using surveys for varied purposes. The advertising department wants to know the *pull* of advertising space. Executives responsible for the paper's appearance may check on *legibility* of type, measuring the relative ease of reading, or *reader-acceptance* of color photos or tinted paper. Of special interest to all newsmen are the following:

Readability and Readership

These should not be confused.

Readability is concerned with rapid comprehension of what's printed. It involves choice of words, rhetoric, punctuation, lengths of sentences and paragraphs and other points already discussed in a previous chapter. Dr. Rudolf Flesch, authority on scientific readability, has defined it for the newsman as "trying to write every story so that the average newspaper reader will read, understand and remember it."

Readership measures the number of people who do read the paper. Circulation figures are helpful but they do not throw much light on what types of news, departments, pages, even specific newsstories and headlines which catch and hold the reader's eye. By measuring *reader-traffic,* reader-ship surveys set up many a stop or go signal for alert newsmen.

For regular features, such as a comic strip or a column, newspapers often use the *drop-out* method to determine readership. Still legend in one Chicago news office is its switchboard tie-up when readers telephoned their protests at the three-day absence of "Little Orphan Annie." Some 50,000 letters are said also to have poured in.

The *drop-out* has limited usefulness and conclusions based on its results should be weighted by the fact that only an articulate minority respond. It is of no help in anticipating readership of new news coverage, for who could praise or protest omission of what he does not know exists? Probable acceptance of an innovation, however, can be learned through check-ups before and after *trial-runs* of the feature in what sometimes are called *pre-tests.*

Small-Town Readership

Weekly newspapers have a special news field, often limited by competition from papers in adjoining communities or nearby cities. How a survey can help a weekly editor sharpen his understanding of his opportunities is illustrated by a typical study of the *Examiner* at Coolidge, Ariz. This weekly has slightly more than 1,000 subscribers and 100 of them were interviewed by journalism students from the University of Arizona. The study revealed:

Of 108 subscribers queried, 100 (about evenly divided between men and women) had read the paper four days after publication.

Average size of family—2.87 members 12 years or over, signifying a probable readership triple the circulation figures.

Forty-two per cent regularly lent their paper to neighbors.

A few subscribers kept back copies for a year; the average was about three weeks.

The top picture on page 1 got the "liked best" vote from all women and 90 per cent of the men. It depicted a "Salad Bowl" float, local in interest.

Readership throughout averaged 67 per cent for women, 44 per cent for men.

The five stories of prime interest to men were all on page 1, and (in this order) told of a new county jail, a coming baseball game, a weather story, post office examinations, and the new county board chairman.

Women liked "locals" best, though they appeared on page 3. Next came stories about a baby born to a local Chinese couple (page 9), a wedding (page 9), births (page 5) and four from one family on a jury (page 1).

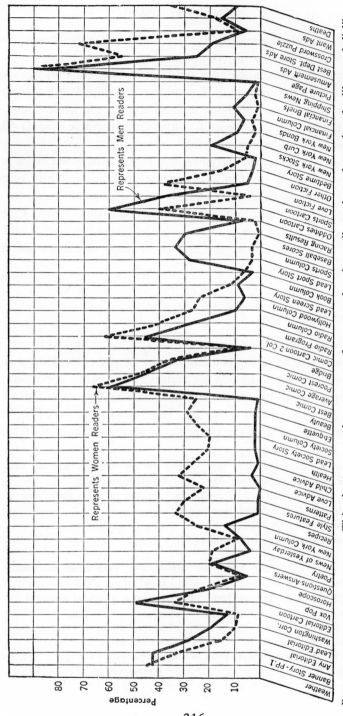

The chart shows a vertical axis labeled "Percentage" with values 10, 20, 30, 40, 50, 60, 70, 80. The horizontal categories from bottom to top include: Weather, Banner Story – pp. 1, Any Editorial, Lead Editorial, Washington Corr., Editorial Cartoon, Vox Pop, Horoscope, Questions-Answers, Poetry, News of Yesterday, New York Column, Recipes, Style Features, Patterns, Love Advice, Child Advice, Health, Lead Society Story, Society Column, Etiquette, Beauty, Best Comic, Average Comic, Poorest Comic, Bridge, Comic Cartoon-2 col., Radio Program, Radio Column, Hollywood Column, Lead Screen Story, Book Column, Lead Sport Story, Sports Column, Baseball Scores, Racing Results, Oddities Cartoon, Sports Cartoon, Love Fiction, Other Fiction, Bedtime Story, New York Stocks, New York Curb, New York Bonds, Financial Column, Financial Briefs, Shipping News, Picture Page, Amusement Ads, Best Dept. Store Ads, Crossword Puzzle, Want Ads, Deaths.

Represents Men Readers
Represents Women Readers

READER INTEREST FLUCTUATES. This chart summarizes returns of a comprehensive poll, made to determine the likes and dislikes of the American daily newspaper reading public. While a careful study of these statistics will reveal many interesting data, the student should remember that this chart is but a generalization, that communities will vary, times change—and the public is fickle.

316

Typical City Readership

Various colleges and universities have conducted readership studies for newspapers, but the most comprehensive study to date is "The Continuing Study of Newspaper Reading," conducted by the Advertising Research Foundation in cooperation with the Bureau of Advertising of the American Newspaper Publishers Association.[1]

Started in 1939, the Continuing Study has surveyed more than 140 newspapers. In addition, the Advertising Research Foundation, in cooperation with the Agricultural Publishers Association, studied farm publications, and, in cooperation with the Weekly Newspaper Bureau of the National Editorial Association, studied weekly newspapers.

Since 1945, dailies in western states have conducted readership studies sponsored by the Hometown Daily Newspaper Publishers Promotion Committee.

Among data of special interest to newsmen are the following points.

Outranking in attention even the highest scoring newsstories are picture pages and outstanding news photos. Large pictures tend to get more interest than smaller ones.

Men favor pictures of events; women prefer people.

Page 1 is most interesting and picture pages come second both for men and women. Men put sports third; women give that place to society.

Serious national events—such as a war—increase reading of editorials while comics, society and sports fall off somewhat.

Society gets more readership in small cities than in large ones but the opposite is true of radio and television programs and news.

Readership of inside pages does not drop progressively. It varies, often depending on advertising.

Quantitative or Qualitative?

Most readership surveys are *quantitative*. They seek statistical answers to such questions as "What type of news is read by whom?" or "How many read it?" When the query becomes "Why?" or "How deep does the interest run?" the study becomes *qualitative*.

"Why" it might be asked, "do subscribers read news from Europe? How intensely are they interested? Does such news influence their opinions? If it were omitted, would they protest by canceling their subscriptions?"

---

[1] Material herewith presented is from copyrighted publications by special permission.

When studies seek reactions to such questions they become *depth surveys*. These are difficult to make properly and even more difficult to interpret correctly. But they can sensitize alert newsmen to trends and shifts in public interest, opinion and fancy.

Typical Depth Studies

In Pittsburgh, newspaper readers were queried as to their reliance on rival *media* for making up their minds on public issues. Answers corroborated the importance of the daily press' visual-record function for they came out in this order: newspapers 805, television 119, radio 118, magazines 57.

"What headlines do you most want to see tomorrow morning?" was a seemingly artless question put to people of Portland, Maine, in a study run by Dr. Ernest Dichter. Returns grouped for psychological reasons (several respondents gave more than one answer) follow:

—50 per cent favored easing of international tensions through mutual understanding and non-military methods. Typical headlines: **"Civilization Has Commenced"** and **"U.S. and Russia Outlaw War."**

—30 per cent were "for peace" but did not suggest headlines.

—15 per cent sought passive-violent solutions. **"Red Army Revolts."**

—12 per cent wanted rough action. **"Drop Atomic Bombs on Moscow"** and **"U.S. and U.N. Declare War."**

—9 per cent were for passive-peaceful solutions. **"Russia Gives up Communism"** and **"Politbureau Converted to Christianity."**

Checking these returns against other studies, Dr. Dichter concluded that "Moral and emotional security are more important to Americans than financial security"—which may or may not run counter to stereotyped opinions held in newsrooms. He also thought it significant that a majority of responses indicated a deep desire that individual and national policy be based on a moral foundation—which may be both cause and effect of increasing space given by newspapers to religious news.

Statistics Aren't Brains

No cure-all for editorial ills was introduced when modern surveys were developed. They are not infallible. If the sample is inadequate, if queries are not wisely formulated, if questioners lack skill, then data inevitably will lead to erroneous conclusions. Moreover, it must always be remembered that human nature cannot be reduced to a simple formula and that "the average man" exists only as an abstraction in the mind.

Newspapering is both a science and an art. "The findings of readership surveys should never be applied as a strait-jacket to creative efforts," warns Chilton R. Bush, head of the Institute of Journalistic Studies of Stanford University. "The findings should be used more for the purpose of checking the effectiveness of copy that has been created, and less as a guide as to how to create copy."

How Surveys Help Editors

Surveys can tell us some things, but not everything, about consumers. Most of the studies, for instance, do not indicate how much of the story is read, or more important, what the reader does as a result of his reading. Editors know that readers do not read everything. Surveys can help show what is best read and what is least read. Such information can help the managing editor re-evaluate the paper's contents. If the sports pages, for instance, show few if any women readers, he can suggest that the sports editor try to broaden coverage to include women-participating sports. But if the crossword puzzle shows a low 10 per cent readership, the managing editor knows better than to incur the wrath of the avid fans by leaving out that feature.

Surveys Are Tools Only

Well-conceived and skillfully executed studies are proving a useful tool for newspapermen. For too long, most newspapers were edited in the "footprints of dead editors." Readership studies have exploded some long-held beliefs and invite further examination of legendary practices. Research until recently has been shamefully neglected in the newspaper business. As a tool of research, readership studies provide answers based upon investigation. More important, they challenge the attention of open-minded men who write and prepare copy or direct the news operation of a newspaper.

The old-time editor felt he had an innate judgment about what his readers wanted. Today's editor can fortify his decisions with scientific studies. That still isn't enough, however. If editors will merchandise their product, they will develop reader interest, no matter what subject they present.

For example, do readers have a scant knowledge of foreign news because they are not interested in the topic or because newspapers have not done enough to stimulate their interest in foreign affairs? One answer was given by the foreign news committee of the Associated Press Managing Editors.

The mass of readers have no constitutional prejudice against foreign news— they could be persuaded to read it if we wouldn't scare them off. They are the men and women who sometimes wonder what is happening to their tax money; the mothers with sons in Germany or Japan; the young men and women who roll up their sleeves when the bloodmobile comes to town; the former GI's who served in North Africa or Burma; the churchgoers who keep the foreign missions going. If we can catch the attention of these people by our treatment of foreign news, we can heighten the intensity of their interest in our newspapers. There is every reason for us to strive for this result, whether we are interested solely in circulation or in enlightened citizenship or both.

Pointing out that news magazines, radio and television are making imaginative use of foreign news to seduce the mass audience, the committee concluded, "The world is our beat. By intelligent and imaginative treatment of world affairs, we can intensify reader interest in our news columns."

What Readers Want

Newspaper readers aren't journalistic technicians. Most of them don't know a good headline from a bad one or good typography from poor typography. When an editor changes type faces in his newspaper, he has to call that fact to the readers' attention. "This type is easier to read than the old type," he announces.

Readers accept the judgment even if they don't know what constitutes readable type. But they reject what is hard to read, whether the difficulty be in poor type, heavy writing, or unfamiliar content. Many times they know whether the facts are accurate or complete; sometimes they know whether the paper is missing the news. They are not discerning readers. They pay little attention to where the dispatch was filed and by whom. But let the paper commit an error of fact, sometimes even trivial, and the newspaper will soon find out that readers are watching its performance closely. Worse, readers have a tendency to remember the mistakes and to offer a blanket condemnation of the paper—"this paper never gets anything right."

The reader wants one thing above all else from his newspaper—truth.

Some readers accept their newspaper because nothing better is available. Some respect their newspaper because of its record for accuracy, completeness, fairness. All newspapers aspire to the distinction claimed for the Manchester *Guardian* by its promotion department. It quotes the old story in England about the Lancashire clergyman who began his sermon: "Oh Lord, as thou wilt have read in yesterday's Manchester *Guardian*. . . ."

21 What Editors Should Offer to the Reader

The duty of the newspaper is to comfort the afflicted and to afflict the comfortable.—Finley Peter Dunne (1867–1936), *Chicago humorist and newspaperman.*

I would rather live in a country with newspapers and without government, than in a country with a government but without newspapers.—Thomas Jefferson (1743–1826), *author of the* Declaration of Independence.

Profits Aren't Everything

Every editor should face up to the fact that journalism as a whole and his own paper in particular have a responsibility to society. The preceding chapter explored the realistic problem of what people *do* read. It is now pertinent to consider what editors *should* offer to the reader.

The "Sage of Emporia," William Allen White (late editor of the Emporia, Kan., *Gazette*) has bequeathed to the journalistic profession his credo on this point:

An editor is really a trustee, entitled to his profits if they are clean and decent to the fullest extent that he may make them, but not entitled to make his profits at the community's loss. Unless he can give the public some valuable thing—information, guidance, or entertainment—he has no right to his profits.

The newspaper responsibility to the public, in general terms, were enumerated by the Hutchins *Commission on Freedom of the Press* as follows:

1. A truthful, comprehensive and intelligent account of the day's events in a context which gives them meaning.
2. A forum for the exchange of comment and criticism.

3. A means of projecting the opinions and attitudes of the groups in society to one another.

4. A method of presenting and clarifying the goals and values of the society.

5. A way of reaching every member of the society by the currents of information, thought and feeling which the press supplies.

What's Fit to Print?

What newspapers offer varies not only because of what ideas and ideals are in the editors' minds but because newspapers are designed to appeal to different audiences.

The editor of a small-town weekly or daily is personally close to his subscribers. He often thinks of his audience as the whole community, a homogeneous totality. Editors of larger papers are inclined to be more selective, a point well illustrated by the *Times* and the *Daily News* in New York.

The case for the *Times* was stated in a symposium by Turner Catledge, managing editor:[1]

It is perfectly obvious that no newspaper can print actually all the news. Every day the New York *Times* receives more than one million words of news copy. It normally uses no more than 150,000. Therefore, a staggering job every day is to select what we can truly present. So, our term, "all the news," means, basically, the vital news on important and interesting subjects and events—news that is significant and necessary to people who need to be informed.

By the same token, just as a newspaper cannot print all the news in volume, it does not attempt to publish for a vague "everyone." Every newspaper selects its audience by practice, whether deliberately or not. And it selects the news that meets the demands of that audience.

The New York *Times* selected its audience when it committed itself to publish a paper devoted entirely to the news rather than partly to news and partly to entertainment. . . . We fundamentally believe that the private lives of public characters may be, within bounds, legitimate public business. But the private lives of private persons are their own business. The twilight zone, of course, gives us trouble. . . . Down through the years "All the News That's Fit to Print" has proved itself to be astonishingly resilient. It encompasses changes as it points to wider horizons. It implies no dogma. It is an everlasting challenge to the staff of The New York *Times*. It is, as someone has put it, "A silent monitor of the copydesk."

Now for the philosophy underlying the New York *Daily News* as reported by Richard W. Clarke, executive editor:

[1]"What's Fit to Print?" in *The Bulletin of the American Society of Newspaper Editors*, Oct. 1, 1954.

Because it addresses itself to an audience considerably larger than that of The New York *Times,* the New York *News* cannot be as highly selective in deciding what is fit to print. I agree with Mr. Catledge that no newspaper can print all the news. Our problem of choice and condensation is considerably greater than his, since our straight news content in the daily paper is about 20,000 words, out of a total of 500,000 available to us. That means we use four per cent of the gross compared with 15 per cent used by the *Times.*

In this relatively scant wordage we try to give our readers an accurate idea of what is going on in the world, with emphasis on matters which affect the great mass of Americans and especially New Yorkers. We feel, however, that our readers are entitled to some entertainment, even in the news columns. Accordingly, we devote space to stories which the *Times* would consider so trivial as to be unworthy of its notice.

These include unusual happenings in which the central figures are unknown to the public, but whose adventures and misadventures are typical of life in a great city. We believe our readers are intensely interested in knowing what happens to the man, woman, child or animal who might live next door. They are less concerned with the activities of statesmen in foreign lands.

In our presentation we attempt to give the most accurate possible account of what happened, in text and pictures. If a murder is the subject, and a photograph of the victim is available, we do not hesitate to use it, even if some gore is in evidence. This is not an effort to harrow, horrify, or sicken our readers. It is done to show them what really happened.

Most editors, of course, strive for the maximum circulation available, but they do not seek the lowest common denominator of mass appeal in order to attract that circulation. Actually, they cater to individual group interests and still try to serve a general audience, usually with the intention of elevating public tastes and interests.

What Newspapers Print

What kinds of topics (and in what proportion) do newspapers offer? The answer was supplied in a cooperative content study of representative American dailies undertaken prior to the 1948 presidential election. Discounting the disproportion of political news because of the interest in the election, the results nevertheless reveal some pattern of newspaper content.[1]

Following is the average percentage of total non-advertising space (excluding opinion and pictorial matter) in 10 categories for 60 daily newspapers in the United States:

[1] Content of Selected U.S. Dailies, Oct. 23–Nov. 1, 1948. Bulletin 16, Department of Agricultural Journalism, College of Agriculture, University of Wisconsin.

Government and political activity (politics, official acts of
non-military branches of government in the United
States, official acts of military branches of government,
foreign relations diplomatic activity, foreign politics and
government, acts of war) .... 13.2 per cent
Economic activity (labor, agriculture, commerce, etc.) 7.4
Crime and vice 1.7
Accidents, natural disasters, fires 1.6
Religion and church affairs 1.3
Education, science, philanthropy 3.0
Arts, literature, leisure-time activities (excluding comics) 6.4
Society, the family and the individual (vital statistics, soci-
ety, club activities) 11.0
Sports 11.8
Miscellaneous (human interest stories, weather) 5.6
Total non-advertising, excluding pictorial and opinion ma-
terial .... 63.0 per cent

It might be interesting to compare this content study with one conducted by the Syracuse University School of Journalism which measured the Associated Press TTS relay wire of the New York State AP service from July 21 through July 27, 1954, as reported in *Editor and Publisher*:

Percentage breakdown by categories of what AP sent on the relay wire on the six days to 24 member papers on the circuit

	By number of lines transmitted
Government, politics, economic	29 per cent
Sports	16
Foreign datelined material	14
Crime, accident, disaster	10
Foreign news, with domestic dateline	9.9
Miscellany	8
Human interest	7
Cultural, scientific, educational	3

What the 24 papers used of each category

	By lines used
Sports	59 per cent
Foreign datelined material	46
Government, politics, economic	37
Foreign news, with domestic dateline	36
Human interest	35
Cultural, scientific, educational	34
Crime, accidents, disaster	34
Miscellany	12

Readers Don't Edit Newspapers

Which of these categories were read most widely? For the answer we turn again to the Continuing Study of Newspaper Reading of the Johnstown (Pa.) *Tribune* in 1945. Crime was the most widely read general newsstory by both men and women, despite the fact the story appeared on page 30. Another crime story was third on the list for men readers and sixth on the list for women readers. Economic activity, accidents and governmental activities were the other best-read categories of general news for both sexes. Of the best-read general newsstories for both sexes, only three appeared on the front page.

Reader preference, therefore, does not necessarily determine newspaper content. For one thing, there could be a diminishing return in readership if newspapers printed too much of one category. Readers may enjoy reading some crime stories, but it is doubtful if they would buy a newspaper packed with crime stories. Secondly, editors, perhaps unconsciously, feel an obligation to society to raise the level of news interests.

The Press and the Public

Society says to the newspaperman:

Because you fill a vital need, we *allow* you to exist. More, we encourage you and freely grant you the incentive of profit. We even aid you by protecting "property rights" in news through copyright laws. Not only are special privileges of the mails accorded you, but we keep a watchful eye on the other channels of communication—the telegraph, radio, and television—lest a monopoly make difficult your successful operation. We but ask that you do not damage or defame the character of an individual; if you do, he is entitled to redress under the laws of libel. If you seriously interfere with the administration of justice, it is possible to declare you in contempt of court, but we are reluctant to do that or, indeed, to put any legal restraint upon you. We even forego the right to license you, for we have dire memories of the abuse of press licensing in England under Charles II. Except in time of national emergency, we waive censorship.

Nevertheless, you operate under many extra-legal checks and balances inherent in a competitive economy. If you long displease your public, you sign your own death warrant. If you notably offend mores or morals, you lose favor. If you are "kept" by special interests, you risk the loss of confidence and patronage. If you grow old, fat and timid and fail to keep identified with the welfare of community, state and nation, you may be usurped by a paper that is young, supple and courageous.

In short, the sources of a newspaper's income show clearly that it is a private commercial enterprise, but the character of the material it sells makes it a *quasi* public utility. Thus, we may say a *newspaper is a private business enterprise that functions as a public institution.*

Properly to fill its role, the newspaper has basic responsibilities, one selfish and four social. They are: *First, self-preservation; second, to provide reliable information; third, to offer wise guidance; fourth, to entertain; fifth, to give public service.*

1. Self-Preservation.   Its critics frequently forget that a newspaper operates under the imperatives faced by any other profit-making enterprise in a capitalist economy. It must pay its way. Only if it gives the public what the public will read and pay for does its *white space* have value for advertisers. The reader's pennies bring the advertiser's dollars. Both are needed to pay the bills.

If a newspaper fails to hold its readers, it faces a realistic dilemma. One horn is labeled: bankruptcy or forced sale. The other calls for "an angel"—who may be the advertiser, one or many; a "pressure group" such as a labor union, a trade association, a political party, or any "interest" with an ax to grind and cash to pay the newspaper to turn the grindstone.

Only the financially stable paper *can* be consistently independent. It is the weak one, harassed by bill collectors and Saturday night payrolls, that is likely to menace the community. A newspaper worthy of its name must stand on its own financial feet. That is its first responsibility—and a necessity if it is to serve society.

2. Informing the Public.   The first social function of the press is to give the news. This is, as was noted in Chapter 1, the newspaper's distinguishing mark. If news presentation is to win reader favor, it must have three qualities. They, the three A's of Journalism, are: *Adequacy, Accuracy, Acceptability.*

Adequacy. This is a relative term, for newspaper fields vary in size and substance. Adequacy concerns time as well as space. The public insists upon the latest; if it is not forthcoming the paper may expect criticism expressed in terms of cancellations. The stated aim of the London *Times* is to be first but not the hastiest with the news, to be serious without dullness or solemnity; to persuade and not to dogmatise; to be emphatic without becoming hysterical, to be graphic without sensationalism; to give the story and to reject the "stunt"; to miss nothing that is amusing and to keep the trivial in proportion; to give the news faithfully and fully without "featuring" the worst side of human nature.

Accuracy. When any considerable number of readers say, "But you can't believe what you see in *that* paper," it is on the road to the poorhouse. A reputation for inaccuracy may be caused by sloppy reporting or it may arise from a distortion of facts through an emphasis keyed to the bias of an editor. Whatever their cause, inaccuracies sap the life fluid of a newspaper.

Acceptability. The New York *Times* publishes "all the news fit to print." "The slogan is a statement of an ideal. It is not the claim of accomplishment. When it first appeared in an editorial on Oct. 25, 1896, it was, in fact, a war cry of the new publisher. Adolph S. Ochs had just entered the New York newspaper field to find it populated largely by journals dominated by strong and provocative characters. Much of the news in many of the New York papers in those days reflected the personal bias of publishers and editors; Mr. Ochs looked around to see where he could best fit. Both as an ideal and as simply good business, he decided to dedicate his paper to printing 'all the news.' This meant, most of all, the news of every side of an issue. Mr. Ochs also wrote in his creed that The New York *Times* would seek to present the news 'in a concise and attractive form, in a language that is parliamentary in good society.' In other words, news that was 'fit to print.' " [1]

The words *taste* and *decency* connote what is permissible at a given time and place.

Acceptability also has to do with the manner of presentation. Readers expect news to be written clearly and displayed brightly.

3. Guidance.   The distinction between reporting in depth and opinionated writing was emphasized in Chapter 2 but it is appropriate to mention again that if the reader is given all the facts and in their proper context he will be able to draw his own conclusions and act wisely.

Newspapers no longer have an exclusive claim to overt news. Television, for instance, can bring the news picture almost simultaneously to the consumer. Newspapers should meet this challenge by providing scope and interpretation.

Television forces the news reporter to be meticulously accurate. The viewer is at the scene along with the reporter. What he sees, of course, is one picture but not necessarily the whole picture of the news. That is where the newspaper has its opportunity.

Radio and television and the newspaper, in fact, complement each other. Radio and television provide the immediate, and whet the consumer's appetite for details and depth—which the newspaper supplies.

True reporting is not a stenographic account but an audited account of the news. *But it cannot be opinion masquerading as news.* Here is how two New York columnists "reported" Mr. Justice Black's first day on the bench:

[1] "What's Fit to Print?" *Bulletin of the American Society of Newspaper Editors,* Oct. 1, 1954.

Possibly it would not be too much to say he was wary. One might easily misread any man's expression under extraordinary circumstances. One might attribute to a central figure in any drama an expression not actually there. But one could not help feeling there was uneasiness in Mr. Black's countenance. He looked as if he feared that any moment someone might arise and say, "I forbid the banns."

But Mr. Justice Black in these matters is not a sensitive man. . . . He looked with satisfaction at a group of admiring relatives and friends and then gazed placidly about the court room. . . . He gave just a sufficient number of his thin-lipped smiles in response to the courtesy of the pages to prove he was thoroughly at ease and to prophesy pleasant association during the long years in which he expects to be a Justice.

Explanatory writing is dangerous when it fails to draw the line between objective and subjective news. The following headlines, which appeared in rival papers in the same city on the same day, show what happens when newspapers editorialize the news:

**Latimore to Face
Trial in Perjury**

**Latimore Upheld
In Court's Ruling**

"All of us in the news business," wrote Elmer Davis in *But We Were Born Free* (Bobbs-Merrill), "ought to remember that our primary responsibility is to the man who buys his newspaper, or turns on his radio, expecting us to give him in so far as is humanly possible, not only the truth and nothing but the truth, but the whole truth."

The Fact-Opinion Spectrum.   Of straight news and of opinion which seeks to guide the reader, one cannot say, as did Kipling of East and West, "and never the twain shall meet." They do. The gradation goes from the straight, factual story to the editorial. *News crusades* guide opinion. *Background* provides significance. *Signed news articles* interpret factually. *Signed columns* comment and explain. *Feature stories* embroider the news, playing up the human interest elements. *Reviews* and *editorials* express outright opinion.

Confusion of thinking will be avoided if these and other forms of newswriting are oriented to this fact-opinion spectrum:

4. Entertainment. Newspapers early adapted to their ends the "all work and no play makes Jack a dull boy" principle. Ancestors of entertainment features of a modern newspaper are the *miscellany* and *fillers* of Ben Franklin's day. Now under entertainment can be bracketed a considerable portion of metropolitan newspaper content, nor is it absent from the cross-road's printed diary.

Comic strips, informational articles, advice columns, sports stories, movie reviews—the list of entertainment features in a metropolitan newspaper runs long. Many of them are timeless, as good tomorrow as yesterday. Others hinge on the day's news.

5. Public Service. The newspaper is neither a public utility nor common carrier; it has complete control of what it prints or what it prefers not to print. Public service, however, plays a major role in a newspaper's function. The newspaper sponsors or promotes civic and charitable enterprises, boosts worthwhile drives, initiates benefits of all types and for all purposes. They range from Community Chest promotion to spelling bees.

Few papers in our country, however, can match the performance of some of the Japanese newspapers in public service activities as reported in *Editor and Publisher*:

> Every week the three major newspapers in Japan produce newsreels which are shown in movie houses all over the country. They award cash prizes to scholars, scientists, writers and others, give money to help scholars, professors and research scientists. In case of big fires or disasters, these major papers immediately dispatch their medical teams, together with relief goods and donations, to give aid to the victims. Frequently they offer free medical aid to the destitute. *Asahi Shimbun* maintains a full-sized hospital.
>
> Almost 80 per cent of the eminent Western scholars, scientists, musicians and men of letters who visited Japan recently have been invited there by these papers as their guests. They sponsor elaborate exhibitions of art, concerts and recitals by internationally known musicians, national athletic and baseball meets, lecture meetings, public forums, musical concerts, cinema shows, once in awhile fashion shows and organize a fair or exposition on a large scale. Four papers have their own professional baseball teams.

22   Running the Desk

The journalist's opportunity is beyond estimate. To him is given the keys of every city, the entry to every family, the ear of every citizen when he is in the most receptive moods, powers of approach and persuasion beyond those of the Protestant pastor or the Catholic confessor. He is no man's priest, but his words carry wider and further than the priest's for he preaches the gospel of humanity. His is not a king, but he nourishes and trains the king, for the land is ruled by the public opinion he evokes and shapes.—Whitelaw Reid (1837–1913), *former editor,* New York *Tribune.*

Slotmen Must Be Versatile

The man in the slot generally earns his position because he knows news, understands the paper's operation, knows typography and makeup, has the ability to write headlines and, probably most important, knows how to cope with personality problems.

He must be a person who won't panic when a big story breaks near deadline or when the managing editor barks an order for sudden changes. He can't sit in the slot unless he can make decisions quickly, keep copy moving, judge headlines and spot errors the deskmen miss. He can be an easy-going, mild-mannered person or a rough slave-driver as long as he can satisfy the other editors and the composing room.

He is the arbiter on spelling, style, grammar, policy, headlines and even story content. He arranges the working days and hours for the men and women on the rim; he keeps records of overtime and holiday work; he recommends copyeditors for promotions or pay increases and for dismissals. He is an executive in that he is in charge of the desk; he is a technician in that he handles copy, writes heads and keeps a slugsheet; he is a psychologist in that he must know how to cope with all the whims and quirks of the odd lot surrounding him.

Human Nature—Even Around the Rim

The close contact between desk chief and copyeditors raises all sorts of personality problems. Rotations can be made on the desk of the metropolitan paper so that the same copyeditors do not have to work with each other day after day. Rotation of the men in the slot also affords a welcome relief to the rim-men.

Some copyeditors do not take kindly to criticism no matter how cordially it is given. Some resent having their headlines changed by the slotman, insist that their head will "go" even if the count obviously is wrong and greet each piece of copy with cynicism.

But the slotman is not "one big duodenal ulcer enveloped in reversed porcupine hide." He learns the interests, specialties and capabilities of everyone on the rim and tries, whenever possible, to deal each the copy befitting his interests. He tests new men with inside and minor stories until they demonstrate they are ready to handle the more important stories. He reserves the stories demanding feature headlines for deskmen who have a knack for writing feature heads. The danger here, of course, is that he may overlook the abilities of a deskman by not giving him an opportunity to demonstrate his talents.

Experience makes a good copyeditor. He becomes a joy to the slotman when he can move copy, compose lively headlines, remember to mark all the instructions to the printer and catch errors that may get by inept copyeditors. He prepares himself for the job of editing raw copy by reading thoroughly his own newspaper, the opposition, news magazines and books.

Read the Papers

Most copydesks work in spurts. Copyeditors handle a huge volume of copy, then sit and wait for the various editors to start filling copy baskets again. During the waiting period, the deskman is expected to read newspapers, his own or others. When a new edition hits the desk, all hands grab a copy. If the copyeditor finds a typographical error, he clips out the item, pastes it on a sheet of copypaper, marks the correction in the margin, writes Cx at the top and hands the corrected piece to the slotman.

If the error occurs in copy handled by another department, the deskman calls that to the attention of the head of the desk. "Wonder if sports caught these reversed lines?" he inquires. If the sports desk hasn't caught the error, it will appreciate the tip.

A thorough reading of the paper will show up hordes of errors, especially in first editions which lack proofreading. Among the many possible errors are these: two stories covering the same item; wrong cutline; lines are dropped or transposed; page numbers don't coincide with those listed in the index; wrong font of type appears in headline or text; story has the wrong headline; continued line indicates the wrong page; slugline left on the story; story ends in the middle of a sentence; lead is repeated; spelling in headline and text do not jibe. Doubtless many of these errors already have been caught on proofs and corrections are on the way for the next edition. But not all will have been caught. The alert copyeditor, who can spot and correct typographical errors, helps make his newspaper a more readable product.

Edition Changes

As soon as the first edition comes to the newsroom, the desk chief starts getting orders for changes. The lead story may drop down on the page and another story put on the line. Both require headline changes.

New head orders may be oral but usually they are written on sheets of copy paper. The slotman transfers the order to the copyeditor who finds the original story in the paper, writes a new headline and turns in the headline copy and the order to the slotman. Unless the news editor has taken care of the "kill" on the original head, the copyeditor pastes the headline clipping on a sheet of copy paper, marks it to be "killed" and sends the marker along with the revised head. Sometimes the banner story retains its original position for the next edition but the line is rewritten to emphasize another angle, to improve the original or to give the new edition a fresh approach.

The slotman must be thoroughly familiar with edition times and with the circulation areas of each edition. Sometimes, a minor state story is rushed along ahead of a more important local story simply because the state story is good for one edition only whereas the local story can keep until the home edition, if necessary.

Editions Permit Second Guessing

The metropolitan newspaper has it over the smaller daily because the former has an opportunity for second guessing. Errors in the first edition are cleaned up for later editions, the time gap between editions gives the various editors an opportunity to re-evaluate news, make heads and leads crisper, bring news up to date. A first edition is bound to have some errors because part of the material has been "railroaded," *i.e.,* not proofread. There should be no excuse for typographical errors in the final edition.

The Slotman Sets the Tone

On the copydesk chiefs of the various departments rests the responsibility of producing a well-edited newspaper. They create the spirit of the desk. Word soon gets around whether the slotman operates a desk that lets anything get by or whether his desk is "rough." He can spoil a conscientious copyeditor with his own lackadaisical attitude or he can build high standards by insisting that editing be thorough. To develop a desk that does a real editing job, the desk chief must have the backing of his superiors. He must have the authority to overrule the city and other desks on matters of editing. He must have the authority to amend the copy of the prima donnas on the staff. He must have the authority to remove inept copyeditors who won't edit to his standards.

It doesn't take an expert to tell the difference between a well-edited and a poorly edited newspaper. Weak editing shows up both in the broad handling of news as well as in the less important details.

Give the Reader a Break

Even though most readers don't understand the mechanics of the headline, they can tell whether the headline conveys the story properly and makes the meaning instantly clear.

A committee in the state house of representatives passes a bill imposing a heavy penalty on a person convicted for the first time of drunken driving. The headline says, accurately but clumsily:

**Hewett's 'Drunk
Driving' Bill
Wins First Okay**

The reader's immediate impression from the first line is that a state representative is drunk. Subsequent lines alter the impression, but the reader still has to read the lead to find out what the story is about. Had the headline-writer spent more time juggling words, the reader would have been spared the problem of juggling ideas.

Too many stories fail to answer questions the reader raises as he goes through the story. Notice the unanswered questions in the following account:

Six men died and five others were hospitalized here Tuesday morning when a flash fire (*what kind is that?*) roared through one of Midtown's oldest hotels (*how old?*) in the subfreezing (*how cold?*) dawn, causing damage estimated (*by whom?*) at $50,000.

Officials (*who?*) termed it "the worst loss of life in Midtown's history." (*what was the previous record?*)

The 35-room hotel was almost completely occupied (*exactly how many?*) when the fire broke out shortly before dawn (*what time?*), the fire chief (*what's his name?*) said.

The victims, all of whom died of smoke suffocation, were identified (*how? by whom?*) as follows: etc.

Sometimes the readers go through a story in its entirety, then wonder if the copyeditor who wrote the headline had done the same thing. Notice this example from a metropolitan newspaper:

Coffee Breaks Pastor's Sermon

A "coffee break" right in the middle of his sermon was called Sunday by the Rev. Ivan Welty, pastor of the Sixth Avenue Community Congregational Church, 3250 E. Sixth ave.

The doughnut dunking festivities were in honor of Mrs. Kate Peterson of 42 S. Cook st., a "longtime loyal worker at the church" who was celebrating her birthday.

Members of the congregation, however, contained their appetites while the pastor finished his sermon. It was entitled, "Bread and Stone."

"The coffee," explained Rev. Mr. Welty, "was not included in the sermon as such."

The last two paragraphs of the story make a lie of the lead and the headline. How is the reader to judge a newspaper that falsifies the news?

The Press and Its Critics

Lapses in newspaper judgment and taste provide fuel for the critics of the press, many of whom would like to limit the influence of the press. Indeed, many of those who profess to believe in the constitutional guarantee of press liberty seek to restrict the press by classifying news or by closing the news sources altogether.

From its beginning the press has had its critics. More than a century ago James Fenimore Cooper, the novelist, penned this:

As the newspaper press of this country now exists, it would seem to have been devised by the great agent of mischief to depress and destroy all that is good, and to elevate and advocate all that is evil in the nation. The little truth that is urged is usually urged coarsely. . . . Every honest man appears to admit that the press is fast getting to be intolerable. While escaping from the tyranny of foreign aristocrats, we have created in our midst a tyranny of a character so insupportable that a change of some sort is becoming more . . . indispensable every day.

By Max P. Milians, Milians Newspaper Service; courtesy of Editor and Publisher

IT ALL DEPENDS ON THE POINT OF VIEW

Later critics have continued in a like vein, asserting that the newspaper is "a circus barker pointing a finger at the latest sensation." Many agree with Critic Silas Bent that ". . . with an eye to the main chance of dividends, the press has forgotten the base of its liberties and is no longer devoted to public service."

Little concern is expressed by such critics that newspapers discharge their first responsibility, which is to preserve themselves so that they may then inform, guide and entertain their readers. Frequently, suggestions are made for "improving the press" which obviously are impractical for an institution which, like the grocery store, must pay its bills before it can serve anyone. Yet, not even its most ardent defenders maintain the press is perfection, and it is apropos at this point to assay some of the charges against newspapers.

They are that newspapers: (1) print unreliable or colored news; (2) are superficial—are more interested in the foam on the news stream than in its main currents; (3) are sensational; (4) invade personal privacy; and (5) interfere with administration of justice.

1. Unreliability. No newspaper of repute condones sloppy reporting, but in the pressure of newspaper-making there is not always time or opportunity to verify news. What to do in such cases is a question calling for sound news discrimination and judgment.

The simplest method of coping with such problems is to cite sources of information. Thomas Jefferson once expressed the hope that newspapers would label stories as (1) truth, (2) probabilities, (3) possibilities, and (4) lies. The *Daily Pantagraph,* of Bloomington, Ill., did for a while use such a system, with modifications.

2. Superficialities. Gossip is not a modern phenomenon, a fact curiously revealed by the word "trivial" (*tri,* three, *via,* road). Ancient Romans evidently were wont to gather where three roads met and to talk about three-legged calves and escapades of maids and other commonplaces, even as twentieth-century folk do at village stores and city clubs. It is doubtful if any newspaper, relying on mill-run people for support, could long exist without providing raw materials for gossip. People want it, newspapers supply it.

So, newspapers have gone far in their efforts to capitalize upon the common denominators of news interest. Some too far, unquestionably. But a reaction is in evidence, caused in part by changing interests of the public and in part by a reasoned belief of newspapers that they should present more news of consequence. The patent importance of science in everyday life has titillated curiosity, and many newspapers and press services are responding with articles on the fascinating ramifications back of ordinary facts and events.

"Newspapers," said Arthur Robb, former editor of *Editor and Publisher,* "can't feed sociological analyses of crime to the millions whose education stops, or used to, at the eighth grade." But the following that has been won by serious columnists and other interpretive writers suggests that newspapers have overlooked actual or potential interests of an important part of the reading public. *Pig iron*—as serious news is often called—might better be termed unworked *ore.*

Readers can be interested in cleverly written news of women and men who are notable not because they went wrong but because they achieved. Church news is not always about a wayward clergyman; even the page of church announcements can be made attractive. Labor news need not always be about spectacular strikes, or financial news that of bank failures and absconding tellers. Sports editors know and tell more news than that of kayos and 10th-inning victories.

A liking for news of consequence, like that for olives, is largely an acquired taste—a triumph of intelligence over prejudice, passion, desires and indifference. If left to free choice, hardly one child in 50 would learn the multiplication table; yet even mathematics can be made interesting. News of significance seldom makes copy by itself. It requires an editor with insight to sense it and a reporter with mastery of his tools to present it in such a way as to catch the eye and hold attention.

3. Sensationalism and Overplay. Sensationalism is the frosting on the cake of the trivial. It is the opposite of socialization. A newspaper is said to be sensational when to such topics as business and labor problems, foreign affairs and books it gives less *play* than it accords to crime, sex, social affairs and the like.

Mechanical errors and careless writing force readers to the conclusion that newspapers do not place a high enough premium on accuracy. Deliberate overplay, sensationalism and distortion all prove, to many readers, that some newspapers lack responsibility. Even the more respected papers occasionally fall into the trap of irresponsibility by rushing into print with premature stories.

In a radio interview with Fulton Lewis Jr., ex-Major G. Racey Jordan accused Harry Hopkins of having ordered a shipment of uranium to Russia.

"Deadpan" stories repeated the accusation and unqualified headlines shouted: **Hopkins Accused of Giving Reds A-Secrets** or **Atom Gift to Russ Told** or **Shipment of A-Bomb Secrets to Reds Revealed.** The more responsible papers withheld judgment until the truth could be determined. Testimony by Lt. Gen. Leslie Groves proved the accusation groundless. Retractions were printed; some newspapers admitted editorially they had "laid an egg." But damage was done, nevertheless, because some readers surely missed the followup and remembered only the original indictment.

It is news when a woman (a widely known Hollywood star) has a child by one man while she is still legally married to another. It is something else when newspapers glorify illicit romance with expressions like "glamorous actress" and "romantic artist" and portray the woman as the martyred heroine who was "behaving with grace and courage." Lamenting the newspaper treatment of the Ingrid Bergman-Rosselini affair, the editor of the trade paper *Editor & Publisher* protested, "We never thought of ourselves as prudish. But if being ashamed of the nauseating newspaper treatment of this shoddy story is being prudish, then we are that. It seems to us the good taste of most American editors was strictly gustatory this time."

Such lapses in judgment crop up (frequently in the more conservative papers as well as in the sensational ones) year after year. Any panel of conscientious editors can list the year's record of the most overplayed stories. For 1954 a panel of editors (named by the editor of the *Bulletin of the American Society of Newspaper Editors*) picked the Sheppard murder trial, the DiMaggio-Monroe separation and the McCarthy-Pentagon hearings as the most overplayed stories of the year. Quoting from the judgments:

Sheppard trial: "Many editors, bound by outmoded news concepts, fail to make allowances for changes in public taste and interests. We suspect that through sensational treatment some papers lost more in reader respect and confidence than they could possibly have gained by increased street sales. The police-court mentality was far too much in evidence in handling the Sheppard story."

Marilyn Monroe's case: "The most overplayed single story was undoubtedly the Marilyn-Joe episode which was generally treated like a life-or-death issue. The fact that the Hollywood publicity characters leaped into the picture and milked it for extra gallons with delightful staging was further indication of the actual value of the thing."

McCarthy hearing: "McCarthy was the most overworked subject, both in news and editorial, during the year just closed. Here was a topic filled with sound and fury and lacking in real substance. Like Fourth of July fireworks, the McCarthy issue has exploded impressively, filled the political heavens with trailing sparks and fallen back to earth a burned out shell."

Achieving Fair Play

Recognizing that fair play is impossible in reporting charges of Communist sympathies unless precautions are taken to guard against loose charges, irresponsible utterances and attempts at character assassination by "spokesmen," official or otherwise, Editor Palmer Hoyt issued the following memorandum to the managing editor of the Denver *Post*:

One: Instruct the news staff always to evaluate the source of the charge.

Two: Ask the news staff to weigh the story and see what they would do with it if official immunity were lacking.

Three: Discuss with the news staff the general proposition of whether or not the *Post* can withhold publication of this particular moot story until proper proof or a qualifying answer can be obtained from the person, organization or group accused.

Four: Ask the news staff whether they of their own knowledge know a doubtful charge to be false, and to apply any reasonable doubt they may have to the treatment of the story.

Five: In connection with banner lines or other headlines on this type of story, ask the news staff to determine whether wording is used as shock treatment or to summarize the facts.

It is obvious that many charges made by reckless or impulsive public officials cannot and should not be ignored, but it seems to me that newsstories and headlines can be presented in such a manner that the reading public will be able to measure the real worth or value and true meaning of the stories.

4. Personal Privacy. A fourth and commonly vehement criticism of the press is that it has invaded and shows no respect for the "inalienable right of the individual to privacy." Although the right to be left alone is still not clearly defined in law, the case for it was well stated in a historic article published in 1890 in the *Harvard Law Review* by Prof. Samuel Warren and Louis D. Brandeis, who later was to become a Justice of the United States Supreme Court. With remarkable prescience, they, in part, said:

Instantaneous photographs and newspaper enterprise have invaded the sacred precincts of private and domestic life; and numerous mechanical devices threaten to make good the prediction that "what is whispered in the closet, shall be proclaimed from the housetops." For years there has been a feeling that the law must afford some remedy for the unauthorized circulation of portraits of private persons; and the evil of invasion of privacy by the newspapers, long keenly felt, has been but recently discussed by an able writer. The question whether our law will recognize and protect "The Right of Privacy" in the circulation of portraits and in other respects must soon come before our courts for consideration.

Of the desirability—indeed of the necessity—of some such protection, there can, it is believed, be no doubt. The press is overstepping in every direction the obvious bounds of propriety and decency. Gossip is no longer the resource of the idle and the rich, but has become a trade, which is pursued with industry as well as effrontery. To satisfy a prurient taste, the details of sexual relations are spread broadcast in the columns of the daily papers. To occupy the indolent, column upon column is filled with idle gossip, which can only be procured by intrusion upon the domestic circle. The intensity and complexity of life, attendant upon advancing civilization, have rendered necessary some retreat from the world, and man, under the refining influence of culture, has become more sensitive to publicity, so that solitude and privacy have become more essential to the individual. But modern enterprise and invention have, through invasions upon his privacy, subjected him to mental pain and distress, far greater than could be inflicted by mere bodily injury. Nor is the harm wrought by such invasions confined to the suffering of those who may be made the subjects of journalistic or other enterprise. In this, as in other branches of commerce, the supply creates the demand. Each crop of unseemly gossip, thus harvested, becomes the seed of more, and in direct proportion to its circulation, results in a lowering of social standards and of morality.

Clearly, the right of individuals to lead their own lives imposes the need for self-restraint and good judgment upon those who fill newspapers' columns—if they would avoid restrictive legislation. No undeviating rule can be given, for cases vary. A newsman cannot always yield to the often insincere request, "Please don't publish that," nor should he publish anything or everything. What to do he must decide, in the light of what he conceives to be his responsibility to the public, his profession and his employer.

5. Obstructing Justice. England, birthplace of the freedom of the press, does not regard as inconsistent with that concept a prohibition upon "newspapers trying cases" before courts have done so. In the United States, however, newspapers possess—or have arrogated unto themselves—the privilege of reporting cases in progress and even expressing opinions about them. A tide of resentment is running in legal circles against sensational court reporting, however, which may prelude an attempt to regulate it by law.

The complaint, in the words of Professor-Emeritus Hugh E. Willis, of the School of Law of Indiana University, is:

The newspapers discuss the criminal act. They refer to those under suspicion. They discuss the merits of the case and follow the case from its first inception until its final conclusion. As a result, it is practically impossible often to apprehend the guilty, to find juries who have not already formed an opinion, and to obtain witnesses who are unbiased and to conduct a trial free from outside influences.

The Newsman's Choice

No universal rules can be laid down, for each community, each paper, each story makes a new problem. In that fact are the rudiments that tend to make journalism a profession, even an art. What an individual newsman will attempt to achieve is a choice for him alone to make.

In practice, many a compromise must be made. A "hireling of the press," which is to say, anyone not in position to formulate his newspaper's policy, must largely conform to the dictates of those over him—or seek a new job. Yet today's reporter or copyeditor becomes tomorrow's editor. And those who make newspapers will, by their acts, formulate the answer to the question of whether the American newspaper is to retain its privileged position or is to be increasingly hedged by popular sentiment crystallized into law.

It Takes Leadership

"Primarily, the responsibility for a well-written, well-edited newspaper lies with the guy who is running the newsroom—usually the managing editor—and with nobody else. And in order to do it, he has to be about 90 per cent leader and 10 per cent boss."

Those words came from Wade Franklin, chief of the copydesk of the Chicago *Sun-Times,* who gave this example in *The Guild Reporter*:

Some years ago the Chicago *Daily News* editorial department was run by a quiet, retiring, modest and gentle man named Henry Justin Smith, and under his direction the paper became just about the best written paper anyone ever read.

Smith did it by working closely with his men; paying particular attention to those in whom he saw a talent that could be developed. He counseled them. He encouraged them. He pointed out how it could have been done better, and he let them feel his pride when they did a good job.

He, himself, was a master craftsman, and in the atmosphere of vigorous scholarship that he created, these writers thrived. Such men as Ben Hecht and Paul Scott Mowrer and Bob Casey and many others.

Of course, everybody didn't take to this.

The paper is being run these days by Smith's exact opposite, a lusty, tireless man who drives himself harder than anyone else.

Yet he, too, has a highly readable paper, one so fresh and provocative that readers hate to miss a single issue. I don't know whether he can write or not, but he knows exactly what he wants and he makes sure he gets it. It is not what Smith wanted at all; it might not even be considered well written by Smith's standards.

But the newspaper reader understands it. He can't help reading it, and if the paper doesn't answer thoroughly all questions, the electorate should understand, it at least gives the people a good general idea of what's going on.

This editor gets results from his staff by an infectious enthusiasm for the news, and by soaking up ideas like a sponge. He is always seeking the fresh approach and so are his co-workers. The whole office avoids the routine like the plague, and everyone knows that every idea, no matter how screwy, will get a full hearing and, more likely than not, a tryout.

This type of editing is like Smith's in that it is inspired at the top, and creates an atmosphere in which the obvious talents of any newspaper shop could grow. Men who want a career on a newspaper are lucky to be working with such an editor—even though they don't always agree with him.

Copydesk Responsibility

The copydesk, by itself, cannot reform a newspaper. But it can be a strong force in improving newspaper performance. Headlines can accent the dramatic without distorting the news. Deskmen can tone down or qualify loose statements. At least they can protest to the slotman who, in turn, can take offending copy directly to the news editors and, if necessary, to the publisher. If a reporter knows his copy can't get by an authoritative copydesk without challenge, he will begin to improve his stories.

That's "subbing" at its best. The copyeditor who is afraid to challenge copy has no place on the rim; the slotman who won't back up an alert deskman doesn't deserve a position of authority. Whenever the "anything goes" attitude takes over, the paper becomes a junkyard.

Idealism on the copydesk need not be vacated. Both the slotman and the copyeditors have to measure copy by its relative importance. For instance, a promotional piece slugged for page 1 comes to the desk. At one glance the copyeditor sees that it has little or no news value. "This stuff's all puff," he might comment to the slotman. "Yeah, I know," replies the chief, "but the city side wants it." The deskman should handle it the best way he can, glorifying the story with a good head. Let him save his indignation for the story that really matters with the readers.

The copyeditor is proud of his newspaper because part of it is his product. If good editing can make it a better newspaper, he has his challenge. If it is a paper with high standards, he is gratified that he has a part in maintaining that performance. The copydesk is at the heart of the newspaper operation. There, too, is part of the newspaper's soul.

APPENDICES

I. NEWSPAPER TERMS

Newspaper men, like other craftsmen, have a language of their own. It consists of slang, technical terms of the editorial rooms, the print shop and the pressroom, with some of the characteristic abbreviations and contractions that have been found useful. The competent copyeditor must be familiar with all these, as they form a kind of universal newspaper language that facilitates work. Following are some of the words and expressions most frequently used.

A

ABC—Abbreviation for Audit Bureau of Circulations, an organization compiling statistics on circulation.

Ad—Abbreviation for advertisement; generally, display advertisements.

Add—Additional news matter; matter to be added at end of newsstory as Add at End Fire, Add 1 Fire, Add 2 Fire, etc. Also used in adding to lead of "running story," or to insert, as Add 1 Lead Fire, Add 1 Insert A Fire, etc.

Ad-side—That part of the newspaper composing room devoted to the setting in type of advertisements.

Advance—A story about something not yet happened, hence often to be held for a specified release date.

Agate—Type 5½ or 6 points in depth; smallest used by modern newspaper. Column lengths and advertising space are generally measured in agate lines.

This is 5½ point type, or AGATE.

Ag. b.f.—Agate boldface type; blackfaced agate.

Agony column—The personal want-ad column.

Alley—An aisle in a print shop, as ad-alley, linotype alley, Sunday alley.

All in hand—When all copy has been given out to compositors it is said to be *all in hand.*

All up—When copy is set it is *all up.*

A.M.—A morning newspaper.

Angle—A *slant* or special aspect of a story.

Angle bars—Printing press attachments that turn paper into folder or in new direction.

AP—Associated Press.

Art—General term for all newspaper illustrations.

Assignment—Any news-gathering task allotted to a reporter. He may be assigned to obtain a newsstory, or one angle of such a story, or pictures, etc.

Assignment book—The city editor's record of assignments given out to reporters. Usually there are "day" and "night" books.

Astonisher—Newspaper slang for exclamation mark.

Ax-grinder—An editorial dressed up as news.

B

Backroom—The mechanical section of a small newspaper plant, as distinguished from the *front office.*

Bad break—Term used when body type begins new column with scant line, or quad line, causing awkward appearance. Also when long story finishes a column on end of paragraph, giving reader erroneous impression story is at an end.

Bank—Table on which type is kept; also lower portion of headline.

Banner—A headline stretching over the top of a page. Also called "streamer," "line," or "ribbon."

Bastard type—Type that does not conform to the standard point system.

Beat—Newspaper slang for a news item that is the exclusive property of one paper; a *scoop;* also applied to special territory assigned to reporters, as city hall beat, federal building beat, police beat.

Ben Day—The name applied to a

347

mechanical process for shading zinc line engravings.

B.f.—Abbreviation for bold face or black face type.

Black and white—Reproduction in one color only, as distinguished from two or more colors.

Blanket head—A headline topping all the columns occupied by a given story or newspaper department. It may *blanket* both text and pictures.

Bleed—A cut *bleeds* when it runs to the edge of a sheet. Cuts often bleed in magazines, seldom in newspapers.

Blind interviews—An interview story in which the interviewed person is not revealed, *e.g.,* "a highly placed official" or "a spokesman for——." Also called a *lamp-post interview.*

Blooper—Irritating or egregious error.

Body type—The type in which the greater part of the newspaper text is set, generally 7 or 8 point.

Boilerplate—Name applied to news matter and features purchased from syndicates in the form of thin metal plates which are attached to metal bases when it is desired to print them.

Boil it down—A copydesk expression for reducing wordage of a story.

Border—Strips of type metal used to form boxes about headline or story. These borders come in many forms— stars, dots, wavy lines, double lines, etc.

Box head—A headline inclosed by thin strips of metal forming a box.

Box story—A newsstory or feature inclosed by a "box."

Break—The point at which a story turns from one column to another; a story *breaks* when it becomes available for publication; news is said to *break* when it happens.

Bromide—A hackneyed expression; a *stereotype*; a *cliché.*

Bug—Any type ornament used in a fancy headline or by the side of a cut or layout; also a Morse telegrapher's sending apparatus.

Bulldog—Name given an early edition or one printed out of regular hours.

Bulletin—Last minute news regarding some important development in a story; it is generally set in heavier type than the body of the story and precedes it. The headline on it reads simply "Bulletin."

Each newspaper has its own typography for bulletins.

Bullpup—Name given first mail-edition of Sunday newspapers.

Bun—Wire symbol for bulletin.

Byline—A signature to precede a newsstory, as "By John Smith."

Byline story—Any signed story in the newspaper.

C

Cablese—Abbreviated or coded copy sent by cable.

C. and l.c.—Abbreviation for capital and lower case letters.

Canned copy—Copy released by press agents.

Caps—Abbreviation for capital letters.

Caption—Literally, any heading, but used specifically in regard to picture headings and accompanying text. Usually over a picture, whereas a *cutline* goes under a picture.

Case—The type cabinet at which the printer works.

Catchline—A guideline or slugline.

Chairman—Printers' union title for head of office branch, or chapel.

Chalk plate—Plate used for making engraving in process now little used. Metal plate is coated with chalk, in which engraving is scratched, and molten metal is cast on finished product.

Challenge—A copyeditor may challenge a story, *i.e.,* question its authenticity, to the head-of-the-desk.

Chapel—Unit of printers' union.

Chase—Metal frame, equipped with *footstick, clamps* or *quoins,* into which are placed type and halftones making one complete newspaper page; it is a *form* in the completed stage.

Chaser—An extra edition, usually following the final home edition.

Check up—A copyeditor may check up or verify a story.

Cheesecake—The slang news photographers commonly use for pictures generous in revelation of female legs.

Circus makeup—A method of making up a newspaper's pages in which the columns are broken up by many headlines of various sizes, and many kinds of type are used, creating a rather freakish effect.

City editor—The editor in charge of

the city room; one who handles local news.

City room—The room in which local news is handled.

Clean proof—Proof needing few corrections.

Clips—Abbreviations for clippings from current newspapers or from files in morgue.

Clipsheet—A sheet, usually printed, containing several publicity stories which can be clipped.

Col.—Abbreviation for column.

Coloroto—Rotogravure in colors.

Color separation—Eliminating, from each negative or plate in a color set, those portions which print only in other colors.

Comp.—A compositor or typesetter.

Combination plate—Halftone and line reproduction combined in one engraving.

Condensed type—Narrow type, as opposed to that of standard width.

This is 8-point Cheltenham bold CONDENSED

Here is a sample of the same STANDARD

Copy—The term applied to all news manuscript; also, any illustrations to be reproduced by photoengraving.

Copyboy—The boy who carries copy from copydesk to composing room and runs other errands; an *office boy.*

Copycutter—A composing room functionary who divides the work of typesetting among the various linotype operators. He derives his name from the fact that he *cuts* the news manuscript into small portions, enabling it to be set more rapidly by division of labor than would be the case if each operator were given a complete story of varying length.

Copyholder—In proofroom practice one proofreader holds the proof of the type matter and makes corrections and a second one holds the copy and reads it aloud for comparison purposes.

Correspondent—A person, often working on a *string,* who is authorized to send news from out-of-town points.

Cover—To get all available news about an event.

Credit line—A line giving source of copy or illustration.

Crossbars—Printing press attachments for guiding or turning the print paper.

Crossline—A line of the headline centered, separating decks or banks.

Crusade—A newspaper campaign for a reform.

Cub—A beginning reporter.

Cut—Any metal plate bearing a newspaper illustration. *To cut* a story is to eliminate some of its type. Thus a copyeditor may be directed to "cut ten agate lines out of the fire story," meaning that the story must be shortened by space equal to ten agate lines in order to confine it to the room available in the page. To *cut in* a story is to reduce it to a certain space.

Cut-in letter—Large initial letter beginning a paragraph. See *Stick-up initial* or *Initial cap.*

Cutline—The caption for a cut, consisting of *overlines* and/or *underlines.*

Cutoff—A *rule* placed across one or more columns to separate boxes, cuts, layouts, page datelines and advertisements from the rest of the page. The cutoff rule is intended to guide the reader and avoid confusion. A double cutoff consists of two rules together, in some cases a light one and a heavy one.

D

Dagger—A reference mark.

Dateline—The line at the top of each page, giving the date on which the newspaper is published; also the line giving the point of origin of a telegraph, cable or radio story.

Dash—A short line separating parts of head, stories, etc.; a punctuation mark.

Day side—A newspaper employe working days is on the day side.

Dead bank—Composing room term applied to the *rack* on which is placed type no longer available for use, whether in the form of stories, parts of stories, or headlines.

Deadline—The last moment to get copy in for an edition.

Deal—The head of a copydesk passes out or *deals* copy to his copyeditors.

Deck—A bank, *i.e.,* a section of a headline.

Desk—A copydesk.

Desk editor—An editor directing reporters or copyeditors.

Devil—The printer's apprentice.

Dingbat—Printer's terms for ornaments used in headline or with cuts. Also a boxed story, generally one spread over a number of columns.

Dinky dash—A special form of dash used in lieu of subheads, or to separate a number of short items.

District man—A reporter covering a district of a community, often a *legman*.

Dog-watch—After the newspaper has finished issuing its regular editions for the day, and staff and deskmen have gone home, one copyeditor generally is kept on duty to watch for stories suitable for replates and extra editions. He is sometimes called the dog-watch man, or the lobster-trick man, and will have working under him one or two reporters and the necessary mechanical force.

Dope—Advance newsstory material, mostly gossip and rumors.

Dope story—Forecast or "think piece."

Double leading—If a story does not fill the required space, it is *leaded* (lĕded) *out,* by placing thin strips of metal, from one to three points thick, between the linotype slugs. If one lead between lines is not enough, two leads are used; this is *double leading*. First-page articles and editorials often are double leaded.

Doublet—Item, word or passage accidentally set twice and repeated in same paper. Same as *dupe*.

Double truck—A two-page advertisement or editorial layout made up as a single unit.

Down style—The newspaper style in which a minimum of capital letters is used.

Dragon's blood—A red powder used in etching zinc, to prevent undercutting.

Drop head—Headline accompanying a streamer line and based on the same story; also called a *read out*.

Droplines—Stepped lines, such as those that make up the top part of a headline:

TWO DROPLINES
FORM THIS HEAD

Dummy—Diagram or *layout* of a newspaper or magazine page, showing the position each story and picture is to have.

Dump—Type is always dumped, *e.g.,* into galleys.

Dupe—Contraction of duplicate. News items identical as to facts, printed by mistake in the same copy of a newspaper, are *dupes*. Same as *doublet*. Also, carbon copies of newsstories.

E

Ears—Little boxes on either side of the newspaper title plate on first page; generally they carry weather prediction, circulation figures, edition name or some like feature as text.

Editorialize—To express an opinion in a newsstory or headline.

Electrotype—A duplicate of a photoengraving, cast from a mat made from the original cut.

Em—The square of any given size of type; formerly it was the space occupied by the letter M. An *en* is one half the width of an em. Ems pica (12-point) are used by the printer in measuring column width and the length of type lines.

Etaoinshrdlu—A pi line made by the compositor running a finger down a row of keys on his typesetting machine.

Exchanges—Where one newspaper exchanges copies with another, these copies are called *exchanges,* which are examined and studied regularly. Most large papers have an exchange editor to perform this duty.

Exclusive—A newsstory is exclusive when it is the property of only one newspaper—a *scoop*.

F

Fake—A falsified story.

Fat head—A headline too large for space allowed for it.

Feature—To give special prominence to a story. Any story that may not be news, strictly regarded, yet is timely and interesting may be called a feature. The word is also used to denominate the most important or interesting element in a story.

File—A correspondent *files* a story when he dispatches it by wire or by radio. All newspapers keep *files* of their back copies.

Filler—Short items that may be placed almost anywhere on the page, as distinguished from stories bearing top heads.

First-day story—A story published for the first time; a story dealing with something that has just happened.

Fingernails—Printer's slang for parentheses. Also called "parens."

Fix—Correct; a fix is a correction.

Flag—The first-page nameplate of the newspaper; the editorial heading; a lead sticking up in the midst of a column of type to warn the printer that a correction or an addition is on the way.

Flash—A bulletin by telephone, telegraph, or radio that conveys the first brief word of an event that has just taken place.

Flimsy—A thin, carbon copy of a newsstory.

Flop—An illustration reversed in an engraving is said to be *flopped*.

Flush and indent—A direction to printers, meaning set the first line of the copy flush, without paragraph indention, and indent the remainder one em or more at the left.

Flush head—A headline set flush to the left with a ragged ending of lines to the right.

Fold—The point at which the newspaper page is folded in half. All important news is *played* above this fold.

Folio—A page; the page number.

Follow, follow up—A follow story is one based on a story previously published; it gives later developments. Same as a second-day story. Also, a subsidiary story following a big lead, and relating to the same or a similar subject.

Follow copy—Directions to printers, meaning set the copy exactly as it is written. May also be used in referring proof back to proofroom for correction.

Folo—Abbreviation of *follow*.

Font—A complete set of type of one size and style.

Footstick—The heavy metal bar at the bottom of a chase, used in locking it. The footstick provides purchase for the *quoins* or *screws* used to clamp the *form* shut.

Form—In newspaper parlance, a page of type, locked within a chase and ready for the press.

Fotog—Abbreviation for news photographer.

Frisket—A paper mask used to protect a photograph while it is being airbrushed.

Front office—The section of a small newspaper plant where the public is met, as distinguished from the *backroom*.

Fudge box or jigger—A mechanical contrivance consisting of a clamp in which linotype slugs can be locked and the whole then sent to press as a part of the first page. The fudge box is used for late news bulletins and sports scores. It obviates the necessity of frequent replates and makes for increased speed in presswork.

Furniture—Pieces of wood or metal of less height than type which are packed around the type, if needed, to make it possible to lock up and *justify* a form.

Future—A note about a story that will develop later; kept by the editor in a *futures book*.

FYI—"for your information."

G

Galley—Metal tray on which printer keeps type ready for use.

Glossy—A shiny photographic print —preferred by photoengravers.

Goodnight—A reporter takes a goodnight from his boss when he goes off duty; the word is also used to indicate when the news section of a paper is closed.

Graf—Paragraph.

Grapevine—Miscellaneous time copy, as good six months hence as today, which is edited, headed up, set in type, and stowed away against a time when emergency filler is needed. Also called "plug" copy.

Graveyard shift—Same as *dog-watch* or *lobster-trick*.

Green proof—First proof taken, therefore, proof that is not yet corrected and .hat carries typographical errors.

Guideline—The indispensable *slug* or title given each newsstory as a guide to both copyeditor and printer. Thus, a political story might be called "Pol," and each section would be so marked, while the headline would bear the same designation; for example, "Add 1 Pol," "Add 2 Pol," "Pol 8 head," "Pol 2 head," "Insert Pol," "Precede Pol." Each guideline is calculated to give a hint as to the nature of the story.

H

Hairline boxes—Shallow little one-column boxes made of border rule that prints in extremely fine lines.

Half stick—matter set in one half-column measure.

Halftone—See photoengraving.

Handout—Copy supplied by press agent.

Hanging indent—Matter set with top line full and flush and remainder indented one em at left.

Head—Headline.

Head-of-desk—Person in charge of copydesk, whether city editor, one of his assistants, or copyeditor.

Hellbox—Box or other receptacle where discarded type and furniture are thrown.

H.I.—Abbreviation for human interest.

High leads—Leads (lĕds) sticking up in the columns in such fashion that they will print. It is the printer's business to push them down so they will not show.

High lines—Lines of uneven depth cast by faulty linotype; when they appear in print they are particularly black.

Highlights—The most nearly white portions of a photograph or halftone.

Hold for release—Term endorsed on copy that is not to be published until a specified time.

Hold presses—When news of superlative importance breaks, the presses may be held until it can be put in type.

Hole—Any vacant space on a page.

Hook, spike—Discarded copy is placed on the hook, or spiked, by the city editor or head of the desk. Also, linotype operators work "from the hook" on which the copycutter places the various *takes* of a story.

Human interest—Any pleasant little news oddity about people; stories with conversation and action, but not necessarily with *straight news*.

H.T.C., H.T.K.—Head to come, or "hed to kum," endorsed on copy indicates the story is *running* and headline will follow.

I

Indent—Type matter is indented when the usual paragraph form is disregarded and lines are begun at some specified distance inward from the margins. Thus matter may be indented one em at the end of each line, creating a little white space area and emphasizing the text so

treated. Matter also is indented for initials of varying size.

Index—An index of the day's news, usually on the front page.

Initial cap—Two- or three-line capital letter at beginning of paragraph.

I.N.S.—International News Service.

Insert—Matter intended to be incorporated within the body of a story after the latter has been sent to the composing room.

Intertype—Trade name for a typesetting machine very similar to the Linotype.

Interview—A story based on an interview.

Italics—Type in which letters and characters slant to the right. First used in 1501 in an edition of Virgil by Aldus Manutius and dedicated by him to the Italian states of that time.

Itals—Abbreviation for italics.

J

Jim dash—Hairline (usually 3 picas) between the deck and the story.

Jump—The continuation of a newsstory from one page to another under another head. The part that is continued is called the *jump* and the whole story is a *jump story*.

Jump heads—Headlines for a story that is continued from one page to another. Also called "runover."

Jumplines—The continuation lines of a story jumped from one page to another: "Continued on Page 12," "Continued from Page 1."

Justifying, justification—Spacing out the type so that form may be locked up; spacing out a single line of type to fill the required column width.

K

Kicker—An overline over the headline.

Kill—Type is killed when it is discarded as useless and thrown into the hellbox. To kill copy is to destroy it.

L

Label head—A dull, lifeless headline with no more interest or originality than the label of a tomato can.

L.C.—Abbreviation for lower case, meaning small letters, not capitals.

Lead (*lēed*)—Introductory sentences or paragraphs of newsstory; the big news-story of the day; there may be substitute leads (sub leads) or new leads, adds to lead, and inserts in lead.

Lead (leed)—A tip which may lead to a story.

Lead (lĕd)—Thin metal strips one, two, and three points thick, used to space out lines of type; also the process of spacing out. The rule of the expert printer is always to lead out from the tops of the columns and a bit around subheads, or short dashes; never between paragraphs to any great extent.

Leaders (leeders)—A row of dots, often used in statistical work, sports summaries, etc.

Legman, legger—A reporter who gets the information and telephones it to a *rewrite* man at the home office.

Library—A newspaper's collection of books, files, etc.; a *morgue.*

Ligature—A single type containing two or more letters, a syllable, an entire word, thus: *ff, fi, ing, the.* Some cuts, such as a miniature reproduction of a newspaper's nameplate, or a signature, are also called ligatures.

Line engraving—See photoengraving.

Linos—Abbreviation for linotype, a typesetting machine.

Lobster-trick—See *Dog-watch.*

Local—A local newsstory; often a brief item, a *personal.*

Localize—To stress the local angle of a story.

Local news room—The *city room,* the workshop of the city staff.

Ludlow—A machine (typograph) casting slugs from hand set matrices, from 6 to 72 points in size. Generally used for display advertising or headlines.

M

Magazine—That part of a typesetting machine which contains the brass matrices of the different letters and characters. Every time the operator presses a key on the keyboard, he releases a matrix from the magazine.

Makeready—Arranging a form so that all elements will print uniformly.

Makeup—The art of arranging pictures and news matter in the most effective and artistic manner throughout the paper.

Makeup man—The printer who makes up or assembles one or more pages. He is not to be confused with the editorial worker known as the *makeup editor,* often called the news editor, who plans the makeup.

Markets—The general name given to the pages or columns devoted to news of the financial, grain, livestock and produce markets. Market boxes are characteristic to these pages and market tables are set in agate type.

Masthead—The matter printed in every issue of a newspaper, usually at the top of the editorial column, stating the title, publisher, place of publication, etc., from the nautical term indicating the top of the mast from which a flag is flown, hence also called *flag.*

Mat—Abbreviation for matrix.

Matrix—The little brass mold used in linotype, monotype and typograph machines for type casting Also, the papier-mâché impression of a photoengraving or a page of type upon which metal may be cast.

M.E.—The managing editor.

Merg.—A linotype, abbreviated from Mergenthaler, the inventor of the linotype.

Mill—A reporter's typewriter.

Milline rate—Advertising rate per agate line per million copies circulated.

Minion—Seven-point type, used by some newspapers as a body type.

This is 7-point modern type.
THIS IS THE SAME TYPE, CAPITALS.
THIS IS THE SAME TYPE, SMALL CAPITALS.
This is the same type, italics.
This is 7-point type or MINION, UPPER CASE and lower case.

Miscellany—The name applied by country newspapers to plate matter consisting of miscellaneous filler items, short and long, in handy shape to fill space on dull days.

Monotype—A type-casting machine that makes a single character at a time, as opposed to the full line of the linotype machine.

More—Written at the bottom of a page of copy indicates *more to come.*

Morgue—The newspaper's repository for clippings, photos and all types of reference material.

Morse code—The code used by telegraphers.

Mortise—A cut-away section of a photoengraving into which type can be inserted.

Mug shots—Closeup of faces.

Must—When "must" is written on copy by the proper executive, it must be published. BOM means business office must.

N

Nameplate—The large heading giving the paper's name, on the front page.

News summary—An index or a summary of the day's news, usually on the front page.

Night side—Newspaper employes on night shifts are on the night side.

Nonpareil—Six-point type. See *Agate*. Also, the unit of measurement for type widths in newspaper composing rooms—thus a cut may be 50 agate lines deep and 20 nonpareils wide. The pica (12 point) unit is used generally for display advertising widths. Also nonpareil slugs for spacing between columns.

This is 6-point type, or NONPAREIL.

O

Obit, obituary—A biography of a dead person.

Op. ed.—Page opposite the editorial page.

Outlined cut—A halftone of which the background has been cut away. See *vignette*.

Overhead—News sent by telegraph or telephone.

Overline—The caption above the cut.

Overs, overset—Type set in excess of the amount allotted and therefore crowded out of the paper for lack of room. Each editor—city, telegraph, cable, and sports—is given a stipulated amount of space for his news; any type in excess of this is *overmatter, overset, overs.* Where there is an insufficient quantity of matter in type, the paper is *underset.*

P

Pad—To make a story long by padding it out with words.

Page proof—The proof of an entire page, taken only in exceptional cases to guard against serious mistake.

Parens—Abbreviation for parentheses.

Patent insides—Name given to *ready-*

print inside pages formerly bought from service agencies and syndicates by country papers. See *Boilerplate.*

Phat, fat—To phat type is to hold it for possible repetition; it is then called phatted type. A fat take or a fat page is a take or page with many cuts or other matter that does not require setting, making the printer's work easy. Fat type is extended type and thin type is extra-condensed. A fat line is a line that cannot be set in the allotted space; a thin line is a line that is too scant.

Phillips' code—A system of abbreviated Morse Code symbols by old-time telegraphers. To them, "prans" meant "the President today sent the following nominations to the senate."

Photocomposition—Type composed on film rather than on metal.

Photoengraving—A picture photographed on metal, which is then given relief for printing reproduction by being etched either chemically or electrolytically. A *halftone* is a photoengraving photographed through a screen, with the dots in the light sections etched away to offer little printing surface. A *line engraving* or *zinc etching* is a *photoengraving* made without *photographing* it through a screen.

Pi—Type that is mixed, disarranged and therefore impossible to use; a jumbled heap of type, as when a page form is dropped and broken up.

Pica—Twelve-point type; see *Em, ems pica.*

Pickup—Type already set that is to be incorporated with a new lead or other fresh matter—"End new lead; pick up old story as trimmed and corrected."

Pig iron—Heavy, serious newspaper copy.

P.I.O.—Public Information Officer; also P.R.O. or Public Relations Officer.

Pix—Abbreviation for pictures; any newspaper illustrations.

Planer—The wooden block used by printers to smooth down the surface of a form filled with type as it is being locked up.

Plate—A page of type cast in metal ready to be locked on to the press.

Play Up—To give prominence to.

Plug—Filler copy.

P.M.—An afternoon paper.

Point—The unit of measurement in

which type sizes are designated; approximately 1/72 of an inch.

Police blotter—The police sergeant's record from which police news is taken by the reporter.

Policy story—A story written to serve the publisher's policy.

Pork—Matter saved from one edition and reprinted in another. Also used with regard to time copy.

P.R.—Public relations.

Precede—Matter intended to precede a newsstory. It may be a bulletin or merely some pleasant or noteworthy feature of the main story; it may be inclosed in a box or it may be plain type.

Press agent—A person hired by an institution, corporation, actor, etc., to *contact* the press and secure publicity. He issues *releases*.

Profile—Biographical sketch.

Proof—An impression of type taken on paper for the purpose of making corrections and alterations.

Proofreader—One who corrects mistakes in typesetting by reading proofs and sending them back to the printer for revision.

Public relations—The science and art of attitude control; a *public relations man* seeks to create public favor for the interest hiring him. His field is broader than that of the press agent. See *P.I.O.*

Puff—A personal publicity story.

Pull—Proofs are always pulled from the type.

Pull in—To publish matter without waiting for the proofroom's typographical corrections is to *pull in* the type. This is rarely done except in emergency cases where the story is important, press time is near and there is need for great haste. Such type is also said to be *railroaded*.

Punch—Stories and headlines with punch are those with vigor, strength, snap, instantaneous appeal. Punch words are short and full of action—nab, trap, plot, etc.

Put to bed—A paper has been put to bed when plates or type have been *locked up* and the press is *ready to roll*.

Q

Q-A stuff—Question and answer copy, as in court proceedings. Question and answer are run in one paragraph without quotes.

Quad—A blank type character or space the width of which equals its height.

Query—A brief mail or telegraphic synopsis of a story sent to a newspaper by a correspondent, who also states the number of words available, as: "Seven killed, ten hurt in powder mill explosion here—1,000." The news executive then orders the quantity desired and the correspondent is paid on this basis.

Quotes—Quotation marks; a part of a story quoted.

R

Rack—Cabinet in which galleys of type are kept.

Railroad—To rush copy to the composing room without reading it carefully; the copyeditor pauses only to see that it contains no dangerous or inaccurate statements and to write subheads and a headline. See *Pull in*.

Register—Correct relative position of two or more colors printed from a set of plates.

Release copy—Copy that is not to be published until a certain release date. Important documents of state, such as the president's message, come to the newspaper in this form.

Replate—To recast a page of type to insert an important but late story.

Retouching—Altering photographs by painting or airbrushing.

Reverse plate—Reversing the color values so that black is white and vice versa.

Revise—A second proof of type, made after it has been corrected, taken for checking purposes.

Rewrite—Each large newspaper has a battery of rewrite men, picked for their ability as writers, who receive information over the telephone and write it up, rewrite poorly written stories of all kinds and boil down the matter received from news agencies.

Rim—The outer edge of the copydesk *horseshoe*, where copyeditors sit, as opposed to the slot, or inside where the executive or *sit-in* man has his post.

Ring—To draw a ring around some word or symbol in news manuscript; a ring around an abbreviation indicates to the printer that it should be spelled out; in other cases it means the word should be abbreviated; some copyeditors "ring" each period.

Ring bank—The composing room stands at which corrections are made in type.

Ring machine—Linotype machine devoted to purposes of making type corrections.

Ring man—Printer who corrects type.

Roto—Abbreviation for rotogravure.

Roundup—Comprehensive story from several sources.

Routing—Removing non-essential metal from non-printing parts of a plate.

Rule for insert—A direction to the printer, meaning that he shall turn a rule as a sign that type already set shall be picked up and incorporated with the story.

Run—A story already printed has been run; a reporter's run is his *beat* or the route he takes on his regular coverage.

Run-around—Body of type to be set around odd-measure cut, as in fiction or feature magazine.

Run flat—To set the manuscript in type as it stands, without revision. When this direction is given to a copyeditor, it means that he shall leave the story unchanged.

Run in—To incorporate two sentences or more into one; to incorporate a long list of names or like matter into one paragraph.

Running stories—These are stories sent to the composing room in short sections, each of which ends with the end of a sentence or paragraph and is marked "more," to signify that additional copy is to be sent along.

Rush—Copy to be handled quickly is so marked.

S

Sacred cows—Personalities or institutions given special newspaper favor.

Schedule—The list of available stories and pictures compiled each day by the city, telegraph, cable, sports and news editors; the draft of a page, showing each story and picture in the position in which it is to appear; a *dummy* page, with the heads, type and pictures pasted in as they will appear.

Scoop—A story that is the exclusive property of one newspaper, possession of which means a victory over a competitor; a *beat*.

Second-day story—A follow story based on one that already has appeared. This type of story also carries a second-day head, conveying the hint that it records not a fresh event, but developments.

Second front page—The front page of a second section.

Sectional story—A story sent to the printer in *takes* or one with various angles played up under different headlines.

See copy—A direction to the proofroom, meaning look up the original manuscript and compare it with proof, which appears to be wrong or to have something omitted.

Set and hold for release—A direction to the printer to set matter in type and hold for orders.

Set flush—This order means to set without paragraph indent or margin. Lines may be set flush to the left or to the right, but generally it is the former.

Shank—The main body or stem of a unit of type.

Short—A brief item; a *filler*.

Shoulder—The top surface of type, on which the character is made.

Shouts—Slang for exclamation marks. See *astonisher*.

Sit-in man—The assistant who substitutes for the city editor or other news executive as head of the copydesk.

Sked—Abbreviation for schedule.

Skeletonize—In copy sent by wire unnecessary words are omitted, hence it is skeletonized.

Skyline—Headline across top of page over nameplate. Also called over-title and over-the-roof.

Slant—An angle of a story, a story is *slanted* when a certain aspect is played up for policy or other reasons.

Sleuth—Newspaper slang for reporter who specializes in stories that require exhaustive investigation, detective work.

Slopover—Type crowded out of a form.

Slot—Copydesks generally are built roughly in the form of a horseshoe. The small enclosure is the slot and here the head-of-the-desk holds forth.

Slotman—The head of the copydesk.

Slug—Linotype line; also strip of

metal thicker than a lead and used for same purpose of spacing out lines. Guidelines also are called slugs and naming a story is termed slugging it.

Slugline—See *Guideline*.

Small caps—Small capital letters, part of each font, as opposed to full size capitals.

THIS LINE IS IN SMALL CAPS.
THIS LINE IS IN REGULAR CAPS.

Soc—Abbreviation for society, used to designate copy intended for society columns.

Space—Blank units of type used to space between words; the linotype operator handspaces between the letters of the words when he finds a line too short for the *spacebands* to fill it out.

Spike—A story is spiked when it is stopped, often by spiking it on spindle.

Split page—A second front page.

Spot news—News obtained firsthand on the spot where it happened, hence fresh and live news.

Spread—An elaborate pictorial layout; a double spread is one across facing pages; a spread may also be a big story and auxiliary stories.

Squib—A short news item; a *filler*.

Standard type—Type of standard width. See *Condensed type*.

Standing boxes—Type boxes that are kept on hand in skeletonized form, ready to be completed when the figures or other data arrive. Standing boxes are kept on hand for baseball scores and elections, in order to facilitate the handling of returns.

Standing ads, tables, etc.—Same as standing boxes and heads.

Standing heads—Headlines that do not change and therefore may be kept on hand ready for instant use.

Step lines—Same as droplines.

Stet—From the Latin, meaning "let it stand." Used to indicate that matter marked for correction or omission is to remain as it was originally.

Stick—The composing stick or type holder used by the printer who sets type by hand. A *stickful* is about two inches of type. When a copyeditor is directed to "trim a stickful" from a story it means that he is to shorten the story by about two inches. The part on linotype machines that holds the type lines is also a stick.

Sticker—A page that is not to be replated.

Stick-up initial—A large initial letter protruding above the normal type line.

Stone—The imposing stone upon which the printer makes up the page; it may be of either stone or metal.

Straight news—A plain recital of news facts with no attempt at featuring or fancy writing or embellishment of any kind.

String—Clippings pasted together in a long strip or in a scrapbook.

Stringer—Correspondent, usually paid on space basis.

Stuff—The raw material of a story.

Sub-Substitute—Sub fire means a new fire story. Also abbreviation for subscription.

Subhead—A one- or two-line head

Sunrise-watch—Same as dog-watch and lobster-trick.

Syndicate—An organization either inside or outside of a newspaper office that buys and sells newspaper and magazine features, such as comics, pictures, department articles, etc.

T

Table—The general term for any tabulation, as of figures.

Take—A small portion of news manuscript or any copy given out to machine operators by the copycutter to be set in type; a small portion of a story sent by the copyeditor to the composing room.

Tape—Perforated paper used in teletype or teletypesetter.

Telephoto—A photograph transmitted by wire.

Think piece—Speculative or opinion story.

Third stick—A direction to the printer to set type one third of a column wide—used in tabulations of various kinds, lists of names, articles, etc.

Thirty—Used in some newspaper offices as closing mark for newsstories.

Tie-back—A sentence or paragraph in a story that *rehashes* or reviews events of a related character.

Tie-in—The part of a story that relates a contemporaneous event, or relevant information, to the news being reported.

Tight paper—A paper so crowded with advertising that the news space must be reduced. It is the opposite of a *wide open* paper.

Time copy—Copy set in type and held for future use.

Tip—A bit of information which leads to a story, hence a *lead*.

Title line—Same as signature and byline.

Toenails—Parentheses.

Tombstone—When heads of the same size are placed side by side they are said to be tombstoned.

Top heads—Headlines intended for the tops of columns only. Generally headlines with banks or decks.

Top lines—The type lines forming the top of a headline.

Tr—Abbreviation of transpose, used when letters, words, sentences or paragraphs are to be changed in position. Matter is "ringed" and connected by lines to indicate changes. Also abbreviation for turn rule.

Trim—A term used when it is desired to have story reduced in length, either in manuscript or in type.

TTS—Abbreviation for teletypesetter.

Turn—A story is said to *turn* when it runs from the bottom of the last column on the first page to the top of the first column on the second page. Such stories require no jump heads, as they *read* from the one page to the other. Also, a story *turns* from one column to another, under a cut, under a box, etc.

Turn rule—Meaning to invert a rule, broad side up, in the body of a story to indicate an alteration or correction is on the way.

Turn story—The story that runs from the last column of the first page to the first column of the second and therefore requires no jump heads.

Two-line initial, two-line figure—Initials and figures that are two average type lines in depth. There are also three- and four-line initials.

Typebook—A book showing various families and sizes of type.

Type high—All type is .918 inch in height—printing height.

U

U. and l.c.—Upper and lower case letters—capitals and small letters.

Underlines—Lines or text to be run beneath cuts, etc.

U.P.—United Press.

Up style—The newspaper style in which many words are initialed with capital letters which would be in lower case when the *down style* is used.

V

Verse style—A direction to the printer, meaning set type after the fashion of poetry.

Vignette—A halftone of an irregular shape bearing little relation to any object in the picture. A *soft vignette* (pronounced veen-yett') fades off into white space. See *Outlined cut.*

W

Widow—A very short word, or part of a word, standing alone on the last line of a paragraph of body type.

Wooden head—Term applied to dull, meaningless headlines that tell nothing.

Wrap up—Complete story, distinguished from a story in takes.

Wrong face, wrong font—Type of different style or size than that specified, occurring in midst of text.

Y

Yellow, yellow journalism—A sensationalized story; a yellow journal specializes in sensationalized stories.

Z

Zinc—Common expression for a zinc etching, a cut without a halftone screen.

II. MARKS USED IN PROOFREADING

Below are the orthodox marks used by proofreaders in making corrections for books and magazines. Usually they are penned in the margins, the marks indicating consecutively the errors in each line.

ꝸ	Take out	ꞈ ꞈ	Quote marks
∧	Insert	ꞈ ꞈ	Single q.; apostrophe
stet}	Let it stand	ꞈ	Comma
#	More space	⊙	Period
‿	Less space	=/	Hyphen
◠	Close up	2	2-em dash
⌐ ⌐	Raise	*w. f.*	Wrong font
⌊ ⌋	Lower	*Ital*	Set in italic
⊏	Move left	══	Use small caps
⊐	Move right	≡	Use capitals
↓	Push down	/ or *l.c.*	Use lower case
×	Bad letter	*rom*	Use Roman type
□	Quad space	⌐⌐ *tr.*}	Transpose
¶	Paragraph	↓	Superior figure
no¶	No paragraph	⌃	inferior figure
═	Straighten line	*bf.*	Boldface (or spl.)
℥	Turn over	⸍/	Use this mark

Newspapers have developed a somewhat simplified and quicker usage as indicated below.

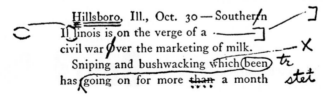

Prooofreaders' marks are to be differentiated from those used by copy-editors.

III.   HEADLINES FOR CLASS EXERCISES

Most newspapers have schedules, or charts, on which the copyeditor will find headlines designated by a number or typeface and size. If such a chart is not available, the copyeditor can paste one up for his own use. Here are a few headlines, taken from a typical newspaper headline chart.

#2 (14-point Vogue extrabold)
Maximum count 21 units.

**Illegally Parked Cars
Belong to City Police**

#3 (18-point Vogue extrabold)
Maximum count 14½ units.

**Sorry, General,
No One at Home**

#4 (18-point Vogue extrabold)
Maximum count 14½ units.

**Woman Phones
For Date With
Funeral Home**

#5 (24-point Vogue extrabold)
Maximum count 12 units.

**Russ Papers
Rap British,
U. S. Plans**

#6 (30-point Vogue bold)
Maximum count 10 units.

**High Court
Upholds
Motorist**

#7 (30-point Vogue bold italic)
Maximum count 9½ units. With overline in 14-point Vogue extrabold caps.

BASTILLE DAY

*French
Celebrate
Revolution*

#8 (36-point Medium Gothic)
Maximum count 10½ units.

**Board Cuts
Big Lawns
Water Fee**

#22 (18-point Vogue extrabold caps)
     Maximum count 24 units.

TRANSPORTATION OFFICIALS
HERE FOR TWO-DAY MEET

#23 (30-point Vogue extrabold)
     Maximum count 19½ units.

Children's Army Joins
Egypt's Insect War

#24 (30-point Vogue bold)
     Maximum count 21 units.

Mayor, Denver Leaders
Sketch Centennial Plan

#25 (36-point Kabel bold italic)
     Maximum count 19. With overline in 18-point Vogue extrabold caps.

A ENERGY FOR FUTURE?

Natural Gas to Heat
Air Force Academy

#26 (36-point Vogue extrabold)
     Maximum count 12 units.

Prominent
Racing Men
Direct Track

IV. HOW TO FIND IT: THE JOURNALIST'S REFERENCE GUIDE

Most newspapers, except the larger metropolitan dailies, have too few books. Their libraries usually consist of a dictionary, an almanac, an atlas, the city directory, telephone directory, postal guide, congressional directory and the Bible. Generally, these are well-worn with use. Other references would be used widely, too, if they were available.

Reference departments of local libraries are cooperative when the reporter or editor calls for information. But reference books should be at the newspaper office and reporters and deskmen should know how to use them.

The following list is selective rather than exhaustive. The standard bibliographies like Constance Winchell's *Guide to Reference Books* and Mudge's *Guide to Reference Books* should be examined by all journalists. They show where useful information on all subjects can be obtained. Guides to new reference works appear periodically in magazines such as the *Saturday Review*.

BIOGRAPHIES

>   *Who's Who*
>   *Who's Who in America* (with Supplements)
>   *Current Biography*
>   *Biography Index*
>   *Dictionary of American Biography*
>   *Dictionary of National Biography* (British)
>   *Century Cyclopedia of Names*
>   *International Who's Who*
>   *World Biography*
>   *Webster's Biographical Dictionary*
>   *Who Knows—and What*
>   Regional:
>   *Who's Who in New England*
>   *Who's Who on the Pacific Coast*
>   *Who's Who in the Midwest*
>   *Who's Who in the East*
>   Specialized:
>   *Who's Who in the United Nations*
>   *Who's Who in Colored America*
>   *Who's Who in American Jewry*
>   *Who's Who in American Art*
>   *Who's Who in Commerce and Industry*
>   *Who's Who in Labor*
>   *Who's Who in Law*
>   *Who's Who in Engineering*
>   *The American Catholic Who's Who*
>   *American Men in Government*
>   *Twentieth Century Authors*

Cattell's Directory of American Scholars
Cattell's Leaders in Education
Cattell's American Men of Science

FACT DICTIONARIES

The World Almanac and Book of Facts
Information Please Almanac
Statesman's Yearbook
Whitaker's Almanack
Standard Dictionary of Facts
Facts on File
Keller's Dictionary of Dates

ENCYCLOPEDIAS

New International Yearbook
Lincoln Library of Essential Information
Encyclopedia Americana
Encyclopaedia Britannica
Collier's Encyclopedia
Columbia Encyclopedia

ATLASES

Columbia Lippincott Gazeteer of the World
Rand, McNally Standard World Atlas
Rand, McNally Commercial Atlas and Marketing Guide
Hammond's New Comprehensive World Atlas
Webster's Geographical Dictionary
American Guide Series
London Times Survey Atlas of the World
Sheperd's Historical Atlas
Lewis and Campbell's American Oxford Atlas
Alsberg's American Guide
Pan American Yearbook

INDEXES AND DIRECTORIES

Reader's Guide to Periodical Literature
International Index to Periodicals
Index to Legal Periodicals
Index to Labor Articles
Annual Magazine Subject Index
Education Index
Agricultural Index
The Art Index
Engineering Index
Public Affairs Information Service
New York Times Index
Official Index (*London Times*)
N. W. Ayer & Son's Directory of Newspapers and Periodicals
Editor & Publisher Yearbook
Broadcasting and Telecasting Yearbook
Variety Yearbook
Ulrich's Periodicals Directory
Willing's Press Guide (British)

Union List of Files Available in the United States and Canada
Severance's Guide to the Current Periodicals and Serials of the United States
and Canada

WORDS, STYLE

New Century Dictionary
Century Cyclopedia of Names
Funk and Wagnalls' New Standard Dictionary
Webster's New International Dictionary
Roget's Thesaurus of Words
Mencken's The American Language
Fowler's Modern English Usage
Fowler's Dictionary of American English
Webster's Dictionary of Synonyms
Allen's Synonyms and Antonyms
Crabb's English Synonyms
Perrin's Index to English
The Concise Oxford Edition of Current English
Concise Dictionary of English Idioms
Dictionary of Foreign Words and Phrases
The American Thesaurus of Slang
Word Finder
The Verb Finder
American Dialect Dictionary
U. S. Printing Office Manual of Style
University of Chicago Manual of Style
Lasky's Proofreading and Copy-preparation
Nicholson's Manual of Copyright Practice for Writers, Publishers and Agents
Woolley's New Handbook of Composition
Colby's Practice Handbook of Better English
Leggett, Mead and Charvat, Handbook for Writers
For Radio and Television newsrooms:
Greet's World Words
NBC Handbook of Pronunciation
Henneke's Radio Announcer's Handbook
Vizetelly's Deskbook of 25,000 Words Frequently Mispronounced
Place-name Pronunciation Guides (now available for most of the states)

QUOTATIONS, PROVERBS

Bartlett's Familiar Quotations
Stevenson's Home Book of Quotations
Stevenson's Home Book of Proverbs
Benet's Readers' Encyclopedia
Everyman's Dictionary of Quotations and Proverbs
Mencken's New Dictionary of Quotations
Grant's Dictionary of Foreign Phrases and Classical Quotations
Hoyt's Cyclopedia of Practical Quotations
Brewer's Dictionary of Phrase and Fable
Oxford Dictionary of Nursery Rhymes
Oxford Dictionary of Quotations

SPECIALIZED YEARBOOKS

Arts

Grove's Dictionary of Music and Musicians
Thompson's International Cyclopedia of Music and Musicians

The Record Guide
The Theater Book of the Year
The Theater Handbook
Wolf's Dictionary of the Arts
Gardner's Art Through the Ages
Bryan's Dictionary of Painters and Engravers
Encyclopedia of the Arts
International Motion Picture Almanac
Variety Yearbook
Religion
Ferm's Encyclopedia of Religion
Yearbook of American Churches
Handbook of Denominations in the United States
Hastings' Encyclopedia of Religion and Ethics
New Schaff-Herzog Encyclopedia of Religious Knowledge
Israel Yearbook
Catholic Encyclopedia
A Protestant Dictionary
Funk and Wagnalls' Jewish Encyclopedia
Douglas' American Book of Days
The Holy Bible (Douay-Rheims translation)
The Holy Bible (King James version)
The Bible and Concordance
The Interpreter's Bible
Cruden's Concordance
Science
Van Nostrand's Scientific Encyclopedia
Beadnell's Dictionary of Scientific Terms
Dorland's American Illustrated Medical Dictionary
A Dictionary of Biology
Warren's Dictionary of Psychology
Cobb's Guide to Medicine
White's The Farmers Handbook
Social Sciences
Encyclopedia of the Social Sciences
Fairchild's Dictionary of Sociology
United Nations Handbook
Dolivet's The United Nations
Yearbook of World Affairs
Dictionary of American Politics
A Dictionary of International Affairs
Encyclopedia of Europe
Langer's Encyclopedia of World History
Dictionary of United States History
Social Work Yearbook
Dictionary of Modern Economics
Masters' Handbook of International Organizations in the Americas
White and Levine's Elementary Statistics for Journalists
Handbook of Labor Unions
Yearbook of American Labor
Patman's Our American Government
Directory of Agencies in Race Relations
Negro Handbook
Negro Yearbook
Hodges' Handbook of American Indians
Municipal Yearbook
Book of the States

State yearbooks (including Bluebooks, Legislative Manuals, etc.)
Congressional Directory
Congressional Record
House Manual
Public Affairs Information Service
How to Get It from the Government
Statistical Abstract of the United States
United States Code
United States Postal Guide
Postal Manual

Law

Ballentine's Law Dictionary
Bouvier's Law Dictionary and Concise Encyclopedia
Black's Law Dictionary
Clark's Summary of American Law
Brandt's How to Find the Law
U.S. Laws
State codes and annotated statutes.

Military

The Army Almanac
The Official Army Register
Navy Yearbook
The Navy Register
The Air Force Register
Jane's Fighting Ships
Jane's All the World's Aircraft

Sports

Spalding's Official Athletic Almanac
Cummings' Dictionary of Sports
Menke's New Encyclopedia of Sports
Fleisher's All-time Record Book
Turkin and Thompson's Official Encyclopedia of Baseball
Hunter's Encyclopedia
The Sporting News (annual edition)

Index

GALVESTON COMMUNITY COLLEGE LIBRARY